Lecture Notes in Artificial Intellig

Edited by J. G. Carbonell and J. Siekmann

Subseries of Lecture Notes in Computer Science

T0238185

Lutz Maicher   Jack Park (Eds.)

Charting the Topic Maps Research and Applications Landscape

First International Workshop
on Topic Maps Research and Applications, TMRA 2005
Leipzig, Germany, October 6-7, 2005
Revised Selected Papers

 Springer

Series Editors

Jaime G. Carbonell, Carnegie Mellon University, Pittsburgh, PA, USA
Jörg Siekmann, University of Saarland, Saarbrücken, Germany

Volume Editors

Lutz Maicher
Universität Leipzig
Institut für Informatik
Augustusplatz 10-11, 04109 Leipzig, Germany
E-mail: maicher@informatik.uni-leipzig.de

Jack Park
SRI International
Menlo Park, CA 94025, USA
E-mail: jack.park@sri.com

Library of Congress Control Number: 200692782

CR Subject Classification (1998): I.2, H.4, H.3, J.1, K.3-4

LNCS Sublibrary: SL 7 – Artificial Intelligence

ISSN   0302-9743
ISBN-10   3-540-32527-1 Springer Berlin Heidelberg New York
ISBN-13   978-3-540-32527-7 Springer Berlin Heidelberg New York

Springer is a part of Springer Science+Business Media

springer.com

© Springer-Verlag Berlin Heidelberg 2006
Printed in Germany

Typesetting: Camera-ready by author, data conversion by Scientific Publishing Services, Chennai, India
Printed on acid-free paper   SPIN: 11676904   06/3142   5 4 3 2 1 0

Preface

The papers in this volume were presented at the workshop "Topic Map Research and Applications 2005" held on October 6-7, 2005, in Leipzig. TMRA 2005 was the first workshop of an annual series of international workshops dedicated to topic maps in research and industry.

As the motto "Charting the Topic Maps Research and Applications Landscape" suggests, the aim of TMRA 2005 was to identify the primary open issues in research, learn about who is working on what, bring together researchers and application pioneers, stimulate the systematic tackling of such issues, and foster the exchange of ideas in a stimulating setting. Besides the scientific track, open-space sessions were foreseen as playgrounds for visionaries. A report from this look into future is added to this volume.

TMRA 2005 was organised by the Zentrum für Informations-, Wissens- und Dienstleistungsmanagement Leipzig to support exchange of experiences, results, and technology in the field of topic maps. The 24 papers (1 invited, 17 full papers, 5 work-in-progress reports, and 1 report on the open-space sessions) presented at TMRA 2005 and in the present volume were selected from more than 35 submissions. Every submission was carefully reviewed by three members of the Program Committee. Before publishing, the editors introduced an additional editorial loop after the workshop to ensure the highest quality and latest insights.

We would like to thank all those who contributed to this book for their excellent work and their great cooperation. Susanne Bunzel deserves special gratitude for her great effort and perfect work at the workshop site.

We wish to acknowledge the substantial help provided by our sponsors: Emnekart Norge, the Medienstiftung der Sparkasse Leipzig, Ontopia, and Jubik.

We hope all participants enjoyed a successful workshop, made a lot of new contacts, held fruitful discussions helping to solve current research problems, and had a pleasant stay in Leipzig. Last but not least we hope to see you again at TMRA'2006 which will be held in October 2006 in Leipzig.

December 2005   Lutz Maicher (Chair)
                                                                        Jack Park

Organization

TMRA 2005 was organized by the Zentrum für Informations-, Wissens- und Dienstleistungsmanagement (ZIWD) in Leipzig, Germany.

Steering Committee
Lutz Maicher (Chair)

Program Committee
Murray Altheim
Robert Barta
Karsten Böhm
Patrick Durusau
Lars Marius Garshol
Gerhard Heyer
Larry Kerschberg
Steve Newcomb
Lutz Maicher
Sung Hyon Myaeng
Jack Park
Thomas B. Passin
Thomas Schwotzer
Alexander Sigel
Bernard Vatant

Sponsoring Institutions
Emnekart Norge
Medienstiftung der Sparkasse Leipzig
Ontopia, Oslo
Jubik, Berlin

Table of Contents

Topic Mapping: A View of the Road Ahead[*]

Jack Park

SRI International, Menlo Park, California 94025
jack.park@sri.com

Abstract. Topic mapping plays several important roles in augmentation of human cognitive capabilities and relational thinking. We summarize three such roles as resource indexing, culture fusion, and modeling. Based on a working hypothesis that combinations of technologies can benefit topic mapping capabilities, we sketch a proposed marriage between Conceptual Graphs and the TMRM variant, Subject Maps. The marriage of technologies is shown to be one of several ways forward for topic mapping.

1 Introduction

When we seek for connection, we restore the world to wholeness. Our seemingly separate lives become meaningful as we discover how truly necessary we are to each other.

– Margaret J. Wheatley[1]

In this talk, I propose to briefly sketch three use cases for topic/subject maps. My goal is to paint a kind of picture of the present state of the art. I will then form a working hypothesis from which this talk will imagine a path, one among many possible paths, for future developments in topic mapping. The largest sense in which this talk paints a story is that knowledge work, a problem solving human endeavor, is an exercise in *relational thinking.* We create and manipulate information resources, some of which represent static phenomena and objects, those which almost never change. Some of those information resources represent dynamic phenomena and objects, where subjects change, relationships between subjects change, and some changes occur relatively slowly while others occur at a rapid pace.

Relational thinking is based on the principle that, to understand any network of entities, we need to understand the relationships between the nodes in that network. I would add to that *text book* definition of relational thinking that we need, also, to pay attention to the nodes themselves in the sense that we always agree on the identity of the subjects those nodes represent. That's unadulterated *topic map speak*, something that permeates the rest of my talk. Indeed, topic maps represent a class of knowledge representation schemes, among the simplest possible architectures, that facilitate

---

[*] Keynote address presented to the International Workshop on Topic Maps Research and Applications, Leipzing, Germany, 6 October, 2005.
[1] Wheatley quote: In *Leadership and the New Science,* Barrett-Koehler Publishers, San Francisco, 1999.

L. Maicher and J. Park (Eds.): TMRA 2005, LNAI 3873, pp. 1–13, 2006.

representation of subject identity combined with representation of relationships among subjects.

Consider a recent news item[2], due to which our understandings of the mechanisms of immune response are now subject to possible revision. The news item suggests that, with ever improving sensor technology, a new mechanism within the immune system has been discovered. The discovery is that tunnels are formed between immune cells, for which we have few, if any, theories, models, or present understandings. Present immune response theories speak in terms of message passing among immune cells by means of various cytokines secreted by one cell and binding to the receptor sites on other cells. The new discovery suggests that molecular messages might be sent through tiny tunnels forged between cells. The number of subjects related to immune mechanisms has grown, and new relationships among those subjects now exist, while other relationships may have changed in other ways. This news item animates a primary motivation behind my talk, that we are in the midst of ever-changing, ever more complex relational situations, about which we need to maintain our organizational and inferential capabilities. For a brief look at scholarly work that influences this talk, I'll turn now to the story of one individual who saw these changes coming and spawned a new line of thinking that provides a means by which we can think about discoveries such as those revealed by improvements in sensor technology.

Nicholas Rashevsky, in his 1954 paper "Topology and Life: In Search of General Principles in Biology and Sociology" [10], said that we had neither sensors sufficiently powerful nor the representational mechanisms appropriate to formation of models of complex systems in sufficient detail to fully understand them, much less create and manipulate life itself. Rashevsky launched a program we now call *Relational Biology*, which argues that we need to evolve ever more powerful tools of relational thinking. Shortly, I'll show how Robert Rosen continued the inquiry started by Rashevsky. The field of relational biology grew at the same time that humans were beginning to recognize the need to think of complex systems as something other than machines; there began a shift away from simple Newtonian mechanics as a means of thinking about things toward a more holistic approach, a relational approach. I hope to convey the message that I see augmented subject maps as useful contributions to the emerging armamentarium of tools for relational thinking.

How do we presently conduct relational thinking? It is said[3] that *language* is the longest running open source project in the universe. With language, we tell stories, we communicate, among other means, by conversation. If we consider our day-to-day activities with productivity tools as *dialogs* with those tools, then we can cast our thinking in terms of *conversation theory* [11] due to Gordon Pask[4]. Conversation theory models speakers and listeners engaged in dialog. Each participant has a *domain model*, a knowledge base from which all speaking occurs and in which all interpretations of incoming information streams occur (Fig. 1 illustrates a conversation).

Each participant has a *listener model*, a kind of knowledge base that provides guidance in selection of ways from which the speaker chooses to present information to the listener. If the listener is a child, words chosen are those appropriate to some imagined vocabulary that is different from the vocabulary appropriate to an adult listener.

[2] News Item: http://www.sciencedaily.com/releases/2005/09/050929083640.htm
[3] I attribute this assertion to Patrick McKercher.
[4] Gordon Pask: http://www2.venus.co.uk/gordonpask/

Fig. 1. A Conversation

If we allow that one participant in a conversation is sometimes a computer program, a productivity tool, it follows that there is an opportunity to turn our productivity tools into the kind of listener/speaker with which we would otherwise prefer to converse. Indeed, it remains a seductive notion[5] that if our relational thinking tools *behave* more like humans during our interactions with them, they will prove even more valuable. This implies implementation of domain and listener models, at least to the extent that our productivity tools can *behave* in a fashion appropriate to the conduct of conversations. The domain of discourse in which productivity tools operate varies. Each domain involves possibly large quantities of possibly heterogeneous information resources, all sorts of document types, media types, and so forth. Topic maps, and their more recent counterpart, *subject maps*, provide us with a means by which we can organize information resources associated with various subjects according to the needs dictated by different users playing the role of listener when querying the map. If the map is a component in a productivity tool, then we have taken a first step in augmenting human cognitive capabilities by adding relational thinking tools to the conversation.

Let thoughts of conversation theory, relational thinking, and topic maps serve as a framework for the rest of this talk. That framework is based on the notion that one logical direction for future research and development in the topic mapping community is that of augmentation of human cognitive capabilities through improved productivity tools.I will offer a proposal for a means by which our tools for relational thinking can be improved. I will start with a sketch of three use cases for subject maps within such tools. From those use cases, I will propose a new direction of research,

---

[5] Seductive notion: Thanks to Lutz Maicher for reminding me of this notion in personal communication, 28 October, 2005.

one in which we consider the marriage of subject maps with other tools known to support relational thinking. In all that follows, the diagrams and words I offer represent my own interpretations of the TMRM specifications as variously offered and continuously evolving.

1.1 Use Case: Indexing Information Resources

Indexing information resources is the original use case for topic maps. This is the classical *back of the book* indexing approach implemented, first, in SGML topic maps, and later in XML topic maps [5] using the XTM standard[6]. More recently, the TMRM [1] is evolving to create a flexible version of the topic mapping paradigm, now called subject maps.

In this use case, the key elements of topic mapping, topics, associations, and occurrences are applied to the indexing task by creating a topic map that resides completely *outside* the information resources, just as the index at the back of a book resides outside the content of the book, providing pointers into the book's contents for each subject indexed.

By way of contrast, the TMRM, subject mapping as implemented in the Versavant[7] reference platform, uses a *subject proxy* as its key object for performance of the same indexing task. It is outside the scope of this talk to discuss the implementation details of the TMRM, but some aspects of that implementation will be illustrated in Section 2 below. To anticipate, a subject proxy serves as a container for all of the properties associated with a subject. Properties include those which serve to *identify* the subject, and all of the other properties, including *castings* of the subject into roles in defined relationships.

1.2 Use Case: Culture Fusion

> *People are human Rosetta stones which can (but don't always) bridge universes of discourse.*
>
> –Patrick Durusau[8]

> *If a person wants to allow his/her ability to serve as a Rosetta stone for multiple (always specific) universes of discourse to be exploited by as many other people as possible, and without constantly answering the telephone and/or e-mail, she/he can codify her/his Rosetta stone-ness as a TMA.* [Topic Map Application].*Thus, the subject maps paradigm shows a way to make *human* understandings about *human* universes of discourse widely machine exploitable.*
>
> –Steven R. Newcomb[9]

I like to think of this use case as a second *primary* use case for topic/subject mapping. Culture fusion implies codifying personal Rosetta stones, personal world views, into a

---

[6] XTM: http://www.topicmaps.org/

[7] Versavant: http://www.versavant.org/

[8] Durusau quote: Personal communication, 23 September, 2005.

[9] Newcomb quote: Personal communication, 23 September, 2005.

subject map such that all interested parties can derive shared understandings of specific universes of discourse. Consider a subject map which is designed to *federate* several research databases in some discipline, say, neurophysiology. In the chosen domain, it is known that researchers who develop individual databases may not use the same naming conventions or other terminology to talk about subjects, each of which is also potentially a subject in other databases. Through the flexibility of naming conventions in topic and subject mapping, it is possible that, once subject identities are agreed upon among those workers for which databases will be federated, understanding of the ways in which each research database represents various phenomena and objects will evolve much closer to a kind of consensus reality. In this case, we see personal Rosetta stones being mapped to a common organizing and viewing framework, the subject map, creating and maintaining a kind of *just for me* [8] reality.

"Just for me" refers to the notion that individuals work best when they are able to maintain their personal ontologies and world views, and to record those world views, e.g. names for things and relationships among things, in such a fashion that the *just for us* notion of semantic interoperability is maintained within individual research communities. That is to say, mapping a research database to a topic map may, or may not map highly personal information resources into a public map. Workers using individual research databases do not necessarily share their private view, just those associated with the need to publish their work. Whatever culture exists and is reflected in world views in the database is maintained, not sacrificed to the larger subject map. The example chosen here illustrates the nature of culture fusion: different research cultures federating their results to the larger research community while preserving the individuality of individual research groups. To the extent that each database is federated, bridges between cultures are formed.

Consider a different kind of culture fusion, one in which storytelling permits individuals and groups to share world views. This scenario illustrates a particular marriage of technologies involving topic maps. In this case, the technologies coupled with topic maps are storytelling and dialog mapping[10]. A graphical illustration of dialog mapping is Fig. 2. I call this marriage Augmented Storytelling[11]. Here, stories are substituted for research databases, and a kind of online collaborative discussion arena, dialog mapping, is added to the mix.

A topic map federates stories by mapping them in great detail, the detail being based on fine-grained addressability of information resource available in each story. Here, I am arguing for making, say, each paragraph, each figure, table, or multimedia resource in a given story directly addressable. Thus, it should be possible to isolate an individual paragraph within a story. With that addressability, it is now possible to present each resource on its own webpage, a place on the web where people can congregate and discuss aspects of the resource using a dialog map, and they can richly *decorate* that resource with links to other resources. Links to other resources involve a kind of ontology of link types, precisely what associations in topic maps provide. Thus, each individually-addressable information resources within each story can be a role player in one or more associations other information resources found in the same story or elsewhere on the web – any other addressable information resource.

---

[10] Dialog Mapping: http://www.compendiuminstitute.org/
[11] Augmented Storytelling: http://www.nexist.org/nsc2004/

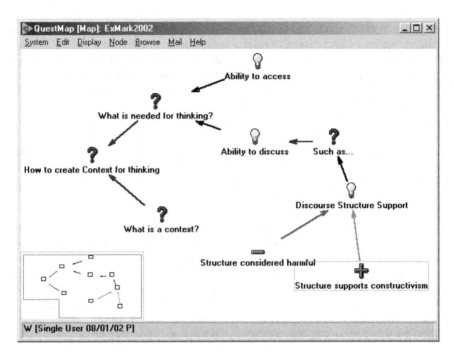

Fig. 2. A Dialog Map of a simple conversation

At the same time, that information resource can be the subject of discussion or debate using dialog mapping. Original authors can take the results of discussions and, where deemed appropriate, edit that resource to suit new ideas and world views, or correct mistakes found during discussions. It should be no surprise that the dialog map turns out to provide subjects for the topic map. Thus, the topic map serves to federate the stories crafted by individuals, while, at the same time, federating the discussions people are having about those stories.

1.3 Use Case: Modeling

When you come to the fork in the road, take it.

–Yogi Berra

Topic mapping is already about modeling domain knowledge as a means of organizing information resources. That's the historical perspective. What does that leave us in terms of a bright and productive future? It leaves us with a fork in the road. Let's take it.

Consider the immune response mechanism mentioned earlier, a newly-discovered tunnel that forms between immune cells and through which molecular messages are passed. We already know how to model such actors (subjects) and relationships (also subjects) in our subject maps. Now, we want to *reason* about those subjects to extend our knowledge and understandings. There is a clear opportunity to use analogical reasoning in order to form hypotheses from which we can design and conduct experiments and produce theories, even therapies that, in this case, involve immune

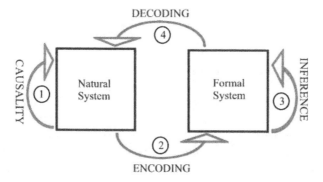

Fig. 3. The Rosen Modeling Relation[12]

response modification. That opportunity exists because similar tunneling mechanisms exist elsewhere in the physiology of animals. Let us now imagine ways in which we can *extend* the existing subject maps modeling tools such that we facilitate forms of reasoning not present in the existing topic maps technology.

My thoughts on modeling return to the relational biology program started by Rashevsky, mentioned earlier. That program eventually led to the work of Robert Rosen [2], and his *modeling relation*. Fig. 2 illustrates Rosen's modeling relation. Rosen continued the Rashevsky inquiry by adapting a topological algebra[13] to the representation of complex, anticipatory systems, of which all living things are instances. As an aside, there are several practitioners of topic mapping who foster the intuition that subject maps might eventually be shown to be similar to that topological algebra in ways that allow topic maps to inherit analytical tools from that algebra.

The kind of modeling I am proposing is that of the *formal system* of Fig. 3, in which we map encodings from *natural systems*, the world 'out there', into a formal system. We tailor the relationships represented in the formal system in such a way that inferences in that formal system mirror, in some sense, causality that exists in the natural system being modeled. In some sense, I am claiming that our subject maps, when suitably enhanced, can play important roles in such modeling activities. Which roles? It is natural to expect that a central role of a subject map is to maintain subject organization and context in which the reasoning systems of our formal models operate.

How might we enhance our subject maps? Below, I will offer a modest proposal, one in which the technology of conceptual graphs [3] is married with subject maps [1]. First, I offer the working hypothesis that animates this talk.

1.4 An Hypothesis

The words for my hypothesis were thoughtfully supplied to me by Bernard Vatant[14]. The hypothesis merely summarizes the kinds of things I have stated above, opening a door through which one path to the future follows.

---

[12] Modeling Relation: Copied with permission from http://www.panmere.com/ rosen/ faq mr1.htm

[13] Topological algebra: Category Theory.

[14] Bernard Vatant: personal communication, 30 September, 2005.

Nothing can better satisfy the needs of augmentation of human cognition and relational thinking than the fusion of technologies.

2   A Marriage of Technologies

Conceptual Graph technology offers a way to express what some people call *microtheories*[15], tiny structures which encapsulate some contextualized statement. The intuition here is that the assertion model of subject maps performs much the same thing, and, therefore, if we were to substitute a conceptual graph for an assertion in a subject map, we bring to the table a new ability, the ability to perform important kinds of inferences different from those presently available in our subject maps.

Before I launch into a marriage of technologies, let me introduce an existing open source software project, one that provides me with a sense of perspective. I will soon sketch a marriage of conceptual graphs (CG) with subject maps. In order to visualize and plan for the results of such a marriage, I find it useful to define the implementation platforms before trying to imagine a means by which a marriage will or can happen. I have chosen the Amine-platform[16] project as a basis for the conceptual graphs component of this marriage. I will likely implement a subject maps engine within that project. Amine-platform, implemented in Java™, is a rather complete and always evolving platform. The program includes a Prolog interpreter and other tools necessary to begin to imagine a rich environment for performing inferences in the formal models created by the marriage and within the content and context of the subject map. The rest of Section 2 will sketch two approaches to a marriage of the two technologies. One approach will be sketched in some detail in order to illuminate the issues involved, ending with a result that suggests the approach is not satisfactory. Another approach will be only lightly sketched, and remains thought to be a suitable approach to the marriage. I'll leave it as an exercise for those who access this talk, including myself, to explore live implementations of these and other topic maps marriage ideas.

We turn now to descriptions of specific means by which a conceptual graph structure might be coupled into the subject map architecture. What does a conceptual graph look like? Consider Fig. 4, which models the statement:

Tom believes that Mary wants to marry a sailor.

A CG is a directed graph. The particular CG of Fig. 4 contains 3 assertions:

1.   a belief
2.   a want
3.   a situation (marriage)

Our goal is to find a way to find a way to splice this structure into a subject map. We now look at two candidate approaches to the necessary coupling of two architectures.

---

[15] Microtheories: e.g. http://www.opencyc.org/OpenCyc_org/doc/tut/Foundations/Microtheories

[16] AminePlatform: http://amine-platform.sourceforge.net/

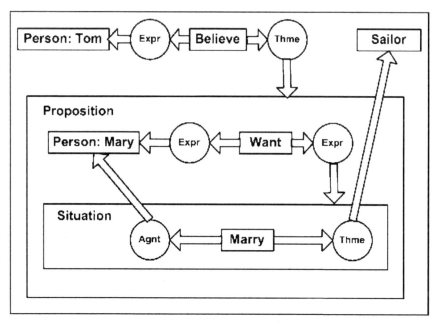

Fig. 4. Conceptual Graph: Tom believes that Mary wants to marry a sailor[17]

2.1 Conceptual Graphs as an Assertion Pattern in Subject Maps

In this approach, we quite literally implement a conceptual graph as an *assertion*. To develop a solid intuition of the assertion model, let us first look at the *association* model of topic maps, and then compare that with the assertion model of the TMRM. Consider Fig. 5, a diagram of the association model of XTM. Each topic node has its subject identity annotated in the oval callout nodes. The visual ontology I use in these illustrations is that a callout-like node, one with a pointer emerging from it, represents subject identity to the node to which it points. In the case of Fig. 7, a node actually provides subject identity by, in fact, serving as the node to which it points.

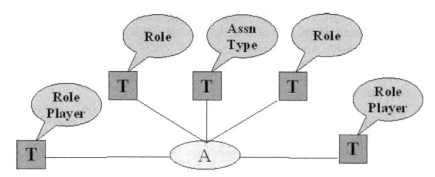

Fig. 5. The Association Model of XTM

---

[17] Figure 3 used with permission of the author [9].

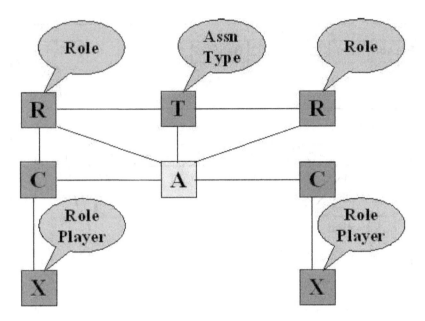

Fig. 6. The Assertion Model of TMRM[18]

In Fig. 5, we see that the association node itself, the A node, is not a topic node, as are the T nodes. Let us hold that fact in mind as we look at the *assertion* model of the TMRM. Consider Fig 6, the assertion model as a diagram.

In Fig. 6, each node is a subject proxy. As such, each node derives a subject identity property based on the nature of its situation in the assertion graph. R-nodes gain subject identity according to the *role type*, T-nodes gain subject identity according to the *assertion type*, X-nodes retain the subject identity of the *role players*, and the A-node gains its subject identity from the totality of the assertion in which it resides. C-nodes are *casting* nodes; they cast role players into the assertion. In some sense, they play the role of allowing one to *see the subject cast as a role player*.

Let us now return to our CG diagram and imagine it as if the nodes in the CG have been implemented in nodes appropriate to a subject map application. We see that in Fig. 7.

The diagram is a bit more complicated, given the number of nodes necessary to express the statement. Here, we see A-nodes lending subject identity to, or, in fact, serving as the X-nodes in other assertions. In fact, Fig. 7 shows that it takes three assertions to model one statement, and some of those assertions nest inside others. Thus, we see the requirement that nested assertions lend subject identity or X-node properties to parent assertions.

That concludes a sketch of an approach to a marriage of two technologies, conceptual graphs and subject maps, which morphs the conceptual graph into the assertion model of the TMRM. If we perform a *post mortem* on this sketch, it will reveal that this approach is unhelpful, possibly not useful at all on the strength of two key points:

---

[18] The particular assertion model sketched has come to be known as *BigAssert*, and it is just one of several ways in which assertions can be implemented.

1. The CG structure is that of a directed graph, whereas the assertion graph of a subject map is not directed.
2. The difference in graph structure implies that, essentially, all of the software available in the chosen platform, Amine-platform, will have to be completely rewritten.

Those two points imply that the proposal to rewrite a conceptual graph as an assertion is a non-starter, that we need to look for a different means by which a CG structure can be made to interoperate within a subject map. Next, I will sketch a candidate coupling.

2.2 Conceptual Graphs as Conceptual Graphs Spliced into Subject Maps

I just took the time to sketch in some detail a means by which a graph in the assertion model might be made to function as a conceptual graph. I did so in order to expose some of the details of subject maps that are germane to the working hypothesis of this

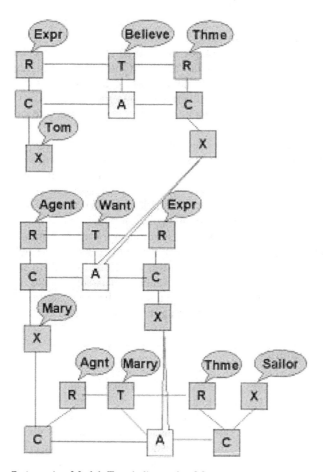

Fig. 7. Assertion Model: Tom believes that Mary wants to marry a sailor

talk. That approach meant that the conceptual graph structure, itself, might have to be morphed from a directed to a not directed graph, meaning the software package chosen for prototyping these ideas would have to be modified in complex ways. We lose the "rapid application prototyping" opportunity.

Suppose, instead, that we consider ways in which the *ontology* component of the Amine-platform software could be adapted to satisfy the architectural requirements of a subject map. After all, the primary function of the Amine-platform is manipulations on conceptual graphs, and the primary function of a subject map in that context is maintenance of subject identity and context. We are going to have to write a subject map engine in any case; let us just imagine that this can be accomplished in a fashion that suits the needs of the Amine-platform, as well as those of a subject map. Since it is the intent of this talk to sketch a candidate view of the road ahead for topic mapping (and not serve as a cookbook for that view), I am going to leave it as an exercise for motivated readers (including me) to explore this option further.

3 Summary and Conclusions

I believe that I have put forth sufficient information to, at the very least, suggest a justification for the claim that the topic maps paradigm can better satisfy the needs of augmentation of human cognition and relational thinking through fusion with other technologies. To do so, I sketched one scenario, called Augmented Storytelling, in which topic maps are married to dialog maps and to storytelling as a means of culture fusion in that one arena where humanity has done its best information transfer, storytelling.

At the same time, I made a modest proposal that subject maps appear to be well suited to a marriage with an important and powerful relational modeling technology, conceptual graphs. That marriage, I believe, leads to the ability to use subject maps to manage the subjects and context in which rich inferences are performed on those relationships between various subjects in the subject map that are represented in the conceptual graphs form and operated on by the conceptual graphs engine.

As a closing thought, to the extent that stories are used as a means of describing natural processes, and to the extent that we will eventually be able to automate reading stories and transforming those stories into formal models, I see a very bright future for topic maps performing the organizational support for modeling large, complex, and urgent problems. I proposed a fork in the road, and I suggested a means by which we can take that fork. I think Yogi Berra would be pleased.

Acknowledgements

Preparing a keynote address to be presented to a distinguished audience is a rare and humbling experience. The experience forces one to draw forth from all of the reserves, both mental and social, one has at one's disposal. I am not able to lay claim to an original thought in this talk, other than, perhaps, some novelty in the particular suggestions I have made. But, those suggestions are always a conceptual combination of ideas I have gleaned from many great minds. I am most pleased to acknowledge the gifts of many individuals, some of which contribute directly to the content of this talk, and some of which have provided me with the intellectually rich environments necessary to hatch ideas and massage them into something coherent from which the talk is created. At the outset, Patrick Durusau and Steven Newcomb have looked closely over my shoulder while this talk was crafted. Indeed, any misinformation I might portray in this talk is solely my responsibility, possibly due to misinterpretations of information given to me, or outright ignorance on my part. Bernard Vatant has always been a great conversationalist on things technical and, in particular, things related to topic mapping and this talk. John Sowa, creator of the conceptual graphs paradigm and author [6], offered comments on an early draft of my thoughts that found their way into this talk. I am greatly indebted to all of the co-authors of the XML Topic Maps book [5], one of which is my son John L. Park, one of which is my daughter, Nefer L. Park, and another of which is my technical editor on that work, Sam Hunting. I acknowledge the many contributions of Steve Pepper, particularly his "TAO of Topic Maps" [4], an important paper that many of us have used to promote topic mapping. Jeff Conklin, Murray Altheim, Judith Rosen , and Douglas Bowden have contributed valuable ideas along the way, for which I am grateful. The working environment at SRI International, working with Adam Cheyer and the CALO team, has lent me the support necessary to take these thoughts into the research community. My friends Glen and Helen Haydon have provided the richest intellectual and social environment for thought and creativity I can imagine. Finally, I am deeply grateful to Lutz Maicher for the invitation to deliver this keynote address.

References

1. Durusau, Patrick, and Steven R. Newcomb, "Topic Maps Reference Model," latest and historical versions accessible from http://www.isotopicmaps.org/tmmm/
2. Rosen, Robert, *Life Itself,* Columbia University Press, 1991.
3. Sowa, John F., Editor, "Conceptual Graphs International Standard," on the web at: http://www.jfsowa.com/cg/cgstand.htm
4. Pepper, Steve, "The TAO of Topic Maps", on the web at: http://www.ontopia.net/topic-maps/materials/tao.html
5. Park, Jack, and Sam Hunting, Editors. *XML Topic Maps: Creating and Using Topic Maps for the Web,"* Addison-Wesley, 2002.
6. Sowa, John F., *Knowledge Representation: Logical, Philosophical, and Computational Foundations,* Brooks/Cole, 2000.
7. Corbett, Dan, *Reasoning and Unification over Conceptual Graphs,* Kluwer Academic Publishers, New York, 2003.
8. Park, Jack and Adam Cheyer, "Just for Me: Topic Maps and Ontologies," International Workshop on Topic Maps Research and Applications, Leipzig, Germany, 7 October, 2005, in these proceedings.
9. Sowa, John F., "Architectures for Intelligent Systems," IBM Systems Journal, vol. 41, no.3, pp. 331-349, 2002.
10. Rashevsky, Nicholas, "Topology and Life: In Search of General Principles in Biology and Sociology",*Bull. Math. Biophys. 16,* 317-348. 1954.
11. McI. Boyd, Gary, "Reflections on the Conversation Theory of Gordon Pask," on the web at http://artsandscience.concordia.ca/edtech/ETEC606/paskboyd.html

Metamorphosis – A Topic Maps Based Environment to Handle Heterogeneous Information Resources

José Carlos Ramalho, Giovani Rubert Librelotto, and Pedro Rangel Henriques

Departamento de Informática – Universidade do Minho,
Campus de Gualtar 4710-057 – Braga – Portugal
{jcr, grl, prh}@di.uminho.pt

Abstract. Nowadays, data handled by an institution or company is spread out by more than one database and lots of documents of different types. To extract the information implicit in that data, it is necessary to pick parts from those various archives. To obtain a general overview, those information slices should be integrated. Different approaches can be followed to achieve that integration, ranging from the merge of resources till the fusion of the extracted parts. In this paper, we introduce Metamorphosis – a Topic Maps oriented environment that enables a conceptual navigation among heterogenous information systems – and we argue that Metamorphosis can be used to achieve, via Topic Maps, the referred semantic integration.

1 Introduction

Daily, a lot of data is produced by every institution or company. To satisfy the storage requirements, these organizations use most of the times relational databases, which are quite efficient to save and to manipulate structured data. Unstructured data (appearing inside documents) is stored in plain or annotated text files.

There is a problem when these organizations require an integrated view of their heterogeneous information systems. It is necessary to query/exploit every data source, but the access to each information system is different. In this situation, there is a need for an approach that extracts the information from those resources and fuses it. Usually this is achieved either by extracting data and loading it into a central repository that does the integration before analysis, or by merging the information extracted separately from each resource into a central knowledge base.

We use Topic to address the the problem of information integration mainly because it is the international industry standard – ISO/IEC 13250 – for semantic information integration and secondly because of its pure abstract nature (enabling the specification of every sort of ontologies). We are using successfully, for some years, this technology for classification and integration of documents in some use case scenarios [LRH03a, LRH04a].

L. Maicher and J. Park (Eds.): TMRA 2005, LNAI 3873, pp. 14–25, 2006.

In most semantic or knowledge based applications an ontology is composed of two parts. The classification structure or or semantic network and the catalog. The semantic network is composed of abstract concepts and their relations. The catalog is made of concrete information items. Throughout the paper when we refer to the term ontology we are considering the whole thing, the semantic network populated with catalog's information items.

However, the process of ontology creation is complex, time consuming, and it requires a lot of human and financial resources: it is necessary to specify the entire semantic network and all the information items that are going to populate it. In an Enterprise Information Integration scenario this can mean the manual extraction of many information items from several and different information sources.

To overcome this problem, we developed Metamorphosis. Metamorphosis is composed of several modules with different aims:

Metamorphosis Repository (MMRep). This is the central component and its purposes are the storage of Topic Maps (for the moment it imports and exports Topic Maps in XTM syntax). All the other components interact with MMRep (section 3 will detail this component).

Topic Map Discovery (TMDiscovery). TMDiscovery is a Topic Map driven browser and can be seen as a web interface to the MMRep (section 4).

Topic Map Extractor (Oveia). This component (still a prototype) automates the task of Topic Map harvesting; It enables the user to specify the extraction task and generates a Topic Map in XTM syntax that can be uploaded into MMRep (section 5).

Topic Map Validator (XTChe). XTChe is an implementation prototype of TMCL (*Topic Map Constraint Language*). It is not yet full integrated but in a near future TMDiscovery will have the power to change the Topic Map (insertion and deletion of topics), and then this module will ensure the preservation of the initial intended semantics (section 6).

In this paper we claim that with Metamorphosis the semantic integration of a set of heterogeneous information sources is possible to achieve. In order to achieve this we propose the following methodology:

1. Look at the information resources and decide how your conceptual view should look like;
2. Choose what information bits must be extracted in order to produce that conceptual view;
3. Specify the extraction task using Oveia;
4. Upload the generated Topic Map into MMRep;
5. Browse it with TMDiscovery and use this interface to access the information resources.

With this methodology the original information resources are kept unchanged and we can have as many different interfaces to access it as we want. We just have to create/generate/specify a Topic Map for each one.

In spite of its advantages MetaMorphosis should be used with some judgement. If your are dealing with frozen information sources, like historic databases, you will not have any problem. But if you are dealing with sources that are still changing you must be careful in defining the conceptual network, you should keep it above the level where the changes occur otherwise you will have to create a new Topic Map each time a change occurs.

The remainder of the paper is structured in the following sections: next section (sec.2) will introduce Metamorphosis, then a description of each module is presented with some detail (MMRep in sec.3, Oveia in sec.5, XTche in sec.6 and TMDiscovery in sec.4). Before the concluding remarks (sec.8) we present a real world case study to consolidate our proposal — *"Emigration Museum"* (sec.7).

2   Metamorphosis

The main idea behind Metamorphosis is close the gap between Topic Map technology and its users. Metamorphosis is being developed to become a Topic Map workbench easy to use and accessible to a common user (we are not there yet).

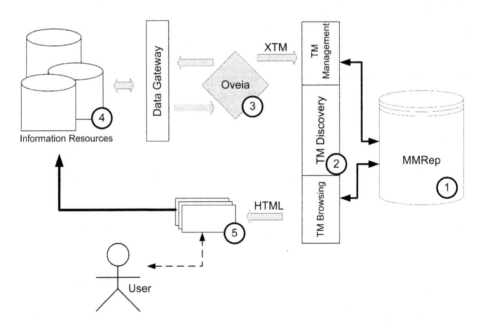

Fig. 1. Metamorphosis Functional Diagram

Figure 1 shows the usage scenario proposed in this paper. It illustrates some of the interaction between the system components, information resources and users.

1. MetaMorphosis Repository is the component that takes care of Topic Map storage and management.

2. TMDiscovery is the browser that allows users to navigate inside the Topic Maps stored in MMRep.
3. Oveia is a processor that eases the job of building topic maps. It implements some extraction mechanisms with which is possible to populate an ontology.
4. Information resources that we want to access.
5. Web interface driven by a topic map stored in MMRep that provides access to information resources.

Metamorphosis can be used to prototype web interfaces or to expose information systems on the web. To do this the user only needs to specify a topic map for each view he wants. Information integration is accomplished by concept integration in the topic map: to integrate two information systems we need to specify the two sets of concepts in the same topic map and specify the associations that will materialize that integration.

In the next sections we are going to discuss the main components of this workbench prototype: Metamorphosis Repository, Topic Map Discovery, Oveia and XTChe.

3 Metamorphosis Repository

Although XTM is a good format for interchange it is not so good for storage. When we refer to storage we are meaning the capability of storing a Topic Map and efficiently being able to query it. XTM is easy to process and for instance to translate it into another format. But querying XTM is complex. The Topic Map model is not hierarchical, every relation is materialized as a reference. Gathering all the information about a topic is very complex.

The obvious choice for storage is a database. For this case we had three options: an XML database [Bou05], an Object Oriented Database [Lea00] or a Relational Database. Since the Topic Map model does not match the XML model XML databases were discarded. Almost for the same reasons OO databases were also discarded. That left us with the relational model as the target for our storage solution.

The next step would be the specification of a Topic Map Relational Model. We have considered two approaches: look at the Topic Map Reference Model [Kip03, DN05] and derive the relational model from it or look at the XTM model and work from there. We decided to work over the XTM model and see if we could reach a model similar to the Topic Map Reference Model.

3.1 Data Model

First, we looked at the XTM model and raised the following subject list (and correspondent content model):

- $topicMap = (topic|association|mergeMap)*$
- $topic = (instanceOf|subjectIdentity|baseName|occurrence)*$
- $instanceOf = (topicRef|subjectIndicatorRef)$

- $subjectIdentity = resourceRef|(topicRef|subjectIndicatorRef)*$
- $baseName = (scope?|(topicRef|subjectIndicatorRef|resourceRef) + |baseNameString|variant*)$
- $scope = (topicRef|subjectIndicatorRef|resourceRef)+$
- $variant = (parameters, variantName?, variant*)$
- $parameters = (topicRef|subjectIndicatorRef)+$
- $variantName = (resourceRef|resourceData)$
- $occurrence = (instanceOf?, scope?, (resourceRef|resourceData))$
- $scope = (topicRef|subjectIndicatorRef|resourceRef)+$
- $association = (instanceOf?, scope?, member+)$
- $member = (roleSpec?, (topicRef|subjectIndicatorRef|resourceRef)*)$
- $mergeMap = (topicRef|subjectIndicatorRef|resourceRef)*$

After some exercise with the leaf nodes of this list we end with the following types that cover any element in a topic map:

$(topicRef|subjectIndicatorRef|resourceRef)$
$(topicRef|subjectIndicatorRef)$
$(resourceRef|resourceData)$
$resourceRef$
$baseNameString$

This result means that any Topic Map node can be represented with one of this five types. To store any of this five types we only need a triple: identifier, value and type. Consider the following example:

Stored Values		
Id	**Type**	**Value**
"TR982"	"topicRef"	"#University"
"SIR500"	"subjectIndicatorRef"	"http://www.uminho.pt"
"BNS32"	"baseNameString"	"U. Minho"
"RD444"	"resourceData"	"UM is ..."
"RR486"	"resourceRef"	"http://www.uminho.pt/students"

This exercise enabled us to simplify the model and to reach the relational model showing in Fig.2.

With this specification we have implemented a Topic Map Repository that is the core component of Metamorphosis. In the following sections we will give some details about the integration of the other components with the repository.

4   Topic Map Discovery

Topic Map Discovery is an API that is being developed in order to work with the repository. For the moment it is composed of two parts: a topic map manager and a browser.

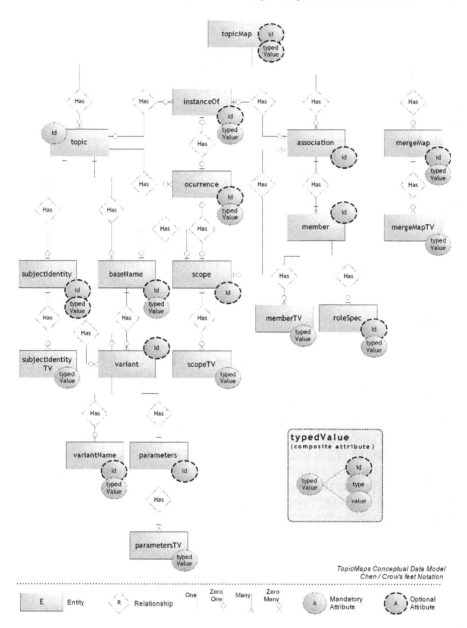

Fig. 2. Relational model schema

The topic map manager lets you upload and download topic maps in XTM syntax and delete a topic map from the repository (soon it will enable the user to edit stored topic maps).

The browser gives the user an interface to navigate inside any of the stored topic maps. So far we have developed the following interfaces:

Topic Maps - is the browser entry point and shows a list of all stored topic maps.

Ontology Index - gives you a structured view of a topic map showing the abstract concepts: topic types, association types, occurrence types and association role types.

Individuals Index - lists all non-type topics in alphabetical order.

Full Index - lists all named topics.

Topic View - lists a subset of the available information about a topic; for the moment: the basenames, its type, all the associations it participates in together with the other members and their roles, internal occurrences and external occurrences.

Association View - lists the names associated with the association and all its descendants.

We say that TMDiscovery is still a prototype because it has no control over users, there are no log or login components. However it will be freely available in a trial basis in the next days.

5   Oveia

The ontology extractor, Oveia (more details in [LSRH04]), is based on ISO/IEC 13250 Topic Maps [BBN99]. Oveia extracts information fragments from heterogeneous information systems according to an XSDS specification and builds the topic map according to an ontology specified in XS4TM language [LRH03b, LRH04b]. The Oveia architecture is shown in figure 3 and it is composed of five components. The dataset extractor receives an XSDS specification, providing metadata about the physical data sources that will be used to query each source in order to get the data needed for the ontology construction, and generates the intermediate representation (called datasets), containing the data (in a unified representation) extracted from resources. The XS4TM processor takes as input these datasets and an XS4TM specification generating a topic map, in XTM syntax.

5.1   XSDS — XML Specification for Data Sources

Oveia supports the concept of extraction drivers. A driver extracts data from a data source and stores it in an intermediate representation, called datasets. XSDS language defines the transformations and filters over the data sources. XSDS gives precise information about each data source that should be scanned to extract topics and associations.

An XSDS specification has two parts: *datasources* and *datasets*. The first one defines the path to the physical resources. Each resource is defined in a *<datasource>* element. This element has a set of attributes that indicates which extraction driver will be used and provides values for the corresponding parameters.

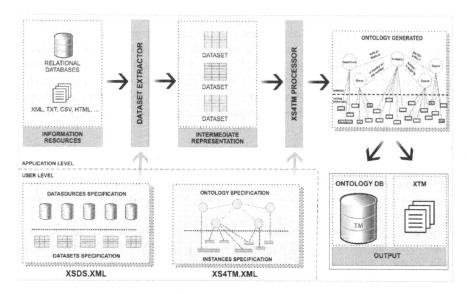

Fig. 3. Oveia Architecture

The second part of this specification is defined in a *<datasets>* element. It declares which data (record fields or DTD elements) must be extracted from each datasource. Each *datasource* can be used to specify the extraction of several *datasets*.

5.2   Datasets: Intermediate Representation

The *datasets* compose the intermediate representation that contains the extracted data from the resources. Each *dataset* has a relation to an entity in these resources and it is represented through a table, where each line is a record following the structure specified in XSDS. The *datasets* representation guarantees that Oveia sees an uniform data structure that represents all the participating resources.

The *dataset* declaration is composed of a query to extract the data from the resources. Each dataset has an unique identifier. This identifier will be used throughout the architecture to reference a particular *dataset*.

The fundamental idea is that all objects have labels that describe their meaning. For instance, the following object represents a member's category: $<1, PhD>$, where the string 1 is a identifier of this category, and PhD is a human-readable label. The *datasets* are very simple, while providing the expressive power and flexibility needed for integrating information from disparate sources.

5.3   Dataset Extractor

The *Dataset Extractor* is a processor that scans the input data sources to get desired data into the *datasets*, in agreement with an XSDS specification.

The *Dataset Extractor* is composed of several extraction drivers (at moment, two), each one responsible for handling a specific type of source. The driver uses the appropriate technology to make the connection (e.g. JDBC, Java DataBase Connectivity, for databases, and an XML parser for annotated documents), and then the extraction of data is expressed in the query language adequate to the type of source in use: SQL will be used to extract information from a relational database while XPath will be used for the extraction in XML documents. Finally, the extracted data is stored in the *datasets*.

5.4   XS4TM — XML Specification for Topic Maps

XS4TM is a domain specific language conceived to specify the process of ontology extraction from information systems; in our case, from the dataset intermediate representation.

Looking at a topic map an ontology designer can think of it as having two distinct parts: an ontology and an object catalog (instances). The ontology is defined by topic types, association types, occurrence types, role types, etc. The catalog is composed by a set of pointers to information objects that are present in the resources and are linked to the ontology. So:

Ontology. The definition of the ontology requires in XS4TM the same effort as in XTM; it is necessary to specify every topic type, association type, occurrence type, ...;

Instances. The instances definition describes each topic and association that will be extracted from the intermediate representation; these will correspond to queries that will return lists of values; each value will turn in a topic.

The XS4TM Context Free Grammar is based in XTM 1.0 [PM01]. The *ontology* and *instances* elements have the same syntax as the *topicMap* element in XTM model.

The XS4TM language is intended to make the specification of Topic Maps extraction more flexible. However, the use of XS4TM is not much more difficult because this language is an extension of the XTM standard; it means the XS4TM DTD includes and augments the XTM DTD. In XS4TM, the ontology is specified like in XTM: with the same elements and attributes. So, if the designer knows XTM syntax, he does not need to learn another syntax to specify an ontology in XS4TM.

5.5   XS4TM Processor

This component uses the XS4TM specification and retrieves the information it needs to build the ontology from the *datasets*. It is an interpreter that takes advantage of the information organization in datasets (an internal universal representation for extracted data) and generates all the associations between the relevant topics according to XS4TM.

The XS4TM processor's behavior can be described in three steps: reads the the XS4TM specification and extracts from the datasets the topics and associations found; creates the topic map as an XTM file.

The status of this component is still prototype. The work that will integrate it with the repository is starting.

6   XTche – A Topic Map Semantics Validator

This component was already presented at Extreme Markup 2005 ([RLH05]). It will be integrated in Metamorphosis when editing capabilities become a reality. Until then it will remain a prototype as it is.

7   Emigration Museum: A Case Study

During the last centuries a huge number of Portuguese people (women and mainly men) left the country to go away to work abroad. Until the middle of twentieth century, the most important destination for emigrants was Brazil (an old Portuguese colony and a very large and rich country). Becoming rich, many of them came back and did notable things with real social impact; they constructed manor houses and palaces, schools, hospitals, churches, factories, and they developed the industry and commerce. As there are plenty of documents and evidences about those emigrants and the outcomes of there lives, a group of Historians in Fafe (a town in the North of Portugal) decided to create a virtual museum devoted to the Brazilian Emigration; after a first prototyped version(www.museu-emigrantes.org), we were involved in the conception of the information system.

The aim is to create a website that provides as many information as possible about each emigrant. The system should allow multiple navigation paths (offering various ways to handle the information) so that different views over the acquired knowledge are allowed. So, this museum on the Web should provide, not only data on individuals, but also knowledge about the social influence of their character and activities, in some geographical place at a certain date. To achieve that second, and main objective, it should be possible to cross data, exploiting the relations between the different information items (or units). Some interesting topics are: emigrant name; birth place and date; travel destination, departure and return dates, carrier; marital status; passport number; psychological profile; social or laboral event; industrial or commercial business; etc. Some important associations are: is; has; buy; creates; pays; offers; develops; etc.

However, as told above, the available resources, that should be exploited to extract the relevant data, are of many different kinds (official or technical records, literary documents, physical evidences, etc.), and are also available in different types of support: databases, annotated documents, and so on. For this case study we considered only three information sources: *travel diaries*, full of details written by the emigrant during the long (ship) trips; *biographical notes*, found in old almanacs, very rich in data concerning the character and social impact of the emigrant; *passport records*, obtained from the Portuguese foreign affairs bureau with factual data about travels. The first two are archived as XML documents (instances of two different document types), and the third one is a database.

In order to implement such an information system we could design a very large central repository, and impose that all the resources are consulted in order to extract the data to populate that huge database. Instead of that, we followed a completely different approach. We decided to use Metamorphosis to keep the data sources as they are and to generate a website where the visitor can start by accessing a topic and then navigate over the knowledge following the relations included in the underlying ontology.

Oveia was fed with: (a) the XSDS structural and physical description of the XML documents (*travel diaries*, and *biographical notes*), and the database (*passport records*) to be parsed to extract the relevant information bits to build topics; and (b) the XS4TM specification of the topic map to be built (notice that this TM corresponds to the ontology defined for the Emigration Museum). After some minutes, Oveia produced a 1,14MBytes (35588lines) XTM file containing a topic map with 1043 topics (instances of 25 topic types) and 1541 associations (instances of 32 association types). This topic map was then uploaded into MMRep and TMDiscovery allows users to browse the information accessing any item without needing to care about its origin. One of the pages, displaying the topic *emigrant*—that plays a role in 27 associations (of 12 different types)—is the most evident example of the knowledge integration achieved.

8   Conclusion

This paper describes the integration of heterogeneous information systems using the ontology paradigm, in order to generate an homogeneous view of these resources. The proposal is an environment, called **Metamorphosis**, for the automatic construction of Topic Maps with data extracted from the various data sources, and a semantic browser to navigate among the information resources.

Although developed for use in our main working area – XML documents processing applied to Public Archives and Virtual Museums – we are convinced that **Metamorphosis** can be applied with similar success in the general area of information system for data integration, analysis, and knowledge exploitation.

In the near future Metamorphosis will suffer several improvements. TMDiscovery will be able to edit topic maps. The inference engine behind the browser will be improved (for instance to give information about subtyping at any level). Oveia will be integrated in the management component of TMDiscovery. A friendly user-interface to write XS4TM and XSDS specifications is under development. **Metamorphosis** will be tested with new case studies, and we will conceive an easy and systematic way to verify the generated topic map against the actual sources and specifications. To assure the absolute correctness of this environment, each module should be formally validated.

As XTche specification language is based on XML Schema language, one of our next concerns is the implementation of the XTM-Skeleton-Extractor. The idea is to infer from the schema that specifies the constraints the basic specification of the Topic Map that we want to validate; this specification will be the skeleton that the user can complete to obtain the XS4TM specification (the second Oveia's input).

References

[BBN99]   Michel Biezunsky, Martin Bryan, and Steve Newcomb. ISO/IEC 13250 - Topic Maps. ISO/IEC JTC 1/SC34, December 1999. http://www.y12.doe.gov/sgml/sc34/document/0129.pdf.

[Bou05]   Ronald Bourret. Xml and databases. Website, Sptember 2005. http://www.rpbourret.com/xml/XMLAndDatabases.htm.

[DN05]   Patrick Durusau and Steve Newcomb. Topic maps - reference model. ISO/IEC JTC1/SC34 Committee draft, February 2005. http://www.isotopicmaps.org/TMRM/TMRM-5.0/TMRM-5.0.html.

[Kip03]   Neill A. Kipp. A mathematical formalism for the topic maps reference model. Draft paper submitted to ISO/IEC JTC1/SC34 Committee, October 2003. http://www.isotopicmaps.org/tmrm/0441.htm.

[Lea00]   N. Leavitt. Whatever happened to object-oriented databases? *IEEE Computer*, August 2000.

[LRH03a] Giovani R. Librelotto, Jos C. Ramalho, and Pedro R. Henriques. ADRIAN – a platform for e-learning content production. In *Second International Conference on Multimedia and Information & Communication Technologies in Education*, 2003.

[LRH03b] Giovani R. Librelotto, Jos C. Ramalho, and Pedro R. Henriques. TM-Builder: Um Construtor de Ontologias baseado em Topic Maps. In *XXIX Conferencia Latinoamericana de Informtica*, La Paz, Bolvia, 2003.

[LRH04a] Giovani R. Librelotto, Jos C. Ramalho, and Pedro R. Henriques. ADRIAN E-Learning Content Production (creating online exams). In *VIII International Conference on Electronic Publishing*, Braslia, Brasil, 2004.

[LRH04b] Giovani Rubert Librelotto, Jos Carlos Ramalho, and Pedro Rangel Henriques. Extrao de Topic Maps no Oveia: Especificao e Processamento. In Mauricio Solar, David Fernndez-Baca, and Ernesto Cuadros-Vargas, editors, *30ma Conferencia Latinoamericana de Informtica (CLEI2004)*, pages 451–460. Sociedad Peruana de Computacin, September 2004. ISBN 9972-9876-2-0.

[LSRH04] Giovani Rubert Librelotto, Weber Souza, Jos Carlos Ramalho, and Pedro Rangel Henriques. Using the Ontology Paradigm to Integrate Information Systems. In *International Conference on Knowledge Engineering and Decision Support*, pages 497–504, Porto, Portugal, 2004.

[PM01]   Steve Pepper and Graham Moore. XML Topic Maps (XTM) 1.0. TopicMaps.Org Specification, August 2001. http://www.topicmaps.org/xtm/1.0/

[RLH05]   José Carlos Ramalho, Giovani Librelotto, and Pedro Rangel Henriques. Constraining topic maps: A tmcl declarative implementation. In *Extreme Markup Languages 2005*, Montral, Canada, August 2005.

Concept Glossary Manager – Topic Maps Engine and Navigator

Jakub Strychowski

Rodan Systems S.A, Sopot, Poland

Abstract. The Office Objects Concept Glossary Manager (CGM), which has been designed by the author as a software component of the ICONS system, helps to create, edit and visualize topic maps. Interesting features of the CGM are distributed topic maps processing, user rights management, topic states and versions management, ontology driven generative user interfaces and Topic Maps Script Language (TMSL). This paper also overviews an example application of the component. In the final section some weaknesses of the CGM are identified and possible improvements are suggested.

1 Introduction

The ICONS project realized under the European Commission's Fifth Framework Program focused on bringing together into a coherent, web-based system architecture the advanced research results, technologies, and standards, in order to develop and further exploit the knowledge-based, multimedia content management platform [ICONS] [Staniszkis]. One of the ICONS components is the Concept Glossary Manager (CGM), whose main functions include storing, processing and visualizing sets of concepts.

In order to be well understood, the word "concept" should be defined. From the perspective of the Concept Glossary Manager, a concept holds informations about a real or abstract subject. A subject can be described by names and definitions written in various languages, links to external resources and relations with other subjects. The Topic Maps ISO standard [Biezunski] [Park] was selected as a base solution for architectonic issues of the Concept Glossary Manager, because the structure of a concept is similar to the standardized structure of a topic.

In fact, the Concept Glossary Manager is a software module which helps to create, edit and visualize topic maps. The module consists of the following components:

- **Topic Maps Engine.** The engine manages topic maps stored in relational databases or on remote Topic Maps Servers, imports and exports XTM files, controls user permissions, provides searching and querying functions, and so on.
- **Topic Maps Navigator.** A Web application based on the Struts technology, which allows for a visualization and **modification** of topic maps. From a user's point of view, the navigator is a thin client application which works

L. Maicher and J. Park (Eds.): TMRA 2005, LNAI 3873, pp. 26–41, 2006.

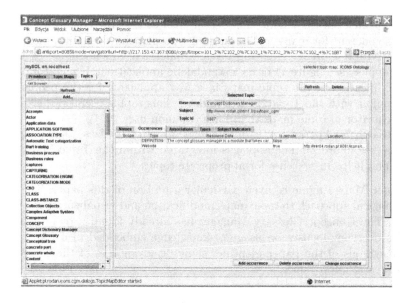

Fig. 1. The Topic Maps Editor in action

in a Web browser. The major advantage of the navigator is its rich flexibility ensured by generative, ontology-driven user interfaces.
- **Topic Maps Server.** A system service (a daemon) sharing topic maps between many processes, hosts and applets. The server uses a single instance of the engine to persist topic maps, and serves persisted topic maps to the

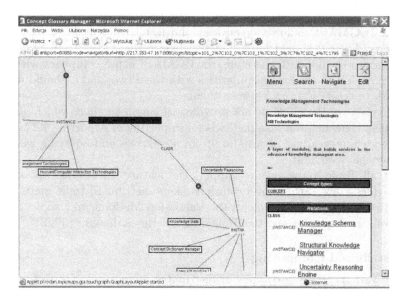

Fig. 2. The TouchGraph Applet in action

other instances of the engine. The server ensures that the content of a topic map is coherent for many clients running in a distributed environment.

- **Topic Maps Editor.** A Swing based application which can be executed as an applet (see figure 1) or as a standalone application. The editor allows for modification of the topic maps in a way applicable for the people who are familiar with the Topic Maps standard. This tool is useful rather for an administrator of topic maps than for a common user.
- **TouchGraph Applet.** A simple applet which visualizes topic maps as graphs (see figure 2). The applet is integrated within the Topic Map Navigator and helps in searches for appropriate topics.

The Topic Maps Engine is given particular attention in this paper. The idea of an ontological approach to topic maps modification and visualization is briefly described. The Concept Glossary Manager has already found a real-life application. Its overview focuses on usage of knowledge embedded in a topic map. The final sections of the paper identifies some disadvantages of the CGM and proposes several improvements.

2   Concept Glossary Manager – Topic Maps Engine

When the ICONS project started, the TM4J engine was proposed as the core of the Concept Glossary Manager design. Unfortunately, at the beginning of 2002, this open source project had some serious bugs and problems with an efficiency during the large topic maps tests. Therefore, a decision about developing a new topic maps engine was taken.

The main part of the CGM is the Topic Maps Engine. The whole background work of the engine, including a relational databases access, a distributed communication, and so on, is encapsulated by a set of Java interfaces. An API of the engine (CGMAPI), allows for an easy and intuitive creation of topic map applications. The CGM had been designed before the TMAPI [Barta] standardization process finished, therefore, the CGMAPI is not compliant with this standard now. There are many similarities with these two, and it should not be a hard task to create a proxy between them.

The interfaces of the CGM do not provide just simple methods which operate on topic map elements, but also methods for importing or exporting XTM files, full text searching, reading information from hierarchies and querying with the Tolog language [Garshol].

Almost all Topic Maps engines support the features mentioned above, but CGM provides a few rather novel solutions like a distributed topic maps management, a user rights management, the Validation Mechanism, a topics states and versions management and the Topic Maps Script Language (TMSL).

2.1   Distributed Computing

There are various levels and types of distributed computing architectures. In this paper, a distributed system denotes a set of computers working on a shared topic map.

One of the objectives for the Concept Glossary Manager design, is that a programmer who uses this tool, should not worry if his code runs in either a standalone system or a distributed system. The CGM realizes this objective thanks to different implementations of the CGMAPI. A configuration of the CGM decides which of the implementations should be used in an application. If the configuration defines a connection to a topic map server, the application uses the "remote" implementation. In this implementation, all operations, which read or modify topic maps, are executed in a networked environment.

A running instance of the "remote" implementation, which is connected to a topic map server, is called as a client of this server. If the client needs to read or write any fragment of a topic map, the topic map server receives a request from the client. All data sent and received during a request execution has a binary form of a list of bytes. An operation type, operation parameters and a return value are serialized before sending and deserialized after a reception of data. The serialized data are sent through a communication medium.

The Concept Glossary Manager can support many communication mediums. The abstract implementation of topic map server and client can be used for a creation of a specific implementation. Any working implementation should extends the abstract one providing methods for establishing connections and sending or receiving lists of bytes. The abstract implementation assures such tasks as a topic map objects serialization and deserialization, a client request executions and a broadcasting of topic map modifications.

The CGM provides two implementations of the communication medium: the implementation based on the standard sockets technology, and the implementation based on the non-blocking sockets technology. The major advantage of the non-blocking sockets is that a server does not require a separate thread for each connected client. From an efficiency point of view, a number of threads is important for many machines working as servers. The disadvantage of the non-blocking sockets is that some versions of JVMs (Java Virtual Machines) contain major bugs in implementations of this technology. Both implementation of the communication medium mentioned above can be mixed, and some experiments with different JVM versions and different operating systems have shown that it is safe to use the non-blocking implementation for a server side and the standard socket based implementation for a client side.

One of disadvantages of a socket based implementation is that a TCP/IP port should be available on client and server machines. This disadvantage is specially important for a user who uses applets. There is no guaranty that a firewall does not block the communication port on an end-user workstation. This disadvantage should not occur for the HTTP based implementation which is planned for the realization. This implementation will use the Servlets technology for a realization of a topic map server. In fact, the HTTP protocol bases on the sockets technology, but it is much easer for a configuration in a target application environment. On the other hand, the HTTP protocol involves an extra processing and increases an average size of transferred data sets.

A topic maps server may use any implementation of the CGMAPI for an execution of received requests. For example, the "jdbc" implementation can be used for a topic maps persistency in a relational database. From the server point of view, it is not important what kind of implementation is used. For example, the server can also use the "remote" implementation, and requests can be passed from one server to another. A server which works in such a configuration is called as a "broker". The broker can increase an efficiency because the "remote" implementation buffers the content of a topic map. If a group of clients works in a long distance from a base server (for example in another city), the broker established for this group can reduce a number of requests passed from one city to another while topic maps reading.

Topic map servers use the asynchronous method for a populating of changes between clients. For each connected client, a server holds a packet of informations about changes. If any modification occurs, the server adds information about changes to all packets. A client updates its buffers reading the packet from the server in parametrized intervals. The packet could be also sent as a part of a return value for a client request. Major disadvantages of this approach are a delay between client synchronizations and no support for distributed transactions. From the other side, the server does not require to wait for a synchronization and transaction can be quickly finished. This feature increases an efficiency and a scalability of distributed systems. Using the synchronized method, the server must wait for updates on all clients before finishing the transaction what is much less efficient.

Data sets transferred between clients and topic map servers may contain topics, lists of topics, names of topics and so on. The content of a transferred data set depends on a type of invoked operation. For example, if a client creates new occurrence, following data are sent to the server: the operation code, the system identifier of a target topic, the system identifier of a topic denoting type of the occurrence, the occurrence data, the boolean flag denoting an in-line status of the occurrence, the system identifier of a scope. The form of information transferred by the CGM is concise and an average size of data sent in single request is rather small.

One of disadvantages of the CGM is that the communication protocol is not an open standard and it is hardly depended on the CGMAPI and the Java language. Therefore, if a communication between different topic maps available systems is required, more accurate approaches like TMRAP [TMRAP] and TMIP [TMIP] should be used. The approach used by the CGM focuses rather on a high efficiency, a programming transparency and a full CGMAPI support on the client side.

2.2   User Rights Management

One of the most important features of the CGM is its support for a user rights management. An ontology defines user rights for, inter alia, creation, modification, visibility of a topic map constructs. The ontology describes the structure of a knowledge represented by a topic map. The CGM stores the ontology as a part of the topic map, therefore, it is possible to transfer the main content of the topic map and its ontology together.

The Topic Maps Navigator uses the specialized implementation of the CGMAPI called "filtered". This implementation, prevent from returning a topic or an association if a user has no rights to see them. In addition, if the user has no rights for a modification of a topic map element, the API can throw an access denied exception. These features are very useful in real life applications, where some users should not see or modify some parts of informations stored in topic maps, particularly, the ontology should be controlled only by a knowledge engineer. The "filtered" implementation filters input parameters and result values. It also blocks forbidden operations. This implementation uses another implementation (for example jdbc, remote) to perform all operations before filtering.

A topic map stores a user rights specification as a set of topics and associations. There are a few simple rules which determine user rights for topics and associations:

– Users and users groups are represented as topics. A user membership in a group is represented as an association. Users groups can be also members of other groups.
– Rights types like "modify", "deactivate", "create" are represented by topics belonging to the class "right type".
– Members of the group called "Administrators" have all rights to all elements of the topic map. Users from other groups have only rights declared in the form of the following associations:
– Users rights for topics are defined as associations between these topics or their classes, users or users groups, and rights types.
– Users rights for associations are defined as associations between types of these associations, users or users groups, and rights types.

The CGM provides also more sophisticated solutions like rights for fragments of hierarchies, topics and associations owners, rights for topics representing accounts of users. It is also possible to define rights for topic names and occurrences.

The User Rights Management Mechanism works parallely to the scoping mechanism. Scopes are good for filtering individual objects. They are not so good if we think about specifying rights for a set of objects described by a certain type. More over, a topic is not described by a scope, therefore it is a problem to set rights for a topic itself. Each topic can belong to many types. In this context, types could be used similarly to scopes but this is not a smart solution. Security informations represented in a form of topic types can hardly obscure an inheritance tree.

The major problem we can find, if scopes and topic types are used for a user rights definition, is the scalability problem. For example, if a topic map contains X topics representing subjects from the class S, and we want to say that users belonging to the "user group A" can modify these topics, we need to add to X topics a type informing about a modification right for the "user group A". This approach is not efficient at all (for example if X equals 10 000 we have to execute 10 000 operations when the definitions of rights are changing). In fact, the knowledge required for inferring rights for any member of the "user group A" can be represented by a single association between topic denoting class S and the "user group A".

In the CGM, rights definitions can be managed by an administrator in the Topic Maps Navigator. In fact, every user who has rights for a modification of a topic map fragment related to the user management, can modify rights definitions using the Navigator.

2.3   Validation Mechanisms

Although, the User Rights Management Mechanism controls an access to the content of a topic map, in some cases more complex mechanism is required. In real life applications, permissions for a modification of any topic or association can depend on a knowledge which can be inferred from the content of a topic map or other data processed in these applications. In these situations the Validation Mechanism can be helpful.

The Validation Mechanism allows to execute a "validator" which can check if a user has privileges for a topic map element creation, modification, deletion, and so on. The CGM uses two kinds of validators: Java validators, and TMSL validators.

A Java validator is a Java class which implements either TMTopicValidator or TMAssociationValidator interfaces from the CGMAPI. Both interfaces contain methods which are executed by the Validation Mechanism while topics or associations are created, modified, and so one. Implementations of these method should check if a certain action can be realized, and if not, the methods should return a set of error messages.

Any Java validator should be registered in the ontology of a topic map. Each topic representing a class in the ontology contains an in-line occurrence holding a list of names of Java classes. Each name from the list denotes a Java validator which is executed while an action is performed on topics or associations belonging to this class. It is possible to turn on or turn off the validator on-line in the Topic Maps Navigator modifying the occurrence value in the ontology.

The TMTopicValidator and TMAssociationValidator interfaces contain also methods which are execute after (also before) topic or association creation, modification, and so on. In this context, Java validators can be seen as plugins or triggers responding for events generated by the Validation Mechanism. Thanks to this feature, when the content of a topic map changes, an application can perform other actions.

TMSL validators use the TMSL language, which is described below, to perform a validation. A TMSL validator is represented in the ontology as a topic. Such topic contains an in-line occurrence holding the TMSL code of the validator. The certain type of associations can be used for the TMSL validator assignment to the type of topics or associations for which validator should be used. The Validation Mechanism executes TMSL validators like it does with the Java validators. The major advantage is that a TMSL validator can be created, modified, assigned while an application is running. It is not necessary to compile the code of the validator during an application deployment what is necessary for the Java validators.

The Validation Mechanisms had been implemented before the draft of the TMCL language [TMCL] became a mature project. Many tasks done by validators (and schemes defined in an ontology) could be replaced by the TMCL nowadays, but the Validation Mechanism offers furthermore a possibility of a topic maps engine integration with the rest part of an application.

2.4   Topics and Associations States Management

An important feature of the CGM is the Topics and Associations States Management. Users do not want to destroy an outdated information preferring to keep historical topics, and associations. Such historical data should be accessible through user interfaces, and capable for reactivation. More over, historical data should be stored as a part of a topic map what guarantee that actual and archive content can be processed similarly.

An "inactive topic" is a typical topic described by some features which denotes its inactive state (markers of inactive state). In the CGM the inactive topic can be marked by the topics type "inactive topic" or an in-line occurrence denoting if the topic is active or inactive. The inactive topic is also described by a deactivation date in a form of in-line occurrence. An inactive association is marked by a certain theme added to its scope.

It is possible to describe the state of a topic in other ways but the markers presented here seems naturally and smart. For example, in another approach, we can mark inactive state changing the type of an inactive topic ("person" to "fired person" or "death person") but this approach is not very general. Topics can have many types, and each of these types is probably described in an ontology. If we change the type of a topic, we loose a knowledge about this topic unless the ontology stores also informations about an inactive version of a topic class. If, in some cases, the state of a topic should be inferred from other informations, a validator can change state of the topic using proposed markers.

All operations required for a states management can be done by any topic maps engine which provides functions for a scope based filtering, manipulations on types, scopes and occurrence. This solution is not very comfortable for a programmer. Therefore, the CGMAPI provides many functions which can check the state of a topic and return active or inactive list of topics, for example:

```
boolean TMTopic:isActive();
boolean TMAssociation:isActive();
TMReadOnlyContainer TMTopicMap:getTopics();
TMReadOnlyContainer TMRole.getPlayers();
Collection TMReadOnlyContainer:getAllActive();
Collection TMReadOnlyContainer:getAllInactive();
Collection TMReadOnlyContainer:getAll();
Iterator TMReadOnlyContainer:iterateActive();
Iterator TMReadOnlyContainer:iterateInactive();
```

```
Iterator TMReadOnlyContainer:iterator();
Collection TMTopix:getRelatedTopics(
    assType, thisTopicRole, targetRole, boolean onlyActive);
Collection TMHierarchyDefinition:getAllChildren(
    TMTopic parent, boolean onlyActive);
```

The CGMAPI provides also specialized functions for an activation and deactivation of topics and associations. Additionally, the CGM buffers information about states of topics and associations what increases a processing efficiency. The Topic Maps Navigator also supports states management providing controls for filtering by states, and buttons which allows for a modification of the state of a topic or an association.

The CGM supports also the Topics Versioning Mechanism. Main assumption for this mechanism is that any subject can be represented by an active topic and many inactive topics. Old representations of the subject are stored as inactive topics which have added prefixes to identifiers and names to prevent merging. All old versions of a topic are chained by the associations so it is easy to get complete list of versions.

This approach to the topics versioning has many disadvantages, and the major one is that this solution is not coherent with the topic map model where a single subject should be presented by a single topic. In fact, this disadvantage is a result of problems with time representation in a topic map. Subjects are changing in time, we can use scopes to express this for names, occurrences, and associations but for example what if a scope, type or subject indicator is changing? How to save many old versions of these? We can use a reification processes for this task but this is not very smart solution, because a number of separate topics created for many points of time can seriously increase the size of a topic map, and decrease an efficiency. The problem of adding meta-data like time points, real numbers (for example the strength of an association) require a wider discussion and exceed the scope of this article.

2.5   Topic Maps Script Language

The Topic Maps community well knows such languages as the Tolog, the TMQL [TMQL] and the TMCL [TMCL]. Somebody could ask; why we need another topic maps language? Unfortunately, as I now there is no a standardized language which provides all functionality we need in real life applications of Topic Maps. Main problem is that the TMQL and the TMCL are not completed yet (august 2005). Some holes in the current standards, like update commands in the TMQL, and rules in the TMCL, must be temporary replaced by other solutions. Therefore the TMSL language has been created.

The TMSL language has many similarities with the JavaScript language. Syntaxes of these languages extend the Java grammar. The JavaScript adds some functionalities useful for a web-pages creation, and the TMSL adds functionalities useful for a topic maps processing. The main assumption for the TMSL language is that a Java code should embed TMQL constructs.

The CGM realizes only a prototype of this language, but almost all Java-like constructs and the Select statement from the TMQL language works in this implementation. The prototype contains also many additional functions like topic maps manipulation functions, mathematical functions, strings functions and so on. It is also possible to add other functions to an execution context of the TMSL. For example the Validation Mechanism adds functions "getValidation-Action" and "getValidatedAssociation", which are useful for a creation of the TMSL validators.

The CGM uses the ANTRL tool for a code parsing. The syntax of the TMSL extends the java.g grammar file which is published in the Internet. Thanks to the ANTLR, the TMSL syntax can be extended without major problems. Although the TMSL prototype works, there are many things to do with this language. Especially, more TMQL constructs should be implemented, and an integration of the TMCL should be done. Also some Java constructs like classes definitions should be added. There are some plans for moving the TMSL implementation from the CGMAPI to the TMAPI. This step will allow for an integration of the TMSL with other engines like the TM4J. Many programmers prefer the structural programming and the TMSL could become a good starting point for a learning of TMQL constructs. I hope that the TMSL will become an open source project.

Currently, the CGM uses the TMSL for a programming of reports and TMSL validators. A report is a table of data generated by a Tolog or TMSL code. The ontology of a topic map represents the report in form of a topic whose in-line occurrence holds the code. When a user of the Topic Maps Navigator selects this topic, he can see a result of a report execution. The report can be also executed from the context of a topic previously selected by the user. For example, it is possible to generate a list of workers older than 50 years and employed in the currently displayed organizational unit.

The following listing shows the example code of a TMSL validator. This validator is assigned (in an ontology) to the topic representing a type of associations between instances of classes "Person" and "Category". If a user changes an association having this type, the Validation Mechanism executes the validator. A validation process pass if the validator does not return an error message. If the validation code returns an error string, the user cannot finish invoked action. This example presents some constructs derived from the Java language and the Select expression from the TMQL. The Select operator returns a two-dimensional array of objects. An index operator (for example tab[i][2]), or specialized arrays functions like "size" or "getColumn" can make manipulations on the returned array.

```
action = getValidationAction();
if (action == "create" || action == "makeActive"
                       || action == "modify")
{

   using mytm for i"http://www.rodan.pl/psi/mytm#";
```

```
ass = getValidatedAssociation();
oldAss = getValidatedAssociation(false);

person = rolePlayer(ass, mytm:person-assigned-to-category);
category = rolePlayer(ass, mytm:category-assigned-to-person);
personRole = rolePlayer(ass, mytm:role-of-person-in-category);

if (personRole == mytm:investigator){
  table = select count($UNIT) where
    mytm:employment(
        person : mytm:employee,
        $UNIT : mytm:employer,
    ),
    mytm:unit-categories(
        $UNIT : mytm:unit-having-category,
        category : mytm:category-belonging-to-unit,
        mytm:main-unit: mytm:unit-function-for-category
    );
  if (table[0][0] == 0){
    return "Investigator must be employed "
           + "in the main unit of the category!";
  }
 }
}
```

3   An Ontology Driven Topic Maps Visualization and Modification

A modification of a topic map could be a hard task for a user who might not even be aware that such standard as "Topic Maps" exists. It is not easy to assure a topic map flexibility and, at the same time, provide user interfaces for the people which have only basic skills in the Internet browsers usage. Naturally one can develop specialized forms for editing topics having specific types but at a cost of loosing flexibility. For example, if somebody wanted to add to a form an additional field representing new type of topic names, a programmer would have to change a code, a script generating html, recompile, test and redeploy an application possible in many hosts. This is a very costly and time consuming process. The Topic Maps Navigator (figure 3) deals with this problem providing the User Interfaces Generative Mechanism. The UI Generative Mechanism provides user interfaces for editing topics and their associations using a knowledge inscribed in the ontology of a topic map. The ontology is a set of topics and associations defining structures of other topics. The ontology says for example what names and occurrences an instance of a specific class can have, which and how many topics can play a specific role, which roles can be used by a specific association. The ontology defines also scopes, default values, formats for topic

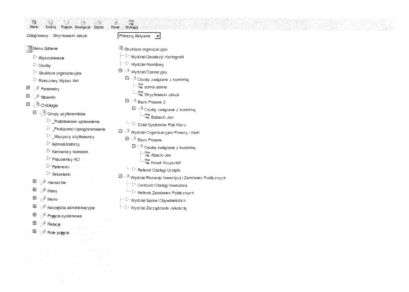

Fig. 3. The Navigator displaying an example hierarchy

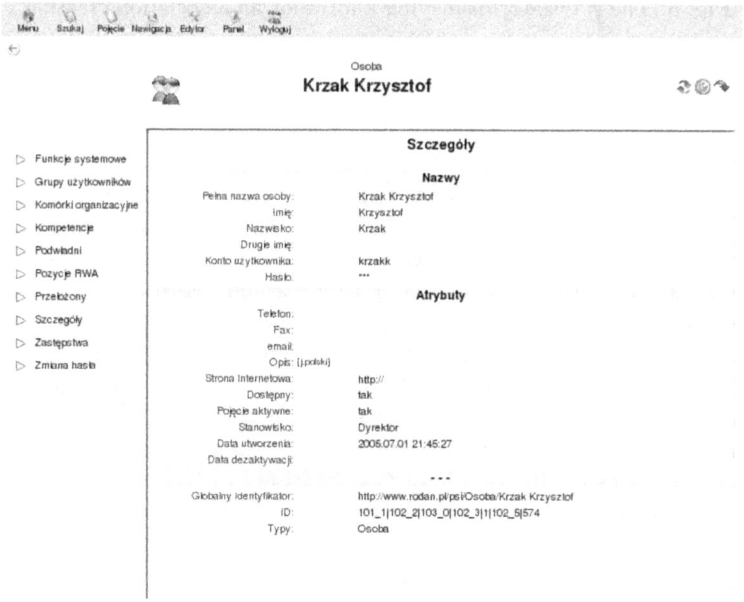

Fig. 4. The Navigator displaying details of an example topic

names and occurrences. Many of these assertions can be written in the form of a TMCL code. A tool allowing for an ontology exporting to the TMCL or an ontology importing from the TMCL could be interesting improvements of the CGM.

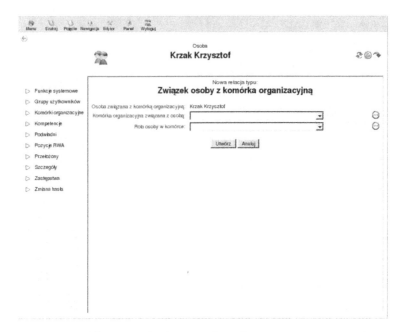

Fig. 5. The Navigator displaying a form for an association creation

The knowledge available thanks to an ontology is used for a generation of specialized forms for a visualization and modification of topics (figure 4) or associations (figure 5). A navigation in a topic map is also controlled by the ontology. An entry point to the topic map is a concrete topic called "Main menu". This topic creates relations with other topics – menu positions. The Topic Maps Navigator generates the menu as a vertical list of selectable topics. If a user selects a topic which represents a topics type, instances of this type will be displayed. If the user selects a topic which represents a hierarchy, a visualization of this hierarchy will be displayed. A hierarchy is a tree structure which has a root topic and children topics available through a traversing on associations having specified type. The main menu can also contain the Tolog or TMSL reports and "sub-menus" defined similarly to the main menu. One of the sub-menus is a topic called "Ontology" which consists of elements providing generative interfaces for the ontology modification.

The main advantage of this generative, ontology-driven approach is rich flexibility, because any modification of the ontology immediately cause a generation of new specialized forms for the users which are not familiar with the Topic Maps.

4   An Example Application of the CGM

A Polish government – Council of the European Union interoperability is an important factor of the EU enlargement success. The European Exchange of Documents – Poland (EWD–P) system is an application responsible for an elaboration of official Polish standpoints to proposals of new procedures and regulations in the EU.

The CGM plays important role in the EWD-P system as a module which manages a knowledge about a domain of this application. The topic map of this system stores informations about an organizational structure of the Polish government. These informations are used by a workflow engine which controls processes of elaborating Polish standpoints. A lot of decisions made by the workflow engine depends on informations provided by the topic map. Polish and EU taxonomies of documents, organizational units and people are represented as topics and associations. Such knowledge allows to send incoming documents to right people distributed in many Polish departments.

The EWD–P system stores all EU documents received from U32Mail system (this system distributes the EU documents to all countries which are united within the EU). Each document is described by an envelope – a meta data object. One of attributes of this object is a list of categories into which this document belongs. The topic map holds a list of all possible EU categories in a form of topics belonging to the class "EU category".

Unfortunately, the Polish governmental units use a different categorization for the documents. While the EU categories are organized as a flat list, the Polish categories are organized as a hierarchy. More over, each EU category can have many Polish equivalents. This mapping between the flat list of the EU categories and the hierarchical Polish taxonomy is represented in the topic map as a set of associations between topics. The subject based mapping cannot be used here, because a single subject from the EU taxonomy can be represented by many, more accurate subjects, in the Polish taxonomy.

Each Polish category could have many people and organizational units responsible for documents belonging to these categories. All relations between the categories and the people or units are also represented as associations. This knowledge allows to determine people and units which should receive incoming documents.

The ontology of a EWD-P system defines a terminology used in this system. In this context, the CGM plays a role of a dictionary manager. Each dictionary used in the EWD-P is represented by a topic in the Topic Map. Instances of this topic stand for elements of the dictionary. Although many systems has their own dictionaries modules it is beneficial to have coherent environment to store dictionaries as a part of a knowledge base in the widely sense. Other important advantage is a common user interface allowing to manage dictionaries in generative forms. The CGM supports hierarchies therefore its usage as a medium for hierarchical dictionaries gives many efforts. Building dictionaries based on the CGM allows to focus on the semantic of a system rather then technical and visualization aspects. Naturally, the fact that a system terminology is stored in the topic map gives many advantages for developers, for example: describing terms by in–line or linked occurrences, internationalization, scoping and so one.

The content of the topic map is managed by office workers in the Office of the Committee for European Integration in Warsaw and the Permanent Representation of the Republic of Poland to the European Union in Brussels. They use the Topic Map Navigator to create taxonomies, mappings, organizational structure, and other informations held by the topic map. They do not know anything about Topic Maps standard, but they are able to fulfill their tasks thanks to the specialized interfaces generated by the Ontology-Driven Generative Mechanism.

More details about the EWD-P and the role of the CGM within this system can be found in [Blizniuk].

5   Possible Extensions and Improvements

The Concept Glossary Manager does not support distributed transactions, consequently, a topic map modification cannot be bounded in a transaction which covers many different components and hosts. This problem can be solved by adding a support for the JTA (Java Transactions API).

The whole content of a topic map is buffered by a running engine. This feature can involve a lot of a system memory consumption for huge topic maps (from 50000 topics on). To deal with this problem the implementations of the CGMAPI should be rebuilt. The more sophisticated caching – for example based on JBossCache [JBossCache] – can solve this problem.

6   Conclusions

The Concept Glossary Manager is a powerful tool for a representation and manipulation of structural informations. The generative, ontology-driven user interfaces allows rapidly develop modules responsible for a declarative knowledge management. This approach has been successfully implemented and applied to real-life cases.

Novel functions like the user rights management, the ontology-driven topic maps management in a Web environment, the topics states and versions management and the TMSL language could be very helpful in real life applications.

Nowadays, the CGM is a stable solution used as a part of many applications and products developed by the Rodan Systems. The CGM is not distributed as a standalone product, but in a few months it will be available as a part of the OfficeObjects DocMan [DocMan].

Smart, generative, ontological user interfaces available within the Topic Map Navigator could considerable decrease development time of any Intranet, WEB-based application. The first version of the EWD–P system was developed in 4 months. More then 35% acceptance test cases for the whole system was based on the Topic Map Navigator. An ontology manages a visualization process of topics, association and hierarchies. The generative mechanism provides a lot of UI forms. Thanks to the CGM, a development time of the EWD–P system was substantially decreased.

References

[Ahmed]   Kal Ahmed: TM4J Developer's Guide. http://tm4j.org/tm4j/docs/devguide, (2002)

[Barta]   Robert Barta, Oliver Leimig: An Introduction to TMAPI. O'Reilly Media Inc. (XML.COM), February 02, (2005)

[Biezunski]   M. Biezunski, S. Newcomb, and M. Bryan: ISO 13250: Guide to the topic map standards. ISO/IEC JTCl/SC34, (2002)

[Blizniuk]   Blizniuk G., Momotko M., Nowicki B., Strychowski J: The EWD-P system. Polish government – European Commission Interoperability Achieved. HICSS-38, the 38th Hawaii International Conference on System Sciences, Big Island, Hawaii, January 3-6, (2005)

[DocMan]   http://www.rodan.pl/en/produkty/officeobjects/?dzial=docman

[Garshol]   Lars Marius Garshol: Tolog – A topic map query language. Ontopia AS, http://www.ontopia.net/omnigator/docs/query/tutorial.htm. (2003)

[ICONS]   http://www.icons.rodan.pl/

[JBossCache]   http://www.jboss.org/products/jbosscache

[Park]   Jack Park, Sam Hunting: XML Topic Maps – Creating and Using Topic Maps for the Web. Addison-Wesley, Boston, (2003)

[Staniszkis]   Staniszkis Eliza., Nowicki Bartosz: ICONS based Knowledge Management in the Process of Structural Funds Projects Preparation. eChallenges e-2004 Conference, Vienna, Austria, October, (2004)

[TMCL]   Graham Moore, Dmitry Bogachev, Mary Nishikawa, JTC1 / SC34: ISO N458 – Topic Maps Constraint Language. ISO/IEC JTC1/SC34, (2005)

[TMIP]   Robert Barta: TMIP, A RESTful Topic Maps Interaction Protocol Extreme Markup Languages (2005)

[TMQL]   Lars Marius Garshol, Robert Barta, JTC1 / SC34: ISO 18048 – Topic Maps Query Language. ISO/IEC JTC1/SC34, (2005)

[TMRAP]   Steve Pepper, Graham Moore, JTC1 / SC34: Topic Maps Remote Access Protocol. ISO/IEC JTC1/SC34, (2004)

Application Framework Based on Topic Maps

Motomu Naito[1] and Frederic Andres[2]

[1] Knowledge Synergy Inc.,
3-747-4-203 Kusunokidai Tokorozawa,
Saitama 359-0037, Japan
motom@green.ocn.ne.jp
http://www.knowledge-syergy.com
[2] National Institute of Informatics,
2-1-2 Hitotsubashi, Chiyoda-ku,
Tokyo, 101-8430, Japan
andres@nii.ac.jp
http://www.nii.ac.jp/

Abstract. One of the most interesting aspects of subject-centric information processing as services is the relationship between resources and subjects. Especially Topic Maps and Published Subjects are core elements of the infrastructure of relationship management. This paper proposes an Application Framework based on Topic Maps. The Application Framework will make possible to realize subject-centric processing. Furthermore in the framework, we can express the semantic distance between topics based on a relationship cost between two nodes of the Topic Map. This paper also introduces some challenges such as software development process and semantic management. Finally, we will overview the on-going on development of the Application Framework to manage those subjects.

1 Introduction

Many people are almost drowning to the information tsunami. It is important to provide services to the end-users for finding required information when it is needed.

For that purpose, the information system should not only handle information resources as the target objects, but the system should also handle subjects related to the information resources. Most important and valuable things for end-users are concepts (= subjects) or knowledge included in the information resource.

In recent circumstances of glut of information, there is an infinite variety of information to be required according to positions, situations, people and so on. And also requested information change according to view, timing, granularity and so on. Advanced information systems include some preliminary services to systemize and organize the information and the knowledge based on the subjects from various points of view.

Topic Maps has enough power to solve such a difficult condition. It is reasonable to adopt Topic Maps as basic technology for information systems to

L. Maicher and J. Park (Eds.): TMRA 2005, LNAI 3873, pp. 42–52, 2006.

manage various information and knowledge. But it is usually very expensive and need long term to develop the information systems. Most of those information systems have similar structure and similar functions. If there are many ready-made functional components and if we can use and assemble them to develop the information systems, we can develop high quality systems with lower cost and shorter term.

This paper proposes an Application Framework based on Topic Maps. The Application Framework can be built easily by using existing components if those components comply with ISO Topic Maps standards. Once the Application Framework is built, we can use it for various purposes and applications. The Application Framework can be built up using currently available technology and consists of various functional components. We can select and replace each component according to the feature of the information systems and the evolution of the technology. Those functional components are, for example input, store, retrieval, and output functions. In addition, more specialized and sophisticated functions can be added to the Framework such as the similarity measurement between topic nodes. Semantic distance between nodes of Topic Maps has been introduced to improve and enhance the search through the relationships between subjects and resources.

In the reminder of the paper, section 2 overviews some key technologies such as Topic Maps and Published Subjects which can be used to realize identification, collocation and organization of the information/knowledge based on the subjects. In section 3, we describe an Application Framework based on Topic Maps which can be constructed using those technologies and functional components. Section 4 describes the semantic metric approach to enhance the meaning of relationship. Section 5 addresses our challenge. Finally section 6 concludes and addresses future works along the framework.

2   Technical Elements

Let us introduce currently available technical elements which are basic technology to build up the Application Framework. Those technical elements are the following.

- Topic Maps
- Published Subjects
- Ontology
- Fragment Exchange Protocol
- Query Language

2.1   Topic Maps

Topic Maps is a technology to target to process subjects (concepts). In Topic Maps subjects, relationships between subjects and relationships between subjects and information resources can be modeled and be processed in computers. Subject is represented by topic, relationship between subjects is represented by association and relationship between subject and information resource represented by occurrence [1]. Topic Maps make possible to realize the subject centric processing.

2.2 Published Subjects

The "Published Subjects" mechanism enables any person and any computer to identify subjects (topics or concepts). And the "Published Subjects" are permanently published on networks and are aimed at making easy to share/exchange Topic Maps. Recently, the role of the "Published Subjects" is not only easing to merge between Topic Maps, but also enabling interoperability between OWL/RDF and Topic Maps [2]. Subject indicators are the information resources which describe subjects, and the subjects can be identified by using unique URI or IRI. Subject indicator which is published is called Published Subject Indicator (PSI).

Fig. 1 shows an example of PSI. An information resource which describes dolphin, sea animal related to whale is a Subject Indicator of "dolphin". It indicates dolphin a concept of real world object in computer. If the Subject Indicator is located in "http:www.knowledge-synergy.com/PSI/dolphin", we can use the address to indicate a concept of dolphin. Then it clarifies the subject we are talking about.

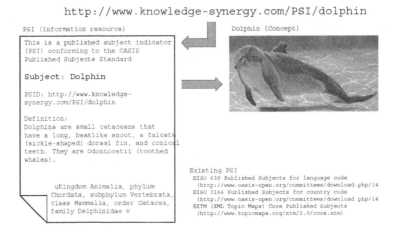

Fig. 1. An example of PSI

2.3 Ontology

Some guidelines for making ontology are shown in Ontology Engineering [3]. We can apply those guidelines to make Topic Maps, for example what is "is-a" relation, "part-of" relation, "role attribute", etc. and to recognize and distinguish those relations.

Recently, various ontology were created or have been created, such as UNSPSC (Universal Standard Products and Services Classification), SWEET (Semantic Web for Earth and Environmental Terminology), ISO 12207 SLCP (Software Life Cycle Process), and so on. These ontologies can be used as Published Subjects and Schema of Topic Maps, if a unique identifier (URI or IRI) is given for each concept in the ontology and if they are published on the network permanently.

2.4   Fragment Exchange Protocol

More and more resources such as Topic Maps, RDF, Published Subjects and Ontology are publishing on the network. It is natural that people want to exchange, update, merge and filter such resources' fragments. If we can realize those operations, related information resources become more useful. From now on, it is necessary to specify the protocol for remote access to those resources. There is no standard at this moment though, there are some proposals. Two candidate proposals are TMRAP (Topic Maps Remote Access Protocol) [4] from Ontopia, TopicMapster [5] from Kal Ahmed and TMIP (Topic Map Interaction Protocol) [6] from Robert Barta.

2.5   Query Language

As there is SQL in a relational database, standardization of a query language mapping a graph structure data model like Topic Maps is progressing. TMQL (Topic Maps Query Language) [7] is being created by ISO. TMQL has three kinds of queries, i.e. path expressions, select queries and FLWOR queries. Using these queries, we will be able to get more powerful way to find what we need and to make diversified outputs. Although it is a basic need to query and update Topic Maps, standardizing process of TMQL have not finished yet. In the meantime, we can use tolog.

3   Application Framework Based on Topic Maps

By using the technical elements described above, it becomes possible to connect information and knowledge on the network seamlessly, to organize and navigate them based on the subjects. Those technical elements have potential to realize collocation and one stop shopping according to the subjects [8].

In order to realize the above-mentioned knowledge sharing structure generally, We propose Application Framework based on Topic Maps. OKS (Ontopia Knowledge Suite) [9] has already exist as a suite of Topic Maps software. OKS has functions to develop Topic Maps Applications and functional components. OKS also has functional components such as Topic Maps engine, Topic Maps storage, Topic Maps browser, etc. Applications can be constructed using functional components which OKS originally have and which is developed by OKS. The Application Framework is a framework to construct application using functional components for example from OKS and functional components which was made by any other way.

3.1 Functional Component

The Application Framework is configured by several functional components and many applications are configured by the same kinds of components. Examples of those functional components are given as follows:

- Input function
    - Generate Topic Maps function is to generate Topic Maps from XML file, EXCEL file, etc.
    - Entry/Edit Topic Maps function is to entry or edit Topic Maps in the screen directly.
    - Information resources registry function is to register information resources.
- Store function is to store Topic Maps to RDBMS, XML DB, etc.
- Retrieve function is to retrieve Topic Maps constructs from memory, RDBMS, XML DB, etc.
- Fragment exchange and merge function is to exchange Topic Maps Fragment with other server and different type of storage and to merge them.
- output/display function is to output or display Topic Maps to file, printer, screen, etc.
    - Topic Maps to HTML translation function is to translate Topic Maps Fragment to HTML format.
    - Topic Maps to PDF translation function is to Translate Topic Maps Fragment to PDF format.
    - Information resources output function is to output resources to designated place.

Furthermore, we can build in more specialized and sophisticated ones such as the components for measuring and indexing "Semantic Distance" in Topic Maps. We describe this theme in the next section.

Fig. 2 shows the architecture of Application Framework based on Topic Maps.

3.2 Standardized Interface Between Components

If those components have loosely coupling structure, we can select and replace each component according to the purposes and the features of applications. In order to make it possible, each component needs to comply with some standard interface. Those standards are as follows:

- ISO/IEC 13250 Part-3 XML Syntax would be applicable between Topic Maps engine and Input/Output functional components.
- Plug-in would be applicable between Topic Maps engine and Input/Display functional components.
- Application Programming Interface would be applicable between Topic Maps engine and Input/Output functional components.
- Fragment Exchange Protocol would be applicable between Topic Maps engine and Topic Maps storage.

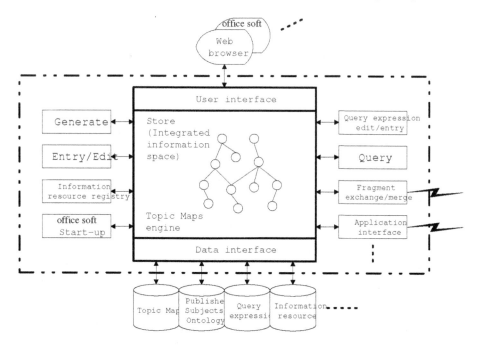

Fig. 2. Application Framework

Depending non how things go, some more standards, for example, graphic notation for Topic Maps, Metadata for Published Subjects will be needed. It is very
important for the Application Framework to make up and maintain good and
proper standards.

3.3 Expanding Alternative

Many software which can be used as functional component already exist. We
expect that more and more components will emerge, and including the capability
to interact with each other. Of course we can also use XSLT engine and FO engine
as one of the components.

We can classify those software in two categories, i.e. "purchasable" software
and open source software. The examples of the former are OKS (Ontopia Knowledge Suite), TMCore05 [10], etc. and the examples of the latter are TM4J [11],
TM4L [12], etc. Both categories are important, because according to our experience some customers prefer open source software, while other customers prefer
"purchasable" software as they want someone to have responsibility of those
components.

Using those components, it possible to build required application easily compare to build it from scratch. We only need to develop the components which
do not exist. Once the Application Framework is built, we can use it for various
purposes and applications. And we can enjoy the merits of Topic Maps more
easily at a lower price.

4   Semantic Distance in Topic Maps

The basic motivation in adding semantic distances to Topic Maps graph is directly the reduction of the semantic gap in understanding the semantic structure of Topic Maps along the previous research [14]. Providing a semantic metric to the Topic Maps will, for example, enable to point out that the semantic similarity is smaller between mandala and labyrinth than between mandala and maze. If subject nodes are in the same level group of topic nodes and have the same relations on the subject located at the immediate upper level group of topic nodes, then those subject nodes are semantically very close.

For a given Topic Map, the semantic distance between two adjacent nodes $\alpha_{i,l}$ and $\alpha_{j,l-1}$ is defined by the following:

$$S(\alpha_{i,l}, \alpha_{j,l-1}) = D_{inter} \times D_{intra} \times W(\alpha_{i,l}, \alpha_{j,l-1}) \tag{1}$$

Where $\alpha_{i,l}$ and $\alpha_{j,l-1}$ are the ith and the jth nodes located at the level l and l-1 group of nodes belonging to the Topic Maps respectively, D_{inter} is the inter-level discrimination weight to maintain the semantic distance between two levels of the Topic Maps, D_{intra} is the intra-level discrimination weight within a single level of the Topic Maps, and W is the semantic path cost between $\alpha_{i,l}$ and $\alpha_{j,l-1}$. In the Topic map implementation inside protege, we mainly manipulate the member-of relation among nodes. In our experiments, the weight of this relation is 1.5. Further evaluations with end users will enable to introduce a learning phase to tune D_{inter} and D_{intra} and will provide both qualitative and quantitative assessments regarding the semantic distance metric. Fig. 3 shows a Topic Map about Buddhism enriched by Semantic Distances.

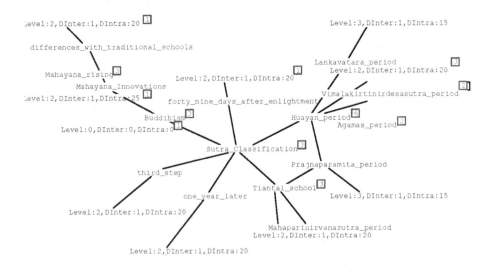

Fig. 3. Topic Map enriched by Semantic Distances

5   Our Challenge

As an information system development in accordance with the idea of the Application Framework based on Topic Maps, we introduce one of our challenge to develop knowledge management environment which supports the activities related to software life cycle.

5.1   Background

In software life cycle, there are many subjects and they are related each other intricately. Those are for example software, software life cycle processes, organizations, projects, person, formation, information technologies, business logic, documents, customers, standards, etc. it is very important challenge to construct the suitable management system for the organizations which engage in software development, maintenance and operation. Topic Maps is one of the most suitable technologies to solve such a problem.

Fig. 4 shows the model of relationships between subjects. In the figure, the circles represent the upper level subjects (the cluster of subjects) in which there are many specific subjects.

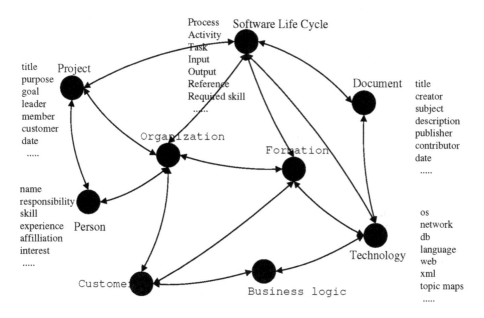

Fig. 4. Relationships between subjects

5.2   Purpose

The purpose of this challenge is to apply the Application Framework based on Topic Maps to construct the management environment of those subjects, their relationships and related information resources. And it also purposes to provide the environment to our customers.

5.3 Approach

Huge efforts have being made until now. People still continue to effort to manage various subjects and their complicated relationship in software life cycle. Because of those people's efforts, it already exist a lot of knowledge (ontologies) concerning the activities. We can use those existing knowledge. We give in the followings some examples:

- ISO/IEC 12207 Software life cycle processes (SLCP) for process model
- Capability Maturity Model (CMM) for evaluation of organization's maturity level of their software development processes
- Unified Modeling Language (UML) for analysis and design
- Software factories for software development

We decided to adopt SLCP as the core knowledge of software life cycle. The reasons we select this is that this standard not only describes the major component processes of a complete software life cycle and the high-level relations that govern their interactions, but also covers the life cycle of software from conceptualization of ideas through retirement. In concrete terms, SLCP describes the following life-cycle processes:

- Primary Processes:
  - Acquisition, Supply, Development, Operation, and Maintenance
- Supporting Processes:
  - Documentation, Configuration Management, Quality Assurance, Verification, Validation, Joint Review, Audit, and Problem Resolution.
- Organization Processes:
  - Management, Infrastructure, Improvement, and Training.

Each process is broken down to several activities, and each activity is again broken down to several tasks. SLCP also describes how to tailor the standard for a project.

In order to develop knowledge management environment for software life cycle, we made Topic Map of SLCP. Processes, activities, tasks and documents are represented as Topics, we also made subject indicators for them, and relationships between processes, activities, tasks and documents are represented as Associations in the Topic Map. The SLCP Topic Map is template and a tailored Topic Map is requested for each real project. When we implement some activities or tasks, thanks of the Topic Map we can get the necessary knowledge i.e. input documents, guidelines, manuals, check list, etc. easily. We can also understand immediately what and how we should make output in the activities or tasks. Next, we made another Topic Maps such as person, project, organization, technology, customer, etc. We also made subject indicators for them. For this application we need the following functional components at least:

- Input/Edit function for SLCP, person, project, etc.
- Registry function for documents

- Topic Maps engine function for handle all Topic Maps related to the software life cycle.
- Topic Maps storage function for all Topic Maps in the domain.
- Topic Maps query function for the subjects and relationships of them in the domain.
- Display/Output function for the subjects, relationships, and information resources.
- etc.

At this moment, we are using OKS for Topic Maps engine and storage. We are also using OKS to develop Input/Edit, Registry and Display functions. We are planning to develop Output function and another Input function using FO engine and XSLT engine.

5.4   Expected Benefit

As a result, we are expecting we can systematically store a lot of information and knowledge of software life cycle. We are also expecting we can access, share, offer and reuse those information and knowledge, even more we can create new information and knowledge from various points of view with various expressions. Users can systematize and organize information and knowledge with their viewpoint by themselves. We can provide this environment for our users. Our users and we can use this for many purposes. For example, the purposes are:

- project management
- process control (workflow management)
- activities, tasks implementation support
- content management
- internal audit for ISO 9000
- maturity evaluation
- skill transfer
- etc.

6   Conclusion

By combining those technical elements, we mentioned above organically, we think it is possible to organize the information/knowledge based not only on the information resources itself but on the subjects included in the resources. Thereby, the find and the accessibility of information/knowledge will be significantly improved.

We proposed in this paper an Application Framework based on Topic Maps using those technologies. As many applications consist of very similar functions, by only replacing the contents by more specific Topic Map, we can apply the Application Framework to various domains. It will enable to provide to the end users a larger accessible and sharable contents. Currently, the development of the Application Framework is going on. More specialized and sophisticated components such as "Semantic Distance Estimation" measuring the semantic distance of topic relationships has been evaluated in religion field and can be added in our Framework to provide semantically-richer Topic Maps. In the near future we would also like to evaluate synergistic effect between Bayesian Network [13] and Topic Maps.

References

1. Steve Pepper: The TAO of Topic Maps : Finding the Way in the Age of Infoglut, http://www.ontopia.net/topicmaps/materials/tao.html.
2. Steve Pepper, Sylvia Schwab: Curing the Web's Identity Crisis : Subject Indicators for RDF, http://www.ontopia.net/topicmaps/materials/identitycrisis.html.
3. Riichiro Mizoguchi: Science of Intelligence: Ontology Engineering, Ohmsha, ISBN4-274-20017-5.
4. Lars Marius Garshol: TMRAP - Topic Maps Remote Access Protocol, http://www.informatik.uni-leipzig.de/ tmra05/PRES/LMGa.pdf.
5. Kal Ahmed: TMShare - Topic Map Fragment Exchange In a Peer-To-Peer Application, http://www.techquila.com/topicmapster.html.
6. Robert Barta: TMIP, Topic Map Interaction Protocol 0.3, Specification, http://astma.it.bond.edu.au/tmip-specification.dbk.
7. Robert Barta, Lars Marius Garshol: Topic Map Query Language (TMQL), http://www.isotopicmaps.org/tmql/.
8. Lars Marius Garshol: Metadata? Thesauri? Taxonomies? Topic Maps: Making sense of it all!, http://www.ontopia.net/topicmaps/materials/tm-vs-thesauri.html.
9. Ontopia: The Ontopia Knowledge Suite, http://www.ontopia.net/solutions/products.html.
10. NetworkedPlanet: TMCore05, http://www.networkedplanet.com/products/index.html.
11. TM4J Project: TM4J - Topic Maps For Java, http://tm4j.sourceforge.net/.
12. Winston-Salem State University: TOPIC MAPS 4 E-LEARNING, http://compsci.wssu.edu/iis/NSDL/.
13. Bayesia: Bayesian Network, http://www.bayesia.com/.
14. Frederic Andres and Motomu Naito: Dynamic Topic Mapping Using Latent Semantic Indexing"in IEEE International Conference on Information Technology and Applications Sydney 4th-7th July, 2005. pp 220-225.

TMRAP – Topic Maps Remote Access Protocol

Lars Marius Garshol

Ontopia AS, Oslo, Norway
larsga@ontopia.net
http://www.ontopia.net

Abstract. This paper describes TMRAP, an abstract web service interface for remote access to topic maps. It can be used to access a topic
map repository to query or update a topic map, or to listen for updates
to parts of a topic map. An HTTP binding for the interface is presented
in this paper; a SOAP binding will be produced in the future.

1 Introduction

The current stack of Topic Maps standards (data model, interchange syntax,
constraint language, and query language) is well suited to building interoperable
Topic Maps applications, given that they meet one restriction. That is, applications must be restricted to a single server, because no standardized means for
applications to connect to each other over the network currently exists. As has
been argued [Moore03], this is unacceptable.

This paper presents TMRAP, a proposed web service interface that aims to
make it possible for Topic Maps applications to interoperate over the network,
and for systems not based on Topic Maps to connect to Topic Maps servers to add
or retrieve data. The version of TMRAP presented in this paper is an extension
of the original TMRAP 0.2[Moore04], but is not backwards compatible.

It should be noted that TMRAP is not a standard, but a private proposal,
implemented in commercial software. The interface may be freely implemented
in other systems.

1.1 Use Cases

Designing a web service interface is not like designing an API. Clients using
a web service should be able to perform a single task as a single operation,
since the overhead of invoking operations is substantial. This is not the case in
an API, which has a much higher granularity, since with an API the cost of
invoking individual operations is negligible by comparison. This implies that a
web service must to a much greater degree make assumptions about the uses to
which it will be put, which again implies that a clear picture of the use cases a
web service will satisfy is essential to its design.

The use cases which TMRAP was designed to meet are presented in this section. Due to space limitations, the web service is then presented with no explicit
arguments as to why it must take the form it does to satisfy these use cases.

L. Maicher and J. Park (Eds.): TMRA 2005, LNAI 3873, pp. 53–68, 2006.

Nearly all use of TMRAP involves interchanging fragments of Topic Maps data, which may or may not be processed using Topic Maps-aware tools. If the producer/consumer is not using a Topic Maps-aware tool, using a developer-friendly syntax such as TM/XML may be more suitable [Garshol05]. TMRAP allows the client to choose what syntax to receive Topic Maps fragments in.

Connecting portals. A simple, but very powerful example, described in [Pepper04], is that of connecting two portals, A and B, both of which have topic pages about the same topic. When the user navigates to the page for the topic on A, A can send B a request, asking if it knows about this topic. On receipt of a positive answer A can insert a link to the topic page for the same topic in B. TMRAP supports this scenario, and even allows the two portals to share Topic Maps data.

Applications working with fragments. A more complex example would be an application that works with only a limited subset (a fragment) of the complete topic map held by the server. An example of this scenario would be when a Topic Maps server is integrated into a portal not based on Topic Maps, running on a different server, which retrieves Topic Maps fragments from the server for presentation when needed. The portal may also submit searches to the Topic Maps server, and present the responses to the user.

Integrating with other applications. A very common use of TMRAP would be to use it to integrate a Topic Maps application with one that is not based on Topic Maps, for example a traditional Content Management System (CMS). The CMS maintains metadata about information resources in the CMS. The topic map contains the key metadata from the CMS, together with much additional information (such as what the resources are about (their subjects), and information about the subjects). The CMS would then need to create, update, and delete topics representing the resources as information about these is updated/changed in the CMS [Garshol02b].

This topic map could then be edited in a separate topic map editor to further classify and describe the documents in the CMS. The CMS could also retrieve fragments for these topics and display them (including associations to topics that only exist in the topic map) in a portal rendered from the CMS data.

Creating "knowledge hubs". One very interesting use case is creating "knowledge hubs" where information from many sources is brought together and integrated. This is effectively a form of Enterprise Information Integration (EII) [Halevy05].

In this scenario, information providers invoke operations on a Topic Maps server to add information coming from outside sources, and the server then integrates this information into the existing topic map. Consumers can then query the integrated topic map and retrieve fragments of information extracted from the topic map.

2   The Abstract Interface

This section defines the abstract interface conceptually, without reference to any specific technology other than Topic Maps. This enables the same design to be used with separate bindings to different technologies, such as HTTP and SOAP. The interface can return fragments representing topics as well as query results from the tolog query language [Garshol05b]; these can be in any Topic Maps syntax, chosen by the client. Authentication and access control are left to the specific bindings.

2.1   Concepts

The interface distinguishes between two actors: a server, containing a topic map repository, and a client. The topic map repository on the server contains any number of individual topic maps, each identified by a unique handle, which is a syntactically opaque string. The server provides access to the repository through a number of operations, each described in a separate section below. No assumptions are made about the client.

Operations are of two kinds: server operations, and callbacks to the client from the server. Each set of operations has a separate section below.

Error handling. If a request is in error (incorrect parameters, tolog or fragment syntax error, no topics found, etc) this must be reported to the client. Erroneous requests must not cause any state changes on the server, whether to the topic map or to the list of registered client listeners. The details of error reporting are left to the protocol bindings.

2.2   Server Operations

Server operations are invoked by the client, and the interface does not dictate what triggers an operation; this is left to the discretion of the client.

The get-topic operation. This operation is used to get a fragment representing a single topic. The parameters to the operation are shown in table 1 on the following page.

If the topicmap parameter is provided the topic maps identified by it are queried, otherwise the server decides which topic maps are queried. The rationale for this is that if the client knows that it wants to query a specific topic map it can do so. The most common use case, however, is that the client simply knows that it wants information on a specific topic. In this case it can ask a known TMRAP server without having to worry about the internal structure of that server.

There are many possible means by which the server might determine which topic maps to operate on, such as operating on all, on a default topic map, on all currently loaded topic maps, on all topic maps to which the client has access rights, etc. As there are many ways to decide this, and as the decision strictly speaking does not affect interoperability, the mechanisms for determining this are left undefined.

Table 1. The `get-topic` operation

Parameter	Required?	Repeatable?	Type?	Description
item	no	yes	URI	An item identifier of the sought topic.
subject	no	yes	URI	A subject locator of the sought topic.
identifier	no	yes	URI	A subject identifier of the sought topic.
topicmap	no	yes	String	A topic map handle.
syntax	no	no	String	A string identifying the syntax used in the fragment.
view	no	no	String	A string identifying the view used to define the fragment.

A set of topics is returned containing, for each queried topic map, all topics matching the parameters. The matching topics are all topics which have one of the URIs in `item` as an item identifier, one of the URIs in `subject` as a subject locator, or one of the URIs in `identifier` as a subject identifier.

The set of topics found can have any cardinality. However, all of the topics found are merged into a single topic (in the returned fragment; the state on the server should not change), as the semantics of the operation is to return a single topic. It follows from this that the identifiers passed in the parameters all identify a single subject, and so even if multiple topics may be found (in the same or in different topic maps) they must necessarily all represent the same subject. A fragment representing the merged topic is returned in the syntax specified in the `syntax` parameter. The default will be to use XTM, but other alternatives are possible, as described in 2.4 on page 63.

A challenge in extracting fragments from topic maps is knowing where to stop. Every topic is defined by means of other topics; its associated topics, topic type, association types, occurrence types, name scopes, and so on are all topics. For each of these topics one might conceivably include just the identity, the identity and the names, or a full fragment, and it is not obvious which of these options best serve the needs of users.

Analysis of the use cases suggests that there are situations where each of these possibilities may be what users want, and in some cases even finer-grained control may be needed. The `view` parameter can be used to specify what should be included in the fragment returned. The requested topic will always be included in full; the view applies to the topics referenced by it. The possible values of this parameter are:

- **stub**: only a single identifier will be included, as defined in [Garshol02]. (This is the default view.)
- **names**: the identity and the names will be included.
- **complete**: complete fragments are included, but topics referenced from these fragments will use the **stub** view.

It is also possible to define custom views with TM-Views [Garshol05] and reference these using the `view` parameter. It is assumed that the views will have been registered with the TMRAP server before the request is received. There is no support for using multiple views when querying multiple topic maps since the client in any case receives a single fragment. That is, to the client there is only one view.

The get-tolog Operation. This operation is used to get an XML document representing the results of a tolog query, either as a fragment or as an explicit representation of the result. The parameters to the operation are shown in table 2.

Table 2. The get-tolog operation

Parameter	Required?	Repeatable?	Type?	Description
tolog	yes	no	String	A tolog query.
topicmap	yes	no	String	A topic map handle.
syntax	no	no	String	A syntax identifier.
view	no	no	String	View identifier.

This operation has two modes of operation: if the requested **syntax** is tolog there are no restrictions on the query, and an XML structure giving the actual query results is returned. Otherwise, the query must produce only a single column containing only topics, and all topics in the result are output in the same way as for the **get-topic** operation, except that they are not merged (as there is no implication that all topics found by a single tolog query must represent the same subject).

A request against the Opera topic map requesting tolog syntax using the **stub** view and the following query

```
select $COMPOSER, count($OPERA) from
 composed-by($OPERA : opera, $COMPOSER : composer)
order by $OPERA desc limit 2?
```

would produce the following result:

```
<result xmlns:x="http://www.topicmaps.org/xtm/1.0/"
        xmlns:l="http://www.w3.org/1999/xlink">
  <head>
    <column>COMPOSER</column>
    <column>OPERA</column>
  </head>
  <body>
    <row>
      <value>
        <x:subjectIndicatorRef
            l:href="http://en.wikipedia.org/wiki/Verdi"/>
      </value>
      <value>28</value>
```

```
      </row>
      <row>
        <value>
          <x:subjectIndicatorRef
              l:href="http://en.wikipedia.org/wiki/Mascagni"/>
        </value>
        <value>16</value>
      </row>
    </body>
</result>
```

When the syntax is tolog, the fragments within the `value` elements are included using XTM.

The RELAX-NG schema [ISO19757-2] for tolog query results is:

```
start =
  element result {
    element head {
      element column { text }*
    },
    element body {
      element row {
        element value { any }*
      }*
    }
  }


# using wildcard here as there are many alternatives for the
# fragments, and specifying them  all is complex
any = (text | element * { anyatt*, any })*
anyatt = attribute * { text }
```

The add-fragment operation. This operation is used to import a topic map fragment into the repository. The parameters to the operation are shown in table 3 on the next page.

The fragment is imported into the identified topic map. Usually this will be used to create a single topic, but the operation is deliberately not restricted

Table 3. The add-fragment operation

Parameter	Required?	Repeatable?	Type?	Description
syntax	yes	no	String	A string identifying the syntax used in the fragment.
fragment	yes	no	String	A fragment representing part of a topic map.
topicmap	yes	no	String	A topic map handle.

to only this. Implementations will most likely have limits on the sizes of the fragments they accept.

Formally, the operation deserializes the received fragment into a TMDM instance [ISO13250-2], then merges that instance into the TMDM instance identified in the `topicmap` parameter, using normal TMDM merging rules.

The `delete-topic` operation. This operation is used to delete a topic from a topic map in the repository. The parameters to the operation are shown in table 4.

Table 4. The `delete-topic` operation

Parameter	Required?	Repeatable?	Type?	Description
item	no	yes	URI	An item identifier of the sought topic.
subject	no	yes	URI	A subject locator of the sought topic.
identifier	no	yes	URI	A subject identifier of the sought topic.
topicmap	no	yes	String	A topic map handle.

All topics in the selected topic map(s) which match the parameters are deleted. Deleting a topic means removing all its base names, variants, and occurrences, as well as all associations in which it plays a role. The topic will also be removed wherever it is used as a scope or type, but the scoped and typed topic map constructs are left undeleted.

The rationale for deleting all associations is that after removing one role from the association unary associations are invalid, while binary associations are meaningless. Associations of higher arities might still be meaningful, but in the interest of simplicity they are treated the same way. Several years of experience with this operation (in an API, admittedly) suggests that in practice this works very well.

The `get-topic-page` Operation. This operation is used to ask the server whether it has any pages for a specific topic. The pages in question might be pages in some Topic Maps application that can display the topic to a user (known as "view pages"), or pages where the user can edit the topic (known as "edit pages"), or other kinds of pages.

The `get-topic-page` operation is really meant to satisfy the portal integration use case mentioned above, and in particular the scenario described in [Pepper04] as "VISIT", where one portal dynamically links to the topic page for the same topic in another portal.

The parameters to the operation are shown in table 5 on the next page.

The response from the request is a topic map describing the structure on the server. The response must contain at least what is described here, but the decision to return a topic map rather than some custom XML format means that the

Table 5. The `get-topic-page` operation

Parameter	Required?	Repeatable?	Type?	Description
item	no	yes	URI	An item identifier of the sought topic.
subject	no	yes	URI	A subject locator of the sought topic.
identifier	no	yes	URI	A subject identifier of the sought topic.
topicmap	yes	no	String	A topic map handle.
syntax	yes	no	String	A string identifying the syntax to be used in the response.

operation is inherently extensible. In the following, the prefix `rap` is to be understood as the subject indentifier namespace `http://psi.ontopia.net/tmrap/`.

The response must include the following:

- A topic of type `rap:server`, representing the server.
- One topic of type `rap:topicmap` for each topic map in which one or more matching topics were found. Each topic map must have exactly one occurrence of type `rap:handle` containing the topic map handle. Each topic map must have a `rap:contained-in` association to the server it's hosted on.
- A single topic containing the results of merging all matching topics. Only identifiers and names need be included.
- For each view and edit page for this topic on the server a topic of type `rap:view-page` or `rap:edit-page`, with the URI of the page as the subject locator of the topic. Each page must also have a `rap:contained-in` association to the topic map it is rendered from.

Note that if no topics are matched the response will contain only the server topic.

An example might help clarify this. The result of asking Ontopia's online demo server (once it's set up) for the topic "Japan" would give the following result (when querying the `i18n.ltm` topic map) in TM/XML.

```
<topic-pages xmlns="http://psi.ontopia.net/tmrap/"
             xmlns:tm="http://psi.ontopia.net/xml/tm-xml/"
             xmlns:iso="http://psi.topicmaps.com/iso13250/"
             xmlns:oasis="http://psi.oasis-open.org/iso/3166/#">

  <server id="online-demo">
    <iso:topic-name>
      <tm:value>Ontopia Omnigator online demo</tm:value>
    </iso:topic-name>
  </server>

  <topicmap id="i18n.ltm">
    <iso:topic-name>
      <tm:value>Scripts and languages</tm:value>
```

```
    </iso:topic-name>
    <handle datatype="http://www.w3.org/2001/XMLSchema#anyURI"
        >i18n.ltm</handle>
    <contained-in role="containee" otherrole="container"
                  topicref="online-demo"/>
  </topicmap>

  <oasis:country>
    <tm:identifier>http://psi.oasis-open.org/iso/3166/#392
        </tm:identifier>
    <iso:topic-name>
      <tm:value>Japan</tm:value>
    </iso:topic-name>
  </oasis:country>

  <view-page id="p1">
    <tm:locator>http://www.ontopia...?tm=i18n.ltm&id=japan
        </tm:locator>
    <contained-in role="containee" otherrole="container"
                  topicref="i18n.ltm"/>
  </view-page>
</topic-pages>
```

The add-type-listener operation. This operation is used to register a client to receive callbacks for all updates to topics of a specific type. The parameters to the operation are shown in table 6.

Table 6. The add-type-listener operation

Parameter	Required?	Repeatable?	Type?	Description
item	no	yes	URI	An item identifier of the sought topic.
subject	no	yes	URI	A subject locator of the sought topic.
identifier	no	yes	URI	A subject identifier of the sought topic.
topicmap	yes	no	String	A topic map handle.
client	yes	no	Handle	The client handle is defined by the binding.
syntax	no	no	String	A string identifying the syntax to be used in notifications.

All topics matching the parameters are found in the identified topic map. It is an error if this is not exactly one topic. This means that one will get an error message if the topic type is not found on the server, or if what the client considered to be one topic is more than one topic to the server.

Every time a topic that is an instance of this type is created, modified, or deleted the corresponding client operation is triggered on all clients. Registrations are persistent until explicitly removed.

The `syntax` parameter is used by the client to indicate what syntax it would like to receive notifications in. All `topic-created` and `topic-updated` notifications must use this syntax. The default is XTM.

The `remove-type-listener` operation. This operation is used to unregister a client that has already registered with the `add-type-listener` request so that update callbacks are no longer received. The parameters to the operation are shown in table 7.

Table 7. The `remove-type-listener` operation

Parameter	Required?	Repeatable?	Type?	Description
item	no	yes	URI	An item identifier of the sought topic.
subject	no	yes	URI	A subject locator of the sought topic.
identifier	no	yes	URI	A subject identifier of the sought topic.
topicmap	yes	no	String	A topic map handle.
client	yes	no	Handle	The client handle is defined by the binding.

All topics matching the parameters are found in the identified topic map. It is an error if this is not exactly one topic. This client is then removed as one of the clients registered to receive callbacks for this topic type. It is an error if this client is not registered previously.

2.3   Client Operations

The operations in this section are operations on the client invoked by the server in response to the client registering itself using the `add-type-listener` operation.

The `topic-created` operation. This operation is invoked by the server every time a topic of a type which the client has registered itself as a listener for is created. The parameters are shown in table 8.

Table 8. The `topic-created` operation

Parameter	Required?	Repeatable?	Type?	Description
server	yes	no	URI	The URI of the server.
topicmap	yes	no	String	A topic map handle.
fragment	yes	no	String	A fragment representing the created topic.

Table 9. The `topic-updated` operation

Parameter	Required?	'Repeatable?	'Type?	Description
server	yes	no	URI	The URI of the server.
topicmap	yes	no	String	A topic map handle.
fragment	yes	no	String	A fragment representing the updated topic.

The fragment provided contains the created topic (in the syntax requested by the client). The interface does not require any specific behaviour from the client in response to the request.

The `topic-updated` operation. This operation is invoked by the server every time a topic is updated of a type which the client has registered itself as a listener for. The parameters are shown in table 9.

The fragment provided contains the updated topic as it was after the update, in the syntax requested by the client. The interface does not require any specific behaviour from the client in response to the request.

Note that the change to the topic may be to the identifiers, in which case the client may not be able to tell which topic has changed. For this reason the server must include any identifiers removed or added in the update in the notification, but the removed identifiers must be omitted in following update notifications.

The `topic-deleted` operation. This operation is invoked by the server every time a topic is deleted of a type which the client has registered itself as a listener for. The parameters are shown in table 10.

Table 10. The `topic-deleted` operation

Parameter	Required?	Repeatable?	Type?	Description
server	yes	no	URI	The URI of the server.
topicmap	yes	no	String	A topic map handle.
item	no	yes	URI	An item identifier of the deleted topic.
subject	no	yes	URI	A subject locator of the deleted topic.
identifier	no	yes	URI	A subject identifier of the deleted topic.

The identifiers given identify the deleted topic to the client. No specific behaviour is required from the client.

2.4   Syntax Identifiers

The syntaxes are identified by their MIME types [RFC2045]. The valid alternatives are shown in table 11 on the next page. If no syntax is specified, the default is to produce an XTM fragment as defined in [Garshol02].

Table 11. Topic map syntax MIME types

Syntax	MIME type
XTM	application/x-xtm
LTM	text/x-ltm
AsTMa=	text/x-astma
TM/XML	text/x-tmxml
tolog	text/x-tolog

The TM/XML syntax is described in [Garshol05].

3   The HTTP Binding

An HTTP binding of the TMRAP abstract interface could take several approaches. It could use SOAP [SOAP]; it could take a RESTful approach [Fielding00]; or it could aim for a more straightforward, traditional HTTP approach. As mentioned in the abstract, this paper opts for the last of these, but there are plans to add SOAP support in the future.

3.1   To REST or Not to REST

REST is best thought of as a style guide for creating web services, famously defined by [Fielding00]. The argument for not using it in TMRAP is that it recommends using the HTTP methods (GET, PUT, etc) to operate directly on resources exposed on the web. It could be described as object-oriented instead of the traditional procedural approach, where URIs represent resources (or objects) instead of procedures.

It should be quite clear from the operations provided that TMRAP is very much in the traditional camp, and not at all REST-like. The rationale is that, perhaps somewhat perversely, Topic Maps provide no easily addressable isolated resources to expose and operate on. Further, REST makes heavy demands on the underlying HTTP infrastructure, which may not always support everything that is needed very well (URL mapping of complex URLs, obscure HTTP operations, etc etc).

In short, the argument generally put forward for REST is elegance [Barta05], whereas the argument against it in this paper is lack of elegance for this particular purpose, as well as a desire to avoid infrastructure problems.

3.2   The Binding Itself

The general approach taken by the binding is simple: server and client endpoints are defined using HTTP URIs. Each operation has a separate URI obtained by concatenating the endpoint URI with the operation name. Each parameter becomes a URI query parameter in the traditional `?foo=1&bar=2&baz=3` syntax.

Authentication and access control are not considered part of the HTTP binding, but are provided by the application server itself, using the normal HTTP mechanisms.

It's tempting to map the `syntax` parameter to the `Accept` header in HTTP, but for this to provide any benefit it requires the user to learn the syntax for specifying alternatives, and it requires implementations to do the same. Few HTTP client libraries provide any support for this, and so it seems better to map `syntax` in the same way as the other parameters.

All operations which make modifications (this includes the client operations) must be accessed using the POST method, while all operations which only retrieve information must use GET. (This means that the `fragment` parameter will automatically travel in the request body, as with POST all parameters are transmitted in the body.)

If errors occur, as defined above, the server must return an HTTP response with response code 400 ("Bad Request"). Including an informative error message in the response is encouraged.

4   Related Work

Substantial work has already been done in this area, and so the charge might be made against TMRAP that it needlessly proliferates the number of alternative interfaces. To answer this charge we review related work.

The most complete and well-documented alternative Topic Maps interface proposal to date is clearly TMIP[Barta05]. This protocol takes a REST-based approach, and is entirely dependent on TMQL (which is not yet stable). It supports retrieval of fragments in various syntaxes, and updates to selected topics. There is no explicit support for deletion and creation, however, although there are hints as to how these might be achieved. There is no support for events.

An alternative is the Topic Maps Service[NetworkedPlanet05] web service based on SOAP and WSDL. This service provides predefined methods for returning topic fragments by certain criteria (topics by type, topic by id, topic by subject identifier, hierarhices, etc), and also for updates and deletes. There is also support for retrieving fragments by means of TMRQL queries. There is no support for events, and TMRQL is unsuitable for our purposes as it requires the topic maps to be stored in specific SQL databases [Barta05b].

A third alternative is the SPARQL Protocol for RDF[SPARQL], which is based on RDF and the RDF query language SPARQL. The protocol is abstract, and has a standard WSDL binding. The present version only provides support for running SPARQL queries and returning the results.

Other related work is reviewed by [Barta05], of which the most relevant are Shark[Schwotzer04] and [Thompson04]. Shark is designed for mobile handheld units, and so has rather different design considerations. [Thompson04] is interesting, but based on the as-yet unstable TMQL, REST-based, and not described in any detail.

As should be evident, no interface currently exists that, in our opinion, meets all our use cases. In particular, no other interface provides event callbacks. Of the Topic Maps-based proposals, two use TMQL (which is unstable), the third uses TMRQL (which is unsuitable), and the fourth (Shark) is intended for a different environment.

Some protocols [Barta05] provide operations not found in TMRAP that allow clients to get information about the server. Such information might include which topic maps are available, which formats are supported by the server, etc. Such operations have been left out of TMRAP as there is nothing in the use cases to suggest that it would be useful. Introspection operations only seem useful in cases where clients are looking servers up in some form of registry and connecting to them dynamically. However, the use cases all involve interaction between a client and a server already known to the person (or tool) configuring the client, and so support for this does not seem necessary.

5   Conclusion

In this article is presented the design of a Topic Maps web service interface that is based on stable and documented technologies, and which, we believe, satisfies a number of important use cases, and thus opens the possibility for Topic Maps applications that are more open and accessible than what has been seen thus far.

5.1   Further Work

The web service interface will be implemented in the commercial Ontopia Knowledge Suite (OKS) over the coming months, and used in a number of different projects. Further revisions will be made if experience with usage in these projects indicate that revisions are needed.

In addition, it is thought that special requests that allow legacy data (XML that is not a Topic Maps syntax, CSV files, etc) to be imported into a topic map may well be needed. That is, clients may wish to add fragments of data to a topic map that is not in any Topic Maps syntax. In these cases, it may be easiest for the server to handle the conversion into Topic Maps, and so special requests may be added that allow legacy data to be imported directly into the server. (One assumes that some form of conversion tool or configuration will already have been installed on the server.)

Finally, it is possible that support will be added for subscription to RSS channels containing topic map update information. Enabling the listener mechanism to support more fine-grained subscription, possibly via tolog queries, is also being considered.

References

[Barta05]   *TMIP, A RESTful Topic Maps Interaction Protocol*; Barta, R.; Extreme Markup 2005, Montral, Canada. http://www.mulberrytech.com/Extreme/Proceedings/html/2005/Barta01/EML2005Barta01.html

[Barta05b]	*SQL as TM Query Language? No, thanks!*; Barta, R.; private blog entry, undated. http://topicmaps.it.bond.edu.au/docs/38?style=printable
[Fielding00]	*Architectural Styles and the Design of Network-based Software Architectures*; Fielding, R. T.; Doctoral dissertation, University of California, Irvine, 2000. http://www.ics.uci.edu/ fielding/pubs/dissertation/top.htm
[Halevy05]	*Enterprise Information Integration: Successes, Challenges and Controversies*; Halevy, A., Ashish, N., Bitton, D., Carey, M., Draper, D., Pollock, J., Rosenthal, A., Sikka, V.; Proceedings of SIGACM-SIGMOD '05 Baltimore, USA; 778-787. http://www.cs.washington.edu/homes/alon/files/eiisigmod05.pdf
[Garshol02]	*XTM Fragment Interchange 0.1*; Garshol, L. M.; Ontopia Technical Report 2002-09-23. http://www.ontopia.net/topicmaps/materials/xtm-fragments.html
[Garshol02b]	*Topic maps in content management – The rise of the ITMS*; Garshol, L. M.; Proceedings of XML 2002, IDEAlliance, Baltimore, USA; 2002-12-08. http://www.ontopia.net/topicmaps/materials/itms.html
[Garshol05]	*TM/XML – Representing Topic Maps in XML*; Garshol, L. M., Bogachev, D.; forthcoming, to be published in proceedings of TMRA'05.
[Garshol05b]	*tolog – a topic maps query language*; Garshol, L. M., forthcoming, to be published in proceedings of TMRA'05.
[ISO13250-2]	ISO 13250-3: Topic Maps – Data Model; International Organization for Standardization; Geneva. http://www.isotopicmaps.org/sam/sam-model/
[ISO19757-2]	ISO 19757-2: Document Schema Definition Languages (DSDL) – Part 2: Regular-grammar- based validation – RELAX NG; International Organization for Standardization; Geneva. http://www.y12.doe.gov/sgml/sc34/document/0362_files/relaxng-is.pdf
[Moore03]	*Semantic Web Servers*; Moore, G.; Extreme Markup 2003, Montral, Canada. http://www. ontopia.net/topicmaps/materials/semantic-web-servers.ppt
[Moore04]	*Topic Maps Remote Access Protocol*; Moore, G.; 2004-04-06, Ontopia. http://www.jtc1sc34.org/repository/0507.htm
[NetworkedPlanet05]	*Topic Map Web Services*; Moore, G., Ahmed, Kal; NetworkedPlanet. Available on 2005-08-12 from http://www.networkedplanet.com/technology/webservices/intro.html
[Pepper04]	*Seamless Knowledge–Spontaneous Knowledge Federation using TMRAP*; Pepper, S., Garshol, L. M.; Extreme Markup 2004, Montral, Canada. http://www.ontopia.net/topicmaps/materials/ Seamless+Knowledge+with+TMRAP.ppt
[RFC2045]	*Multipurpose Internet Mail Extensions (MIME) Part One: Format of Internet Message Bodies*; Freed, N., Borenstein, N.; IETF RFC 2045; November 1996; http://www.isi.edu/in-notes/rfc2045.txt

[SOAP]   *SOAP Version 1.2 Part 1: Messaging Framework*; Gudgin, M.,
                    Hadley, M., Mendelsohn, N., Moreau, J., Frystyk Nielsen, H.;
                    W3C Recommendation; 24 June 2003.
                    http://www.w3.org/TR/2003/REC-soap12-part1-20030624/

[Schwotzer04]   *Shark - a System for Management, Synchronization and Ex-
                    change of Knowledge in Mobile User Groups*; Schwotzer, T.,
                    Geihs, K.; Technical Report, Intelligent Networks and Man-
                    agement of Distributed Systems, TU Berlin; http://ivs.tu-
                    berlin.de/ thsc/Shark_IKnow.pdf

[SPARQL]   *SPARQL Protocol for RDF*; Grant Clark, K.; W3C Work-
                    ing Draft 27 May 2005; http://www.w3.org/TR/rdf-sparql-
                    protocol/

[Thompson04]   *Scalable, document-centric addressing of semantic stores using
                    the XPointer Framework and the REST architectural style*;
                    Thompson, B., Moore, G., Parsia, B., Bebee, B. R.; Extreme
                    Markup 2004, Montral, Canada.
                    http://www.mulberrytech.com/Extreme/Proceedings/
                    html/2004/Thompson01/ EML2004Thompson01.html

Replication of Published Subject Indicator as Thesaurus by Means of LDAP

Thomas Schwotzer and Agnes Cebulla

University of Technology, Berlin
thsc@cs.tu-berlin.de, mail@agnes-cebulla.de

Abstract. Published subject indicators (PSI) are public available descriptions of non-addressable subjects. PSI sets can be used as shared vocabulary. Different Topic Map authors can use the same PSI sets to assure that topics dealing with the same subjects are recognized as identical topics by arbitrary Topic Map engines. There is no standardized structure for PSIs or PSI sets. There is no concept for distributed and replicated PSI sets. Both are required features from several application classes. This paper describes how thesauri can be used as a schema for PSI sets and how existing thesauri can be converted to Topic Maps. It is also explained how LDAP can be used as replication platform for PSI sets.

1 Introduction

Topic Maps are structured around two core concepts: subjects and information resources (IR). The later are defined as entities that can automatically be processed by computers and there exist algorithms that can decide whether two IRs are identical or not. Subjects are things about which a Topic Maps author is interested to store knowledge. Addressable subjects are information resources (like web pages, online documents etc.). All other subjects are non-addressable subjects, e.g. Hamlet, the Soviet Union, the concept of peace.

Subjects are not stored in Topic Maps directly. Topics are used instead as placeholders for subjects. One topic can be a placeholder for only one subject. Any topic can have a link to its subject. This is straightforward for addressable subject. Non-addressable subject whereas cannot be linked per definition because there is no IR which can be addressed. Subject Indicators (SI) are used to overcome this problem. A SI is an IR that describes a subject. Whenever a SI was made publicly available it is called a Published Subject Indicator (PSI). A collection of PSIs is called a PSI set. There are no constraints for PSI formats or structure. A PSI can be plain text, a picture, a topic in a XML Topic Map etc.

PSI sets can be used by different Topic Maps authors to define which topics are placeholders for which subject. Thus, in different Topic Maps there can be two topics depicting the same subject. PSIs can be seen as a shared vocabulary.

Another approach for administration of shared vocabularies is a thesaurus which is a collection of concepts and their hierarchical relations. Constructing a thesaurus is a very time consuming task.

L. Maicher and J. Park (Eds.): TMRA 2005, LNAI 3873, pp. 69–76, 2006.

Both PSIs and thesauri are not distributed by itself. Conceptually, PSIs can be accessed via the Internet and thus they are distributed. The same applies to a thesaurus. This is not sufficient for any application class. Some applications require replication of concept systems or namely PSI sets. Furthermore, for a lot of applications it would be helpful having a system that allows using existing PSIs (which are kept up to date by an external site) and which can be extended locally. Such a system will be presented in this paper. It is a combination of a thesaurus (to structure the concepts), Topic Maps as a representation format and LDAP as a replication platform.

2   An Example Describing the Challenge of Distributed PSIs

Imagine a software company called X produces a Topic Map Engine (TME). They decided to use Topic Maps (of course) to structure internal knowledge. Probably, the subject "Topic Maps" will be of special interest as well as the subject "X's TME". Two subject indicators are required because neither "Topic Maps" nor "X's TME" is an addressable subject. The company also decides to publish their SIs. Imagine another company called Y makes projects with Topic Maps especially in distributed environments. They have also decided structuring internal knowledge with Topic Maps. They are aware of company X which has a high reputation in their business field. Therefore, they plan to re-use PSIs defined by X and are going to add additional concepts like "Distributed Topic Maps" etc. Technically, it looks easy. Y defines its own concepts as PSIs and defines links to concepts of X which shall be re-used. Thus, Y can also introduce derived concepts from X, e.g. "Distributed Topic Maps" might be a sub-concept of "Topic Maps".

Unfortunately, this approach wouldn't lead to the wished results. X can change and fully reorganize its PSIs whenever it likes. Moreover, Y wouldn't even get a notification in this case. Thus, Y has absolutely no way to assure consistency in its own knowledge base. Alternately, Y could make a copy of all concepts of X and add its own PSIs. This approach assures consistency because changes in X' PSIs doesn't harm Y's copy. On the other hand side, corrections in X' PSIs are not propagated to Y's PSIs. Thus, after making the copy, Y is fully responsible for any PSI. Neither the link nor the copy approach lead to wished results. A replication approach is required.

3   LDAP – A Distributed Directory Service

LDAP (Lightweight Directory Access Protocol) [RFC-2251] was derived from DAP (Directory Access Protocol) which is a protocol for the X.500 standard. DAP is a rather complex standard based on the OSI Protocol Stack. LDAP is the result of the need for a less complex TCP/IP based protocol to access directories. It has reduced functionality but is more popular then its predecessor DAP.

A LDAP directory contains entries which can have relations. In LDAP, a schema describes the structure of entries and possible relation types between them. The probably best known and most frequently utilised schema is the schema for structuring information of persons and organisations: The distinguished name (DN) is a mandatory attribute of an entry and unique in the whole LDAP tree. An entry for a person has additional attributes like user ID, password or telephone number. The common name (CN) attribute allows the definition of a human readable name. Furthermore, e-mail address, title and similar attributes can be described in such an entry. Since all entries in LDAP can be organised hierarchically, there are nodes for organisations which have sub nodes for sub organisations and/or employees.

LDAP administrators are free to define their own schema. LDAP allows replication. It is also possible to get a copy from a LDAP server and to extend this directory locally. Any changes from a remote server are propagated if wished. LDAP has the necessary features that are needed for the replication of PSIs. Unfortunately, there is no common schema for PSI sets. But there is a well known and standardised structure for organising concepts: Thesaurus.

4   Thesaurus

The word thesaurus is derived from the Greek noun *thesaurus* which means treasure. The term thesaurus is now used to depict a well-organized structure of concepts. The are a couple of existing thesauri on the Internet, e.g. Thesaurus of Sociological Indexing Terms[1], Life Sciences Thesaurus[2], The Astronomy Thesaurus [3], ASIS Thesaurus of Information Science[4], INFODATA Thesaurus[5], UNESCO Thesaurus[6] and others. The construction of a thesaurus is a very time consuming task. According to Dagobert Soergel, it took one and a half year to define the „Thesaurus of Engineering Terms (USA)" [SOE-69, S.33].

There are standards defining thesaurus structures [ISO 2788, DIN-1463-1]. Each concept in a thesaurus has a so-called *descriptor* which is the name of a concept. There are also *non-descriptors* which are synonyms or the name in another language. Relations between concepts can also be defined.

5   The General Integration Concept

The concept is based on the assumption that a thesaurus can and shall be used as a PSI set for a distributed Topic Map application. Each entry in a thesaurus can be transformed into an entry in the LDAP directory, since both support a hierarchical structure and attributes for each entry. The next chapter explains the details of the required LDAP schema and the transformation. This transformation is a one-to-one function which means that users can choose whether to change concepts with a thesaurus or an LDAP editor. Any change can be transformed to the other schema.

LDAP is a distributed system. Thus, the thesaurus became a *distributed* thesaurus after transformation. LDAP can manage replicated and distributed changes in its

---

[1] http://md1.csa.com/edit/sociothes.html

[2] http://md1.csa.com/edit/lscthes.html

[3] http://msowww.anu.edu.au/library/thesaurus/

[4] http://www.asis.org/Publications/Thesaurus/isframe.htm

[5] http://www.infodata-edepot.de/thesaurus/START.HTM

[6] http://databases.unesco.org/thesaurus/

entries. That means, that also a thesaurus could be distributed, e.g. in a company. Working groups or single individuals could be responsible for parts of the thesaurus and would be allowed to change entries. LDAP automatically publishes changes to any other node in the network.

Each LDAP entry can be addressed. Topic Map authors can use addresses of LDAP entries as locators for subject identifiers. Moreover, LDAP implementations provide flexible and fast search capabilities which help to find the appropriate subject descriptions. It is also possible to transform LDAP entries into a Topic Map if required for example to easily compare two entries for their equality without having to leave the Topic Map context. The idea is straightforward: Entries becomes topics, relations between entries are mapped to associations and entry attributes are either mapped to names or to (inline) occurrences, see section 7 for details.

Figure 1 gives an overview of all three components.

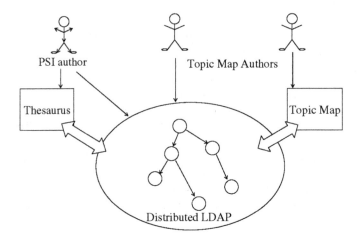

Fig. 1. Distributed Published Subject Identifier

There are several approaches for distributed Topic Maps, e.g. TMShare [Ah03], federated Topic Maps [Ba04], Remote Topic Map Access Protocol [PG04], Shark [Sc04]. All these approaches focus on distribution on Topic Maps and try to hide distribution details from the Topic Map application.

But TM applications don't end in themselves. They are means to support distributed knowledge intensive processes [BBC02, Cu03]. Such processes require a shared vocabulary [MS05, MW04]. But this vocabulary cannot be assumed to be static. It is in a permanent flux. A contradiction must be solved: Establishing a shared vocabulary which can be changed by any user. A solution can only be a compromise, e.g. providing a nearly static core vocabulary which can be changed only by dedicated users and allow adding new terms by others. Such a solution can be achieved by the proposed concept of distributed PSIs by means of LDAP.

The next two chapters describe the details of the transformation processes.

6 Thesaurus Goes LDAP

To map a thesaurus in a LDAP based directory a new LDAP schema is required. Since the thesaurus has a rather simple structure the schema will consist of only one main class, the 'term' which represents one entry in a thesaurus. An entry in a thesaurus has standardised attributes like the 'currentTerm', 'usedFor' or 'relatedTerms' which describe the entry with its preferred name, other synonyms and related entries. These attributes can be easily taken over into the very flexible LDAP schema. For administrative reasons a few other attributes will be added to the thesaurus schema for example the 'author' of the entry and a numeric 'id'.

Once the schema for the thesaurus is configured for usage, the thesaurus entries can be inserted into the directory. Existing thesauri should be transformed into the text-based LDIF format (LDAP Data Interchange Format) [RFC-2849] which allows importing large amounts of data into the directory. Thesauri have a predefined structure therefore a transformation into the LDIF format is an easy process no matter which format the thesaurus has originally. A newly created thesaurus can also be inserted manually or with the proper API for example the Java Naming and Directory Interface (JNDI).

There are various tools for inserting and editing the data in a LDAP directory. One of them that also supports LDIF operations as well as a graphical tree view of the whole directory is the JXplorer. Depending of the size of a thesaurus groups of editors should be defined who either can change the data in the whole tree or only in parts of it. The larger the thesaurus the more editors are needed who specialise only in certain sections. For Topic Maps the idea of one large thesaurus instead of many differently

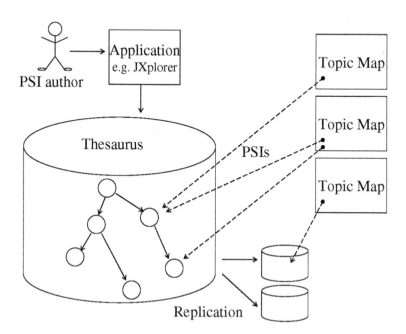

Fig. 2. Usage of PSIs within a LDAP thesaurus

structured PSI sets would mean that the process of merging Topic Maps will become easier. Figure 2 illustrates the use of PSIs within a thesaurus or its replicas.

Replication of a thesaurus in the directory is configurable at any time, so that all changes are being propagated to other servers. It has to be considered if the whole thesaurus should be replicated or only sub trees, which is also possible. If no replication is needed the data can also be exported into the LDIF format and imported to another server, provided that the same schema is also on the targeted server.

7 LDAP Goes Topic Map PSIs

It was already mentioned that a thesaurus distributed by replication of a LDAP based directory would provide several advantages when used as a PSI set for defining topics in a Topic Map. The current lack of syntax for the structure of a PSI makes it impossible to efficiently compare two PSIs for the same topic in two different Topic Maps. A LDAP thesaurus provides two ways of proving the equality of two PSIs, the first one are the attributes that are standardized. They can be easily compared to each other, especially the attributes for related terms and synonyms since they base on keywords and not on arbitrary text. The second way to compare two PSIs is to analyse their position in the hierarchical directory tree. The path consists of all higher ranked terms and gives information about the derivation of the current term.

Once a distributed vocabulary for Topic Maps is available, a web-based search for specific PSIs must be provided as well as a way to export PSI sets and single PSIs into a Topic Map for comparisons or other use. With JNDI as one of the possible APIs the access to the directory is possible.

Figure 3 shows a search or export process within the LDAP thesaurus based on an application that uses JNDI to access the directory.

LDAP is known for its fast search capabilities. No matter how large a thesaurus becomes a keyword search can quickly provide the Topic Map author with possible results for the use of a PSI in his Topic Map. The results of a search in the directory need to inform the Topic Map author of the description of a PSI so that he can determine which PSI is the one he is searching for and the URI for the PSI in the directory so that he can insert it into his corresponding topic in the Topic Map.

When PSIs from the thesaurus are being used in Topic Maps the URI of a PSI needs to return the PSI with all it's attributes including the complete path in the directory. Since the Topic Map authors already are handling Topic Maps it is self evident to return a Topic Map when a PSI URI is called. This Topic Map containing one topic which is the PSI can now be used to compare the PSI to others that are also in the same format and have the same attributes.

An application that can export a PSI from the directory into a Topic Map can also export either the whole directory or a sub tree into a Topic Map. Each entry in the thesaurus is then a topic in the Topic Map and the hierarchical structure can be provided using associations between topics. Is this exported Topic Map published, other Topic Maps can refer to its topics and use them as PSIs instead of pointing directly into the LDAP thesaurus.

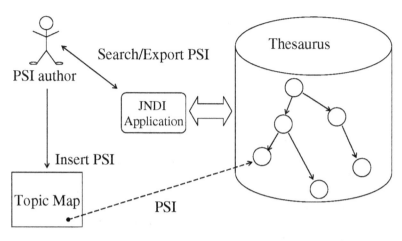

Fig. 3. Search or export PSIs with help of a JNDI Application

The exported Topic Map can also be viewed with a Topic Map viewer and edited by a Topic Map author with an existing tool. If required, the changes can be re-imported into the directory. There would then be no need for a PSI author dealing only with the thesaurus in the LDAP directory. The JNDI-application box shown in Figure 3 can thus be expanded with more functionality depending on the demands of a project.

8 Summary and Outlook

This paper explained a combination of thesauri, LDAP, Topic Maps and PSIs which helps to overcome a couple of current problems: There is no standard PSI editor or thesaurus browser? One of the existing LDAP editors like the JXplorer can be used instead. There are just a few PSI sets public available? Existing thesauri can be converted into Topic Maps and used as PSI sets. There are no tools for replicating and searching distributed PSI sets? The LDAP replication mechanism can be used instead. There is no schema for PSI sets? Standardised thesaurus schemas can be used.

Topic Maps is still an evolving standard. There are stable Topic Map Engine implementations. For a real Topic Map application, there is still a lot of work to do. This paper tried to open the view to two other existing and successful standards. It tried to show, how both standards can be integrated into Topic Map applications to solve the problem of distributed and replicated PSI sets.

The authors hope that this concept is just another brick of the way towards distributed Topic Maps and distributed knowledge management.

References

[Ah03]   Ahmed, K.: TMShare – Topic Map Fragment Exchange in a Peer-to-Peer-Application. In: *Proceedings of XML Europe 2003*, London, (2003).

[Ba04]   Barta, Robert: Virtual and Federated Topic Maps. In: *Proccedings of XML Europe 2004*, Amsterdam (2004).

[BMWC04] Böhm, K.; Maicher, L.; Witschel, H.-F.; Carradori, A.: Moving Topic Maps to Mainstream - - Integration of Topic Map Generation in the User's Working Environment. In: *Proceedings of I-KNOW '04,* Graz, (2004), pp. 241-251.

[CPV03]   Ciancarini, P.; Pirruccio, M.; Vitali, F. et al.: Metadata on the Web. On the integration of RDF and Topic Maps. In: *Proceedings of Extreme Markup Languages 2003,* Montreal, (2003).

[BBC02]   Bonifacio, Matteo; Bouquet, Paolo; Cuel, Roberta: Knowledge-Nodes: the Building Blocks of a Distributed Approach to Knowledge Management. In: *Proceedings of I-KNOW '02,* Graz, (2002), pp. 191-200.

[Cu03]   Cuel, Roberta: A New Methodology for Distributed Knowledge Management Analysis. In: *Proceedings of I-KNOW '03,* Graz, (2003), pp. 531-537.

[JXP3]   JXplorer Java LDAP Browser v3.0, Available at: http://pegacat.com/jxplorer/, Pegacat Computing

[Ke03]   Kent, W.: The unsolvable identity problem. In: *Proceedings of Extreme Markup Languages 2003,* Montreal, (2003).

[MS05]   Maicher, L.; Schwotzer, T.: Distributed Knowledge Management in the Absence of Shared Vocabularies. In: Proceedings of the 5th International Conference on Knowledge Management (I-KNOW '05). Graz, July 2005

[MW04]   Maicher, L.; Witschel, H.-F.: Merging of Distributed Topic Maps based on the Subject Identity Measure (SIM). In: *Proceedings of Leipziger Informatiktage,* Leipzig (2004).

[Oasis]   OASIS: Published Subjects. Introduction and Basic Requirements. Available at: http://www.oasis-open.org/committees/download.php/3050/

[PG04]   Pepper, S.; Garshol, L. M.: Seamless Knowledge – Spontaneous Knowledge Federation using TMRAP. Presentation at: *XML Europe 2004,* Amsterdam (2004). Available at: http://www.ontopia.net/topicmaps/learn_more.html

[RFC-2251] Wahl, M: Request for Comments: Lightweight Directory Access Protocol (v3) Available at: http://www.ietf.org/rfc/rfc2251.txt, Internet Engineering Task Force, 1997

[RFC-2849] Good, Gordon: The LDAP Data Interchange Format (LDIF) - Technical Specification, Network Working Group, iPlanet e-commerce Solutions, 2000

[SH03]   Schulz, S.; Herrmann, K.; Kalcklösch, R.; Schwotzer, T.: Towards Trust-based Knowledge Management in Mobile Communities. In: *Proceedings of AAAI Spring Symposium on Agent-Mediated Knowledge Management,* Stanford, (2003).

[ScGe03] Schwotzer, T, Geihs K..: Shark - a System for Management, Synchronization and Exchange of Knowledge in Mobile User Groups. In: J.UCS 8, Issue 6 (2002)

[Sc04]   Schwotzer, T.: Modelling Distributed Knowledge Management Systems with Topic Maps. In: *Proceedings of I-Know'04,* Graz (2004), pp. 53-60.

[TMDM]   ISO/IEC JTC 1/SC 34: ISO/IEC 13250. Topic Maps – Part 2: Data Model. Latest version available at: http://www.isotopicmaps.org/sam/

[TMRM]   ISO/IEC JTC 1/SC34: Topic Maps – Reference Model. Editor's Draft, Revision 3.1. 01.12.2003. Available at: http://www.isotopicmaps.org/TMRM/TMRM

Topic Map Exchange in the Absence of Shared Vocabularies

Lutz Maicher

University of Leipzig, Department of Computer Science,
Augustusplatz 10-11, D-04109 Leipzig, Germany
maicher@informatik.uni-leipzig.de

Abstract. Topic Maps are the international industry standard for semantic information integration. Appropriate means for Topic Map exchange are crucial for its success as integration technology. Topic Map exchange bases on the governing Subject Equality decision approach, the decision whether two Subject Proxies indicate identical Subjects. This paper discusses the 'absence of shared vocabularies' in the context of these decisions. Thereby, a differentiation between Referential and Structuralist Subject Equality decision approaches is introduced. All existing approaches to Topic Map exchange base on the TMDM. This implies a Referential Subject Equality decision approach and bound to a concrete Subject Map Disclosure (SMD) ontology and Subject Map (SM) vocabulary. This paper introduces a Structuralist Subject Equality decision approach which is called SIM. It allows the exchange of Topic Maps in the absence of a shared SM ontology and SM vocabulary.

1 The Challenge in an Example

Within a cooking peer-to-peer network remote peers exchange recipes documented as Topic Maps[1]. To collect information, peers send Topics which represent the Subjects of interest to remote peers. In the cooking network a Subject might be 'roasted lamb loin'. The remote peers check the availability of information about this Subject and respond with an according Topic Map Fragment. Afterwards, the requesting peer integrates all remote recipes about roasting lamb loins into its local recipe collection.

This works fine if all peers made agreements about how to describe lamb cuts correctly. What happens if a remote peer uses the term lamb saddle instead? Or roasted lamb leg chops? The resulting meals are identical, but the requesting peers will never receive their recipes from distance. This shows that two critical points arise, if semantic agreements are not made by all peers logging into the network: How to request knowledge from remote peers if shared vocabularies are not available? How to integrate (merge) the received information into the local Topic Map?

The solution proposed in this paper allows peers to interact in networks without having the overhead of centrally enforced vocabularies. Our solution detects

---

[1] To avoid ambiguities all terminology concerning Topic Map Technologies is capitalised.

L. Maicher and J. Park (Eds.): TMRA 2005, LNAI 3873, pp. 77–92, 2006.

similarity between Subjects through the similar usage of their proxies. Even if lamb lag chops and lamb loin are represented by different Subject Proxies, in recipe collections these proxies will be used similarly: with bean and rosemary proxies, etc. And the chef will cook roasted lamb loins according to this very good traditional French recipe even if the recipe's author roasted lamb leg chops.

2 Introduction

Peer-to-peer systems for Topic Map exchange envisaged in the introducing example already exist as well as approaches and protocols to Topic Map exchange. But all of them base on the agreement about shared vocabularies within the exchange network.

Our premise is that in practice the centralised enforcement of shared vocabularies has strong limitations. Only the semantic web search engine "swoogle" lists 763 different class definitions of 'person' found in divers ontologies[2]. Because all of the existing Topic Map exchange approaches completely fail if the peers use proprietary vocabularies, solutions for these environments have to be developed.

This paper makes the following contributions:

- Systematisation of the 'absence of shared vocabularies' in the context of Topic Maps Technologies in section 3.
- Description of existing approaches to Topic Map exchange and discussion of their limitations in the absence of shared vocabularies in section 4.
- Discussion of alternative Subject Equality decision approaches besides the Topic Maps Data Model (TMDM, [34]) in section 5.
- Introduction and Assessment of the SIM, a structuralist approach to Subject Equality decisions, which allows the exchange of Topic Maps in the (particular) absence of shared vocabularies in section 6.

3 The Absence of Shared Vocabularies

As sketched in the motivating example, Topic Map exchange is faced with the problem of the 'absence of shared vocabularies'. From a lazy point of view the 'absence of shared vocabularies' is the non-existence of mutual agreements about syntax and semantics of means for assertions about Subjects. This section systematises the notion 'absence of shared vocabularies'.

In section 1.1 the *semanticness* of Topic Maps Technologies is discussed. The semantic kernel of Topic Maps Technologies is examined in respect to the semantics of the vocabulary which will be shared. This supports the discussion about the nature of the necessary mutual semantic agreements. In section 1.2 the nature of Subject Equality decisions is further investigated. In section 1.3 the previous sections are summarised by systemizing the notion 'absence of shared vocabularies' in the context of Topic Map exchange.

---

[2] http://swoogle.umbc.edu [requested: 15th April 2005].

3.1 Semantics in Topic Maps Technologies

Topic Maps are the international industry standard for *semantic* information integration. In a first step the *semanticness* of this technology will be depicted.

From an information science point of view *semantics* means that information systems are aware of the functionality which has to be applied to given data. There have to exist a well defined mapping from the syntax[3] to the semantic domain [18]. The difference between a *semantic technology* and a *non-semantic technology* is that in contrast to the latter one the semantic technology *reveals* the functionality which should be applied to data. In fact, the mapping from syntax to the semantic domain really exists to a sufficient extent. For example, an information system governed by a non-semantic technology applies to the string "<name>Leipzig</name>" an application specific functionality arbitrarily. A semantic technology, however, *reveals* the functionality which has to be applied to such a string.

The *semanticness* of Topic Maps Technologies is defined by the Topic Map Reference Model (TMRM, [9]). Generally, a Subject Map Disclosure[4] discloses (the examples for the TMDM, the common SMD, are given in parenthesises):

1. *SMD Ontology* (defines that Topics have Base Names, Occurrences)
   - *Subject Indication Approach* (defines that Topics indicate the Subjects they represent by Subject Locators and Identifier)
2. *Subject Equality Decision Approach* (defines that Topics having identical Subject Locators or Identifiers indicate identical Subjects)
3. *Subject Viewing Approach* (defines, in example, that the set of Topic Names of a merged Topic is the union of the Topic Name sets of the original Topics).

The only generic semantic functionality of Topic Maps is the following objective: Subject Proxies indicating identical Subjects have to be viewed as merged ones. *Only* this functionality constitutes the *semanticness* of Topic Maps Technologies.

Additionally to this *generic functionality*, a Topic Maps Processing Application (TMPA) performs *application specific functionality*: for example showing a Base Name as a string in the left corner of the screen. The semantics of all those application specific functionality is not revealed by the SMD itself.

This implies that Topic Maps Technologies do not define the semantics of the represented facts (the assertions belonging to Subject Proxies).[5] The definition of these semantics is left to the ontology engineers, which are appropriate for that task. But the ontology engineers should heavily exploit the fact that in Topic Maps all relationships between proxies and their subjects have well defined semantics. That's the uniqueness of Topic Maps which makes them to a real semantic technology.

---

[3] In our cases a specific syntax implies a specific kind of instances of the data model. Therefore the existence of a mapping between these instances and the semantic domain is necessary.

[4] The latest proposal of the TMRM [9] replaces the term "Topic Maps Application".

[5] One might argue, that the creator of a Subject Map Disclosure have to describe the semantics of the Property Classes of the Subject Proxies, i.e. the meaning of the concept 'Occurrence'. But there is no structured way for this semantic modelling and its non-existence does not influence the independent behaviour of a TMPA. Obviously, the definition of the semantics of an Occurrence item (in TMDM) does not influence the behaviour of a TMPA.

As depicted in the listing above the generic semantic functionality of Topic Maps is split into two parts: *Subject Equality Decision* (deciding that Subject Proxies indicate identical Subjects) and *Subject Proxy Viewing* (viewing Subject Proxies indicating identical Subjects as merged ones).

Why this has to be discussed in the context of Topic Map exchange? Section 4 shows that this exchange bases on the request of Subjects. A remote peer requests information by indicating the Subject of interest. The requested peer has to decide whether it can provide a Subject Proxy indicating the identical Subject. This request scenario is the context of this paper. Therefore the Subject Equality decisions will be discussed in further detail.

3.2   The Subject Equality Decision in the Absence of Shared Vocabularies

A Topic Maps Processing Application, an application which processes Subject Maps according to given disclosures, has to do the Subject Equality Decisions as follows[6]:

Subject Equality Decision $_{SMDi}$ (
   Subject Indication$_{SMD1}$ (Subject Identity $_{Subject\ Stage\ 1}$),
   Subject Indication$_{SMD2}$ (Subject Identity $_{Subject\ Stage\ 2}$)) $\Leftrightarrow$
Subject Identity $_{integration\ perspective}$(Subject Stage $_1$, Subject Stage $_2$)

The formalisation asserts, that a TMPA should decide that two Subject Proxies indicate identical Subjects (Subject Equality holds) iff from the current integration perspective the Subject Stages represented by these Subject Proxies belong to the same Subject. Thereby, each Subject Proxy documents the decision about its own identity with the means of the governing Subject Indication approach at documentation time.

As discussed in more detail in [6] section 2.1, Subject Identity is not an absolute "quality" due to the vague nature of Subjects. Rather it is the result of a perspective dependent decision process under uncertainty whether Subject Stages caught at different occasions and from different perspectives [5] belong to the same Subject. (These thoughts are strongly affected by Quine [28], [29]).

The TMPA is governed by a SMD$_i$ which defines the Subject Equality Decision Approach that as to be applied. (The index i does indicate the integration perspective.) This decision has two parameters: the documentation of the Subject Identity of the first Subject Stage (Subject Indication$_{SMD1}$) and the documentation of the Subject Identity of the second Subject Stage (Subject Indication$_{SMD2}$). It is important to outline, that the used Subject Indication Approach for the documentation of the decisions about Subject Identity at documentation time can be governed by a different SMD than the Subject Equality decisions at consumption time. A SMD based on the SIM introduced by this paper might imply such a situation.

Furthermore it is important to outline, that the perspective of the decisions about Subject Identity $_{Subject\ Stage\ 1}$ (at the time of creating the Subject Proxy belonging to Subject Stage 1), Subject Identity $_{Subject\ Stage\ 2}$ (at the time of creating the Subject Proxy belonging to Subject Stage 2) and Subject Identity $_{integration}$ (at the time of the decision

---

[6] For simplification, in the following the Subject Equality Decision concerning only *two* Subject Proxies is discussed.

about Subject Equality) might differ fundamentally. In [6] section 4, the evolution from a more technical perspective at documentation time to a special integration perspective at consumption time is discussed in detail.

The applied approach to Subject Equality decisions defines the semantics of the vocabulary (used to create the Subject Proxies) in respect to the only generic *semantic* functionality of Topic Maps Technologies: viewing Subject Proxies indicating identical Subjects as merged ones.

To understand the semantic implied by the approaches to Subject Equality decisions a side glance to linguistics is useful. Linguists distinguish between the referential and the structuralist paradigm. (Their differences are roughly reflected by the shifting from Wittgenstein's early thoughts to its late ones.) In referential semantics the meaning of a word (as a symbol) is defined by a referent (mostly outside the language) it refers to. According to the structuralist paradigm the meaning of words is only defined by their usage within the language.

Adopting this spadework we will differ between *Referential Subject Equality Decisions* and *Structuralist Subject Equality Decisions*.

The TMDM is a popular SMD adopting an approach to referential Subject Equality decision. If Subject Proxies' sets of Subject Identifiers/Locators comprise identical URLs, they have to be viewed as merged ones. Referring to a discrete 'thing' is the only mean for indicating the intended Subject. This approach enforces a Proxy to make explicit the Subject it intends to represent.

The premise of structuralist Subject Equality decision approaches is that the Subject depends on other Subject Proxies in the Subject Map. For example, the SIM introduced by this paper assumes, that whenever two Subject Proxies are used similarly, the probability that both indicate identical Subjects increases. The Subject is non tangible by any means, because it is emergently defined by relationships between Subject Proxies.

Summarised, the Subject Equality decision has the following structure:

Subject Equality Decision $_{SMDi}$ (
       Subject Indication $_{SMD1}$, Subject Indication $_{SMD2}$,
       Subject Map $_{Subject Proxy1}$, Subject Map $_{Subject Proxy2}$**) ➔ true | false**

The differences between the formalism introduced above have the following rationale. At the point of time the decision about Subject Equality is made, none information about Subject Identity is available. Only the documentation of the result of these decisions can be used. Additionally, the Subject Maps which are the origin of the according Subject Proxies are introduced as parameters. The rational is that at least structuralist Subject Equality approaches might rely on all Subject Proxies from these Subject Maps. At the moment, the decision about Subject Equality is a binary one, whether equality holds or not. In future probabilistic or fuzzy approaches should be investigated.

3.3 Topic Map Exchange and the Absence of Shared Vocabularies

In the following the previous insights are summarised to sketch the possibilities of an absence of shared vocabularies in the context of Topic Map exchange.

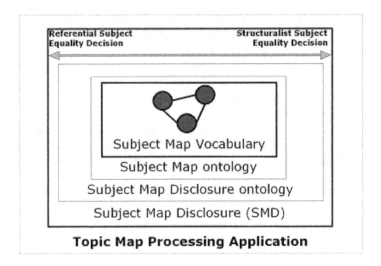

Fig. 1. Vocabularies and the Subject Equality Decision

As shown in Figure 1, the chosen Subject Equality decision approach defines at consumption time the *semantics* of the vocabulary used by the Subject Proxies.

The competition of SMDs between the time of the Subject Equality decision (SMD_i) and the time the according Subject Proxies were created ($SMD_{1,2}$) implies different SMD ontologies which have to be handled. The 'absence of shared vocabularies' can be interpreted as the absence of a shared SMD ontology.

Furthermore each Subject Map (governed by a SMD and its ontology) is restricted by an application specific ontology. For example, the type 'person' can be defined including further constrains for its instances (i.e. by a schema language). This specific ontology is called the SM ontology. The 'absence of shared vocabulary' might include the absence of a shared SM ontology, too.

Finally, inside a Subject Map the vocabulary at the instance level can be constrained, too. The concept of PSIs (Published Subject Identifiers, [33]) enforces, that if two Topic Map authors intend to refer to exactly the same Subject (i.e. a specific book is referred by using the according ISBN), they have to share these published vocabularies. The 'absence of shared vocabulary' might even include the absence of a shared SM vocabulary. The absence of a shared SM vocabulary might be more important in the case a Referential Subject Equality Decision Approach is applied.

The nested relationships between all different kinds of vocabularies imply that the semantic (in the context of Topic Maps Technologies) of a specific vocabulary depends always on all higher layers.

4   Topic Map Exchange – The State of the Art

Topic Map exchange is governed by a one-to-many-to-one problem (1:N:1) [19]. One master requests from N remote peers information about a Subject in interest (1:N).

These remote peers extract their answer set, usually a Subject Map Fragment, from their local Subject Map. After receiving, the master has to integrate these different results into its local repository (N:1). *Request* and *Integration* are the tasks of Topic Map exchange to be solved in the 'absence of shared vocabularies'. Requesting is a retrieval task: retrieve the most appropriate Subject Proxy from a repository.

Request means, that the remote peers might receive Subject Map Fragments with unfamiliar SMD ontology, SM ontology or SM vocabulary. Under this uncertainty they have to decide about Subject Equality. The second part of the request is the specification of the Subject Map Fragment which has to send to the requesting peer.

Integration means, that the master has to decide about Subject Equality in respect to the received Subject Proxies in uncertainty about the used SMD ontology, SM ontology and SM vocabulary. This paper does only focus on the Subject Equality decisions. It leaves out the functionality of Subject Viewing.

In the following existing approaches to Topic Map exchange are introduced, whereby the arising problems in the absence of shared vocabularies are emphasised.

4.1 The Topic Map Remote Access Protocol (TMRAP)

The Topic Map Remote Access Protocol (TMRAP) [10], [14], [25], [27] is proposed by Ontopia[7]. It addresses requirements from distributed Topic Maps Portal integration. If a Topic Map Portal knows other TMRAP supporting Topic Map Portals it is enabled to request all information concerning a given Subject from these applications. The TMRAP bases on the TMDM (as common SMD and SMD ontology). In [16] TMViews as "mechanism for describing what to include when extracting a fragment from a topic map" is introduced. Besides being bounded on the TMDM, TMViews bases on the knowledge about the used SM ontology.

How does TMRAP address the Subject in interest? TMRAP enforces the usage of a shared SM vocabulary. If a Topic Map Portal requests information about a given Subject, it has to declare it by a (set of) Subject Indicators or one Subject Locator. Furthermore, it has the opportunity to request information from a Topic with a specific Source Locator.[8]

Problems arising in the absence of shared vocabularies. That implies that all communicating Portals have to share a SM vocabulary.

4.2 TMShare

TMShare [1] is a P2P information sharing application based on Topic Maps Technology using the JXTA framework[9]. The aim of TMShare is to allow the exchange of Topic Map Fragments in a group of interacting peers. Each peer hosts a set of 'private' Topic Maps in designated back ends. Additionally, it hosts cached Topic Maps which were received from remote peers. TMShare bases on the TMDM.

---

[7] http://www.ontopia.net

[8] Requesting a Topic by its Source Locator is used to in the case the local ID is already known, e.g. from previous requests. For *semantic* integration the request of distributed Topic Fragments by their local IDs is out of interest.

[9] http://www.jxta.org

How to address the Subject of interest? From our perspective, requesting a remote peer is quite similar to the TMRAP. Furthermore it may request for all Topics which satisfy a tolog query [15]. (The latest version of the TMRAP [14] does define this opportunity, too.)

Problems arising in the absence of shared vocabularies. As already discussed concerning the TMRAP all peers have to share the SM vocabulary. Using tolog queries is useful for customising requests. But at least in all cases where dynamic predicates or class definitions are used, the usage of tolog implies that the requesting peer is familiar with the remote peers' SM ontologies. A peer is only able to request the statement

```
performed-by($A : performer, aisha : song)
```

if it is familiar with the Association Type 'performed-by' and the Role Types 'performer' and 'song'.

4.3   The Knowledge Port Approach

Inspired by Bonifacio et al. [7], [8] Schwotzer proposed the Knowledge Port Approach (described in more detail in [31], [21]). Through the Knowledge Port Approach the Topic Map exchange is contextualized. Simplified, Knowledge Ports (KP) are end points of Topic Map exchange channels with the function of input/output filters. The peers store all information as Topic Maps.

How to address the Subject of interest? A peer stores three kinds of Topic Maps. The first reifies the known network structure. The second, called content map, is a Topic Map View about all local information. Additionally, information is useful in dedicated contexts, especially spatial coordinates. Therefore a Point of Interest (POI) map is introduced. Generally, each context should be modelled like the POI map.

The Topic Map exchange takes place between the peer's Knowledge Ports. A requesting peer describes its demand with Topics from its local Topic Maps: its Subject in interest, its current POI, the allowed communication partners within the network. The Knowledge Ports of the requested peers match these demands with their offer. If all communication parameters fit, Topic Map exchange takes place. The Knowledge Port Approach bases on the TMDM.

Problems arising in the absence of shared vocabularies. All communication parameters (context, partners, Subjects in interest) are defined by PSIs within these ports. This is a shared SM vocabulary. Whereby for some parameters PSIs are inevitable (i.e. within the POI map), the definition of the Subject in interest with the help of PSIs delimit the power of the approach. Therefore, in [21] its liaison with the SIM approach is proposed.

4.4   From Federated Topic Maps to TMIP

Barta introduces an approach to federate distributed materialised and non-materialised Topic Maps [3]. This approach was further developed to TMIP, a RESTful Topic Maps Interaction Protocol [4]. TMIP bases on the TMDM.

How to address the Subject in Interest? While introducing Map Spheres TMIP always addresses the Subject in interest by using path expressions of the (future) Topic Maps Query Language (TMQL).

Problems arising in the absence of shared vocabularies. Similar to the tolog requests in TMShare and TMRAP, the path expressions of TMIP are bound to an overall knowledge of the SM ontologies and SM vocabularies of the requested peers.

5 Subject Equality Decision Approaches Besides the TMDM

As shown in Figure 2 different approaches to Subject Equality decisions are imaginable. One has to outline, that each Subject Equality decision approach besides the TMDM implies a proper SMD.

Naturally, all approaches should operate on the data model level instead of the syntax level.

The first important decision is the differentiation between structuralist Subject Equality decision approaches and referential Subject Equality approaches. The latter is materialised by the TMDM. As discussed above, the TMDM enforces that all communication partners have to share the SM vocabulary.

In general, two kinds of structuralist approaches are imaginable. The first interprets a Proxy's Subject as a relative value. The SIM introduced by this paper materialises this approach. Being a relative value means that the Subject Equality between two Subject Proxies depends on the Subject Equality of all other Subject Proxies (which in turn depends on the Subject Equality which has to be decided) in the Subject Maps. Those algorithms do hardly scale.

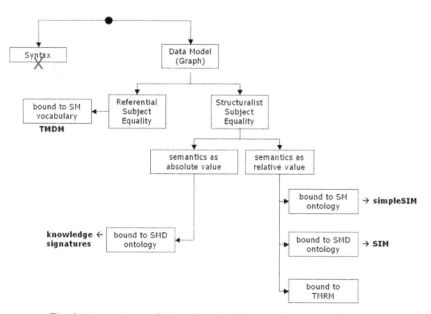

Fig. 2. Approaches to Subject Equality decisions besides the TMDM

For effective retrieval of conceptual graphs Sowa and Majumdar proposed the calculation of feature vectors representing the Subject of a conceptual graph as a concrete value [32]. These vectors are called knowledge signatures of a conceptual graph. The spatial distance between two knowledge signatures define the semantic closeness of the according Subjects. Retrieving of Subjects becomes very efficient. Those knowledge signatures interpret a Proxy's Subject as absolute value.

6 The SIM Approach

We have shown that all existing approaches to Topic Map exchange are bound to the TMDM. To gain more flexibility, we propose the SIM Approach. This is a structuralist Subject Equality decision approach ($SMD_i=SMD_{SIM}$). The SIM approach is independent of a shared SM ontology and SM vocabulary. But all Subject Proxies which are the input of the SIM have to be governed by the TMDM ($SMD_1=SMD_2=TMDM$).

Subject similarity is a weak kind of Subject Equality. The SIM Approach bases on the assumption that if two Subject Proxies interact with similar Subject Proxies in similar ways, the probability of their Subject similarity in the current context increases, too. And if the Subject similarity exceeds a specific threshold, Subject Equality holds.

The SIM Approach has strong relationships to Gentner's Structure-mapping theory. "This structural view of analogy is based on the intuition that analogies are about relation, rather than simple features. No matter what kind of knowledge (causal models, plans, stories, ect.), it is the structural properties (i.e., the interrelationships between the facts) that determine the content of an analogy" [10].

Furthermore, the SIM approach uses insights from schema matching gained by Melnik's et al. [23].

For brevity, the SIM Approach will be introduced in limited detail. The requesting Topic will be called T. The fragment of the requesting Topic Map around T will be called F. The fragment F consists of all Topics and Associations which are influenced by T. Our premise is that the fragment F indicates the Subject which is represented by T. (In future, TMView introduced by [16] might be used to define the fragment properly.)

After the reception of F, the remote peer compares each Topic from F with each Topic in the requested Topic Map and calculates a similarity measure (simDNA') for each pair of Topics.

The calculation is done in two iteration steps. In the first step only the similarity of the topology is exploited. In the second step additionally the similarity of Topics calculated in the first step is used. After the second step, Subject Equality holds for T's most similar Topic from the requested Topic Map, if simDNA' exceeds a specific threshold.

The similarity of two Topics is calculated as follows. Each Topic has a state of interaction with its environment which we will call *simDNAtype*. For example, the simDNAtype 'x13tn' characterises a typed Topic having a Base Name, a Source Locator and a Subject Identifier. The 'x' in the simDNAtype indicates that this Topic is used for typing purposes in one other Topic of the given Topic Map Fragment. A Topic's simDNAtype is valid according the following regular expression:

/x*y*z*w*s*1*2*3*t*n*(\(o\))*(\[a\])*/

x,y,z,w   – the Topic is typing a Topic (x), an Association (y), a Topic
                     Characteristic (z), or an Association Role (w)
s   – the Topic is scoping a Topic Characteristic
1,2,3   – the Topic has a Source Locator (1), a Subject Locator(2),
                     or a Subject Identifier (3)
t   – the Topic is typed
n   – the Topic has a TopicName
o => /(vll)t?s*/ – the Topic has an Occurrence (with OccDNAtype)
a => /a(tp)*/   – the Topic takes part in an Association (with AssDNAtype)

The similarity of a pair of Topics called *simDNA*. It is calculated for each digit of the simDNAtype. The simDNAtype of the *requesting* Topic constrains the simDNA of this pair.

For example, in the first iteration a digit of type 't' can have the values 'X' and '1'. 'X' specifies that the requested Topic is not typed, '1' specifies that the requested Topic is typed, too. In the second level the value '3' is attainable and specifies that the typing Topic of the requested Topic and the typing Topic of the requesting Topic gained sufficient similarity in iteration step 1.

For each digit of the simDNAtype similar rules are defined. The complexity of these rules would go beyond the scope of this paper. The simDNA' is the sum of the digits of the simDNA. Basically, the higher the simDNA', the higher is the similarity of two Topics. Subject Equality holds for a pair of requesting and requested Topics if they gain the highest simDNA' and this simDNA' exceeds a specific threshold.

6.1   Assessment of the SIM Approach

For brevity, only some insights from the evaluation are given. Imagine a Topic Map which is requested by its own Topics. This test we call self assessment. For each requesting Topic the SIM Approach has to response with its "twin" in the requested Topic Map. If for all Topics the twins are returned the recall is 1. The question is the behaviour of the SIM Approach if the requesting Topic and its submitted environment are pruned randomly. What happens if randomly only 40 percent of all Names and 60 percent of the Associations are left in the submitted fragments? What happens if all Names and all Associations are pruned in the submitted fragments? The higher the recall, the better the SIM Approach allows to retrieve Topics in environments with unfamiliar vocabularies.

Fig.3 shows the result of an experiment with a small Topic Map of 20 Topics. The probability of non-pruning Topic Names (probTopNam) and non-pruning Associations (probAss) is iterated in the interval [0,1]. To yield statistically firmed results the calculated recall is the mean of 10 self assessments.

As already predicted, if probTopNam and probAss are 1, the recall is 1, too (see circle number 1). But, if both probabilities are 0, the recall is still 0.53 (see circle number 2). This implies, even in the case of a massive loss of information, when *all* Topic Names and *all* Associations are pruned, the typing information (typing of Topics, typing of Occurrences etc, whereby the typing Topics are pruned, too) and the information inside the Occurrences is sufficient to get the half of all Topics correctly.

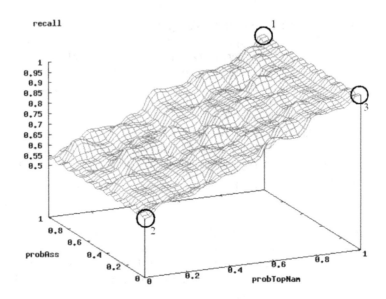

Fig. 3. Iteration: probTopName [0,1], probAss [0,1]

Furthermore, the naming information has more influence on a high recall than the Topics' participation in Associations (see circle 3).

One has to bear in mind that the algorithm neither has knowledge about the used SM ontology and SM vocabulary nor about the human languages used in the Occurrences and Topic Names.

In addition, the results already drastically improve if only some typing information bases on a shared SM ontology. This result implies that a combination of TMDM and SIM might be useful. In a first step, the Subject Equality decisions according the TMDM will be applied. In a second step, this information will be used, to decide for all Subject Proxies were the first decisions failed, whether Subject Equality governed by the SIM might hold.

This experiment sketches the abilities of the SIM Approach for Topic Map exchange in the absence of a shared SM ontology and SM vocabulary.

Problems of the SIM Approach. The SIM Approach has a number of limitations which should be introduced in short detail.

- If F and the requested Topic Map grow, complexity increases significantly.
- Applying the SIM Approach to non-materialised Topic Maps [3] is not possible.
- The SIM Approach does only yield good results, if the assertions of requested and requesting Topics are similar (i.e. the requested Topic Map provides small new information). If the requested Topic Map provides only new information, the SIM Approach fails.
- In cases a requested Topic Map can objectively not provide a Topic similar to a requesting Topic, the SIM Approach tends to post a false Topic. While the recall tends to be high, the precision tends to be low.

- In contrast to the TMDM, the decisions about Subject Equality are not deterministic. The result always depends on the whole requested Topic Map which might change randomly.

7 Related Work

"For computing the similarities, we rely on the intuition that elements of two distinct models are similar when their adjacent elements are similar." [23] Melnik et al. introduce and apply a graph matching approach for schema matching based on flooding of similarity through the graph [23]. Further they give a broad overview about existing matching techniques (which we do not want to rehash), mainly restricted to schema matching [30]. In contrast to the most efforts in information integration working at the schema level, solutions for Topic Maps Technologies should explicitly target to the integration at the instance level.

Our experiments with Melnik's et al. similarity flooding approach in conjunction with Topic Maps revealed substantial problems to provide a structuralist Subject Equality approach which is independent of SMD ontology, SM ontology and SM vocabulary. If Topic Maps are translated into the required directed labelled graphs (i.e. using Garshol's Foundational Model for Topic Maps [26] which is today superseded by the Q model [13]) the number of nodes increases enormously, conjunct with complexity problems. Additionally, nodes which represent the TMDM ontology (i.e. "SOURCE_LOCATOR") exhaust the similarity from the nodes which represent the SM ontology and SM vocabulary. These results showed that Melnik's et al. approach might be very interesting for SMD ontology and SM ontology matching. For the more general case of providing a common structuralist Subject Equality decision method, we had to decide to modify the approach significantly and to bind the SIM to the TMDM ontology.

Falkenhainer et al. report the implementation of Gentner's Structure-mapping theory through the so called Structure-Mapping Engine. The implemented algorithm has the poor complexity of $O(N^2)$, too.

Newcomb introduces the Versavant Project[10] (in early versions at the moment of writing) which provides a Topic Maps Application bus acting as "Subject addressing engine". This bus allows aligning between different SMD ontologies (and probably shifting between referential and structuralist Subject Indication paradigms). Versavant is further described in [24].

Additionally, Vatant introduces the concept of 'Hubjects' [35]. A Hubject is "a hub connecting different representations of a subject inside the same or across different contexts. [..] Hubjects provide neither semantic interpretation of the representations they connect nor absolute indication of the subject." [35]. As far as the sparse literature about Hubjects allows a Subject Equality decision method can be interpreted as a Hubject *class*.

Guo and Yu proposes the idea "that schema mapping and data mapping might be carried out simultaneously in a mutually way." [17]. Encouraged by the positive assessment, the SIM does mutually enhance the matching quality of schema entities and their data instances, too.

---

[10] http://www.versavant.org

Basically, the issues discussed in this paper are strong related to the idea of emergent semantics [1].

In [20] and [22] we introduced a more lightweight version of the SIM Approach (see simpleSIM in Figure 2). This version yielded very good results, but was bounded to a common SM ontology. The new version of SIM is more generic.

8   Conclusions and Further Research

We outlined, that Topic Map exchange heavily depends on the Subject Equality decisions. We discussed this decision in detail, differentiating between a referential and structuralist approaches to Subject Equality decisions. We depicted, that the 'absence of shared vocabularies' might include the absence of shared SMD ontology, SM ontology and SM vocabulary. We introduced the SIM as a structuralist Subject Equality decision approach which is only bound to a shared SMD ontology (the TMDM). In future, the SIM should be disclosed as a SMD_{SIM} on top of the TMDM.

The main challenge of the current SIM Approach is the unbounded complexity. Today, the SIM Approach resembles a broadcast search within the requested Topic Map. The requesting Topic Map Fragments will be compared with each Topic from the requested Topic Map. Inspired from [36], interpreting the request of an appropriate Topic as a retrieval task, it is imaginable that each Topic knows k 'similar' neighbours inside its Topic Map. A requesting Topic will be forwarded through this network until it reaches its merging partner. We assume that only a few hops are sufficient to find this Topic (in contrast to the broadcasting approach today).

Additionally, the idea of Knowledge Signatures introduced by Sowa might be interesting to reduce the complexity.

Furthermore, the usage of the SIM approach might be appropriate to evolve a future TMQL towards a probabilistic query language, like probabilistic Datalog [11]. Such a probabilistic query language might allow requesting remote Topic Maps like:

> $topic_{TM1}(\$TYPE, 0.5\ person_{TM2})?$ – bind all Topics in Topic Map 1 (TM1) to the variable \$TYPE which are with a probability of at least 50% similar to the Topic with id 'person' in Topic Map 2 (TM2).
> $instance\text{-}of_{TM1}(\$TYPE, \$TOPIC), topic_{TM1}(\$TYPE, 0.5\ person_{TM2})?$ – bind all Topics in TM1 to the variable \$TOPIC which are of the types specified by \$TYPE.

Besides these ideas of future research, the SIM applied in the introducing example's cooking network would bring the chef interested in roasting lamb loins to the traditional French recipe for roasted lamb leg chops. Both handles with rosemary, green beans, lamb ...

References

[1]   Aberer, K. et al.: Emergent Semantics Systems. In: Proceedings of ICSNW 2004; LNCS 3226, Springer, (2004).

[2]   Ahmed, K.: TMShare – Topic Map Fragment Exchange in a Peer-to-Peer-Application. In: Proceedings of XML Europe 2003, London; (2003).

[3]   Barta, R.: Virtual and Federated Topic Maps. In: Proceedings of XML Europe 2004, Amsterdam; (2004).

[4]   Barta, R.: TMIP, A RESTful Topic Maps Interaction Protocol. In: Proceedings of Extreme Markup Languages 2005, Montreal; (2005).

[5]   Biezunski, M.: A Matter of Perspectives: Talking About Talking About Topic Maps. In: Proceedings of Extreme Markup Languages 2005, Montreal; (2005).

[6]   Böhm, K.; Maicher, L.: Real-time Generation of Topic Maps from Speech Streams. In: Proceedings of TMRA'05, Leipzig; LNCS 3873, Springer, (2006).

[7]   Bonifacio, M.; Bouquet, P.; Cuel, R.: Knowledge-Nodes: the Building Blocks of a Distributed Approach to Knowledge Management. In: Proceedings of I-KNOW '02, Graz; pp. 191-200, (2002).

[8]   Cuel, R.: A New Methodology for Distributed Knowledge Management Analysis. In: Proceedings of I-KNOW '03, Graz; pp. 531-537, (2003).

[9]   Durusau, P.; Newcomb, S. R.: Topic Maps - Reference Model, 13250-5 version 6.0. Available at: http://www.isotopicmaps.org/tmrm/TMRM_6.0.pdf

[10] Falkenhainer, B.; Forbus, K. D.; Gentner, D.: The Structure-Mapping Engine: Algorithm and Examples. In: Artificial Intelligence, 41, pp. 1-63, (1989).

[11] Fuhr, N.: Probabilistic Datalog - a Logic for Powerful Retrieval Methods. In: Proceedings of SIGIR-95; (1995).

[12] Garshol, L. M.: XTM Fragment Interchange 0.1; Ontopia Technical Report 2002-09-23. Available at: http://www.ontopia.net/topicmaps/materials/xtm-fragments.html

[13] Garshol, L. M.: Q: A model for topic maps: Unifying RDF and topic maps. In: Proceedings of Extreme Markup Languages 2005, Montreal; (2005).

[14] Garshol, L. M.: TMRAP – Topic Maps Remote Access Protocol. In: Proceedings of TMRA'05, Leipzig; Springer LNCS 3873, (2006).

[15] Garshol, L. M.: tolog - a topic maps query language. In: Proceedings of TMRA'05, Leipzig; Springer LNCS 3873, (2006).

[16] Garshol, L. M.; Bogachev, D.: TM/XML - Topic Maps fragments in XML. In: Proceedings of TMRA'05, Leipzig; Springer LNCS 3873, (2006).

[17] Guo, M.; Yu, Y.: Mutual Enhancement of Schema Mapping and Data Mapping. In: Proceedings of the 10th ACM Knowledge Discovery and Data Mining, Seattle; (2004).

[18] Harel, D.; Rumpe, B.: Meaningful Modeling: What's the Semantics of "Semantics"? In: Computer, 37 (10) 64–72, IEEE (2004).

[19] Korthaus, A.; Hildenbrand, T.: Creating a Java- and CORBA-Based Enterprise Knowledge Grid Using Topic Maps. In: Proceedings of the Workshop on Knowledge Grid and Grid Intelligence, Halifax; pp. 207-218, (2003).

[20] Maicher, L.: Subject Identification in Topic Maps in Theory and Practice. In: Proceedings of Berliner XML-Tage 2004, Berlin; (2004).

[21] Maicher, L.; Schwotzer, T.: Distributed Knowledge Management in the Absence of Shared Vocabularies. In: J.UCS - Journal of Universal Computer Science, Volume 11, Special Issue I-Know 2005, Springer, (2005).

[22] Maicher, L.; Witschel, H. F.: Merging of Distributed Topic Maps based on the Subject Identity Measure (SIM). In: Proceedings of LIT'04, Leipzig; pp. 229-238, (2004).

[23] Melnik, S.; Garcia-Molina, H.; Rahm, E.: Similarity Flooding: A Versatile Graph Matching Algorithm and its Application to Schema Matching. In: Proceedings of the 18th International Conference on Data Engineering (ICDE'02), San Jose, California; (2002).

[24] Newcomb, S. R.; Durusau, P.: Multiple Subject Map Patterns for Relationships and TMDM Information Items. In: Proceedings of Extreme Markup Languages 2005, Montreal; (2005).

[25] ISO/IEC JTC 1/SC34: Topic Maps Remote Access Protocol 0.2. Available at: http://www.jtc1sc34.org/repository/0507.htm

[26] ISO/IEC JTC 1/SC34: A Proposed Foundational Model for Topic Maps. Available at: http://www.jtc1sc34.org/repository/0529.htm

[27] Pepper, S.; Garshol, L. M.: Seamless Knowledge – Spontaneous Knowledge Federation using TMRAP. Presentation at: Extreme Markup Languages 2004, Montreal; (2004).

[28] Quine, W. v. O.: Identity, Ostension, and Hypostasis. In: Journal of Philosophy, 47(22), pp.621-633, (1950).

[29] Quine, W. v. O.: Word and Object. MIT Press (1960).

[30] Rahm, E.; Bernstein, P. A.: On Matching Schemas Automatically. Microsoft Technical Report MSR-TR-2001-17. Available at: http://www.research.microsoft.com/pubs/

[31] Schwotzer, T.: Modelling Distributed Knowledge Management Systems with Topic Maps. In: J.UCS - Journal of Universal Computer Science, Volume 10, Special Issue I-Know 2004, pp. 53-60, Springer, (2004).

[32] Sowa, J. F.; Majumdar, A. K.: Analogical Reasoning. In: Aldo, A.; Lex. W.; Ganter, B. et al.: Conceptual Structures for Knowledge Creation and Communication, LNAI 2746, Sprinter, pp. 16-36, (2003).

[33] Pepper, S.; Schwab, S.: Curing the Web's Identity Crisis. Subject Indicators for RDF. Available at: http://www.ontopia.net/topicmaps/materials/identitycrisis.html

[34] ISO/IEC JTC 1/SC34: Information Technology – Topic Maps – Data Model. Final Committee Draft. Available at: http://www.jtc1sc34.org/repository/0588.htm

[35] Vatant, B.: Tools for semantic interoperability: hubjects. Available at: http://www.mondeca.com/lab/bernard/hubjects.pdf, (2005).

[36] Witschel, F.: Content-oriented Topology Restructuring for Search in P2P Networks. Technical report, University of Leipzig, (2005).

Conceptual Modeling of Topic Maps with ORM Versus UML

Are D. Gulbrandsen

The XML group, Center for Information Technology Services,
University of Oslo, Norway
a.d.gulbrandsen@usit.uio.no

Abstract. The paper aims to discuss strengths and weaknesses of using Object Role Modeling (ORM) and UML Class Diagrams for conceptual modeling of Topic Maps. Established evaluation criteria for conceptual modeling languages are used to compare Topic Map ontology modeling with ORM and UML, to try to find if ORM is a good alternative to UML. The paper discusses a few extensions to simplify viewing ORM diagrams of a Topic Map ontology. ORM is also used to model a case ontology to show practical use within an application domain.

1 Introduction

The paper will discuss strengths and weaknesses of using *Object Role Modeling* (ORM) [8] and *UML class diagrams* [21] for Topic Map[1] ontology modeling, to try to find if ORM is a good alternative to UML.

First an overview over related work is presented. Then Topic Map notation for ORM and UML[2] is introduced. In Sect. 3 evaluation criteria for conceptual modeling languages are discussed. Sect. 4 discusses a case ontology where ORM has been used to model and document a Topic Map based documentation system. A few extensions to simplify viewing Topic Map ontologies are also suggested. The paper ends with a short discussion of conclusions and future work.

1.1 Related Work

Conceptual modeling, ontology modeling, and graphical notations for ontologies are not Topic Map centric research areas. Conceptual modeling is well established for database modeling. Ontologies are widely used in Knowledge Representation, Artificial Intelligence and Computer Science [25].

A much used definition of *ontology* is that it is an explicit specification of a conceptualization [18], but in general, the accepted industrial meaning of ontology is synonymous with *conceptual model* [28].

---

[1] The name of the standard is "Topic Maps" (plural). When generalizing I have chosen to use *Topic Map*, and when referring to a particular instance *topic map*.

[2] The paper will use the abreviation UML to mean UML class diagrams, unless something else is stated.

L. Maicher and J. Park (Eds.): TMRA 2005, LNAI 3873, pp. 93–106, 2006.

Ontologies can be categorized on a scale from lightweight to heavyweight [25]. [5] discusses how ontologies can be implemented using Topic Maps. UML and other conceptual modeling techniques are generally considered to be well suited for relatively lightweight ontologies [25] [3].

One of the conclusions of a comparative study of ontology languages and tools [28] is that most of the ontology languages don't have a graphic interface. This is in contrast with modeling efforts in traditional information systems, where graphic representation is always at focus. The study finds several rough parallels between frame-based languages and semantic data languages. It suggests that languages like UML can be extended to support ontology engineering, so that their well-formed graphic representations can be leveraged.

ORM started 25 years ago as *Natural language Information Analysis Method* (NIAM) [9], and is well established as a conceptual modeling tool for relational databases. The ORM dialect in [8] will be used in this paper.

ORM is a conceptual modeling approach that has both verbal and graphical syntax and a sound theoretical foundation of formal logic. In recent years, ORM has gotten much interest as a tool for modeling business rules (see the discussion of metamodels below). It has also been suggested as a tool for ontology modeling [16]. Visio and DogmaModeller are two examples of ORM based tools used for this. For a full survey of these and other ontology editors see [4].

The conceptual modeling methodology, and ORM in particular, have a semantic modeling approach at the core. The model is constructed as a dialectic process, in cooperation with the domain experts and stakeholders. It's considered very important to use concepts in the model that reflect the concepts used for the *Universe of Discourse* (UoD). The domain experts help to break down the information about the UoD to elementary sentences (*facts*) that are represented graphically. The goal is that all constructs can be translated back to elementary sentences in natural language, so that the domain experts can verify the model.

Topic Map Ontology Modeling and Visualization. A variety of notations have been used to model and display Topic Maps, usually a mix between ontology and instance visualization, for example in [24] and [26]. [22] includes one UML class diagram and a few Concept Maps, but does not discuss conceptual modeling of Topic Maps in depth. [23] uses Directed Labelled Graphs and Conceptual Graphs for ontology visualization. The paper will restrict the discussion from instance visualization, and focus on ontology modeling.

There are not many published examples of Topic Map ontologies. UML seem to be the most used notation. It is used for the metamodels *Topic Maps Data Model* (TMDM) [13] and [1].

The main contribution of this paper is the introduction of a compact ORM-based graphical notation for Topic Map Ontology modeling.

Ontology Metamodels. The TMDM standard [13] defines a formal metamodel for Topic Maps, and will be the foundation of the *Topic Map Query Language* (TMQL) [15] and the *Topic Map Constraint Language* (TMCL) [14]. The work on the TMDM is now a *final committee draft*.

There is some very interesting work going on under the umbrella of *Object Management Group* (OMG) *Model Driven Architecture*[3](MDA). A new ORM 2 metamodel, the next generation ORM, is under progress [17] [11]. It is the basis (metamodel) for the emerging OMG specification *Semantics of Business Vocabulary and Business Rules* (SBVR) [19]. The metamodel is compliant with *Meta-Object Facility 2* (MOF), which is the standard meta-metamodel for both SBVR and the *Ontology Definition Metamodel* (ODM) [18].

ODM is an emerging OMG standard for conceptual modeling and ontology development based on MOF and UML. The final specification will include two-way mappings from UML2 and TM to RDFS/OWL. The work within OMG should make it possible to make transformations between ORM 2 and the different MOF compliant metamodels.

We will have to wait for this work to finish before discussing how the different other metamodels corresponds to the Topic Map metamodel. TMCL and TMQL should also be included in a discussion of this. An ORM model is essentially a connected network of object types and relationship types [10]. A conceptual model would be a good basis for making a TMCL schema [14], once the standard get finished. Another possibility could be to generate an ORM model from a TMCL schema for ontology viewing and editing.

2   Topic Map Notation for ORM and UML

The main constructs in Topic Maps are *Topics* (representing *subjects*), *Topic Characteristics* and *Associations*.

In UML the terms *Classes*, *Attributes* and *Associations* are used. ORM is based on only two main constructs: *Objects* and *Relationships*. This correspond to nouns as subject or object, and verbs as predicates in sentences. ORM classifies objects further into *Entity Types* and *Value Types*. An Entity Type corresponds to a Subject; a Value Type corresponds to Topic Characteristics.

For a full introduction to UML and ORM, see [9], [10], [8] and [21]. I will only give a short introduction on how to model the most important Topic Map elements using the two modeling languages.

Fig. 1. A topic representing a subject. In UML a subject is modeled as a class, in ORM as an Entity Type.

In UML an association can be modeled as a simple association, ref fig. 2. It is modeled as a relationship in ORM (also called a sentence). It's possible to reify (objectify) associations in both notations. An objectified relationship in ORM is equivalent to an association class in UML.

---

[3] http://www.omg.org/mda/

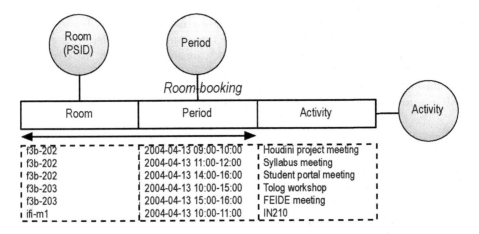

Fig. 2. Associations modeled in UML and ORM with role players and association roles

ORM can model associations of any arity, ref fig. 3. UML can model any arity larger than 1. Fig. 3 is also an example of how to instantiate an ORM diagram. The examples help the domain experts to verify the model. The arrow under room and period in the example is a uniqueness constraint, which restricts the combination of room and period to be unique (a key).

Fig. 3. An example of a ternary Association with association roles

An occurrence is essentially a specialized kind of binary association, where one role player in the association must be a topic and the other an information resource[13]. This is a good explanation of how an occurrence is modeled in ORM. The occurrence type describes the nature of the relationship between the subject and the information resource linked by that occurrence [13].

A topic may have several names of different types. The names can have different scopes, which defines in what context the name is an appropriate label for the subject represented by the topic. The standard states that a basename essentially is a specialized kind of occurrence [13]. I suggest modeling a simple name without variants the same way as an occurrence except that the name plays the *role* of name, see fig. 4.

The name (base name) may have several variant names in different scopes. I suggest modeling variant names by first changing the base name from a value type to an entity type (the equivalent to reifying it), and then making new associations from the base name to each of the variant names.

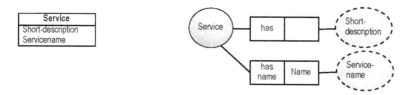

Fig. 4. Occurrence type and Name type are modeled as attributes in UML, and modeled as a value types in ORM

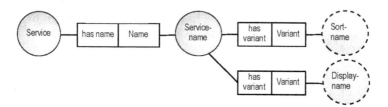

Fig. 5. Service-name with two variant names: sort-name and display-name

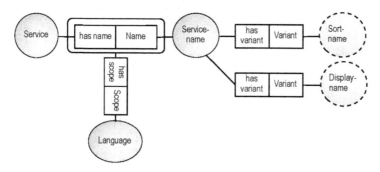

Fig. 6. Suggested notation for scope on name, occurrence or association, by objectifying the relation

Fig. 6 show the suggested notation for scope on names, occurrences and associations. In the case study in the next chapter I suggest modeling scope on association roles as a textual notation inspired by *Linear Topic Map Notation* (LTM) [6]. I think this alternative gives good clarity, ref fig. 8. I will discuss this in more detail discussing the case. I have not found any standard way of expressing scope with UML (when doing a semantic mapping).

3   Evaluation Criteria

Halpin established six conceptual model language criteria, based on earlier research [10], [2], [12], [7]: *Expressibility, Clarity, Semantic stability, Semantic relevance, Validation mechanisms* and *Abstraction mechanisms*.

3.1   Expressibility

It should be possible to express all the relevant aspects of the UoD in the conceptual schema. This is called the 100% principle, and is fundamental for conceptual modeling [7]. Ideally a modeling language should be able to model everything that is needed, but with graphical notations we will have to use the 80/20 principle in practice, and add the rest with a constraint language.

ORM diagrams are graphically more expressive than UML class diagrams, with a richer set of graphical restrictions [8] [10]. Sect. 4.2 discusses this in more detail. However, both notations opens for extensions. UML has the *Object Constraint Language* (OCL) and ORM has the constraint language *ConQuer* [2] and the emerging ORM 2 *FORML* language [11].

3.2   Clarity

The clarity of a language is a measure of how easy it is to understand and use. The language should be unambiguous. Ideally, the meaning of diagrams, or textual expressions in the language, should be intuitively obvious [10].

The example in fig. 7, is taken from [3], chap. 2.1 *Ontologies as class diagrams*, where the author explains how to use UML to model ontologies.

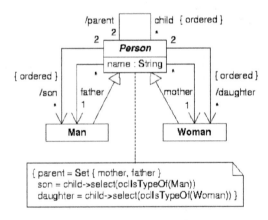

Fig. 7. The family ontology as UML, chap 2.1 [3]

The ORM notation in fig. 8 represents roughly the same model. Compared to the UML notation I feel the ORM diagram is much easier to read. This criterion is quite subjective, and any conclusions will have to be left to the reader.

3.3   Semantic Stability

This is a fundamental difference between ORM and UML. Wherever an attribute is used in UML, ORM uses an association. Attribute-free models and queries are generally more stable, because they are free of changes caused by attributes evolving into other constructs (e.g. associations), or vice versa [10]. ConQuer can

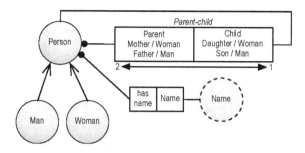

Fig. 8. ORM model of the family ontology

be used to make queries against an ORM model, and can be used for constraints, a parallel to using TMQL constraints in TMCL. There are no side effects on the constraints if the model is changed [2].

In early phases of making a model, it can be hard to decide what should be a topic and what should be characteristics. One example is the changes of servicename from fig. 4 to fig. 5. The best strategy is to postpone this decision to the realization phase [27]. If an attribute needs to be promoted to a class, late in the modeling process, it can be rather expensive [10] [10].

In a topic map, it's not a big issue, because it's possible to reify constructs into topics, with minimal changes to the rest of the information structure in the topic map. In this respect, Topic Maps are semantically stable; the reification should not break any inference rules or queries.

3.4 Semantic Relevance

Only conceptual aspects of the UoD should be taken into account when constructing the conceptual schema. This is also called the conceptualization principle, and is one of the most fundamental principles of conceptual modeling [7]. Any aspects irrelevant to the semantic meaning should be avoided in the conceptual model. One should not have to commit to any implementational choices or efficiency issues at the conceptual level [8].

3.5 Validation Mechanisms

Validation mechanisms allows domain experts to check whether the model matches the UoD. All constructs in an ORM model can be verbalized and checked by testing the sentences on an expert of the UoD. Examples of more advanced automatic validation by simulation is mentioned in [10].

3.6 Abstraction Mechanisms

Abstraction mechanisms allow unwanted details to be removed from immediate consideration. This is very important with large models (e.g. wall-size schema diagrams). Tools can provide additional support to hide and show just the part of the model relevant to a user's immediate needs [10].

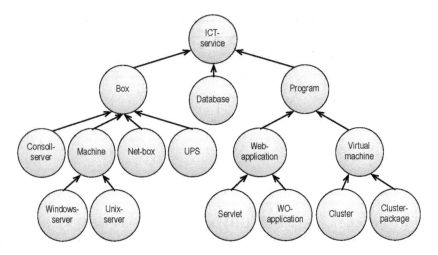

Fig. 9. ORM diagram of ICT-service class hierarchy

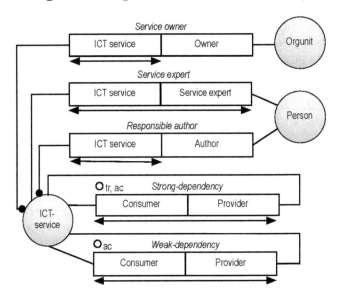

Fig. 10. Main Ontology only showing associations between main entities

Similar abstraction techniques can be applied to both UML and ORM, but ORM diagrams tend to be more detailed and larger than corresponding UML models, so abstraction mechanisms are more often used. For example, a global schema may be modularized into various *views*, see fig. 9 and 10.

It is possible and advisable to generate more compact views when using an ORM model for Ontology visualization. This will improve clarity, and make the model easier to understand, see fig. 11.

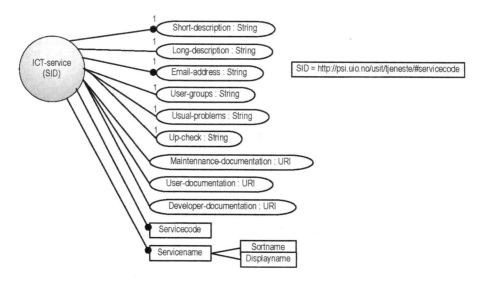

Fig. 11. Detailed and simplified view for the ICT service entity

4   Case Study – The Houston Ontology

The XML-group at the Center for Information Technology Services (USIT) has developed a Topic Map based knowledge base for systems operation, administration and maintenance documentation, which is used by the *Information and Communication Technology* (ICT) control centre, codename *Houston*. Houdini is a web application based on Java and the *Ontopia Knowledge Suite* (OKS) [20].

Much of the information needed already exists in different information systems, and much of the challenge is in systems integration. A server, for instance, is the authoritative source of which operating system version it is running. This information is harvested when running a daily script on the servers.

LTM [6] documents are generated in batch mode from the authoritative sources and saved in a CVS repository. Additional information is edited manually through a normal web interface. The documentation is merged together with the use of Subject Indicators.

The ORM notation has been used to make hypertext-based documentation of the ontology, based on HTML and image maps, as a demonstration of how to use an ORM model for documentation and visualization of an ontology[4].

4.1   Modeling of Class Hierarchy

The main subject for the knowledge base is the ICT-service. Different types of ICT-services form a class hierarchy. This is used both for the classification of services and for object oriented specialization, where a subclass can add required

---

[4] http://folk.uio.no/areg/topicmaps/HoudiniOntology/

documentation attributes. Hardware, for instance, may have a geographical address and picture, while a web application is addressable by a URI.

The notation for a class hierarchy is very similar in UML and ORM; it's just the shapes used for the topics that are different.

4.2   Modeling of Associations and Restrictions

At the core of the ontology are the dependencies between different instances of services, modeled as Topic Map associations. We use the terms *Strong Dependency* and *Weak Dependency*, see fig. 10. Definition of *Strong Dependency*:

If a service X has a strong dependency of service Y and service Y is not functioning, then service X will not function.

One of the key features for the control centre is the dynamic browsing of dependency graphs between dependent services. This is a key feature when planning the maintenance of a service, or in getting an overview of the side effects if a service is failing.

Uniqueness Constraints. The arrows under association roles in figure 10 and 3 are uniqueness constraints. A long arrow corresponds to a many-to-many association and a binary association with two short arrows would correspond to a one-to-one association. With one arrow it depends on the side.

Uniqueness Constraints are usually explained to domain experts by instantiating the roles, like in fig. 3. The combination of values under the arrow has to be unique; that is, it must be usable as a key for the association. In fig. 3 the room-id and period combine to form a key for a room booking.

Mandatory Constraints. ORM uses a black dot connecting some of the associations, ref. fig. 10. This is the mandatory constraint. The dot means that it's mandatory for an ICT service to have a responsible Orgunit.

UML uses a cardinality constraint to cover both uniqueness constraints and mandatory constraints. In ORM it's possible to use a frequency constraint in addition to the other two constraints if for instance one would need to model a 1:3 constraint. ORM has a higher level of expressibility concerning these and other type of restrictions [10]. For full introduction to constraints in ORM vs UML see [10].

Ring Constraints. When two roles in an association are played by the same subject, the path from the first roleplayer, to the role pair and back to the other role player, forms a ring. Ring constraints may be applied to a pair of roles played by the same host type. See the dependency associations in fig. 10 for an example of this. The role pair may also be part of an association with higher arity.

ORM has eight built-in ring constraints: antisymmetric (ans), asymmetric (as), acyclic (ac), irreflexive (ir), intransitive (it), reflexive (ref), symmetric (sym) and transitive (tr). The last three are most often used to derive additional facts.

Strong dependency in fig.10 is defined to be transitive and acyclic. It is also asymmetric, but since acyclic implies asymmetry, this is not declared.

UML does not provide ring constraints built-in, so this has to be specified as OCL constraints.

4.3   Modeling of Scope

A notation for scope on topic characteristics and associations was suggested in fig. 6. A textual notation, inspired by the LTM notation [6], was suggested for modeling scope on association roles in fig. 8.

The family ontology example demonstrated the possibility of modeling association roles with different names depending on which subtypes that play the roles. The scope is written as a slash followed by the type of the scoping topic.

There is limited use of scope in the case ontology until now, and the suggested notations are not yet verified through analysis of the MOF metamodels, so modeling of scope is still an open issue.

If occurrences and names were modeled as classes and not attributes in UML, it would be possible to express scope on topic characteristics with association classes, parallel to what is suggested in fig. 6.

4.4   Modeling Topic Characteristics

One of UMLs advantages is the compact notation that can give better clarity. An ORM diagram tends to have a lot of basic has-sentences, representing occurrences and names, that can be space consuming. The use of relations to model topic characteristics is also a strength however, and it seems like it can be necessary to model topic characteristics as classes in UML, to be able to model variant names and to model scope.

Generated views is an abstraction method that can help make ORM diagrams more compact. It's possible to dynamically generate a simplified view. The view could even be an attribute based UML diagram for visualizing the ontology [10]. It seems like it doesn't have to be a tradeoff between clarity and semantic stability. With views in ORM "we can have our cake and eat it too".

The notation in fig. 11 is suggested as a simplified view for topic characteristics. The basic has-sentence (ORM relation) used to model topic characteristics don't give much useful information, and I think it's both more compact and clearer to view the relations as arcs.

A stretched stippled oval shape is used for occurrences, adding a datatype as a restriction of the occurrence value. The cardinality is also included, and mandatory constraints are modeled as black dots at the end of the arc.

The Subject Identifier (SID) for an instance can be shared by different ontologies to share the subject ID across systems. This is used for merging Topic Maps. Because it is an ID it can be said to form a 1:1 reference scheme for ITC-service, so I have suggested to write the SID in parentheses under the subject, the usual notation for an unique identifier in ORM.

A name can have several variant names in different scope (set of themes). Because of this names with variants have to be modeled as classes in UML, and

UML will have the same problem as ORM with a less compact notation. I have suggested a compact view notation that display names as rectangles.

5   Conclusions and Future Work

It seems that ORM is usable for Topic Map ontology modeling.

A conceptual model would be a good basis for making a TMCL schema, once the standard is finished. An interesting possibility would be to generate an ORM model from a TMCL schema for ontology viewing and editing. The work within OMG will hopefully provide a good basis for implementations.

UML has more widespread use and tool support today, and more developers have learned the modeling language. The use of ORM for *Semantics of Business Vocabulary and Business Rules* (SBVR) will probably lead to both more tool support and more widespread use of ORM.

ORM is more semantically stable than UML, and has better expressibility in some areas, especially concerning constraints. The constraint expressibility should be evaluated against the expressibility of the emerging TMCL standard.

To conclude which notation has the best clarity is the most subjective evaluation criterion, and is left for the reader. Using views in ORM for presentation, and using the abstraction mechanisms available, I see no reason why ORM should be less clear than UML. The best way to find out is probably to use both notations in practice, and get some experience on how easy it is to communicate the ontology to others.

The ORM method puts emphasis on proper naming of roles in associations. The method is built around elementary facts, and a key feature of the method is the ability to translate all parts of the model to natural language sentences. This could make it easier to communicate the model to domain experts than UML, and is a good validation mechanism. This seems to be a main reason why ORM was chosen as the basis for the OMG SBVR specification.

I hope the suggested notation for modeling scope on association roles adds clarity. Modeling of scope is still an open issue however, as the suggested notation is not yet verified through analysis of the MOF metamodels resulting from the OMG specifications discussed in the paper. This has to be left as future work.

The name used for fact types In an ORM model is also used as ID. An unsolved issue is how to specify subject identifiers for the types. Using ORM without solving this will be parallel to using LTM without subject identifiers. The MOF metamodels for ORM 2 and Topic Maps, specified in the OMG specifications, could be a good starting point for working on this.

UML have an advantage of being a more compact notation. ORMs abstraction methods make it possible to generate compact views of an ORM model however, and even display ORM as UML.

The work within OMG promise to make transformations between the different metamodels possible. With the right tool support, switching between using ORM and UML for ontology modeling could one day be possible.

References

1. Ahmed, K.: Topic Map Design Patterns For Information Architecture (2003). http://www.techquila.com/tmsinia.html
2. Bloesch, A. & Halpin, T.: ConQuer: a conceptual query language. Proc. 15th International Conference on Conceptual Modeling ER'96 (Cottbus, Germany). B. Thalheim ed., Springer LNCS 1157 (Oct. 1996) 121-133.
3. Cranefield, S.: Networked Knowledge Representation and Exchange using UML and RDF. Journal of Digital Information, Volume 1 Issue 8 (2001). http://jodi.ecs.soton.ac.uk/Articles/v01/i08/Cranefield/
4. Denny, M.: Ontology Tools Survey, Revisited. Xml.com (2004). http://www.xml.com/pub/a/2004/07/14/onto.html
5. Garshol, L. M.: Metadata? Thesauri? Taxonomies? Topic Maps!. Proceedings of XML Europe 2004, IDEAlliance, April 2004. http://www.ontopia.net/topicmaps/materials/tm-vs-thesauri.html
6. Garshol, L. M.: The Linear Topic Map Notation. Definition and introduction, version 1.3. http://www.ontopia.net/download/ltm.html
7. Griethuysen, J. V. (Ed.): Concepts and Terminology for the Conceptual Schema and the Information Base. Publ. nr. ISO/TC97/SC5/WG3-N695, ANSI, 11 West 42nd Street, New York, NY 10036 (1982).
8. Halpin, T.: Information Modeling and Relational Databases, From Conceptual Analysis to Logical Design. Morgan Kaufman, San Francisco, California, USA (2001). ISBN 1558606726.
9. Hapin, T.: ORM/NIAM Object-Role Modeling. Ch. 4 of Handbook on Architectures of Information Systems, Springer-Verlag, ISBN: 3540644539 (1998). http://www.orm.net/pdf/springer.pdf
10. Halpin, T. & Bloesch, A.: Data modeling in UML and ORM: a comparison. Journal of Database Management, vol. 10, no. 4 (Oct-Dec, 1999), Idea Group Publishing. http://www.orm.net/pdf/JDM99.pdf
11. Halpin, T.: FORML Position paper for W3C Workshop on Rule Languages for Interoperability. W3C Workshop on Rule Languages for Interoperability, 27-28 April 2005. http://www.w3.org/2004/12/rules-ws/paper/32/
12. ter Hofstede, A., Proper, H., van der Weide, T.: Formal definition of a conceptual language for the description and manipulation of information models. Information Systems 18, 7 (1993) 489-523.
13. ISO 13250-2: Topic Maps Data Model (TMDM). International Organization for Standardization (ISO). http://www.isotopicmaps.org/sam/sam-model/
14. ISO 19756: Topic Maps Constraint Language (TMCL). International Organization for Standardization (ISO). http://www.isotopicmaps.org/tmcl/
15. ISO 18048: Topic Map Query Language (TMQL). International Organization for Standardization (ISO). http://www.isotopicmaps.org/tmql/
16. Jarrar, M., Demey J., Meersman R.: On Using Conceptual Data Modeling for Ontology Engineering. Journal on Data Semantics, Vol. 2800, pp.:185-207, LNCS, Springer, ISBN: 3-540-20407-5, (October 2003).
17. Krogstie, J., Halpin, T and Siau, K.: Information Modeling Methods and Methodologies. Idea Group Publishing. ISBN:1591403758 (2005) Chapter 2.
18. Object Management Group (OMG): Ontology Definition Metamodel RFP. OMG Document: ad/2003-03-40, http://ontology.omg.org/ontology_info.htm
19. Object Management Group (OMG): Semantics of Business Vocabulary and Business Rules. OMG Document: dtc/05-11-01 (SBVR draft adopted specification), http://www.omg.org/cgi-bin/apps/doc?dtc/05-11-01.pdf

20. Ontopia: The Ontopia Knowledge Suite. http://www.ontopia.net/
21. Object Management Group (OMG): Unified Modeling Language 2.0 (UML). http://www.uml.org/
22. Park, J. (Ed.): XML Topic Maps: Creating and Using Topic Maps for the Web. Addison Wesley, ISBN: 020174960 (2004).
23. Passin, T. B.: Explorers Guide to the Semantic Web. Manning Publications, ISBN: 1-932394-20-6 (2004).
24. Pepper, S.: The TAO of Topic Maps, Ontopia (2002). http://www.ontopia.net/topicmaps/materials/tao.html
25. Gómez-Pérez, A., Fernández-López, M., Corcho, O. : Ontological Engineering, chapter 1. Springer-Verlag, ISBN: 1-85233-551-3 (2004).
26. Rath, H. H.: The Topic Maps Handbook - an empolis White Paper, Empolis (2003). http://empolis.de/downloads/empolis_TopicMaps_Whitepaper20030206.pdf
27. Skagestein, G. & Normann, R.: Revival of the elementary sentence - or the dark side of UML class diagrams. The Norwegian Conference of informatics (2003). http://www.nik.no/2003/Bidrag/Skagestein.pdf
28. Su, X. & Ilebrekke, L: A Comparative Study of Ontology Languages and Tools. Lecture Notes In Computer Science; Vol. 2348 (2002) Pages: 761 - 765, ISBN:3-540-43738-X.

Topic Maps for Image Collections

Martin Leuenberger, Silke Grossmann, Niklaus Stettler, and Josef Herget

The authors are affiliated to: University of Applied Science Chur,
Department of Information Science, Ringstrasse, CH-7000 Chur
{Martin.Leuenberger, Silke.Grossmann, Niklaus.Stettler,
Josef.Herget}@fh-htwchur.ch
http://www.informationswissenschaft.ch

Abstract. *Living Memory* is an interdisciplinary project running for two years, which is realised in cooperation of several institutions. It aims at developing an information system for a digital collection of different types of visual resources and will combine classical methods of image indexing and retrieval with innovative approaches like content-based image retrieval and the use of topic maps for semantic searching and browsing. This work-in-progress-report outlines the aims of the project and present first results after the period of eleven months.

1 *Living Memory* – Aims of the Project

Living Memory is a cooperative project of applied research running for two years; it is in progress presently. Project partners include the University of Art and Design (HGK) Basel (Department of Visual Communications), the University of Applied Sciences (HTW) Chur (Department of Information Science), and the software company Interaktion, located in Zurich.

The aims are to set up an information system of visual resources and to explore new paths of image cataloguing and retrieval, including the investigation of how topic maps can be made fruitful for the image domain. A topic map representing index terms will be used both as a navigation tool for the user, allowing him to browse the image collection, and as a means to enable semantic searches, allowing the user to choose between "more precision" and "more recall". Special emphasis is laid on the combination of different access options.

The visual resources at hand document a major project of urban planning – the structural alteration of an industrial area, located in Basel, into a research site.[1] In order to create a digital "living memory" of the site, Novartis mandated the HGK to document the process, and since 2003 HGK students have created 600-800 visual resources in different media – photographs, drawings, graphics and videos – per year.[2]

---

[1] The project has been initiated by the pharmaceutical company Novartis, the owner of the site. For more information about the emerging, so called Novartis Campus see http://www.novartis.ch/about_novartis/de/campus_2005/index.shtml.

[2] These include architectural photographs as well as images of special events or everyday scenes like construction workers or Novartis employees at work.

L. Maicher and J. Park (Eds.): TMRA 2005, LNAI 3873, pp. 107–111, 2006.

The project *Living Memory* started in January 2005 and reached its first milestone after eleven months. The following results have been achieved: a database, implemented with the system Cumulus[3], is ready for cataloguing; a first version of both a thesaurus and a topic map have been built; a concept of different access options has been set up.

2   The Semantic Structure of *Living Memory*

The semantic structure of the *Living Memory* information system is formed by three interlocking modules: metadata schema, thesaurus and topic map.

The basis for image description is a metadata schema especially designed for *Living Memory*. For that purpose, existing schemas such as the Dublin Core Metadata Element Set[4], the Categories for the Description of Works of Art[5] and the SEPIA Data Element Set[6] were consulted. Since we expect users of a *Living Memory* information system – mostly image professionals – to search images by a variety of criteria, the schema combines formal metadata, index terms and visual properties. Formal metadata (such as author or medium) and index terms have to be assigned intellectually, visual features (such as contrast or luminance) can be extracted automatically.[7]

A thesaurus drawing mainly on the Art and Architecture Thesaurus (AAT)[8] has been designed; it will serve as a controlled vocabulary for image indexing.[9]

The thesaurus also served as a fundament for the construction of the topic map;[10] it provided the topics and some basic associations: the hierarchical super-/subclass association, synonyms and related terms. However, when converting a thesaurus into a topic map, care must be applied with regard to the hierarchical composition of the thesaurus.[11] Since we did not follow the strict super-/subclass hierarchy of the AAT, but allowed part-of- and affiliated-with-relations[12], as well, every hierarchical relation had to be examined with regard to its semantics. Part-of- and affiliated-with-relations were therefore turned into association types of the topic map.

---

[3]   http://www.canto.de/pro/

[4]   http://dublincore.org/

[5]   http://www.getty.edu/research/conducting_research/standards/cdwa/index.html

[6]   http://www.knaw.nl/ecpa/sepia/workinggroups/wp5/cataloguing.html

[7]   Since the 1990ies, images can be searched for by their inherent features, i.e. colour, texture and form. This is called content-based image retrieval (CBIR). Although the technology has evolved into some commercial products, the results are not yet fully satisfactory. We limited this option to colour features.

[8]   http://www.getty.edu/research/conducting_research/vocabularies/aat. This comprehensive and specialised thesaurus proved to be best suited for our project.

[9]   The thesaurus in its present raw version contains ca. 1'000 terms ranging from concrete entities to abstract concepts, which are divided into several branches.

[10]   Cf. [1], p. 38. The topic map was modelled with the software L4 Modeller by Moresophy (http://www.moresophy.com).

[11]   [3], p. 3.

[12]   Examples are "tree – branch" for the part-of-relation and "architecture – building" for the affiliated-with-relation.

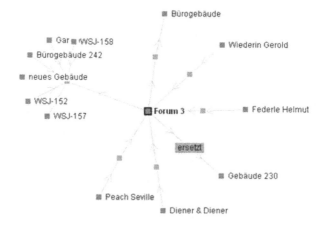

Fig. 1. Extract from the *Living Memory* topic map

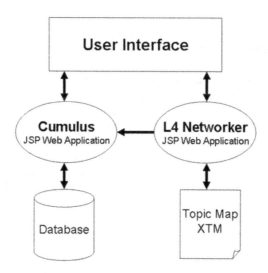

Fig. 2. Architecture of the *Living Memory* information system (arrows signify data transfer)

Accordingly, the topics of the topic map cover the index terms of the thesaurus.[13] The topic map will serve both as a navigation tool for the user (see fig. 1) and as an instrument to enable semantic searches (see sect. 3).

Since the occurrences are stored in the database, every topic will be defined as a database query. This query may be simple; the topic "fence" e.g. will initiate a query for "fence" in the subject term data field of the database. Consequently, every relevant image of a fence will be an occurrence, provided the images have been properly indexed. But the query may also be combined; in fact, topics for image *expression* shall be defined in this way. The question "What makes an image express an idyll?"

---

[13] The topic map will not, however, cover formal metadata like authors or formats of images. Formal search terms can only be found by traditional database queries.

may lead to answers like the following: colour feature A plus colour feature B plus subject term C.[14] By this mechanism, the topic map is connected to the database without redundancy. Fig. 2 shows the basic architecture of the *Living Memory* information system.

3 Access Options

As [2] suggests, users shall be able to combine different search methods, which is supposed to be the most successful approach in image retrieval.[15] We therefore focused on the combination of different levels of image description and methods of image retrieval, rather than pushing one method to extremes.

The following search cases show how the semantic structure supports different access options:

- **Traditional search** can be effected as text-based search (for formal metadata or index terms) or as visual search (for colour features, with the possibility to adjust a value on a scale). Given a set of images as a result, the user may then want to refine his search results, or he may continue the search based on a found image by selecting and combining allocated metadata of the image, including visual properties.
- **Semantic search and browsing** is effected with the aid of the topic map. The user can select the degree of precision (e. g. no related terms, exact match) or recall (e. g. all related terms) of his search. But he may also browse the topic map guided by subject interests. The latter has several advantages for the user: He does not have to be familiar with the logic of the database or description language;[16] moreover, by navigating the topic map he will learn about the semantic context, in which a collection and its single items are embedded, and may find useful items he would not have expected to find in the beginning.

4 Conclusions and Further Work

The basic concepts of access options have been laid down above. These concepts will have to be implemented in a next step. With regard to the topic map, database queries assigning occurrences to the topics will have to be defined. Furthermore, the use of topic maps for semantic searches will have to be worked out in detail: Given a search term, which are the related terms to be included in a query with the choice "more recall"?[17]

---

[14] For the assignation of image expression, the images will have to be interpreted by image professionals. If the experts agree on a set of images to have the expression „idyllic", these images can be analyzed with regard to visual features. If similarities can be found, combined queries can be defined accordingly.

[15] Cf. [2], p. 19ff.

[16] Topic maps may therefore be an appropriate solution for the increasing number of digital archives on the World Wide Web facing users without professional skills in information retrieval or databases.

[17] This will have to be defined for every single topic, probably with the aid of scopes.

Moreover, in the next stage of the project, the design of user interfaces will occupy a central position. Finally, usability tests are due to optimise the emerging prototype of the information system.

References

1. Rath, Hans Holger: *The Topic Maps Handbook. White Paper.* http://www.empolis.com/downloads/empolis_TopicMaps_Whitepaper20030206.pdf
2. Renz, Monika; Renz, Wolfgang: *Neue Verfahren im Bildretrieval. Perspektiven für die Anwendung.* (Contribution to 22th DGI-Online Conference, May 2-4 2000, Frankfurt a.M.) http://users.informatik.haw-hamburg.de/~wr/internFH/Renz_DGIonline.pdf
3. Wielinga, B. J. et al.: *From Thesaurus to Ontology.* http://www.cs.vu.nl/~guus/papers/Wielinga01a.pdf

Real-Time Generation of Topic Maps from Speech Streams

Karsten Böhm and Lutz Maicher

University of Leipzig, Department of Computer Science,
Augustusplatz 10-11, 04109 Leipzig, Germany
{boehm, maicher}@informatik.uni-leipzig.de

Abstract. Topic Maps are means for representing sophisticated, conceptual indexes of any information collection for the purpose of semantic information integration. To properly fulfil this purpose, the generation of Topic Maps has to base on a solid theory. This paper proposes the Observation Principle as the theoretical fundament of a future scientific discipline Topic Maps Engineering. SemanticTalk generates sophisticated, conceptual indexes of speech streams in real-time. Reflecting the Observation Principle, this paper describes how these indexes are created, how they are represented as Topic Maps and how they can be used for semantic information integration purposes.

1 Introduction

The challenges addressed by this paper are described by the following example. Interviews are a very popular technique in qualitative research in a variety of fields, from social sciences to market research. For example, an automotive company observes the interests of its customers with the help of guided interviews. These interviews are continuously repeated with the same customers within intervals of one year. The task of the interviewer from the market research department is the observation of the rise and fall of trends within the time line. Additionally, he has to provide background knowledge about these trends for further investigations.

From our perspective we understand a Topic Map[1] *firstly* as a representation of a sophisticated index of any information collection. *Secondly* a Topic Map has to be generated in order to merge with others to allow semantic information integration.

This paper describes how sophisticated, conceptual indexes can be generated from speech streams automatically in real-time by a software-system called SemanticTalk. Topic Maps Technologies allow it to integrate the concepts observed in the speech-streams with known background knowledge to support the interviewer from the market research department. The paper is based on a solid theory how indexes of any information collection created by any means could be represented as Topic Maps to fulfil their purpose as integration tool.

Besides intellectual approaches to Topic Maps Engineering, the automatic generation of Topic Maps from textual sources is a relatively new area that has been covered

---

[1] To avoid ambiguities all terminology concerning Topic Maps Technologies is capitalized.

L. Maicher and J. Park (Eds.): TMRA 2005, LNAI 3873, pp. 112–124, 2006.

by some research approaches already. The application of such techniques to speech streams in order to provide a real-time generation of Topic Maps from a spoken conversation is a new approach that is presented in this paper.

There are a number of interesting applications imaginable. The most evident is the real-time generation of Topic Maps for the comprehension of the core concepts of conversations in meeting situations. These Topic Maps should be used to link background knowledge to the key concepts of the current conversation by merging in Topic Maps Views (TMV, a set of Subject Proxies [2]) of other relevant information collections. By implementing this automatic process directly onto the speech stream it would be possible to build a Push-System that provides the user with relevant or related information without requiring an explicit search.

The generation of Topic Maps should base on a solid theory. To our best knowledge this theory is not available in the current literature. Therefore we introduce the Observation Principle. This principle is proposed to be the basis of a future scientific discipline Topic Maps Engineering, regardless whether automatic or manual methods are addressed. The Observation Principle bases on a deeper investigation of the Subject Equality Decision Chain. This chain discloses the nature of the semantic core of Topic Maps Technologies: the decision whether two Subject Proxies indicate identical Subjects. This paper discusses the generation of Topic Maps with SemanticTalk in the context of the Observation principle.

This paper makes the following contributions:

- Introduction of the Observation Principle based on a deep investigation of the Subject Equality Decision Chain in section 2,
- Introduction of SemanticTalk as means for the real-time generation of sophisticated indexes of speech-streams in section 3, and
- Reflecting the Observation Principle while representing these indexes as Topic Maps for semantic information integration in section 4.

2   The Observation Principle

Topic Maps are means for representing sophisticated indexes of any information collection for the purpose of semantic information integration. From this perspective, the generation of Topic Maps, whether it is done manually or automatically, needs a solid theory. Our proposal is called Observation Principle. It is introduced in brief by this section. Previously, the Subject Equality Decision Chain is introduced.

2.1   The Subject Equality Decision Chain

As discussed more detailed in [10] the *semanticness* of Topic Maps Technologies is determined through the following objective: Subject Proxies indicating identical Subjects have to be viewed as merged ones. The insight gained from the semanticness discussion in [10] is that the enforcement of this objective is the only semantic feature of Topic Maps. Consequently, Topic Map authors have to be strictly aware to *correctly* define the Subject of their proxies according to their exact intents.

But when do Subject Proxies *indicate identical* Subjects? This decision about Subject Equality is determined by a foregoing process of abstractions, simplifications and decisions. The following thought chain might help to understand the impact of this process on the semanticness of Topic Maps. This Subject Equality Decision Chain reveals the real nature of the decision whether two Subject Proxies indicate identical Subjects.

Basically, within the Subject Equality Decision Chain the separation of *Subject Identity* and *Subject Equality* is introduced. Subject Identity is based on the decision whether Subject Stages caught at different occasions belong to the same Subject. Subject Equality, however, is based on the decision whether Subject Proxies indicate identical Subjects. Simplified, Subject Identity targets to the real world whereby Subject Equality targets to the modelled world each Topic Map represent.

In the following the Subject Equality Decision Chain is described in detail. The subsequent summary defines the six steps of this thought chain:

1. Assumption of a world without any sensory systems,
2. Sensory systems come to stage, catching Subject Stages,
3. Decision about Subject Identity from a given perspective,
4. Decision about Subjectness from the given perspective,
5. Documenting the impressions from the given perspective,
6. Documenting the decision about Subject Identity, and
7. Decision about Subject Equality according to the governing Subject Map Disclosure (SMD, see [5], [10]) at consumption time.

The first step of the Subject Equality Decision Chain is a universe of Subjects. It is assumed, that within this universe all possible Subjects purely *exist*, but they are not recognised and deranged by any sensory system. This absence of any sensory system implies slightness to the very nature of the universe of Subjects. Any suppositions about these Subjects are speculations, because any empirical evidence is impossible to gain. Obviously, discussions about the very nature of Subjects should be left to the philosophy. Caused by the absence of any sensory system, within in the first step the question of Subject Identity or Subject Equality is irrelevant: Subjects solely exist, no one is (or can be) interested in their nature.

As a second step, sensory systems come on stage, trying to investigate the nature of Subjects (even if the "investigated" Subjects do not exist in the physical reality, like a unicorn or the abstract concept of liberty, etc.). Immediately, as a third step the problem of Subject Identity arises. In accordance to Quine's "momentary stages" [13] of things, we assume that the owner of sensory systems observes Subject Stages. *A Subject Stage is a momentary stage of a Subject.* (Simplified, it is an observation of a Subject). For example, a ranger might observe moose at different occasions. He catches different momentary stages. The question is, whether both moose stages belong to the same moose. From this perspective *Subject Identity means that Subjects Stages caught at different occasions belong to the same Subject.* It is important to stress the fact that this definition disburdens from the constraint to make explicit what the Subject is (only its sameness is used as an identifying criteria). For the ranger, the decision about Subject Identity is a judgement whether the caught moose stages belong to the same moose.

Another example is an automatic traffic control indexing the traffic stream by taking pictures from each car passing different points. The question of Subject Identity is, whether two car stages caught at different occasions are the same car [14]. The question of Subject Identity is not compelling whether two car stages caught at different occasions belong to the car with a concrete registration number.

Obviously some philosophical questions remain open. For example, all Subjects alter in time, at least imperceptibly. In this case, is it possible to catch exactly the same Subject twice? The decision about Subject Identity is thus always a decision under uncertainty. As the first step of the thought chain revealed, only the observations gained from the sensory systems are available to judge about Subject Identity. It is compelling that this information is never sufficient to judge about Subject Identity with certainty. Uncertainty is an important aspect of the decision about Subject Identity.

Even in the case that the identity seems to be sure, this certainty is derived from the chosen perspective. Biezunski notes: each "interpretation of any subject is made within certain perspective." [2]. The chosen perspective defines the assertions which should be made later about the Subject. From a child's perspective all car stages caught by the traffic surveillance system belong to the same Subject 'car'. From a toll system's perspective each car stage caught at different occasions belongs to the Subject of a specific toll debtor. The chosen perspective therefore heavily determines the decision about Subject Identity.

What does the fact that the child learns to differentiate car brands and models imply for Subject Identity? It reveals that the decision about Subject Identity is a process. Subject Stages are considered to belong to the same Subject as long as convincing information is received from the sensory system. Even if contradicting information is observed, Subject Identity might be considered as long as this information is not sufficient to disprove the present conviction. Looking at it as a process is an important characteristic of the decision about Subject Identity.

We conclude, that the decisions about Subject Identity is *a perspective dependent discovery processes under uncertainty.*

The next part of the Subject Equality Decision Chain is dedicated to the documentation of the impressions from the sensory systems: changing from the real world to the modelled world, changing from the question of Subject Identity to the question of Subject Equality. It is important to stress the fact, that modelling always implies a loss of information. The fourth step of the thought chain represents the first decision concerning this loss of information: impressions about which Subjects (Stages) should be documented? This is a decision about the *Subjectness* of a given Subject in the current perspective. The child looking at the street catches a lot of Subjects besides cars (SOS-telephones, traffic signs). By heavily repeating the word "car", the child shows that from its current perspective only the caught car stages are noteworthy.

After the decision about Subjectness the impressions should be documented. (This documentation is equal to modelling the caught impressions from the current perspective with the available vocabulary.) For each Subject Stage with 'proved Subjectness' in the current perspective a Subject Proxy has to be created. *Observation Subject Proxies* might be an appropriate name for those proxies. Afterwards, all impressions which should be documented about the recognised Subject Stages have to be documented using the available vocabulary: SMD ontology, Subject Map (SM) ontology and SM vocabulary (see [10] for a further discussion of these terms).

It might be evident to document the decision about Subject Identity simultaneously in the recently created Observation Subject Proxies. The decision about Subject Identity is a process under uncertainty. The conviction about Subject Identity of Subject

Stages might alter in time. Therefore, the creation of additional *Integration Subject Proxies* is proposed. These Subject Proxies only assert that two Observation Subject Proxies indicate identical Subjects. Generally, the decision about Subject Identity has to be documented by using the Subject Indication approach of the governing SMD.

For the moose example this implies that for all times the ranger observes moose stages it has to be created an own Observation Subject Proxy to document the impressions at these occasions. Additionally, an Integration Subject Proxy has to be created to assert that these Proxies indicate identical Subjects from the current perspective. Integration Subject Proxies can be compared to Hubjects as introduced by Vatant [17].

The last step of the Subject Equality Decision Chain is the decision of a Topic Map Processing Application (TMPA) whether two Subject Proxies indicate identical Subjects. As discussed in [10] in more detail, this decision about Subject Equality depends on the governing SMD at consumption time. If the Topic Map Data Model (TMDM, [15]) is the governing SMD, these decisions are simple string comparisons.

2.2 The Observation Principle

The Observation Principle might be a theoretical fundament for a future scientific discipline Topic Maps Engineering. We assume that Topic Maps created according to the Observation Principle are well suited for semantic information integration, the core functionality of Topic Maps Technologies. The Observation Principle postulates that each observation (caught by any provided sensory system) of a Subject Stage *in interest from the chosen perspective* has to be documented by a proper Observation Subject Proxy. The documentation of the decision about the Subject Identity by means of Integration Subject Proxies allows defining the perspective in a proper way. All documentations are constrained by the Subject Indication Approach and the additional vocabulary provided by the governing Subject Map Disclosure (SMD).

1. Observe the information collections in interest (texts, video streams, etc.) by any means and detect Subject Stages.
2. Decide about the Subject Identity of the observed Subject Stages from the chosen perspective.
3. Decide about Subjectness from the chosen perspective.
4. Create Observation Subject Proxies for each Subject Stage in interest.
5. Document all observed information about the Subject Stage with the given vocabulary: SMD ontology, SM ontology, and SM vocabulary.
6. Document the decisions about Subject Identity by the means of Integration Subject Proxies with the provided Subject Indication Approach.

The modus operandi of observations can be a set of NLP methods (like those in SemanticTalk), a human hand-crafting a Topic Map, a mapping approach integrating data from a legacy system like a relational data base or any other function creating any kind of information which can be interpreted as "observations of Subject Stages". It is important to outline, that Topic Maps do only *represent* indexes created for any information collection by any means.

In the following it is discussed, how the SemanticTalk System can be used to apply the Observation Principle. As a first step SemanticTalk is introduced.

3   The SemanticTalk System

SemanticTalk (see figure 1) observes speech streams in real-time with a number of different Natural Language Processing (NLP) methods. It generates sophisticated conceptual indexes of speech streams in real-time. According to the Observation Principle, this bouquet of NLP methods defines a proper SemanticTalk perspective.

This section introduces the technical background of SemanticTalk. The following section discusses how SemanticTalk can be used to represent the created indexes as Topic Maps with the objective of semantic information integration.

SemanticTalk can be used on a single computer. It is implemented as platform-independent client-server architecture to support a multi-user scenario. Several GUIs as well as independent speaker input units, consisting of a standard headset and a client notebook, can be locally distributed and connected via standard networks, for example in a wireless local area network (WLAN). It thus enables the use in dynamic meetings scenarios. A more detailed description of the system can be found in [1].

SemanticTalk provides various interfaces to both data sources and sinks, the most important of which is the input module for free speech, a text mining component called Graph Distiller to automatically assemble static indexes, and the XML-based interface for the bi-directional exchange of structured data.

For speech-to-text conversion, the commercially available dictation system Voice-Pro from Linguatec is used. Although speech recognition is not error free the performance is noteworthy and for our requirements the generated word stream is more than sufficient. Term extraction is performed using a large-scale reference terminology corpus (about 10 million phrases mainly from newspaper papers, automatically generated) as background information (comparable to the general linguistic competence of native speakers). This database can be extended by domain tence of native speakers). This database can be extended by domain specific terminology. This can be derived by processing relevant sets of documents using text mining algorithms. In the case highly specialised domains are investigated this extension is quite useful. While the term 'cancer' might by a key concept in a conversation about everyday life, it is not sufficient selective in a medical conversation about leukaemia. Adding domain specific terminology alters the perspective SemanticTalk takes.

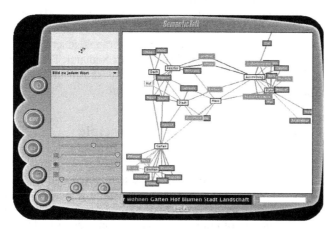

Fig. 1. The user interface of SemanticTalk

Filtering relevant concepts is done by extracting nouns that exceed an adjustable relevance threshold for the domain of discourse. In the next step, relationships between terms selected from the text stream are determined based on term relations in the underlying database. The term is discarded, if no additional terms can be associated with this term within a defined time frame. Otherwise it will be added to the growing conceptual structure (white nodes in figure 1). This index will be continuously updated, as long as the speech stream is analysed. Furthermore, the network is expanded by additional terms that are not present in the voice stream. They are integrated if the strength of the association is above a threshold (grey nodes in figure 1).

In order to generate a conceptual background structure, a module called Graph Distiller is used. It takes one or more text documents as input and generates a corresponding conceptual view on the data. The interconnection of concepts is based on the same principles as described above, but no additional concepts are associated. The output is only a network of domain specific concepts and their relationships. However, there is a significant difference to the process described above, as at any point during the processing only the current word and the history of words is available, no assumptions about the future of the ongoing discourse can be made. In contrast the Graph Distiller benefits from the availability of the complete text material to construct the graph and it is not required to work in real-time. Hence, a more sophisticated and thus more costly algorithm is applied to extract the relevant concepts. Obviously, using the Graph Distiller alters the SemanticTalk perspective slightly.

The extraction algorithm is based on *Difference Analysis* [6]. It applies pure language statistics: the distribution of terms in the given text documents is compared to the distribution of the same terms in the general use of a specified language, for example German. If a term occurs significantly more often in the examined input text documents than in the general language use, it is called a 'key concept of the domain'. The conceptual graph is constructed of only these key concepts. As based on pure statistics, Difference Analysis is language independent. However, it requires a large, representative collection of digital documents. Beyond Difference Analysis, the Graph Distiller optionally provides algorithms as described in [18]. For morphologically rich languages like German, complex noun decomposition and lemmatization particularly improve the output of the Graph Distiller.

SemanticTalk provides a bi-directional interface (import/export) for the Resource Description Framework (RDF), a language representing statements about resources and their relationships. Hence, virtually all kinds of graphs generated in different applications can be used as background information for SemanticTalk. The results of a SemanticTalk sessions can be exported to RDF and as shown in section 4 be further processed to refine and augment the generated structures.

4 SemanticTalk and the Observation Principle

SemanticTalk generates sophisticated conceptual indexes of speech streams. This section provides an illustrative example from the automotive industry. After a brief description of the example setting, section 4.1 depicts how SemanticTalk generates indexes by taking its own perspective. Thereafter, the representation of these indexes as Topic Maps for the purpose of information integration is described in 4.2 and 4.3.

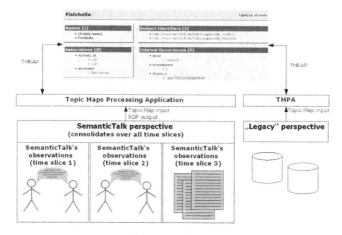

Fig. 2. SemanticTalk and the Observation Principle

The example setting described in figure 2 was used to index ten conversations about the automotive domain at different time epochs (time slices). The goal of the experiment was to show the changes of subjects during time although the domain remains fixed. Additionally to speech streams, other available documents (such as a year's publication of an automotive magazine) were used to extract similar indexes.

4.1 Getting the SemanticTalk Perspective

What does SemanticTalk actually observe? Does it, as the figure 2 might indicate, recognise *Fisichella* as a key concept of the conversation?

To answer to this question accurately, the application of the Observation Principle in SemanticTalk should be investigated in more detail: SemanticTalk observes speech streams and recognises words (or phrases). From the SemanticTalk perspective each word (or phrase) can be interpreted as a Subject Stage. With the help of some linguistic methods (stemming, etc.) a decision is made about the identity (simplified its base form) of each Subject Stage (the observed inflected word form). During the observation of the speech stream the frequency and the use within the context of the utterance is observed. Based on these observations, noticeable usage of a word implies its Subjectness from the current SemanticTalk perspective. As already described in section 3, this perspective depends on the methods and corpora which are applied in detail. If Subjectness is decided, a Subject Proxy is created for each Subject (a node) and all observed impressions, which are in interest from the current perspective, are documented. (In contrast to the proposal in section 2.2, our implementation does not differentiate between Observation and Integration Subject Proxies.)

Coming back to the question about what SemanticTalk really observes? It does not recognise the concept 'Fisichella' as a key concept of the conversation. This might be an interpretation from another perspective which is in interest for integration purposes as discussed in 4.3. SemanticTalk does only observe a noticeable usage of the term 'Fisichella' in the speech stream and this 'noticeable usage of the term Fisichella' is the Subject of an according Subject Proxy.

The same procedure holds for the relationships between the terms, because relationships are represented as Subject Proxy, too ([5]). The Subject of those proxies, the Associations, is the observed noticeable relationship between two terms.

4.2 Creating the SemanticTalk Topic Maps View

As mentioned above, SemanticTalk generates RDF output for the further usage of the created index. As described in figure 2, the next step is the generation of a Topic Map from this output:[2] the SemanticTalk Topic Maps View (SemanticTalk TMV) of the observed conversation. This TMV must be usable for further semantic integration tasks, like integrating background knowledge from marketing, customer and employee databases. The following example assumes the TMDM as the governing SMD.

As discussed in literature, the mapping of RDF and Topic Maps governed by the TMDM should be a semantic mapping [12]. Today, such a semantic mapping is provided by Ontopia's Omnigator[3]. In future a Q engine, as proposed by Garshol [7], might be able to process RDF and Topic Maps simultaneously.

SemanticTalk's RDF output consists of a set of nodes (Subject Proxies for the observations of noticeable usage of terms) and a set of edges (Subject Proxies for the observations of noticeable simultaneously usage of noticeable terms) connecting these nodes. The following listing shows (a part of) the description of a node in RDF:

```
<st:node rdf:ID="node_Fisichella">
  <st:ID>160615</st:ID>
  <st:label>Fisichella</st:label>
  <st:nodelevel>1</st:nodelevel>
  <st:ref_wort_nr rdf:resource="#node_160615"/>
  <st:variant st:index="3" st:type="4" st:weight="0.3176"/>
</st:node>
```

The node with the internal ID '160615' has the label 'Fisichella'. The <st:variant> tag asserts, that the term 'Fisichella' was observed with sufficient relevance only in time slice number 3. This node is semantically mapped into LTM[4] (Linear Topic Maps Notation) as follows. The <st:label> tag is mapped to a Basename and the <st:ref_word_nr> and <rdf:id> tags are mapped to Subject Identifiers. This Subject Indication determines that if a noticeable usage of the same term is detected by the same technique twice, Subject Equality holds. All information about a time slice represented by each <st:variant> tag is represented by a single Topic which is connected to the Topic 'Fisichella' with a typed Association.

```
[id7406 : id7276 = "Fisichella"
    @"http://www.texttech.de/dtd/st/pap#node_160615"
    @"http://www.texttech.de/dtd/st/pap#node_Fisichella"]
    {id7406, id7650, [[160615]]}
id7549( id7406 : id463, id464 : id2195 )
```

---

[2] At the moment, SemanticTalk does only create the indexes in real-time. The generation of Topic Maps based on these indexes is done with the result of conversation observations afterwards. In future, it is desirable that a TMPA becomes the kernel of SemanticTalk.

[3] http://www.ontopia.net

[4] http://www.ontopia.net/download/ltm.html

```
[id464]
   {id464, id1636, [[0.31766722453166335]]}
   {id464, id4378, [[3]]}
   {id464, id787,  [[4]]}
```

Similar semantic mappings are done for the edges. In the example, the only edge of the node 'Fisichella' is a relationship to the node 'Schumacher'. Due to the success of Michael Schumacher in several competitions it is not surprising, that in contrast to 'Fisichella' the term 'Schumacher' was observed in all time slices.

4.3 Integration of Background Knowledge with the SemanticTalk TMV

As shown in figure 2, the last step is the integration of background knowledge (represented as TMVs) with the SemanticTalk TMV. To remind again, the perspective of the generated SemanticTalk TMV is defined as follows: a Subject Proxy documents a noticeable usage of a term detected by SemanticTalk. Subject Identity is given, if this observation of noticeable usage of the same term is done twice by the same algorithm at different occasion.

For integration purposes, the perspective of the integration has to be defined. From the integration perspective the noticeable usage of a term observed by SemanticTalk should be interpreted as the observation of a key concept of the conversation.

For example, the SemanticTalk TMV should be merged with a hand-crafted Topic Map about motor sports. This edited Topic Map might have a Topic which documents observations about Giancarlo Fisichella, the formula one driver. This Topic uses the Published Subject Identifier (PSI) "http://www.formula1-fansite.org/Fisichella" for Subject Indication. In the example the integration perspective is defined as follows: whenever information about the person Giancarlo Fisichella is observed the Subject 'Fisichella' is caught.

From this perspective, Subject Identity holds between the observations documented in the 'Fisichella' Topics of both Topic Maps. This decision should be documented in an Integration Topic Map. The creation of this Integration Topic Map should be governed by the Observation Principle, too.

According to the Observation Principle, an Integration Subject Proxy has to document the decided Subject Identity with the means of Subject Indication provided by the governing SMD. From the current integration perspective, the same Subject is caught, if SemanticTalk observes a noticeable usage of the term 'Fisichella', and if the author of the hand-crafted Topic Map indicates a Subject by the PSI for Giancarlo Fisichella. An appropriate Integration Topic Maps looks as follows:

```
[id @"http://www.formula1-fansite.org/Fisichella"

    @"http://www.texttech.de/dtd/st/pap#node_Fisichella"]
```

The merging of all three Topic Maps (the SemanticTalk TMV, the hand-crafted Topic Map and the Integration Topic Map) governed by the TMDM integrates all relevant information automatically. The advantage of the Integration Topic Map is obvious: in the case the integration perspective changes, the Integration Topic Map can be switched off or changed accordingly to the alterations in the integration perspective. It is apparent that in this connection the concept of Observation and Integration Subject Proxies introduced in 2.2 is applied on a higher semantic level.

For the integration of distributed sources the usage of the Topic Maps Remote Access Protocol (TMRAP) [8] or similar techniques discussed in [10] is recommended.

In most cases, the automatic generation of Integration Topic Maps is not straight-forward. In these cases the application of heuristic methods for the detection of Subject Identity respectively Subject Equality [11], [10] is recommended.

5 Related Research

There exists a substantial body of work on text classification and topic or metadata extraction from multimedia data (information extraction). All of these approaches define their own perspective in respect of the Observation Principle.

Research on sophisticated real-time indexing of speech streams in group meetings as one possible application has so far been very limited. Jebara et al. [9] describe a system that classifies the current focus of the conversation according to a limited number (12) of pre-defined topics. The classifier is trained by initially providing training sets of documents associated with each topic. Real-time analysis of spoken conversation is also reported in DiMicco & Bender [4]. Their focus is on facilitating equal participation in group discussions by visualizing the contributions of each participant. Terms and sentence fragments are associated with a fixed number of categories by a classification component also based on machine learning. None of the above approaches, however, builds up a concept structure by relating the terms spoken. Also, no extraction of semantically related terms is reported.

To our best knowledge there exists no approach that focuses on Topic Maps, fostering the integration of background knowledge to the current conversation. To our best knowledge, there exists no deeper theory related to the creation of Topic Maps, similar to the Observation Principle proposed by this paper. The Observation Principle exclusively focuses on the semantic characteristic of Topic Maps Technologies: viewing Subject Proxies indicating identical Subjects as merged ones.

The work presented in this paper is the advancement of our previous research described in [3].

6 Conclusion and Outlook

We discussed how Topic Maps can be generated from speech streams in real-time by using SemanticTalk. Furthermore, we introduced the Observation Principle based on a deeper investigation of the Subject Equality Decision Chain.

This investigation showed that each automatic generation of Topic Maps is governed by a specific perspective for the observation of digital information collections. The resulting Topic Maps are only the documentations of the observations from these perspectives. It is important to outline, that the interpretation of these observations has to be done in the time of integration with other Topic Maps.

In future, large repositories of Observation Subject Proxies should be investigated by statistical means to detect emergent relationships and concepts inside.

We assume, that it is important to disclose for each Topic Map how the Observation Principle was exactly applied during its generation. This knowledge allows more accurate interpretation in the time the generated Topic Map is used for integration purposes. We foresee theses disclosures as an important feature for the further success of Topic Maps in information integration scenarios. The disclosure of the Topic Map Engineering Process (TMEP) as sketched in [16] is the consequential development in respect to these insights. We assume that further corresponding research will be the advent of the emergence of the scientific discipline *Topic Maps Engineering*.

References

[1] Biemann, C.; Böhm, K.; Heyer, G.; Melz, R.: Automatically Building Concept Structures and Displaying Concept Trails for the Use in Brainstorming Sessions and Content Management Systems, In: Proceedings of I2CS'04, Guadalajara, Mexico; Springer LNCS, (2004).

[2] Biezunski, M.: A Matter of Perspectives: Talking About Talking About Topic Maps. In: Proceedings of Extreme Markup Languages 2005, Montreal; (2005).

[3] Böhm, K.; Maicher, L.; Witschel, H.-F.; Carradori, A.: Moving Topic Maps to Mainstream – Integration of Topic Map Generation in the User's Working Environment. In: Proceedings of I-KNOW '04, Graz; pp. 241-251, (2004).

[4] DiMicco, J. M.; Bender, W.: Second Messenger: In-creasing the Visibility of Minority Viewpoints with a Face-to-face Collaboration Tool. In: Procceedings of Conference on Intelligent User Interfaces, Funchal, Portugal; ACM Press, (2004).

[5] Durusau, P.; Newcomb, S. R. (eds.): Topic Maps - Reference Model version 6.0. Available at: http://www.isotopicmaps.org/tmrm/TMRM_6.0.pdf

[6] Faulstich, L.; Quasthoff, U.; Schmidt, F.; Wolff, C.: Concept Extractor – Ein flexibler und domänen-spezifischer Web Service zur Beschlagwortung von Texten. In: Hammwöhner, R; Wolff, C.; Womser-Hacker, C. (eds.): Proceedings of ISI 2002. Schriften zur Informationswissenschaft 40; Hochschulverband für Informationswissenschaft 2002, Regensburg, (2002).

[7] Garshol, L. M.: Q: A model for topic maps: Unifying RDF and topic maps. In: Proceedings of Extreme Markup Languages 2005, Montreal; (2005).

[8] Garshol, L. M.: TMRAP – Topic Maps Remote Access Protocol. In: Proceedings of First International Workshop on Topic Maps Research and Applications (TMRA'05) Leipzig; Springer LNCS, (2006).

[9] Jebara, T.; Ivanov, Y; Rahimi, A.; Pentland, A.: Tracking conversational context for machine mediation of human discourse. In: AAAI Fall 2000 Symposium - Socially Intelligent Agents, Massachusetts; AAAI Press, (2004).

[10] Maicher, L.: Topic Maps and the Absence of Shared Vocabularies. In: Proceedings of First International Workshop on Topic Maps Research and Applications (TMRA'05) Leipzig; Springer LNCS, (2006).

[11] Maicher, L.; Witschel, H. F.: Merging of Distributed Topic Maps based on the Subject Identity Measure (SIM). In: Proceedings of LIT'04; pp. 229-238, (2004).

[12] Pepper, S.; Vitali, F.; Garshol, L. M.; Gessa, N.; Presutti, V.: A Survey of RDF/Topic Maps Interoperability Proposal. W3C Consortium Working Draft. Available at: http://www.w3.org/TR/2005/WD-rdftm-survey-20050329/

[13] Quine, W. v. O.: Identity, Ostension, and Hypostasis. In: Journal of Philosophy, 47(22), pp.621-633, (1950).

[14] Russell, S.: Identity Uncertainty. In: Proceedings of IFSA-01, Vancouver; (2001).

[15] ISO/IEC: Topic Maps – Part 2: Data Model. Latest version available at: http://www.isotopicmaps.org/sam

[16] Sigel, A.: Report on the open space sessions. In: Proceedings of First International Workshop on Topic Maps Research and Applications (TMRA'05) Leipzig; Springer LNCS, (2006).

[17] Vatant, B.: Tools for semantic interoperability: hubjects. Working report available at: http://www.mondeca.com/lab/bernard/hubjects.pdf

[18] Witschel, H. F.: Terminologie-Extraktion: Möglichkeiten der Kombination statistischer und musterbasierter Verfahren. Ergon, Würzburg, (2004).

A Case for *Polyscopic* Structuring of Information

Rolf Guescini[1], Dino Karabeg[2], and Tommy Nordeng[3]

[1] The Department of Linguistics and Scandinavian Studies, University of Oslo
rolfbg@grace.uio.no
[2] The Department of Informatics, University of Oslo
dino@ifi.uio.no
[3] Cerpus AS, 8342 Alsvg, Norway
tommy@cerpus.com

Abstract. We outline the main elements of what we call *polyscopic* structuring of information and argue that information needs to be structured accordingly. The principles of *polyscopy* may both serve as guidelines for creating Topic Maps, and provide orientation for further development of Topic Maps standards and software.

1 Introduction

Information overload is a clear sign that the development of information technology alone will not make us better informed [1]. At the same time, the characteristic problems of today, such as declining health and non-sustainability, impose urgent new demands on the nature and quality of our informing [2]. Paradoxically, while we call our era 'The Age of Information,' our information may well be our stumbling block.

The Topic Maps community is, of course, aware of this problem, better structuring and use of information being its very reason for existence. In this article we argue that in order to be truly effective, the creation and use of Topic Maps, as well of information in general, needs to be oriented according to a collection of principles which we associate with the word *polyscopy*.

Our argument is organized as follows. In the second section, which follows this introduction, we point at a close analogy between the information overload and the crisis in software industry a half-century ago, to which the solution was found in developing the software engineering methodologies, Structured Programming, Object Orientation and others. In the third, we introduce *polyscopy* as an instance of an analogous, methodological approach to creation and use of information, which allows us to instantiate a similar approach to solution. In the fourth, we argue that the change to *polyscopy* is needed if our information should become suitable for its key new role of orientation provider. In the fifth, we show that *polyscopy* in practice leads to a different and, we claim, better way of accessing information, and we illustrate this claim by describing an application where *polyscopically* structured Topic Maps play a key role. In the sixth,

L. Maicher and J. Park (Eds.): TMRA 2005, LNAI 3873, pp. 125–138, 2006.

we show how *polyscopy* may be implemented within the current Topic Maps standard and we give some ideas for future development.

Related ideas have been proposed by other researchers (see, for example, [3]). The main novelty in our approach is that we first assess what information should be like in order to best serve its purpose, and then develop a methodology which supports such information. We call this approach *information design*[4], [5].

Polyscopy also allows for *designing* concepts, and thereby giving them a meaning which is more precise and perhaps subtly different from their *traditional* meaning. In this text the *designed* concepts are written in italics.

2   Software Engineering and Information Structuring – A Noteworthy Parallel

A parallel with early history of computer programming suggests the approach to handling the information overload which is proposed in this article.

Early software development projects resulted in thousands of lines of 'spaghetti code,' called so because of their chaotic, spaghetti-like structure, which led the industry into a state of crisis. The solution was found in creating programming methodologies, which provided guidelines for structuring programs [6].

Certain basic principles were shared by all methodologies. Since understanding anything large cannot be done in one piece, abstraction and structuring must be used. The programs need to be structured in terms of small, manageable modules. Underlying this subdivision is the key idea, which provided the basis for abstraction, that programming can be done on different 'levels.' The 'high-level modules' should be constructed and understood in terms of 'high-level concepts,' which are more general and less technical than the 'low-level concepts' which are used in 'low-level modules.' This allows anyone to get an initial understanding of the whole program by reading only the highest-level module which, conveniently, is written in a language which everyone can understand. Similarly, more detailed sub-tasks can be understood by focusing on the particular module where they are handled.

The internal structure of the high-level module should reflect the over-all structure of the program. In that way the high-level module naturally serves as a sort of a structured index for finding more detailed information.

The programming methodologies differ from each other regarding the way in which the modules are supposed to be constructed and put together. Each manner of modular organization reflects a specific way of thinking about programming, which characterizes the methodology and serves as the foundation for its methods. Based on the methodologies, high-level programming languages have been developed which support corresponding modular program organization. The generic GOTO program control instruction, which led to spaghetti code by allowing for arbitrary jumps from one context to another, has been replaced with structured control statements such as IF-THEN-ELSE.

The similarity between the information overload and the 1950s crisis in software industry is quite striking. Now as well as then, a new technology emerged which allowed us to overproduce, in both volume and complexity. Now as well as then, the routines which were developed for smaller volumes no longer worked for larger ones. Indeed, it is not difficult to see, from the point of view of our parallel, that the hyper-links are similar to the GOTOs, in the sense that they allow for arbitrary jumps from one context to another. The consequence is that the Internet information tends to be structured in a spaghetti-like manner, similar to early computer programs.

In one respect, however, computer programming and information making are different: When a team of programmers can no longer understand the program they are making, the problem is very easy to detect – the program won't run on the computer. Different programming strategies can then be tried until the one that works best is found. When, however, a generation of people can no longer understand the information they have inherited or created, the problem is a lot more difficult to detect, and a lot less comfortable to experiment with.

Fortunately, in handling the information overload we do not need to depend on experimentation. We can learn from history. Our two situations being similar, we can adapt and apply to information the ideas and techniques which have proven to be instrumental for managing the complexity of computer programming.

The first and most important idea is to base information structuring on a methodology.

3   *Polyscopic* Structuring of Information

Polyscopic Modeling has been proposed as a prototype *information design methodology* [4]. In Polyscopic Modeling terminology the *scope* is the point of view, determined in practice by the choice of the subject, terms of the language, epistemological assumptions, methods for establishing facts, representation techniques etc. The *polyscopic* structuring of information, which is one of the main propositions of this methodology, is based on the insight that the *scope* determines the *view* (our way of looking and communicating determines what we are able to see and express). As the practice which follows from the Polyscopic Modeling Methodology, *polyscopy* employs conscious creation of multiple *scopes* and *views*.

The metaphor of the mountain is used as practical guideline for the practice of *polyscopy*. The triangle is used as ideogram to represent it. Every point on the mountain, and on the triangle, represents a viewpoint or *scope*.

Although while taking a walk on the mountain we can see an infinite variety of landscapes and details of natural life, we are not plagued by the information overload. The reason is obvious: The physiology of our vision is such that we always focus on a single, limited *scope* at a time. We can either see an ant, or a tree, or a forest, but never all of them at once. One of the key ideas in *polyscopy* is to preserve this essential property of our vision also in creation and structuring of information.

We say that a *scope* (and the corresponding *view* or piece of information) is *coherent* if it corresponds to a single way of looking, or metaphorically, to a single viewpoint on the mountain. What we see with our eyes is always *coherent*.

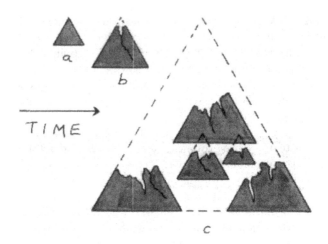

Fig. 1. The Information Fragmenting Ideogram

In *polyscopy* the information is organized into modules in such a way that every module represents a single *coherent view.*

The *scope* just created allows us to understand why we *do* have an overload of man-made information. The Information Fragmenting Ideogram (Fig. 1) suggests that our information is evolving as a collection of 'islands' corresponding to various *informing traditions* (such as molecular biology, sports journalism and Buddhism). Each 'island' is characterized by its own *scope* or collection of *scopes.* If one happens to be living or working on one such 'island,' it is difficult to know what sorts of information exist in other 'islands.' Furthermore, each of the 'islands' is lacking the *high-level* part which would give us an overview of the information it contains, and help us comprehend it. The information overload, suggests this ideogram, is not the result of having too much information, but of having too little *high-level* information which would connect those fragmented pieces together and allow us to make sense of them.

The *polyscopic* information, which is the goal of *polyscopy*, is represented by the Polyscopic Information Ideogram (Fig. 2). The 'i' in the ideogram stands for 'information'. This 'i' is composed as a circle on top of a square. It is suggested that *polyscopic* information consists of two distinct parts: The *high-level* part, represented by the circle, and the *low-level* part, represented by the square.

We have seen that abstraction and modular organization have been the key to managing the complexity of computer programming. Polyscopic Modeling provides three kinds of abstraction for organizing information into modules: *vertical, horizontal* and *structural.*

The *vertical* abstraction, which is symbolized by the circle, can easily be understood as, metaphorically, climbing up the mountain in order to see the simple 'big picture.' As suggested by the circle, the *vertical* abstraction involves rounding off the details and presenting the main point.

The *horizontal* abstraction, which is symbolized by the square, can easily be understood as, metaphorically, looking from a side or as projecting the object

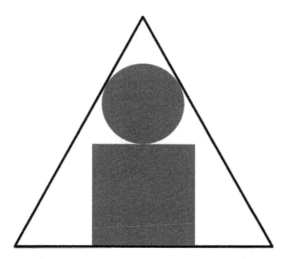

Fig. 2. The Polyscopic Information Ideogram

onto a plane. One again sees a simple picture, but the simplicity is now the result of 'projecting' rather than of 'rounding off.' As suggested by the square, the art of *horizontal* abstraction involves finding a suitable collection of *aspects* (or 'angles of looking') which, like projection planes in technical drawing, give simple and relatively independent (or 'orthogonal') views of the subject, and together give a complete representation of the whole.

The *structural* abstraction, which is symbolized by the triangle, focuses on the relationships which exist among the created *views*. While the *vertical* and the *horizontal* abstraction allow us to create the information modules, the *structural abstraction* allows us to put those modules together.

By inscribing the 'i' in the triangle, it is suggested that the *polyscopic* information is organized based on a structure of *scopes* which the triangle represents. It must be emphasized that the division of information into *levels* does not imply that the modules must be structured as a hierarchy. Indeed, the main point behind the *structural abstraction* is that the structure is an essential property of information, which should neither be removed nor imposed.

Closely related to *structural* abstraction is *polyscopic* navigation. In this context, the principle that the *scope* determines the *view* demands that the user of information be given the capability to choose one out of a number of provided *views* or modules by selecting the corresponding *scope*. As when walking on a mountain one is always aware whether one is looking at a scene from above or from below or from a distance or from close, in *polyscopic* information presentation we support this awareness also in the virtual world. This means that we need to organize the navigation in such a way that the reader has a clear intuitive idea of the *scope*, as if she were walking on the mountain. Visual and other presentation techniques such as animation here have an important role.

The Polyscopic Modeling Methodology provides four criteria to orient the creation and use of information [7]. The one that is most interesting for

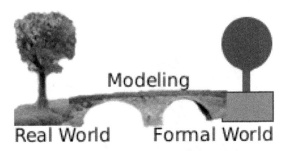

Fig. 3. The *high-level* view of Algorithm Theory course

information structuring is the Perspective Criterion, which postulates that information needs to provide a clear and correct *perspective* (idea of the subject as a whole). Factual truth, which is presently our dominant criterion, directs us to focus on facts and to search for them there where we can find them with largest possible accuracy. This in practice leads to fragmented and *low-level* information. The *perspective* as criterion directs us to seek the information that we are lacking in order to understand the whole, and to present that information in a way which makes the character of the whole and the relevance and the roles of the details clear. In other words, the Perspective Criterion supports the creation and use of *polyscopic* information.

The Polyscopic Modeling Methodology also provides methods for creating *polyscopic* and in particular *high-level* information, as well as prototype examples of such information [5].

For illustration, we now show how an existing body of information, the Algorithm Theory course at the University of Oslo, has been made *polyscopic*. Since this example points at a whole range of problems and possible solutions, in education and elsewhere, we explain it in some detail.

Here is how the algorithm theory has been introduced to the students of the redesigned Algorithm Theory course. What interests us when we study algorithms (and computer science in general) is 'How to solve problems efficiently by using a computer.' But in order to be able to say anything about this question in a precise or academic way, we must first give precise meanings to the real-world notions 'problem' and 'solution,' and define under what conditions a solution may be considered efficient. To that end we create another, 'formal' framework or domain, where only defined or formal concepts exist so that questions can be answered in a rigorous and precise way, and we translate our problem into the language of that domain. Or to use a metaphor (Fig. 3), we take our real-life questions over the modeling bridge into the formal world, we answer them there and we bring the answers back to the real world, where we interpret them and apply the acquired insights in practice.

Contrary to its potential to serve as framework for understanding the main questions about computation in a systematic or academic way, algorithm theory is often considered as an obscure academic pursuit, as 'theory for the sake of theory.' One of the reasons for this misunderstanding is the 'monoscopic' character

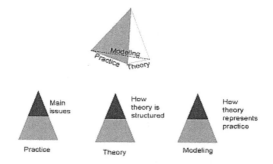

Fig. 4. The structure of Algorithm Theory course

of our information: If one needs to choose a single *scope* to represent algorithm theory, what could be a more natural choice than the algorithm theory itself? The result is that a typical algorithm theory textbook begins with a definition and ends with a theorem. For most computer science students and practitioners, the meaning and purpose of the theorems about 'formal languages' and 'Turing machines' remains rather obscure.

Introducing *polyscopy*, we distinguish three main *aspects* and two main *levels* of algorithm theory (Fig. 4). The 'practice' *aspect* and the 'theory' *aspect* correspond to the two shores of our metaphorical river. The 'modeling' *aspect* corresponds to the bridge.

Standing on the mountain top on the real world side of our bridge, we see only the main practical issues, such as whether there are problems which cannot be solved by algorithms. In the *high-level view* of the modeling *aspect* we examine why the 'formal language' and the 'Turing machine' represent respectively the real-world notions of 'problem' and 'solution.' In the *high-level view* of the theory *aspect* we learn to recognize the main building blocks of the theory.

The students are encouraged to avoid memorizing the theorems and proof techniques and to use the 'mountain-top views' to distinguish and understand the main issues. The *high-level views* provide the motivation for studying the theory, and the context for understanding the details.

After this *polyscopic* re-organization, the course ended up being quite different from what it was before. Notice that this difference reflects not only the way the information is organized and presented, but also the underlying 'philosophy' or approach. In the *traditional* scheme of things, the goal of an algorithm theory course is to teach algorithm theory. In the *designed* course, our goal is to teach what the students most need to know, in a most accessible way.

4   Information as We Need It

As already mentioned, *polyscopy* is founded upon an approach to information creation and use which we are calling *information design*. We now motivate this approach by looking 'from a mountain top' at the way our information presentation developed historically.

The oral tradition, which was the early form of communication, is inherently sequential. Although paper, being two- dimensional, could have been used for implementing a variety of information structures, it was used mainly for making the traditional way of communicating more efficient. In effect, the two- dimensional paper was turned into a one-dimensional sequence of characters and lines, for recording the traditional narratives. Since the printing press also only automated what the traditional scribes were doing, we should then not be surprised if the Internet too has mainly been used for displaying and sharing traditional documents.

The information overload reminds us that such *traditional* way of developing and using information technology (where we simply reproduce in the new technology the sorts of information we have inherited from our ancestors) cannot continue forever. Our *traditional* way of using technology also prevents us from taking real advantage of technology.

Information design is, by definition, an approach to information which is alternative to the *traditional* one. In *information design* the way we create and use information is not automatically inherited but *designed*, aiming to best respond to the needs of contemporary people and society. Information is designed according to state-of-the-art epistemological and methodological insights and by taking advantage of available technology.

Information design is also an initiative to put the *information design* approach to information into practice, which has originated at the University of Oslo.

We can now approach our issue of information structuring from the point of view of *information design* by asking 'What key purposes should information perform in our individual and social lives?' and 'What should information be like in order to best serve those purposes?'

We find that information in our post-traditional, rapidly changing culture needs to fulfill a new role - to allow us to make choices consciously (with awareness of their consequences)[8]. Sustainability is one of the contemporary issues which makes this new role of information vitally important [9]. *Polyscopy* is proposed as a way of creating and using information which suits this new role [10]. By seeing 'from a mountain top' we can comprehend the issues and choose suitable ways of handling them [5]. By consciously seeking to see multiple *aspects*, we can avoid focusing on only one (for example economy) and neglecting others (for example ecology).

5   *Polyscopy* as Orientation for Topic Map Engineering

Every good organization involves an artful combination of freedom and discipline, without which freedom all too easily dissipates into anarchy and chaos. The resolution of the software engineering crisis too involved a change from completely free to a directed structuring of programs. The Object Oriented Methodology, for example, *prescribed* how programs should be organized into modules. The IF-THEN-ELSE statement *restricted* the sequencing control in the interest of clarity. Underlying such prescriptions is an intuitive conception of programming as it should be in order to lead to well-structured programs. In object orientation, programming is conceived of as modeling the real world in terms of objects and the functions they perform for other objects.

Similarly, *polyscopy* is, above all, a conception of a good way of creating and using information, which is founded upon *information design* as approach, as we have just seen. The *information design* as foundation allows us to determine which of the available ways may be considered as 'good.'

From this vantage point we may distinguish three modes of structuring information:

- Linear. This organization is typical for traditional university courses and textbooks. The interaction mode it supports is passive, sequential assimilation by listening or reading.
- Semantic. This organization is characteristic for Topic Maps as they are today. The interaction mode it supports is browsing, guided by free association.
- Polyscopic and semantic. This organization is the substance of our proposal. The interaction mode it supports is to use the *high-level* information as one would use the view from a mountain top, to acquire a quick understanding of the subject as a whole and its main elements, and to direct further inquiry based on this view, aiming at a correct and clear *perspective*.

While the latter two modes share the advantage of providing the information the user wants, thus also engaging her interest and receptiveness, the third mode has the additional advantage that it supports the holistic understanding of phenomena and issues, which, as we have seen, is our prime socio-cultural need. At the same time, by providing the 'mountain top view,' and organizing the details into *aspects* and modules, the *polyscopic* organization allows us to control the overload.

We illustrate the above ideas by describing a real-life example.

'Flexplearn' is the name of a flexible and exploratory university course model developed by the authors, where *polyscopically* structured Topic Maps play a key role [11]. This model has been implemented and used within the University of Oslo Information Design course.

In the Information Design course the students learn in part by co-designing the Information Design course and the course materials.

If the student should venture into a new field and be allowed to learn by exploring actively and freely, what could be more natural than to provide the guidance in terms of a (topic) map? This is exactly how the things are done within Flexplearn. The Topic Maps are used both for organizing the learning resources, as container for student's results, and for recording the student's 'itinerary' through the information design topics for the purpose of the exam (Fig. 5).

The use of *polyscopic* Topic Maps in Flexplearn supports the corresponding style of learning and understanding. At the beginning of the course the student stands 'on top of a mountain' looking at *information design* as a whole, and seeing the main areas of knowledge it consists of. In order to be able to depart from the habits of the tradition and *design* information, one needs to know about

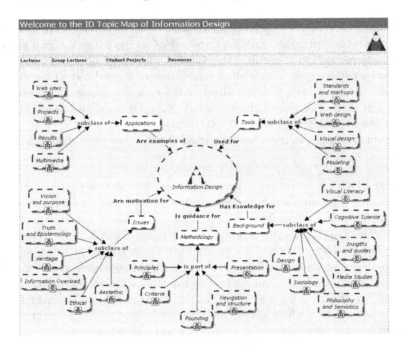

Fig. 5. The Flexplearn taxonomy

the issues which motivate such departure, acquire certain epistemological and other background insights from several traditional disciplines, and be familiar with the technological tools for handling information. From this standpoint, the student can access the information as needed, aiming to gain a functional over-all understanding of *information design.*

The *polyscopic* organization of information also allows us to take care of the prerequisites, which in a traditional course are automatically handled by the fixed order of presentation. By beginning 'from a mountain top' the students naturally acquire an understanding of basic ideas and principles which then serve as background and motivation for more detailed knowledge. While many different learning paths may be taken, each path begins 'from the mountain top' and descends gradually downwards. A simple, hierarchically structured taxonomy (Fig. 5) serves as 'meridians and parallels,' for placing the learning resources and other topics.

6   Implementing *Polyscopic* Topic Maps

As we have seen, many of the constructs described within the polyscopic methodology map readily to Topic Map constructs. To begin with, 'scoping,' one of the strong Topic Maps features, allows us to implement *scopes* in a natural way.

Implementing the *vertical* abstraction should be fairly trivial by using Topic Map constructs. The modules themselves would necessarily have to be implemented by creating topics for each module, while the vertical structure showing the relations between the modules would call for the creation of association types showing the nature of the structural metaphor used. Examples would be "high-level-view" and "low-level-view", "more-detailed" and "less-detailed", "'part-whole' etc. The existence of the "superclass-subclass" concept, specified in XTM 1.0 for the definition of class hierarchies, shows how associations can be used to express hierarchies and other structures which distinguish levels using Topic Maps.

Example

```
/* TOPIC TYPES */
  [high-level-module = "High Level View"]
  [low-level-module = "Low Level View"]
  [high-level = "High Level"]
  [low-level = "Low Level"]

/* ASSOCIATION TYPES */
  [high-low-level
         = "High Level view" /high-level
         = "Low level view" /low-level]
[topic1:high-level-module = "topic1"]
[topic2:low-level-module = "topic2"]

high-low-level(topic1:high-level, topic2:low-level)
```

The *horizontal* abstraction may be implemented by using the inherent scoping abilities of Topic Maps. Here we have, however, several possibilities. Whether to scope the associations or the occurrences depends on the situation and the kind of presentation or document one is designing. If one wants to say anything specific about the scoped entities themselves, such as relating them to other modules, one would have to create topics reifying them, one for each *aspect*, and relate them to the *high-level* topic directly by association, and then scoping the associations used for creating the vertical relations.

On the other hand, if the presentation is content-centered and does not rely on attaching specific associations to the aspects of the subject, it is preferable to put the scope on the occurrences. One would have to create topics for the modules representing the various levels of information within the presentation, and then scope the different occurrences holding the content itself, or the references to content for a given module.

Scoping Occurrences

```
/* TOPIC TYPES */
  [high-level-module = "High Level View"]
  [low-level-module = "Low Level View"]
```

```
/* ASSOCIATION TYPES */
 [high-low-level
        = "High Level view" /high-level
        = "Low level view" /low-level]


/* ASPECTS * /
 [aspect1 : aspect = "Aspect 1"]
 [aspect2 : aspect ="Aspect 2"]
 [aspect3 : aspect = "Aspect 3"]

/* Instance and scoping example*/
[topic = "The subject in question" @"uri.to.psi"]
[topic-h : high-level = "High level view of topic"]
{topic-h, content, [[Content...]]}

[topic-l : topic
    = "Low level module of topic to represent the low level"]
{topic-l, content, [[Content...]]}/aspect1
{topic-l, content, [[Content...]]}/aspect2
{topic-l, content, [[Content...]]}/aspect3

[topic-12 : topic = "Low level module relative to topic-l"]
{topic-12, content, [[Content...]]}/aspect1
{topic-12, content, [[Content...]]}/aspect2
{topic-12, content, [[Content...]]}/aspect3

high-low-level(topic-h : high-level, topic-l : low-level)
high-low-level(topic-l : high-level, topic-12 : low-level)
```

The question remains, however, whether the available Topic Map implementation tools can secure that Topic Map designers, and no less importantly the broader public, will be able to use the Topic Map model to create holistic information as this article envisions it? It may well be the case that in order to develop this possibility to its full potential, high-level constructs will need to be created on top of the existing Topic Map model.

A field study of educational Topic Maps authoring using the TM4L Editor showed that authors generally don't have problems selecting appropriate learning content and resources for their Topic Maps. The difficulties lie, however, in structuring the content by using Topic Map constructs. Topic Map authors are often untrained in information classification and lack controlled vocabularies and support from ontology analysts [12].

Could it be that the creation of some kind of 'Topic Map design pattern' for *polyscopically* designed Topic Maps might help the information designer in her work? By formalizing design insights as a pattern, designers and programmers would be able to talk to each other about them, compare different patterns for a given solution, and develop a reusable 'tool-box.' [13]. Then tools or even software like TM4L could be built around these patterns, making it easier for the practicing designer to concentrate on creating the *high-level* information that is needed. This would also make it easier for authors to create Topic Map content.

7 Conclusion

In the spirit of *polyscopy*, we condense our discussion to a simple and intuitive *high-level view*, by saying that "**We can come out of the information jungle by climbing to a top of a mountain.**" Like the view from a top of a mountain, *polyscopic* information can give us simplicity and clarity, highlight what is large and important, orient our information search and help us not get lost in the information jungle.

We have also advanced a more general proposal, to base the information structuring on a methodology. *Polyscopy*, or Polyscopic Modeling, is an example or a prototype of this approach. The methodological approach may lead Topic Maps engineering through similar developmental stages as the ones we have witnessed in computer programming (the formulation of methodologies, the development of high-level structuring constructs and standards, development of information design environments akin to programming environments and others). Visual and other media, programming, animation, sound and a variety of presentation tools and techniques will naturally be used to give information multiple 'dimensions' and in that way also suitable structure. Dynamically created structures, based on user profile and needs, will be supported. It may be expected that not only the remedy to information overload, but also a far more positive social and cultural role of information will be the result of this development.

References

1. Postman, Neil: Informing Ourselves to Death. Keynote speech at German Informatics Society conference, Stuttgart, October 11, 1990. http://www.mat.upm.es/ jcm/ postman-informing.html
2. Meadows, Dennis, L. et al.:Limits to Growth. Universe Books, New York, 1972.
3. Bush, Vannevar: As We May Think. In: Atlantic Monthly (1945).
4. Karabeg, Dino: Designing Information Design. Information Design Journal 11 (2003/03) 82-90.
5. Karabeg, Dino: Information Design. Book manuscript.
6. O. Dahl, E. Dijkstra, C. Hoare: Structured Programming. Academic Press, (1972).
7. Karabeg, Dino: *Polyscopic* Modeling Definition. In Griffin at al (Ed.): The Turning of the Tide. Selected Readings of the IVLA, (2004).
8. Peccei, Aurelio: The Human Quality. Pergamon Press (1977).
9. Laszlo, Erwin: The Choice: Evolution or Extinction? A Thinking Person's Guide to Global Issues. Putnam (1994).
10. Karabeg, Dino: Information For Conscious Choice. Information Design Journal 11 (2003/03).

11. Karabeg, Dino, Guescini,Rolf, Nordeng, Tommy: Flexible and Exploratory Learning by Polyscopic Topic Maps. 5th IEEE International Conference on Advanced Learning Technologies, ICALT 2005, July 5-8, 2005, Kaohsiung, Taiwan, 946-948. http://www.win.tue.nl/SW-EL/2005/swel05-icalt05/final/W3-2.pdf
12. Dicheva, Darina, Dichev, Christo: Authoring Educational Topic Maps- Can we make it easier?. Proc. IEEE ICALT (2005) 5th IEEE International Conference on Advanced Learning Technologies, ICALT 2005, July 5-8, (2005), Kaohsiung, Taiwan, 216-219.
13. Ahmed, Kal: Beyond PSIs, Topic Map Design Patterns. Extreme Markup Languages, Montreal, Quebec, August 4-8, (2003).

Subject Centric IT in Local Government

Gabriel Hopmans, Peter-Paul Kruijsen, and Roger Dols

Morpheus Software, P.O. Box 240, 6200 AE Maastricht, The Netherlands
{G.Hopmans, P.Kruijsen, R.Dols}@mssm.nl
http://www.mssm.nl

Abstract. This paper illustrates the Topic Maps approach taken in a project for a Dutch Document Management Specialist supporting local Government municipalities. The solution described in the paper is about Access Control Lists in a Topic Map and exploits the advantages of subject based approaches in combination with a Topic Map Ontology. This subject centric IT solution builds on an existing generic model and makes it possible to build Topic Maps portals that become more maintenance free.

1 Introduction

This paper explains ongoing work in a project running for BCT – The Document Store (BCT–TDS[1]), a Dutch Document Management Specialist. This project with the name ON-TOP is about subject centric organization of information that integrates with existing infrastructure and software for municipalities in Dutch Government. With the help of Topic Maps the existing BCT–TDS infrastructure is extended to a portal by which multiple user groups can facilitate their own information. Huge amounts of data and information from several municipalities and a generic model are available and a Topic Maps approach will be used on top of BCT-TDS' Document Management System to integrate quickly and to build a facility function. This Dynamic Information Facility (DIF) offers large, distributed organizations, operating in complex value chains, such as Governmental organizations, an easy way to improve their document management-, information sharing-, and publishing processes.

First we will describe why governmental organizations need to improve their collaboration. Then the next two subsections will show that with an existing generic model for Local Government domain published subjects can help in the integration phases. Subsection 1.4 illustrates our solution to work more subject based and how we can develop topic map portals that become almost maintenance free by using the topic maps ontology and an Access Control List. The last paragraph gives more detail in our future ongoing work.

2 Improving Collaboration Between Governmental Organizations

Dutch governmental organizations need to increase their collaboration, within and between their respective domains. Between all the management systems and the

---

[1] http://www.bct.nl

L. Maicher and J. Park (Eds.): TMRA 2005, LNAI 3873, pp. 139–144, 2006.

webportals of these organisations a lot of information needs to be exchanged and more and more this becomes XML based. BCT-TDS has a lot of information silo's of multiple organisations within their system and they require flexible binding points to fully integrate the organisation value chains. The desire of governmental organizations to 'connect everything' is reinforced by a policy of "demand steering", with varying success so far. An influx of (partly web oriented) new technologies has brought a multitude of communication channels within reach of individual organizations. Using Topic Maps services can be further improved by making organizational borders transparent and providing coherent views on information: it is going to be possible to see where one person is registered within the whole organisation and even if desired where there are dependencies between organisations for this person. From the organization's perspective it is equally important to guard critical dimensions of their services and public outings, such as timeliness, appropriateness and lawfulness through a comprehensive, Topic Maps based, flexible DIF to improve collaboration between organisations. One example is that information about one person become portable and maintained distributed instead of sending multiple items to central repositories.

Topic Maps technology builds on existing IT infrastructures and eases pressure on the strategic level because it avoids the technical and organisational challenges which occur when these infrastructures are integrated. Topic Maps will be a long term guarantee ensuring portability and longevity. Using a bottom up approach with Published Subjects[2] allows for the legitimate continued grip within the responsibilities of organizations while empowering users (e.g. citizens, customers) to construct their own relevant information environment.

3   ON-TOP: Integrating Governmental Organization Processes

Nowadays in the Netherlands, organizations like municipalities need to connect with other organizations. The Government obliges them to enable standardized ways to exchange information. Also, the customers are demanding more and better services and they are becoming more web-aware.

Integration is time consuming, brings organizational stress and is difficult and there is an urgent need for real practical, distributed knowledge management! BCT - TDS initiated ON-TOP with a Topic Maps solution targeting Document Management. Municipalities can not get one global overview on all their different applications and information sources and they have a lack of standardization.

To solve the problem of lack of a global overview, the gaps in their information supply chain have to be closed, while leaving their existing infrastructures intact.

Topic Maps will bring quick wins in the integration phase. The task to deliver one solution to collaborating organizations is still often a repeating process of mapping all internal and external objects and diving into each business process of the organization. Topic Maps provide a solution to all this: standardize all subjects on a meta level, leaving the critical needs of the individual organization in tact.

[2] http://www.ontopia.net/tmp/pubsubj-gentle-intro.htm#s.2

4 Subject Centric Organization with Published Subjects

Within the Local Government domain a generic model[3] has been developed in a program initiated by the Dutch Ministry of Interior Relations fitting to the phase of organizational maturity of a customer organization. In ON-TOP this generic model and
underlying information resources of municipalities are used to develop the Topic
Maps. In a parallel activity the authors defined table-definitions, developed an
ontology and made mappings with all the fields from the table definitions. For the
mapping process itself a new meta-ontology has been developed to facilitate this
process. In all these activities Published Subjects played an important role. With this
extension it is now possible to repeat the whole process again for all the municipalities that are supported by BCT–TDS. When the Topic Maps are generated they are all
merged. Different user groups in the municipality domain are now able to navigate
and search all the objects and subjects in a targeted way.

Within the ON-TOP project the Ontopia Knowledge Suite (OKS) is used, to create
and maintain the TM&PS. In the first phase already duplicates, errors, forms of "hid-
den" information and knowledge were detected and unlocked through the OKS, thus
contributing to improved quality of the information production process.

A next step is to build custom-made applications based on the Topic Map. ON-
TOP focuses on multiple user groups, initially on 3 groups: management/municipal
managers, municipal employees and the customer/web-site-visitors. These groups will
be supported in a first version of the web-application driven by the flexible Topic
Maps model. Subject-centric selections by the user drives the application without
'knowing in advance' which group will be navigating the application and even without having to know what the user wants to know.

In next steps the user groups will be refined. In related work, in the KORVIS project for the municipality of Stuttgart the user group is for municipal managers like

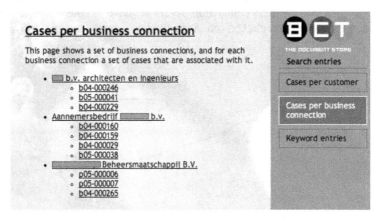

Fig. 1. The first version of the ON-TOP web-application running on the OKS. At the right hand
side three possible search entries. At the left hand side the topics of "cases per business connection" are shown.

---

[3] http://www.egem.nl/kennisbank/architectuurinformatie/integratie/gfozaken

mayors and council members [1]. The user groups have been defined and some first user requirements have been drawn up to find the first navigation paths and search entries for these groups. In the next step a web-application has been developed. Figure 1 shows the result of the first version of the web-application. Using this web-application the user only has to choose search entries to start his navigation paths. In figure 1 the user can browse the "business connections" present in the topic map and can see which "cases" are running for a particular business connection.

5   The Solution: From Application Centric to Subject Centric

Subject centric organization is the more advantageous in policy fields with changing laws and regulations. With TM&PS, collaboration can start immediately, because it builds on the existing data model. The application that has been developed is web enabled, will service different target groups from the same environment, and enable user groups to match their information needs without predefined models.

Currently the project is in a phase wherein more parts of the municipality domain are described in abstract layers which will be further modelled towards the different target groups (e.g. management, employees, "random" visitors, clients, interest groups, etc.). If we focus on the "Building and construction" sector, a visiting user searches for building locations, municipality employees only want to see which cases she/he has to complete tasks and which documents are related to this; while the municipal manager only wants to see bottle-necks within cases with date and time.

For the abstraction layers and the different target groups Access Control Lists have been drawn up. In a Topic Map in the LTM syntax has been described which topics are allowed to be visible for which user group and the navigation paths are defined (see figure 2). In this Topic Map we define which topics are the start and end points of a possible navigation path based on user requirements and which topics are visible for each possible user group. Figure 3 presents the situation where the user has clicked on a particular business connection. Again we have to note that what becomes visible after the user has clicked on a particular concept is just browsing the

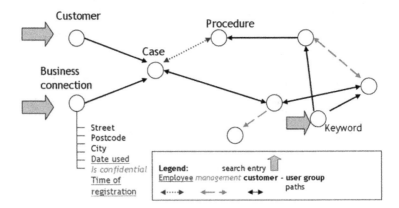

Fig. 2. Navigation paths for different user groups and ACL's for the topics

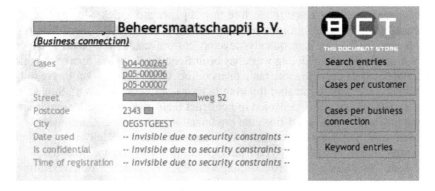

Fig. 3. A particular user group is browsing some concepts. The visiting/customer user is only allowed to see address details on case identifiers.

Topic Map. It is not pre-defined or programmed but just using the same functionality as we know from the Omnigator. Figure 3 shows the information that a "regular/random visiting user" of the website is allowed to see. The user is only allowed to see the address details like the City "Oegstgeest" and the cases for this business connection. Since this is just the first web-application we also see the names of the concepts that this user group is not allowed to see. In this case: "is confidential" is only visible for managers (this is defined in the topic map, see figure 2); and "time of registration" and "Date used" is only visible for the employees user group.

What this first version of the ON-TOP web-application in fact shows is that when the ontology development, modelling and topic maps generation has been finished one can build a Topic Map portal that is almost maintenance free. Management of the topic map ontology and the ACL will be the core. Several organisations can reach consensus upon mutual dependencies in a top-down fashion and one can easily and quickly construct web-applications fulfilling the user needs. The behaviour of the web-application is derived from the navigation paths which are part of the Topic Map. Accessibility to concepts and relations normally needs to be programmed but now they are part of the information layers instead of the application layer. Municipalities or third parties just have to define the search entries thus maintenance is improved.

6   Conclusion and Further Work

In next steps the authors need to define more search entries and how the DIF integrates with existing system functionalities. The facility enables organizations to collaborate working in related subject domains and publish information dynamically, while maintaining the policy objectives. We suspect to find more advantages whe data-sets are merged and we integrate our editor environment to manage taxonomies.

Our topic maps based solution is showing a combined bottom-up and a top down approach. More and more organizations are recognizing that they need to take this two-fold approach in parallel instead of sequentially (see for instance [3]). Topic Maps vendors are fulfilling this need by providing a TM&PS based solution that fits this two-fold approach (like in [4]) better then any other standard.

Advantages that have come to the fore in this paper are: quick wins by generating topic maps from existing information sources; With Topic Maps, the OKS and our solution with ACLs one can quickly develop custom made web-pages and portals when the ontology and modeling work has been finished. With this approach building Topic Maps portals become more maintenance free. Organizations don't have to build new infrastructures, they can start thinking in terms of integration; With Subject Centric Orientation users will be enabled to construct their own information environment (without any supply-side need from the organization). Over time it becomes possible that stable sets of PSI's will emerge as de facto standards especially if organizations or programs like ICTU, EGEM, VNG and OSOSS [5,6,7,8] become involved.

The result becomes even more advantageous when organisations merge results exchange information upon related subjects. Collaborating Municipalities using this DIF in combination with web-services functionalities like TMRAP [9] will be able to put spontaneous knowledge federation in their complex value chains in practise.

References

1. Pepper, S. and Garshol, L. M. : The XML Papers; XML 2002, December 2002, paper is available at http://www.ontopia.net/topicmaps/materials/xmlconf.html
2. Wolf, P. and Krcmar, H. : Topic Maps Technology for Municipal Management Information Systems; 2005, In Proceedings of the 38th Hawaii International Conference on System Sciences – 2005, Technische Universitat München
3. Standpunt Metadata van 'Advies Overheid.nl' onderdeel van ICTU. Guidelines from Advice Organ for Government available at http://advies.overheid.nl/metadata-standpunt/
4. Biezunski, M. and Newcomb, S. : A DRM Perspective: What Topic Maps Bring to the Table; 2005, Available at http://www.infoloom.com/workshops.htm
5. ICTU is founded by the Ministry of the Interiour and Kingdom Affairs to advice governmental organisations, Website available at http://www.ictu.nl/profile.html
6. EGEM is a knowledge platform for municipalities. Website at http://www.egem.nl
7. VNG is an Association of Netherlands Municipalities committed to strengthen democratic local government. Website available at http://www.vng.nl
8. OSOSS is the Dutch program Open Standards and Open Source Software for Government affiliated with ICTU, Website available at: http://www.ososs.nl
9. Garshol, L. M. : TMRAP - Topic Maps Remote Access Protocol; 2006, In Proceedings of TMRA'05, LNCS, Springer.

Just for Me: Topic Maps and Ontologies

Jack Park and Adam Cheyer

SRI International, 333 Ravenswood Ave, Menlo Park, CA 94025
jack.park@sri.com

Abstract. The development of the IRIS semantic desktop platform has provided illumination of some important issues associated with the collection and manipulation of knowledge assets that are organized by an ontology. We explore those issues related to the personalization of the workspace and of the knowledge assets manipulated by IRIS users. We show that a topic map can provide a necessary mediation between the formal organization provided by an ontology to serve the needs of semantic interoperability between workstations and the individual's need to personalize the workspace in a *just for me* fashion.

1 Introduction

Experience of life has taught me that the only thing that is really desirable without a reason for being so is to render ideas and things reasonable.

–C.S. Peirce, *Science* 20 April 1900

Semantic desktop applications [1] exist to facilitate productivity and creativity in knowledge work. Two key use cases facilitated by such applications are *finding* and *reminding*. Both finding and reminding services derive from means by which information resources are organized and turned into knowledge assets. Ontologies are created to provide organizational guidance for local and for networked knowledge work. A new semantic desktop system called IRIS[1] [14] we are building at SRI has provided an opportunity to observe the onset and evolution of an interesting user experience issue. In this paper, we wish to share an interesting finding, a kind of tension that grows out of two distinct requirements for tools applied to knowledge work. Those requirements call for semantic interoperability between knowledge applications, and for user personalization of the workspace, something we label "*just for me*". IRIS can be cast as a kind of topic map for personal knowledge assets, assets which must exist in a networked community. It is in that topic maps context that we find an opportunity to realize a candidate solution to a user's need to personalize the working environment.

To anticipate, the term "just for me" refers to the notion that an individual's workstation must satisfy the user's need to work in a *familiar* environment, describing (naming and relating) things in ways which are familiar to the individual, possibly

---

[1] IRIS: http://www.ai.sri.com/software/IRIS

L. Maicher and J. Park (Eds.): TMRA 2005, LNAI 3873, pp. 145–159, 2006.

less familiar to the networked community. This tension arises from the nature of a continuum which separates two concerns. On one end of that continuum lie representations of the objective universe defined by a consensus and empirical ontology, while at the other end lies representations of the subjective universe of individual users. The concerns are those of semantic interoperability and of usability. If the poles of that continuum are orthogonal, they are more so for some users than others. The closer a user is to the objective end, as the author of the ontology at the objective end would be, the lower the tension; *just for me* might not be an issue at all some users.

With this paper, we hope to open a discussion that centers on human-computer interactions (HCI) as related to the user experience particularly in the context of knowledge workstations such as IRIS. During the ongoing development of the IRIS platform, we continue to bump up against a kind of barrier, a simple one: users bring a lifetime of personally learned *ontology*, an instrument of knowledge organization, to their day-to-day activities with IRIS, while IRIS brings a different ontology, one created with the specific intent to facilitate semantic interoperability across a network, to the very same activities. As we shall show, the personal ontology of the user is often not sufficiently similar to the IRIS-supplied ontology; cognitive dissonance and unsatisfying user experience ensues.

We will argue that the presence of a *personal topic map* can serve as a mediator between the needs of a satisfying user experience with those of semantic interoperability. We suspect that HCI, the design of human-computer interaction experiences for semantic workstations, will eventually rise to be at least as important to the success of semantic desktops as is semantic interoperability among platforms. We believe that it is the specific relationships that topic maps forge between *subject identity* and *names for things* which facilitate the mediation process. In this paper, we take the term *semantic interoperability* to be *context sensitive*. That is, semantic interoperability implies, first, that two agents know how to speak with and listen to each other, where *meanings* are derived from interpretations of messages in agreed-upon ways. Context sensitivity implies understanding of your listener's model of the universe, when you are the speaker. If your listener happens to be applying the same ontology to listening as you are to speaking, semantic interoperability is possible. If, say, the listener is a child and you are an adult, say, scientist, you would be expected to find a vocabulary that matches or is interpretable by the listener. We begin this paper by discussing the issue itself. We then present IRIS, and follow that with a look at related work. Let us look closer at the issue.

2   The *Just for Me* Issue

> *The end goal of all of this research, design, testing and rumination is not just a software system that is easy for people to get. (If that were the case, let's just give people 1s and 0s, it doesn't get much simpler or more generic than that.) The end goal is a data structure that sits firmly upon the deep-seeded, some might say, hard-wired, natural structures of the human information architecture. The stuff of linguistics and grammar.*
>
> –Mimi Yin [12]

Clarifying the lens is more primordial than any particular perceiving or acting

–Mark Szpakowski[2]

In order to frame a discussion about the tension we observe to exist between a user's needs and those of semantic interoperability, let us imagine three conceptual spaces, one which is associated with all the information resources directly or indirectly available to a user, one which is associated with a *model* of those information resources, rendering an otherwise heterogeneous information space into an organized, classified body of information, and the last space, which is the user's *lens* or *view* into the other two spaces. We sketch those three spaces in Figure 1[3].

We have given those spaces the labels

- Documents—the space of all information resources
- Knowledge Structures—structured representations of the information resources
- Topic Maps—a user's *lens* into the other two spaces

The illustration does, indeed, have some of its ancestry in those marvelous illustrations in Steve Pepper's "The TAO of Topic Maps" [6]. But, Figure 1 is different in the sense that it injects an ontology layer between information resources and the topic map. Such a separation, by no means, implies that the topic map does not point into those information resources. Rather, it suggests that there is a marriage of ontologies and topic maps as suggested in Bernard Vatant's paper "Ontology-driven Topic Maps" [7]. Such a marriage contrasts with the case where the topic map *is* the ontology, as described by Eric Freese in Chapter 13 in [2] and by H. Holger Rath in Chapter 14 [2].

The spaces just sketched relate to the issues we develop here in the following sense. There exist the dual needs of *user personalization* of the workspace, and *semantic interoperability* between the databases maintained by individual installations

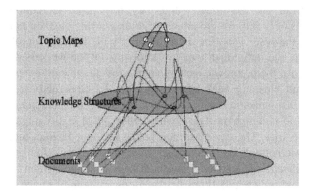

Fig. 1. Conceptual Spaces for Information Architecture

---

[2] Mark Szpakowski: http://collab.blueoxen.net/forums/yak/2005-08/msg00040.html#nid07

[3] This diagram was first conceived during discussions by the first author with Mary Keeler and Howard Liu. In some sense, it represents an interpretation of a Peircian view of inquiry space.

when applied in group settings. In some sense, the *user interface*, labeled a Topic Map in the illustration, can present the universe of information resources available to the user in a *just for me* fashion. The desktop application needs to present those information resources to external applications in a *consensus reality*, we say, semantically interoperable fashion. In both cases, *subject identity* must remain based on consensus reality.

2.1 Just for Me

Just for me is perhaps best viewed as a fractal concept, one that starts at the individual level. Owing to the many relationships between individuals and their work groups, "just for me" morphs into "just for us" (locally), which then morphs (onion skin fashion) to "just for us" (globally). The Topic Maps layer of Figure 1 delineates the context for what follows. It is precisely the topic map, perhaps, the entire user experience associated with interacting with IRIS that constitutes the "just for me" discussion that follows. To anticipate the arguments, "just for me" suggests that the topic map should be user-constructed. The ontology (Knowledge Structures of Figure 1), in the case of IRIS, is constructed by teams of researchers; it could have just as well been constructed by a committee created by an enterprise that uses installations of CALO; indeed, it could be constructed by an individual user in the first place, but that's neither the case for CALO, nor the context of this discussion. The issue is this: entities other than individual users craft the ontology, and users craft their own topic maps. In some cases, the ontology can provide all that is necessary to populate such a topic map; in other cases, the user might see things differently.

It is probably useful to digress for just a moment. Consider the physician, or the scientist, or the lawyer. For those individuals, the ontology is probably already *just for me*. Such users operate closer to the objective end of the continuum mentioned above. They invented it in the first place, and they live in it. Certainly, they might personalize aspects of it, but, for the most part, their ontology is their normal universe of discourse. For the rest of us, for the office users of IRIS, the ontology might or might not represent the individual's way of knowing. Office workers don't generally invent ontologies; for them, knowledge engineers provide the ontologies.

The story behind "just for me" is the story behind constructivist epistemology, which suggests[4] that constructivism is about focusing on *personally constructed* reality as opposed to *ontological* reality, where ontological reality might reflect either fiat or consensus reality. The central notion is that people construct their own reality through social interaction; they construct their own names for things that are identified in social settings, and they construct relationships between those things. It follows that users of semantic desktop workstations are going to have their own way of organizing what they know and their own names for things with which they interact. The tension, as we see it, lies in the fact that the user's constructed reality must co-exist with the group's consensus (ontological) reality. In some cases it co-exists, and in others, tension remains.

---

[4] Statement adapted from http://en.wikipedia.org/wiki/Constructivist_epistemology

Consider a short story. Jared Spool[5] recently spoke to a web designers' meeting, speaking about the conclusions he was able to draw by observing web users purchase cameras online. The problem was framed in the context of a sum of money given to the purchasers, comparing the sum given to the amount of money actually spent on a purchase. He observed that, at most websites—for example, amazon.com—something like 110% of the money given for the purchase was spent on the purchase. One particular website stood out by capturing far more money in the purchase than was originally budgeted by the buyer—the consumer spent more than allocated for the purchase. The analysis is revealing. It goes like this. In spite of all of the many faceted attributes of the cameras displayed, consumers were mostly interested in the pictures they would get from the camera, not with number of pixels, lens speed, and so forth. To most consumers, cameras were a vehicle to get pictures. The site that achieved large sales was the site displaying photos taken by the camera. That site had discovered a *just for me* "sweet spot". The faceted attributes were still there, but those attributes were not the ones those consumers were using to make the purchase. A moral drawn from that story is this: ontologists can design elegant taxonomies, and those may, or may not, satisfy the needs of the consumer (user). It may be that the ontologists simply cannot be expected to "think like a user" or anticipate all of the many ways in which users categorize their personal universe.

The *name for things* issue animates discussions of some existing and emerging techniques. The distinction between name and identity comes together through the emerging notion of *folksonomies*,[6] and the well-known *faceted classification*[7] [12]. While there are some institutional faceted classification schemes in existence,[8] as for example DMOZ,[9] other such schemes are crafted as needed by individuals and group. Those individual activities are indicative of the human need to individualize, or *personalize*, the ways in which information resources are named and identified.

Consider the *delicious*[10] website, where users are encouraged to "tag" various websites. Jon Udell explains[11] this tagging process as a means to associate names for things, websites in this case. He goes further and casts this as a *language evolution* process. Constructivism, indeed! Tagging, as a process, is not without its critics. For instance, L. Jeffrey Zeldman argues[12] that tagging replaces user-centered taxonomies with usage frequency. Tag *clouds* form which separate related topics from each other. Another way to look at tagging is that it is social constructivism at work, where individuals are practicing their "just for me" behaviors, and evolving those behaviors during social interactions. Indeed, Mimi Yin, who works on the Chandler[13] project, has much to say about these issues. In her recent paper "Hierarchies versus Facets versus Tags" [11], she argues, among other things, that hierarchies can become

---

[5] Jared Spool: http://www.uie.com/

[6] Folksonomy: http://en.wikipedia.org/wiki/Folksonomy

[7] Faceted Classification: http://en.wikipedia.org/wiki/Faceted_classification

[8] Just about every online catalog uses facets, e.g., price, shipping weight, lens speed, color, etc.

[9] DMOZ: http://www.dmoz.org/

[10] delicious: http://del.icio.us/

[11] Jon Udell: http://weblog.infoworld.com/udell/gems/delicious.html

[12] Zeldman: http://zeldman.com/daily/0505a.shtml

[13] Chandler: http://www.osafoundation.org/

"messy" and unmaintainable, and that facetted systems don't offer some of the benefits of hierarchies and become too flexible to be useful.

Yin's writing constitutes anecdotal evidence that open questions remain. Adam Mathese, in his paper "Folksonomies—Cooperative Classification and Communication through Shared Metadata," [13] concludes his discussion with the notion that a folksonomy is fundamentally uncontrolled in nature, suffering imprecision and ambiguity, but at the same time, free-form tagging allows for self-organization of information resources.

In the context of IRIS and "just for me", we take the view that tagging really is just for the individual user, and not necessarily for the group, unless the group dynamic chooses to encourage it. The role of a topic map with groups of IRIS users would be to permit personal topic maps to reflect personal naming conventions locally while linking to a group topic map, say, on a server, which reflects consensus naming conventions. Mappings between the two are mediated by subject identity properties reflected in the consensus ontology. At the desktop level, we are certainly not alone in this notion. Murray Altheim has implemented faceted classification in Ceryle [18], a semantic desktop application created to organize those knowledge assets necessary for authorship.

2.2   Tensions Between "Ontology-Driven" and Personal Topic Map

> ...when thinking about ontologies and semantic web it is easy to focus on the requirements of precision and data integration to the exclusion of the requirements for end user navigation
>
> –Dave Reynolds, et al. [17]

Semantic interoperability demands consensus identity, and some consensus names; personal views, *just for me*, call for personal naming conventions alongside consensus subject identity. Let us contrast these views:

- Separate ontology and topic map
  o Topic map, itself, doesn't necessarily have to support consensus names for things
- Topic map as ontology
  o User's *lens* topic map directly supports user names for things along with consensus names for things

While an artificial separation between ontology and topic map appears in those views, it is not the intent of those views to imply that such a separation need exist. A separate ontology and topic map is just one approach to implementation. Indeed, a topic map can represent the ontology in place of serving as a proxy for the subjects of a separate ontology.

If IRIS is to have a topic map,[14] then, in the near term, it will be separate from the ontology. It is not inconceivable that some future version of IRIS could migrate to a

---

[14] A small, focused topic map existed in the original prototype, but was set aside to facilitate evolution of other functionality. A focused topic map means that a small map of specific aspects of the user's world was created as the user entered that world. For instance, a general topic map of all people and of all projects existed in the background, and fragments of those maps appeared, for instance, in the tasks view.

topic map as ontology architecture. For now, the tension exists because IRIS, indeed, all semantic desktop workstations, are, essentially, *just for me* platforms and the intuition is that a topic map can mediate between the interoperability need for a consensus ontology and the user's need for a personal lens into that workspace.

2.3   A Solution: Topic Maps as Mediators

Consider a patient-doctor scenario, the context of which is a vision problem where the patient says "...the world is going *Picasso* on me." The doctor replys with "Well, we call that syndrome *scintillating scotoma*; it's one of the many kinds of migraine headaches people can experience." The doctor is working from a medical ontology, and, based on years of experience, has a pretty good idea of how patients are liable to describe their signs and symptoms. In the simple *office world* of IRIS, let us imagine some office worker relating the proper name *Joseph P. Sixpack* to a favored way to recall that person, say, *Bubba*. The rest of the world doesn't need to know about "Bubba", but, if association of a specific person to a favored name renders the user's life simpler, less hectic, and more productive, then it's useful to provide for such mediation.

Topic maps offer a simple *paradigm* from which a candidate solution to the *just for me* issue emerges. The topic maps paradigm simply suggests that, for each *subject*, there can exist in a given topic map, at most, one *topic*, where a topic is best-imagined as a container, nexus or proxy for the subject, at which all presently-knowable information related to the subject can be found. The nexus concept evokes the image of a topic as a *hub* around which all information resources related to the subject radiate.

While topic mapping, the paradigm, itself, continues to evolve, there remains a core set of notions, a core ontology which guides application developers. Core to topic mapping are the elements: *topic*, and *association*. With those two core elements, a slightly broader ontology grows. We draw on the concept of *scope* to construct a solution to the *just for me* issue.

A scope represents a *context*, and, as such, is, itself, a subject represented by a topic. Names for topics can take scopes. That is, a particular name for some subject might be a string written and scoped in the English, a string written and scoped in the German, and name strings written in other languages, all representations of a name for the subject. Scopes can also be used to provide context other than language. Scoping *Bubba* as a *private* name string in a topic map might mean that this name string will not appear in the public transmission of data between IRIS installations. Using *scoped names* thus permits a user to inject favored names for things.

Using *scoped associations*, a topic map permits a user to inject favored relationships into the knowledgebase without risk of those relationships altering the semantic interoperability of the larger ontology. Topic maps thus provide a useful means by which users of ontology-driven workstations can personalize their working environment.

Implementing a topic map in a semantic desktop application as a means of satisfying a *just for me* requirement avails other potential benefits. For instance, the inherent indexical capabilities of topic maps are suited to many of the needs already satisfied by the ontology. That opens the door to two larger questions: *could a topic map satisfy the need for an ontology*, and *could the ontology satisfy the need for a topic map*? Both, great questions, and each suggests avenues for future research. While other workers are already exploring those questions, we believe the opportunity to implement an ontology as a topic map remains an important opportunity since that one structure can satisfy both semantic interoperability and just for me requirements. For the present work, it is shown that a topic map can mediate between two important needs, those related to user experience, and those related to semantic interoperability between workstations.

We have discussed personalized names for things and personalized relationships between things. Another issue is, and will remain for a long time in the future, that of subject identity. For instance, IRIS exists in an email-rich universe, where the names of unknown (to IRIS) persons appear frequently. CALO provides a framework wherein new persons are isolated and studied by a variety of means, the intent being to disambiguate identities. For instance, one email might come in from, say, jpark@foo.org and another from jackpark@bar.com. A question is this: do both emails refer to the same individual? That is a nontrivial question, and it mirrors the subject identity issues facing topic maps during merging processes. IRIS includes a harvesting framework which includes some tools for name resolution. More powerful tools are included in CALO.

Where does IRIS presently stand in relation to resolving the *just for me* issue? We have cast IRIS as a kind of topic map for personal knowledge assets, assets which must reside in a networked community. We are not claiming that IRIS *is* a topic map in the sense understood in terms of XTM documents, merging tools and so forth. Rather, IRIS continuously orbits in the space of tensions between the necessity to use an ontology to organize information resources for purposes of interoperability between software agents involved in processing those resources and other semantic desktop installations, and between the user's need semantic desktop installations, and between the user's need to capture individual ways of knowing and doing.

3   IRIS

There are several threads related to the background from which IRIS, topic maps, ontologies, and the issue we found. In the end, they all relate to the ever-increasing rate at which sound decisions must be made in the context of ever-increasing amounts of information to process in order to achieve those decisions. Out of the need to index a growing body of software documentation (one form of infoglut), topic maps were created. As Steven R. Newcomb said in his introduction to topic mapping in the book *XML Topic Maps* [2, page 32],

> *Information is both more and less real than the material universe. It's more real because it will survive any physical change; it will outlast any physical manifestation of itself. It's less real because it's ineffable. For example, you can touch a shoe, but you can't touch the notion of "shoe-ness" (that is, what it means to be a shoe). The notion of shoe-ness is probably eternal, but every shoe is ephemeral.*

As topic mapping technology matures and enters mainstream application in ever more complex indexical and organizational situations, user interface issues bubble to the foreground. Indexical and associative applications require attention to two core issues: *subject identity* and *names for things*. Recent innovation on the web,[15] the notion of *social bookmarking*, for instance, is pointing the way toward a web that satisfies a *just for me*[16] requirement. The combination of rising popularity and high level of innovation in this arena strongly suggests that the *just for me* requirement should be investigated at the desktop application level, along with the web.

We now live and work in a networked global village; the term *infoglut* has become the meme that reminds us of the information overload we experience in our daily lives, and about which Vannevar Bush eloquently wrote in his 1945 paper, "As We May Think" [10]. Indeed, it was that paper which inspired Ted Nelson, Douglas Engelbart, and many others to try to find solutions to the infoglut problem and augment human capabilities for solving complex, urgent problems.

IRIS has been developed as part of SRI's CALO[17] project, one of two projects funded under DARPA's "Perceptive Assistant that Learns" (PAL) program.[18] The goal of the PAL program is to develop an enduring personal assistant that "learns in the wild," evolving its abilities more and more through automated machine learning techniques rather than through code changes. In approaching the design and development of IRIS, we took much inspiration from the work of Douglas Engelbart, who performed much of his early work while employed at SRI. While Ted Nelson's Xanadu[19] [3] was arguably the first project to set the stage for modern hyperdocument processors, Engelbart's Augment[20] was the first system to find engagement in group document processing and sharing. In 1968, at the Fall Joint Computer Conference in San Francisco, Engelbart demonstrated Augment before a live audience.[21] Augment displayed many of the capabilities we now want to build into modern semantic desktop applications. Augment, the program, saw commercial application, and is still used today by Dr. Engelbart in his day-to-day activities.

Central to our work is the *augmentation program*, first proposed by J.C.R. Licklider (who funded Engelbart's work) in 1960 [5]. The emphasis of that program was to augment human capabilities with computers, as we see in the Engelbart work, as then compared to the *artificial intelligence program* (AI), in which human capabilities are

---

[15] E.g. http://www.flickr.com/ and http://del.icio.us/

[16] The term *just for me* was first introduced to the first author by Nancy Glock-Grueneich in the context of pedagogy. The context is this: regular school learning is sometimes described as "just in case"; by contrast, constructivist learning is described as "just in time", and Nancy suggests that real learning is best described as "just for me."

[17] CALO is an acronym for "Cognitive Assistant that Learns and Organizes." CALO's name was also inspired by the Latin word *calonis*, which means "soldier's servant" and conjures an image of Radar O'Reilly from the M*A*S*H TV series.

[18] DARPA's PAL program: http://www.darpa.mil/ipto/programs/pal/

[19] Xanadu: http://xanadu.com/

[20] NLS/Augment at the Computer History Museum: http://community.computerhistoryorg/scc/projects/nlsproject/

[21] Videos of the first online document editing project. Found on the web at http://sloan.stanford.edu/ MouseSite/1968Demo.html

mimicked or otherwise provided by computers. CALO represents a blending of the AI and the augmentation programs.

There is a clear and vibrant link between topic maps and the augmentation program. We see opportunities for that link in IRIS, because the program integrates several desktop office productivity tools, such as email, web browsing, calendar, instant messaging, and more. At the same time, IRIS provides a framework that supports aspects of artificial intelligence and machine learning, all in support of aiding the user in assembling, indexing, clustering and otherwise organizing a growing body of knowledge assets.

In order to better understand how IRIS can be cast as a topic map for personal knowledge assets, we now briefly sketch those aspects of IRIS that make up the letters in the name. IRIS is first and foremost an *integration* framework. Whereas in today's packaged applications suites, where only loose data integration exists[22] (usually limited to the clipboard and common look-and-feel for menus and dialog boxes), IRIS strives to integrate data from disparate applications using reified semantic classes and typed relations. For instance, it should be possible to express that *"File F* was presented at *Meeting M* by *Tom Jones,* who is the *Project Manager* of *Project X,"* even if the file manager, calendar program, contact database, and project management software are separately developed third-party applications. In a Topic Maps fashion, there should be a single instance that represents each concept, and all that is knowable about that concept should be directly accessible from that instance [2].

The IRIS framework offers integration services at three levels (Figure 2):

1. Information resources (e.g., an email message, a calendar appointment) and the applications that create and manipulate them must be made accessible to IRIS for instrumentation, automation, and query.
2. A knowledge base (KB) provides the unified data model, persistence store, and query mechanisms across the information resources and semantic relations among them.
3. The IRIS user interface framework allows plug-in applications to embed their own interfaces within IRIS, and to interoperate with global UI services.

The IRIS user interface provides the "shell" for hosting several embedded applications (Figure 3). Two side panels frame the main application window, one for selecting among available applications, the other for displaying and editing semantic links for the selected application object and presenting contextual suggestions from the learning framework. Applications can add toolbars to the IRIS frame, and when selected, an application's menu items are "merged" with IRIS menu functionality present for all applications. IRIS provides an extensible context-sensitive online help system and several methods for querying information resources within and across applications.

IRIS is used to semantically integrate the tools of knowledge work, to form *relationships* between knowledge assets. What do we mean by this? We use the term "semantic" in the sense used by the Semantic Web community, where markup

---

[22] Even within a single application, deep data integration is usually pretty threadbare. Consider Microsoft Outlook: the email addresses displayed in a message are not linkable (or deeply related) to the people records in your contacts folder.

technologies are being wedded to the tools of semantic representation (e.g., ontologies, OWL, RDF). This facilitates putting data on the web in such a way that machines can access it, make meaningful references to it, and perform manipulations on it, including reasoning and inference. In that sense, IRIS provides an OWL-based ontology and backside by which the artifacts of a user's experience such as email messages, calendar events, files on the disk or found on the web, can be stored and related to each other across applications and across users.

When defining the ontology to be used for IRIS, a design choice had to be made: Do we use a small, simple ontology or a complex, more-expressive ontology? We first implemented a fairly large, yet straightforward, ontology. However, the requirement that IRIS interoperate with CALO's reasoning and learning capabilities drove us to adopt CALO's preexisting ontology, which supports roles, events, and complex data structures.

Additionally, IRIS provides a framework for *harvesting* application data and *instrumenting* user actions in IRIS applications. The harvesting of data refers to importing external data into semantic (ontology-based) structures.

One of the key differentiators of IRIS, compared to many semantic desktop systems, is the emphasis on machine learning and the implementation of a plug-and-play learning framework, providing the ability for IRIS to make *inferences*. We see machine learning as one of the solutions around a key issue limiting the Semantic Web's growth and mass adoption: Who is going to enter all of the required links and knowledge?

Prior to the Internet, the last technology that had any real effect on the way people sat down and talked together was the table.

–Clay Shirky[23]

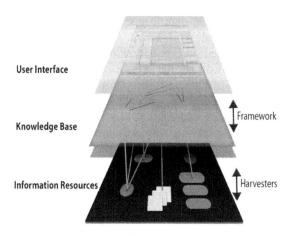

Fig. 2. IRIS Architecture

User Interface

Framework

Knowledge Base

Information Resources

Harvesters

---

[23] Clay Shirky: at Emerging Technology Conference 2003 http://shirky.com/writings/group_ enemy. html

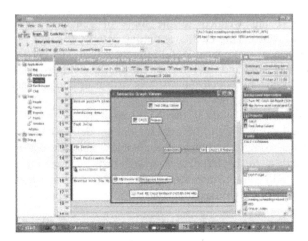

Fig. 3. The IRIS Platform

Sharing information is one of the four key concepts that make up the IRI<u>S</u> vision. We feel that the ability to learn and leverage semantic structure in organizing one's work life will be greatly enhanced in a collaborative setting. Shared structures are essential for both end-user applications, such as team decision making and project management, and for infrastructural components such as machine learning algorithms, which improve when given larger data sets to work on.

4   Related Work

Several projects exist and are similar in spirit and intent to IRIS. We sketch a few of them here,.Two projects of great significance to the personalization of information resources are Lifestreams[24] and WorldBoard.[25] Lifestreams is the vision of David Gelernter, and was developed as a dissertation project by Eric Freeman [15]. WorldBoard is the outgrowth of the vision of Jim Spohrer from his paper "Information in Places" [16]. Whereas Lifestreams speaks mostly to local individual needs, WorldBoard speaks to Global individual and group needs.

While developing IRIS, we explored Haystack[26] from MIT. When we discovered this project [8], we were amazed how well it fit our initial designs for IRIS, in terms of both architecture and user interface design, with the added benefit of being Java-based and open source. We learned much from a visit by Dennis Quan, one of the principal developers, and did, indeed, begin the task of adapting Haystack's significant code base to our framework. For a variety of reasons, we ended up moving in a different direction, but Haystack and Dr. Quan's deep knowledge of the subject gave us a solid start.

---

[24] Lifestreams: http://www.cs.yale.edu/homes/freeman/lifestreams.html
[25] WorldBoard: http://www.worldboard.org/
[26] Haystack: http://haystack.lcs.mit.edu/

The next system we evaluated was the Radar Networks[27] Personal Radar, a very impressive semantic desktop that turned out to share many of the goals and requirements for IRIS: Java-based, ontology-driven, user-centric. We have combined elements of Personal Radar into the IRIS code base.

Well down the path of implementing IRIS, we discovered two additional projects. Gnowsis.[28] Gnowsis [9] appears to offer integration with many of the same third-party applications as IRIS, and to share many similar philosophies regarding application and data integration. MindRaider,[29] is a project arguably close to IRIS, Haystack, and Gnowsis in spirit and intent.

Ontologies have become the *lingua franca* of semantic interoperability. Programs such as Haystack, IRIS, and others are, essentially, driven by ontologies. This means that operations by users, data items such as email messages and calendar events, and communications between different platforms, are all performed in the context of a built-in ontology. Outside of desktops, SHOE [4] represents an early approach to providing for semantic interoperability on the web. SHOE is an ontology-based language. Today, the OWL web ontology language is rapidly becoming a standard for representing ontologies. The IRIS ontology is implemented in OWL.

5 Conclusions

IRIS is the platform that allowed its creators to experience the tensions we have discussed here. The system is now in daily operation as the primary office environment used by several members of the CALO community. In that daily use, and during trials by developers, we continue to encounter users who wish they could add tags or otherwise provide names for objects, or forge relationships between objects such as files on the hard disk and emails or calendar events. A growing awareness of this issue is propagating some rethinking regarding the design of the IRIS knowledgebase. This rethinking allows for the opportunity to implement a topic map linked to the ontology and driven by the user interface. With the addition of a topic map to IRIS, users will be able to provide their own names and relationships, and still remain semantically interoperable with the rest of the community.

We have argued that a *personal topic map*, one that mediates between a user and an ontology, is a candidate solution to the *just for me* issue. We believe that our work with IRIS and CALO supports our claim that semantic desktop applications which use ontologies for semantic interoperability can benefit from the application of personal topic maps. We offer a concluding conjecture that the topic map, itself, might server the role of the ontology, providing both semantic interoperability and *just for me* user support.

Acknowledgements

This work was supported by the Defense Advanced Research Projects Agency (DARPA) under Contract No. NBCHD030010. Any opinions, findings, and conclusions

---

[27] RadarNetworks: http://www.radarnetworks.com/

[28] Gnowsis: http://www.gnowsis.org/

[29] MindRaider: http://mindraider.sourceforge.net/

or recommendations expressed in this material are those of the authors and do not necessarily reflect the views of DARPA or the Department of Interior-National Business Center (DOI-NBC).

We would like to thank those SRI and non-SRI CALO members, too many to name, who are working with us to integrate their cutting-edge technologies into the IRIS learning framework. We also would like to thank the anonymous reviewers, Glen B. Haydon, Patrick Durusau, Ray Perrault, and Josh Levy for comments on an early draft of this paper.

References

1. Decker, Stefan; and Martin Frank, "The Social Semantic Desktop," 2004. On the web at http://www.deri.at/publications/techpapers/documents/DERI-TR-2004-05-02.pdf

2. Park, Jack, Editor, and Sam Hunting, Technical Editor, *XML Topic Maps: Creating and Using Topic Maps for the Web*, Boston, MA. Addison-Wesley, 2003

3. Nelson, Theodor von Holm, "Xanalogical Structure, Needed Now More than Ever: Parallel Documents, Deep Links to Content, Deep Versioning, and Deep Re-Use." ACM Computing Surveys 31(4), December 1999. On the web at http://www.cs.brown.edu/ memex/ACM_ HypertextTestbed/papers/60.html

4. Heflin, Jeff and James Hendler, "Semantic Interoperability on the Web," 2000. On the web at http://www.cs.umd.edu/projects/plus/SHOE/pubs/extreme2000.pdf

5. Licklider, J.C.R., "Man-Computer Symbiosis", 1960. On the web at http://memex.org/ licklider. pdf

6. Pepper, Steve, "The TAO of Topic Maps," Ontopia. On the web at http://www.ontopia.net/ topicmaps/materials/tao.html

7. Vatant, Bernard, "Ontology-driven Topic Maps", XML Europe 2004, Amsterdam, The Netherlands. On the web at http://www.idealliance.org/europe/04/call/xmlpapers/03-03-03.91/ .03-03-03.html

8. Karger, David R., Karun Bakshi, David Huynh, Dennis Quan, and Vineet Sinha, "Haystack: A Customizable General-Purpose Information Management Tool for End Users of Semistructured Data," in CIDR 2005, Asilomar, California. On the web at http://www-db.cs.wisc.edu/ cidr/cidr2005/papers/P02.pdf

9. 9. Sauermann, Leo, "The Gnowsis Semantic Desktop for Information Integration," in IOA 2005, Kaiserlauten, Germany. On the web athttp://www.dfki.uni-kl.de/~sauermann/papers/ Sauermann2005a.pdf

10. Bush, Vannevar, "As We May Think," The Atlantic Monthly, July 1945. On the web at http://www.theatlantic.com/doc/194507/bush

11. Yin, Mimi, "Hierarchy versus Facets versus Tags", July 11, 2005. On the web at http://wiki.osafoundation.org/bin/view/Journal/HierarchyVersusFacetsVersusTags

12. Yin, Mimi, "Preface to Hierarchy Papers", July 14, 2005. On the web at http://wiki. osafoundation.org/bin/view/Journal/PrefaceToHierarchyPapers

13. Mathes, Adam, "Folksonomies – Cooperative Classification and Communication Through Shared Metadata," December 2004. On the web at http://www.adammathes.com/academic/ computer-mediated-communication/folksonomies.html

14. Cheyer, Adam, Jack Park, and Richard Giuli, "IRIS: Integrate. Relate. Infer. Share," submitted to the 1st International Workshop on The Semantic Desktop, Galway, Ireland, 6 November 2005.

15. Freeman, Eric Thomas, "The Lifestreams Software Architecture", Ph.D. Dissertation, Yale University, May 1997. On the web at http://www.cs.yale.edu/homes/freeman/dissertation/etf. pdf
16. Spohrer, James C., "Information In Places", IBM Systems Journal, Vol 38, No 4, 1999. On the web at http://www.research.ibm.com/journal/sj/384/spohrer.html
17. Reynolds, Dave, Paul Shabajee, Steve Cayzer, and Damian Steer, "SWAD-Europe deliverable 12.1.7: Semantic Portals Demonstrator- Lessons Learnt", Sept. 2004. On the web at http://www.w3.org/2001/sw/Europe/reports/demo_2_report/
18. Altheim, Murray, "Ceryle and "Grass Roots" Ontologies," Ceryle Blog, Feb. 10, 2005. On the web at http://www.altheim.com/ceryle/blog

Rebuilding Virtual Study Environments Using Topic Maps

Kamila Olsevicova

Faculty of Informatics and Management, University of Hradec Kralove,
Rokitanskeho 62, Hradec Kralove 50003, Czech Republic
kamila.olsevicova@uhk.cz

Abstract. Virtual study environments are web-based applications where e-courses are delivered. In accordance with the shift towards the semantic web, the conception of separated and narrowly focused e-courses seems to be obsolete and certain new solutions should be offered. The Topic Maps technology is a good candidate to become the core integrative element of the next generation of educational portals with the potential to replace current virtual study environments. In the paper we explain why and how to transform virtual study environments using Topic Maps. Also we present a pilot application.

1 Introduction

The second half of the twentieth century was characterized by the growing influence of information and communication technologies (ICT) on our lives. A significant impact of ICT can be seen in the area of higher education; universities turn their attendance to delivery of e-courses through *virtual study environments* (VSE) that promise to increase the effectiveness of educational processes.

But the broadening palette of offered e-courses brings new challenges and opens serious questions about the management of e-courses and about the future of large repositories of electronic study materials. The introducing of VSE has to be understood as adding a new piece to puzzle of different information systems of the university and strong integration of VSE with other applications is desirable. Therefore the main objectives of this paper are:

o to describe weak points of current virtual study environments in context of their application at university and with respect to understanding university as a natural environment for application of knowledge management principles,
o to suggest a TM solution that would help to minimize detected insufficiencies and would contribute to convergence of virtual study environments and knowledge management systems.

2 Description of Virtual Study Environments

E-learning is defined as transport of knowledge and skills, enabled by computer networks [8], [20], [27]. The main objective of e-learning is to transform educational

L. Maicher and J. Park (Eds.): TMRA 2005, LNAI 3873, pp. 160–168, 2006.

processes with the aim to customize learning to student's needs in term of study style, time and space. E-learning can be realized through different online and offline technologies. The most common online e-learning systems are virtual study environments.

Virtual study environments are widely applicable from the traditional to fully distance education. Today, there are many vendors of VSEs in EU countries and in North America, who provide professional solutions, see [2],[7],[10],[29],[30] and others.

The functionalities of VSE can be divided into five main categories:

o   The core of each e-course is the *study content*, delivered to students in particular e-course. The study content consists of learning objects, i.e. documents in different formats (doc, html, txt, ppt, jpg, gif, mp3...), or executable applications. The learning objects that are utilized in particular e-course inside VSE are arranged in standardized form of lessons, glossaries, indices, image databases etc., that correspond to preferred functionalities of VSE from the pedagogical point of view.

o   The *communication tools* available to all participants of educational processes are e.g. e-mail client, thread discussion, shared whiteboard, chat, voice chat, voice conferences, videoconferences, lists of online users etc. E-commerce applications and tools for synchronization with PDA-devices can be seen as special kinds of communication tools, too.

o   *Classroom management* functionalities are used for management and monitoring student activities inside VSE, delivery of organizational information, organization of assignments etc. Common tools are calendar, notice board, schedule, gradebook, tools for creation of test etc.

o   *Individual student management tools* are available either to student, or to teacher, or to both. Students can manipulate with files inside their private folders, publish self-presentations, access their evaluation records or compare individual results with statistical summaries of the study group. Teachers maintain data in gradebooks or make decisions about visibility of statistics.

o   *The e-course information* can be seen as the envelope of the e-course that informs current or potential users about the e-course. It consists of the e-course description, contacts to authors and teachers, syllabus, pre-requisites, e-course sitemap etc.

It is important to point out how the term e-learning evokes the paradigm shift: we talk about computer assisted "learning", not "teaching", what expresses the effort to stimulate the student's own activity, to the detriment of teacher [11]. The objectivist approach, where the educational process was conducted by teacher and students performed their knowledge level in tests by reproducing facts and information, is replaced by a constructivist theory, based on the idea that students have to build their own systems of knowledge in their minds [24], [27]. Naturally, all students will not develop the same systems of knowledge at the same time and educational institutions must respect this. The accentuation of knowledge structures, their internalization by students and the environments that must enable this internalization – it all makes us to think about adaptation of both constructivist pedagogy and knowledge management

(KM) principles for the area of education and therefore to understand VSE as pure KM solution [12],[13],[14],[18],[20].

3 Weak Points of Virtual Study Environments

Unfortunately, the benefits of virtual study environments applied at universities are accompanied with two categories of insufficiencies: the first category is related to the stored e-content, others are related to learner management. In next two sections we discuss general problems that appear in most VSEs. We do not explore problems that are appearing only in an individual product, but we talk about those of disadvantages coming from the fundamental conception of VSE, that can be remove using our solution, as it is presented in chapters 5 and 6.

3.1 Insufficiencies in Content Management

Five kinds of content management insufficiencies can be observed:

- o *Limited search and navigation possibilities* – if only full-text search was available, for students who are not experts in studied domains it is hard to formulate optimal sets of keywords to locate resources inside VSE. Also, traditional learning objects (word or html files) are not enriched with enough detailed metadata and therefore it is not possible to search for specific formulas, explanations of terms, particular schemas, solved examples etc., but students have to browse numerous documents to find the details that they need. Then, the wandering in plenty of resources can decrease motivation of students, because they see how slow and ineffective their studying process is. It is clear that some better organization of currently separated, unconnected study e-resources would help to eliminate previously explained obstacles. We should think also about integration of links to non-digital resources, such as contacts to human experts inside the university or catalogue of the university library etc [17], [18].
- o *Unnatural organization of stored content* – VSEs are not developed primarily for academic institutions, but for commercial area, e.g. for training of employees. Therefore, users of VSEs are expected to access only one e-course at the moment, with narrow scope and in limited time. But at universities students attend numerous interconnected e-courses during several years. It is common that they need to return to certain themes several times or have to see them from different angles, in different depths. Then, philosophy of separated e-courses is not optimal, and more complex repository of interconnected resources is demanded. From teacher's point of view, better interlinking of e-courses would also change the quality of education in terms of more practical and for students more attractive and meaningful activities such as cross-disciplinary assignments, see e.g. [1].
- o *Lack of support of coordination in content creation* – the independence of e-courses brings the following side-effect: even inside one educational institution, inconsistencies in e-courses appear in case of lack of communication between e-courses designers, there may be duplicities in contents, or

certain themes can be missed because the e-course designer expects them to be explained in colleague's e-course. The digitalization of study materials could simplify the information exchange between teachers, but in practice it does not happen [12],[13],[14],[17],[18]. Although it is matter of communication culture inside the educational institution, it is true that current VSE do not offer anything what could help to improve this situation.

o *Stereotypes in forms of content* – learning objects are often developed by transformation of traditional study texts or teachers notes to the form of web presentations. These transformations are more or less successful in terms of fulfilling pedagogical recommendations related to online study materials and respecting specifics of web media. As [3] or [16] explain, perception of web page is different than perception of printed text. The "digital learners" have got characteristics such as screen literacy, ability to learn by discovering, preferring bricolage before abstract logic etc. Surely, if the study e-materials are not designed in way that attracts readers, it is not the primary failure of VSE. But traditional VSE conception of html-texts makes authors to create electronic study materials in this unpleasant way. Different organization of study content and different access mechanisms should be used in VSE to suit users' real needs.

3.2 Insufficiencies in Learner Management

Although the solution that will be presented in next chapters is focused mainly on overcoming of problems related to content management, it can also be seen as the first step to solving learner-related insufficiencies of VSE.

In e-courses, students usually work alone, so their attendance must be activated and it is important to take care about the effectiveness of their studying by providing continuous feedback, ideally using running questions and tasks. In optimal case, all students' answers and solutions should be checked immediately, and results of evaluation should be presented to students and reused for reasoning about next navigation of students in the study environment to make their education more effective. To do this, there should be brief questions with good ability to recognize students' failures: the information that students succeeded is not valuable for detection of their current needs, while discovering areas where they fail can be reused in design of next path through the e-course. These advanced features, that were already studied and partly implemented in intelligent tutoring systems and intelligent educational systems, still are not included in virtual study environments, for details see [26] and others.

4   Topic Maps Solution for Virtual Study Environment

Most of mentioned insufficiencies of virtual study environments could be eliminated using the Topic Map solution that would serve as a gate to the memory of the university. Students would use the TM application to locate information and knowledge resources related to study programmes. Teachers and managers of the faculty would use it for evaluation of the content of study programmes and answering managerial questions. Moreover, the map would be applicable for comparing specializations of academics at different universities, for discovering strong and weak points in study programmes, for finding research partners etc. Briefly, our TM application would discover knowledge potential of the university and would help to utilize this potential. The scope construct of the TM model would allow distinguishing what resources are accessible to different user groups: study resources can be filtered according language, level of difficulty, access rights.

The proposed TM application should simplify access to different kinds of resources of the educational institution, including educational resources, content repositories, scheduling system, student agenda system, digital libraries, contacts to human experts etc. Therefore the TM solution should cover all information and knowledge resources available at the university and should provide suitable mechanisms for maintaining and updating. We have to respect the fact that numerous digital study materials (learning objects) have already been created and are available in different formats and granularity. We do not think about complete rebuilding current digital resources, their re-formatting, additional digitalization of paper materials etc.

Except the primary goal to improve accessibility of resources at the university, we are motivated also by the idea that natural incorporation of KM principles and developing culture of sharing knowledge and participation on building a kind of "knowledge space" of the university is important for students, who need to be prepared for future carriers in knowledge society.

In VSE, the TM technology is applicable in the following way. Each e-course (that supports course in traditional meaning of this word) is focused on certain discipline that has got its own terminology. This terminology is conceptualized by the discipline (domain) ontology and TM of study resources can be built above this ontology. Such TM visualizes the discipline terminology, what helps students to understand the structure of the studied discipline. Together with the discipline ontology, used for subject categorization of resources, it is possible to apply a kind of e-course ontology for arranging units and elements that together form the e-course content. Through associations in TM teacher can define the recommended order of resources (presentations, documents, exercises etc.) to be studied as well as he does it in the e-course's study content module of today's VSE. Also all other parts of the e-course (students' agenda, evaluation tools, communication tools), can be integrated into the TM application through occurrence elements. All these integrations are motivated by the effort to unify access mechanisms to information.

Reusable domain ontologies are available in web libraries of ontologies, e.g. [4],[15],[23],[25],[15] etc.

5   Pilot Study

For demonstration of our proposed solution, we developed a pilot TM application that captures different information and knowledge resources of the University of Hradec Kralove, Czech Republic, and especially materials related to courses of artificial intelligence (AI) that are taught at the Faculty of Informatics and Management and that already are supported by numerous study materials, digital as well as non-digital. The pilot application operates with three ontologies:

- o The *general ontology* describes information and knowledge resources of the educational and research institution. It helps to incorporate various organizational information that are published on university website, in e-zines of faculties or through different applications (scheduling system, student agenda system) into the single TM application. Also information about staff can be involved, e.g. about research activities of academics, projects in run, upcoming conferences organized by the university.
- o The *course ontology* of concepts and relations from the education area, e.g. instructional theory, psychology etc., forms the backbone of courses' structure captured in TM application. It contains information about study resources, recommended order of courses, suitability of resources with respect to study styles and preferences.
- o The *discipline* ontology of concepts and relations from domain that is studied in particular course that of AI is, in our case, derived from the ACM Computer Classification Schema, where themes, subthemes and descriptors relevant to AI are organized in the tree structure. Subject based categorization of study materials, based on ontology, brings different advantages, e.g. it helps students to internalize the terminology of studied domain during navigating and browsing study resources. The application of the part of the ACM schema means that our TM can be potentially merged with TM built above other parts of ACM schema, so there is a way how to integrate all study materials delivered to students of computer science study programmes.

Following three snapshots illustrate how our pilot application looks like and what types of information can be captured in it. All snapshots come from freeware version of Ontopia Omnigator TM software [19] where our TM application was loaded.

The first snapshot (Fig. 1) shows the page of topic "Agent", corresponding to one of fundamental terms of AI. The associations "ACM CSS category", "Has subcategory" and "Is element of" explain the position of the topic in the ACM CCS

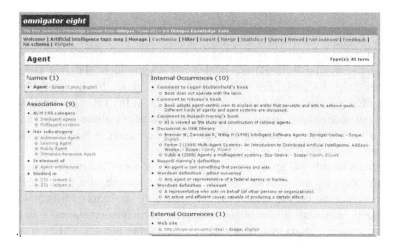

Fig. 1. Snapshot of the topic page "Agent"

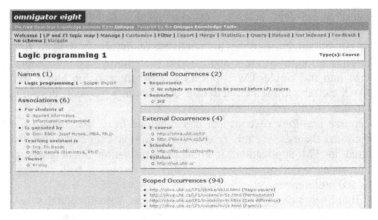

Fig. 2. Snapshot of the topic page "Logic programming 1"

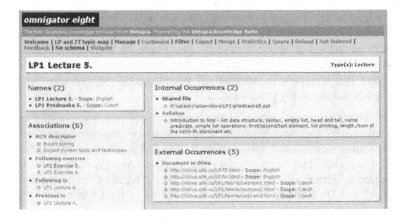

Fig. 3. Snapshot of the topic page "Lecture 5 in LP1 course"

and its relation to other close topics. The course association "Studied in" shows what courses (and particular lectures) are related to "Agent" topic. Internal and external occurrences refer to topic resources: information about books available in the university library, hyperlinks to online web resources, string value information – here, quotations of definitions from the WordNet lexical database [31]. The scopes assigned to occurrences are used to distinguish the languages of resources, knowledge level (expert, beginners), user group (student, teacher).

The second snapshot (Fig. 2) presents the page of topic "Logic programming 1". This page contains information about particular course, i.e. its name, study programmes, names of the guarantee and teaching assistants, prerequisites and recommended semester, list of different kinds of online resources – scheduling application, student agenda system, available e-courses in WebCT VSE).

The last snapshot (Fig. 3) presents the topic page "Lecture 5 in LP1 course", that contains brief syllabus of the lecture, note about location of PowerPoint presentation file stored in shared folders (direct addressing was not possible from our TM browser), hyperlinks to html-pages stored on the WebCT VSE server, where traditional e-courses are provided, hyperlinks to topic pages of previous and following lectures and exercises where content of current lecture is reused etc.

6 Conclusion

In the paper we offered the Topic Maps application designed for the area of university education. Our solution helps to integrate information and knowledge resources of the university and can be understood as the core of the semantic web-based virtual study environments. We suggest using the TM application for covering all digital and non-digital information and knowledge resources, from e-courses over paper resources stored in university libraries towards human experts.

The proposed TM solution is currently in the phase of a pilot study. Its full implementation would be accompanied with numerous obstacles, mainly:

o the need of subject description of all elder documents and resources,
o the need of methodologies for description of all documents created in future,
o the need to capture areas of expertise of academics,
o the problem of updating and maintaining TM after changes in study programmes, organizational practices etc.,
o the lack of trust and motivation of potential users, mainly academics, to work with the TM application and to participate on its construction.

When thinking about our TM application, we have to think also about the position of knowledge engineers in the organizational structure of the university, about adaptation of suitable educational metadata standards etc. For more about the proposed application, see [18].

To be exhaustive, the presented idea is not exceptional: particular aspects of educational applicability of TM already were and are explored, see e.g. [5],[6],[9],[22]. The next development of TM standards will open new possibilities how to expand our idea in different directions.

Acknowledgement

This contribution was supported by KNOMEDIAS, GACR project No. 406/04/2140.

References

1. Baets, W. (ed): Knowledge Management and Maangement of Learning: Extending the Horizons of Knowledge-Based Management, Springers's Integrated Series in Information Systems, Springer Science+Business Media, Inc. (2005)
2. Blackboard website. http://www.blackboard.com (2005)
3. Brown, J.S.: Growing up digital – How the Web Changes Work, Education, and the Ways People Learn. Change, 4 (2000) 10-20
4. DAML Ontology Library website. http://www.daml.org/ontologies/ (2005)

5. Dichev, C., Dicheva, D., Aroyo, L.: Using Topic Maps for Web-based Education, Int. J. of Advanced Technology for Learning, 1 (2004) 1-7

6. EduNuggets website. http://www.cs.ualberta.ca/~stroulia/EduNuggets/ (2005)

7. FirstClass website. http://www.firstclass.com (2005)

8. Kaplan-Lieserson, E.: E-Learing glossary. http://www.learningcircuits.org (2005)

9. Lavik, S., Nordeng, T.W.: BrainBank Learning - building personal topic maps as a strategy for learning, http://idealliance.org/papers/dx_xmle04/papers (2005)

10. LearningSpace website. http://www.lotus.com/home.nsf/tabs/learnspace (2005)

11. Lowerison, G., Gallant, G., Boyd, G.: Learning Objects in Distance Education: Addressing issues of Quality, Learner Control and Accessibility. http://www.cade-aced2003.ca/conference_proceedings/Gallant.pdf (2003)

12. Mikulecka, J., Mikulecky, P.: Knowledge Management in University e-Learning Activities Support. In: Proc. of the 2nd European Conference on e-Learning, Glasgow (2003) 341-346

13. Mikulecky, P., Mikulecka, J.: Knowledge Management Approaches in Higher Education Support. In: Proc. 3rd Int. Conference on Technology in Teaching and Learning in Higher Education (Spirou, C. Ed.), College of Arts and Sciences, National-Louis University, Chicago (2003) 199-203

14. Mikulecky, P., Olsevicova, K.: eCourses Contents Intelligent Management. In: Proc. of the 3rd European Conference on e-Learning, Reading (2004), 225-230

15. Milton, N.: (2002) Personal Knowlege Ontology, PhD thesis. http://www. epistemics.co.uk/staff/nmilton/ontology/ standardframe.htm (2002)

16. Nielsen, J.: Designing Web Usability. NewRiders, Canada (1999)

17. Olsevicova, K.: Development of Topic Maps e-Learning Portal. In Proc. of 4th European Conference on e-Learning, Amsterdam (2005), 333-340

18. Olsevicova, K.: Knowledge management in Virtual Study environments. PhD dissertation, Faculty of Informatics and Management, University of Hradec Kralove (2005)

19. Ontopia website. http://www.ontopia.net (2005)

20. Paquette, G.: Virtual Learning Centers for XXIst century Organizations. In: The Virtual Campus (Verdejo, F., Davies, G. eds.), Athenaeum Press Ltd., UK (1998)

21. Paulsen, M.F.: Online Education Systems: Discussion and Definition of Terms. http://www.nettskolen.com (2002)

22. Project NSDL website. http://www.wssu.edu/iis/nsdl/index.html (2005)

23. Protégé-2000 website. http://protege.stanford.edu (2005)

24. Rochowiak, D.: Ontologies for Education: Templates for intersecting interests. http://isl-garnet.uah.edu/dmr/ontodoc.pdf (2003)

25. Schemaweb SchemaWeb website. http://www.schemaweb.info (2005)

26. Shang, Y., Shi, H., Chen, S.: An Intelligent Distributed Environment for Active Learning. In: Proceedings of the tenth international conference on World Wide Web, Hong Kong (2001) 308-315.

27. Stauffer, K.: Student Modeling and Web-based Learning Systems. http://ccism.pc.athabascau.ca/html/ccism/research/initsm.htm (1996)

28. The eLearning Action Plan. http://europa.eu.int/eur-lex/en/com/cnc/ (2001)

29. TopClass website. http://www.wbtsystems.com (2005)

30. WebCT website. http://www.webct.com (2005)

31. WorNet website. http://wordnet.princeton.edu/ (2005)

Collaborative Software Development and Topic Maps

Markus Ueberall and Oswald Drobnik

Telematics Group, Institute of Computer Science,
Johann-Wolfgang-Goethe University,
D-60054 Frankfurt/Main, Germany
{ueberall, drobnik}@tm.informatik.uni-frankfurt.de

Abstract. This work-in-progress report subsumes our ongoing research to develop a Topic Maps centric, modularised system which supports collaborative software development by combining the merits of Topic Maps for representation, the Semantic Zooming paradigm for navigation/visualisation, and a generic process model for development process steering.

1 Motivation and Objective

The consistent transfer of semantics of requirements from the initial requirements analysis phase to concepts and models used in subsequent development phases is a major problem in software development [6,11].

As far as *collaborative* software development is concerned, communication between, e.g., stakeholders, designers and programmers may be complicated due to different individual viewpoints, interests, and domain knowledge. Phase-related conceptualisation as shown in Fig. 1 may help to organise and mediate their discussions: Conceptual graphs are useful to represent domain knowledge, UML-based diagrams model designs of software components and their interactions, and annotated Java classes may be used to describe classes and interfaces on source level.

Our group has been working with a form of conceptual graphs in conjunction with a collaborative learning environment named CLE [16,17]. So-called "concept graphs" with a fixed, restricted taxonomy of types for concepts and relations proved to be usedul in representing the contents of scientific texts, which had to be evaluated by students during seminars. Starting from individually built concept graphs, groups of students successively developed a joint concept graph representing a common, agreed-on understanding of the texts. CLE supports this task by means of a three-dimensional visualisation interface and a process model.

The experiences gained encouraged us to consider the use of such a tool for collaborative software development as well. In this context, Topic Maps seem to be well-suited for several reasons: E.g., they are lightweight, easy to extend and manipulate, and therefore adequate to represent conceptualisations in

L. Maicher and J. Park (Eds.): TMRA 2005, LNAI 3873, pp. 169–176, 2006.

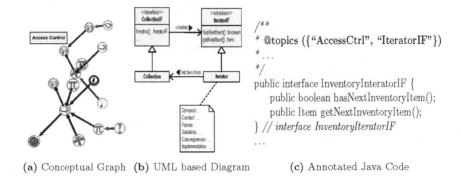

(a) Conceptual Graph (b) UML based Diagram   (c) Annotated Java Code

Fig. 1. Schematic depiction of exemplary phase-related conceptualisations with connected concepts from different development phases

different software development phases. In case that a critical mass of phase-related conceptualisations is either created using Topic Maps based representations in the first place or can be reproduced using Topic Maps, existing, probably isolated development subprocesses may be integrated into a single coherent software development workflow. In this way, the collaboration of stakeholders, designers, and programmers can be improved, which, e.g., results in better documentation.

2   Development Phases and Modelling

Our starting point is illustrated by a simplified scenario from object-oriented development as shown in Fig. 2. During requirements analysis, functional and non-functional requirements are specified by means of concept graphs, possibly reflecting different stakeholder viewpoints. The resulting concepts and relationships must then be mapped to specifications during the design phase. Finally, during the implementation phase, another mapping has to be carried out, in this case (ideally) incorporating given definitions of design patterns. In a sense, development phases hence correspond to different abstraction levels and mappings between them, respectively their concepts.

It is proposed to use a predetermined set of types for concepts (e.g., "question", "problem", "definition", "example") and relationships (e.g., "references", "supports", "contradicts") in order to reduce the complexity of conceptualisations during the requirements analysis phase. Initially, concept graphs are used, because they are very flexible regarding the modelling of concepts and relationships and can easily be annotated. Annotations serve different purposes here, e.g., stakeholders may provide additional details about their viewpoints in a format most convenient to them. Therefore, it is possible to quickly build a coarse-grained overview of relevant topics.

During the design phase, a software architecture has to be developed, e.g., as a set of interacting components, addressing all the concepts and relationships from

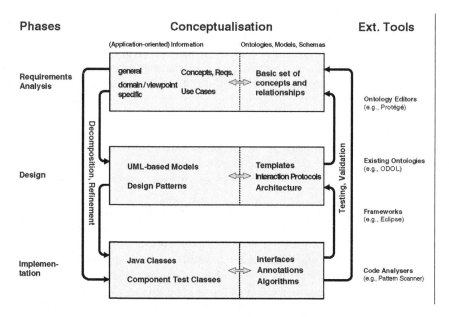

Fig. 2. Simplified view of development phases, related conceptualisations and tools (grey arrows mark interactions of modelling primitives and conceptualisation needs)

the requirements analysis phase. Despite their deficiencies, especially regarding the problem of modelling architectures, we currently see no equivalent alternative to UML based models and schemas during the design phase as they are the *de facto* standard for system modeling (note that we are talking about *conceptualisation* and not *internal representation* here, which is entirely Topic Maps based). However, in order to overcome their rather weak expressiveness, i.e., the lack of means to either model information flow or links to requirements within structured class diagrams, they need to be supplemented by additional sets of templates and constraints which are directly linked to concepts used during adjacent phases of development. Related annotations have to be transformed into a structured format (cf. Fig. 1) from which verifiable assertions or constraints may be derived. In this context, design pattern ontologies may be favourably used.

Eventually, the derived UML based models, combined with models of design patterns and programming language-dependant templates (code fragments), form the basis of semi-automatically generated Java class and interface skeletons used during the implementation phase. On source level, it is essential to be able to map these individual skeletons to corresponding concepts from previous stages of development. This task can be accomplished by means of the recently introduced annotation feature of Java5 [14], which allows to use custom Javadoc comments defining additional semantics that can be interpreted both at compilation and run time. Anchoring topic ids in this way is necessary for true round-trip engineering–that is, any modification of either relevant code fragments or concepts has an immediate, traceable effect on associcated "artefacts" [13]. E.g., either the "iterator" interface or class in Fig. 1 is the result of a refinement after the first concept has been associated with the "access control problem" which is part of the concept graph on the left. Therefore, subsequent elements in the UML diagram as well as derived implementations of this design pattern as shown on the right will automatically inherit this association.

In general, development phases often have to be iterated, enforcing redefinitions of concepts. Hence, the possibility to track individual changes is a crucial requirement–especially in the context of collaborative software development. Advanced version management methodologies offer a solution to this problem by supporting the management of links between different versions of concepts and relationships [7].

In our opinion, the resulting strong interrelation between concepts and the evolutionary changes can be best expressed by means of Topic Maps, incorporating a set of predetermined, possibly domain-specific upper ontologies [12], representable in terms of PSIs. E.g., versioning of relationships between concepts can easily be achieved by means of occurrences and reification as shown in Fig. 3. In order to annotate relationships in the same way as topics, they are automatically reified at first (a). Whenever relations or their associated concepts change, superseded sets of related occurrences can be marked accordingly using a single association (b).

The forementioned aspects will obviously lead to fairly complex Topic Maps, conceivable as process-based, versionised indexes of all involved concepts, referenced resources, etc. Consequently, all mappings have to preserve semantics [5] in order to support navigation within and visualisation of the sets of concepts and relationships.

Either the (unfinished) TMCL [9] or functionally equivalent implementations like XTche [8] can be used to verify the preservation of semantics if assertions and constraints can be expressed through adequate typing and querying of topics and relationships. However, conformance tests regarding non-functional requirements, e.g., a guaranteed response time of application components, may require additional treatments.

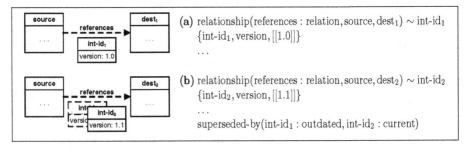

Fig. 3. Versioning of relationships between concepts by means of topic maps (expressed in LTM notation, cf. [4])

3   Underlying Process Model

In order to preserve semantics of conceptualisations throughout all development phases, a process model is needed to organise the evolution of all concepts and relationships in a semantic and constituent way. In Fig. 4, a generic model emphasising collaboration of stakeholders, designers and programmers is outlined, which can be adapted to different development phases. It consists of several intertwined subprocesses for identifying objectives, developing corresponding conceptualisations, and comparing and integrating both individual and joint conceptualisations and their objectives.

Finally, additional iterations of subprocesses are necessary if inconsistencies between conceptualisations or objectives are detected. Such inconsistencies have to be resolved immediately, e.g., by applying techniques as discussed in [15].

Note that, dependent on the role a participant holds, he may not be able to partake actively in all subprocesses. E.g., while programmers should write tests for their own code, it is often required that a team has dedicated testers (ideally, at least one for every two or three programmers) which are solely responsible for the actual code reviews–without their approval, further modifications of (parts of) the code may be blocked.

By use of Topic Maps, both roles and process steps are expandable if all participants agree with modifications. In this context, dynamic loadable Java classes seem to be predestined to add necessary business logic, although they cannot be modified as easily as Topic Maps (Fig. 5).

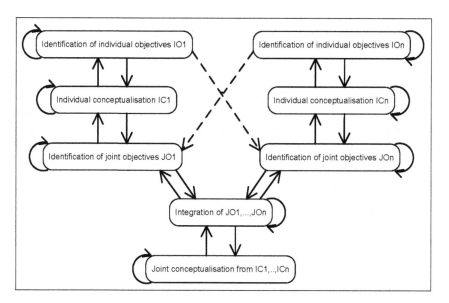

Fig. 4. Overview of the generic process model: Forward and backward transitions represent refinements, validations and verifications between the subprocesses, respectively, while dashed lines highlight additional information flows between participants

```
[role = "Role"]
[stakeholder : role = "Stakeholder" @ "http://.../roles/stakeholder.xml"]
...
[subprocess = "Subprocess"]
[validation : subprocess = "Validation" @ "http://.../subprocesses/validation.xml"]
...
[actions₁ : jar = "..." % "http://.../actions/stakeholder-validation.jar"]
assoc-business-logic(stakeholder : role, validation : subprocess, actions₁ : jar)
...
```

Fig. 5. Simplified definition of subprocesses and roles: Concepts are associated with application-specific business logic by means of dynamically loadable Java classes

4   Visualisation of Conceptualisations

The forementioned process model has to be combined with appropriate visualisation paradigms in order to deal with the complexity of resulting conceptualisations and their associated metadata, e.g., stemming from versioning.

Recall that development phases may be conceived as different abstraction levels of, e.g., viewpoint descriptions. Navigation within this information space can basically be performed in two ways: by filtering and by zooming. In our setting, *semantic zooming* is far more important to orientation than geometric zooming. The former differs from the latter in that eyed objects do not simply change their size, but also their visual appearance, e.g., a document associated with a concept could gradually be visualised by its abstract and a list of keywords. Particularly, the combination of semantic zooming and filtering, i.e., focusing on relevant information, would allow stakeholders to concentrate on their own viewpoints and related constraints when tracing the different development phases.

Topic Maps offer a convenient way to link different abstractions to a concept as well. Both the Topic Map specific scope operator [10] and reification (as demonstrated in Fig. 3) are powerful means to annotate concepts with attributes that can be used for context-based filtering, e.g., based on query languages such as the TMQL which allow for selection of all concepts satisfying given criteria. These attributes have to be provided manually or may be derived semi-automatically applying information retrieval methods on available annotations and linked resources (e.g., individual text documents could automatically be summarised or annotated with keywords).

Graph-based navigation support requires map-specific metadata. Therefore, we investigate possibilities to implement computer-supported semantic zooming operations for a predetermined set of Topic Maps using so-called "hints", i.e., definitions (PSIs) that specify parameters controlling shape and layout, which can be modified like any other concept. In order to use, e.g., different layout algorithms, dynamic loadable Java classes encapsulating additional application logic can be integrated in the same way as demonstrated in Fig. 5. However, as seen from Fig. 1, the use of varying visualisations for different levels of abstraction does require a certain extent of familiarisation.

5   Summary and Outlook

Both the presented modelling approach and the process model are generic and can be expanded. Therefore, development phases and roles can be easily refined and adapted which is necessary in the case of large development projects [1,6]. Likewise, context specific visualisations can be added, so that our approach can be used in other domains as well: E.g., a possible application that suggests itself would be a Topic Map editor. Our process model enforces the review and modification of inconsistent conceptualisations [15], which is an important step towards round-trip engineering [13].

At present, we aim at the integration of existing tools for maintenance of upper ontologies [12] as addressed in Fig. 2 (cf. the right side of each box). Here, OWL based tools are also of interest as a number of mappings between Topic Maps and OWL(-DL) are recently being investigated [2,18] and existing ontologies like ODOL and its associated design pattern matcher [3] seem to fit well into our setting.

In order to provide a proof-of-concept of our approach, we are currently prototyping an Eclipse plugin. In this context, the forementioned matcher may be integrated in order to compare design pattern signatures within the source code with generated annotations derived from previous development phases.

References

1. Broy, M., Rausch, A.: Das neue V-Modell® XT. In: Informatik-Spektrum **28** (3) 220–229. Springer (2005), http://www.springerlink.com/link.asp?id= 1173638386334305
2. Cregan, A.: Building Topic Maps in OWL-DL. Proc. Extreme Markup Languages (2005), http://www.mulberrytech.com/Extreme/Proceedings/xslfo-pdf/2005/ Cregan01/EML2005Cregan01.pdf
3. Dietrich, J., Elgar, C.: A Formal Description of Design Patterns Using OWL. Proc. Australian Software Engineering Conference (2005) 243–250, http://csdl. computer.org/comp/proceedings/aswec/2005/2257/00/22570243abs.htm
4. Garshol, L. M.: The Linear Topic Map Notation: Definition and introduction, version 1.3 (revision 1.21, 2005/09/18), http://www.ontopia.net/download/ ltm.html
5. Harel, D., Rumpe, B.: Meaningful Modeling: What's the Semantics of "Semantics"? In: Computer, **37** (10) 64–72. IEEE (2004), http://www.wisdom.weizmann. ac.il/~dharel/papers/ModSemantics.pdf
6. IEEE Guide to the Software Engineering Body of Knowledge, 2004 Version. ISBN 0-7695-2330-7, http://www.swebok.org/ironman/pdf/SWEBOK_Guide_2004.pdf
7. Kimber, E., Newcomb, S., Newcomb, P.: Version Management as Hypertext Applications: Referent Tracking Documents. Proc. Markup Technologies (1999), http://www.coolheads.com/SRNPUBS/ref-track-docs-paper.pdf
8. Librelotto, G., Ramalho, J., Henriquez, P.: XTche - A Language for Topic Maps Schema and Constraints. Proc. XML (2004), http://www.idealliance.org/ proceedings/xml04/abstracts/paper114.html

9. Moore, G., Nishikawa, M, Bogachev, D.: Topic Map Constraint Language (TMCL) Requirements and Use Cases. Editors Draft (2004/10/16), http://www.isotopic maps.org/tmcl/

10. Pepper, S., Grønmo, G.: Towards a General Theory of Scope. Proc. Extreme Markup Languages (2001), http://www.ontopia.net/topicmaps/materials/scope.htm

11. Sommerville, I.: Software Engineering, 7th edition. Pearson Education (2004), ISBN 0-321-21026-3, http://www.comp.lancs.ac.uk/research/books.html

12. Stuckenschmidt, H., van Harmelen, F.: Information Sharing on the Semantic Web. Springer (2005), ISBN 3-540-20594-2

13. Sendall, S., Küster, J.: Taming Model Round-Trip Engineering. Position Paper, Model-Driven Software Development Workshop, OOPSLA (2004), http://www.softmetaware.com/oopsla2004/sendall.pdf

14. Sun Microsystems, Inc.: Library support for the Java programming language annotation facility, http://java.sun.com/j2se/1.5.0/docs/guide/language/annotations.html

15. Spanoudakis, G., Zisman, A.: Inconsistency Management in Software Engineering: Survey and Open Research Issues. In: Chang, S. (ed.), Handbook of Software Engineering and Knowledge Engineering. World Scientific (2001), ISBN 981-02-4973, http://www.soi.city.ac.uk/~gespan/hseke01.pdf

16. Ueberall, M., Horvath, O., Pendo, A., Drobnik, O.: CLE: A constructivist collaborative learning environment prototype. Unpublished working draft (2002), http://www.tm.informatik.uni-frankfurt.de/~ueberall/cle-uwd.pdf

17. Ueberall, M., Lauer, M., Drobnik, O.: CLE: Eine konstruktivist., kollaborative Lernumgebung. Proc. 1. e-Learning Fachtg. Informatik (DeLFI 2003). Köllen Lecture Notes in Informatics (LNI), P-37 321–330

18. Vatant, B.: Ontology-Driven Topic Maps. Proc. XML Europe (2004), http://www.idealliance.org/europe/04/call/xmlpapers/03-03-03.91/.03-03-03.html

Topic Maps for European Administrative Nomenclature

Gabriel Hopmans[1], Peter-Paul Kruijsen[1], Leon Oud[2], Jelte Verhoeff[2],
Marc Wilhelm Küster[3], and John Clews[4]

[1] Morpheus Software, P.O. Box 240, 6200 AE Maastricht, The Netherlands
{G.Hopmans, P.Kruijsen}@mssm.nl
http://www.mssm.nl
[2] Conclusion, P.O. Box 85030, 3508 AA Utrecht, The Netherlands
{loud, jverhoeff}@conclusion.nl
http://www.conclusion.nl
[3] FH Worms - University of Applied Sciences, Fachbereich Informatik/Telekommunikation,
Erenburgerstraße 19 * D-67549 Worms
kuester@Fh-Worms.de
[4] Keytempo Limited, 8 Avenue Rd, Harrogate, HG2 7PG, United Kingdom
adnomist@uk2.net

Abstract. This work-in-progress report describes the requirements for a
"European Administrative Nomenclature" network. It addresses the research
topic of interoperability between UN and EU reference classifications, Topic
Maps, ebXML Registries and distributed databases. Governmental organisations in Europe will be supported in their administrative terminology with the
help of a Seamless Core Model, Published Subjects and TMRAP.

1 Introduction

Increasingly, mobile European citizens need to interact with national administrations,
and the services that they provide, in several countries (citizen to government, C2G).
European administrations need to exchange information between each other
(government to government, G2G). Differences between national administrations,
their nomenclature, terminology, structures, and centralised information islands
approaches make this difficult. These problems will be addressed with the help of
Topic Maps within ADNOM [1] (Administrative Nomenclature), a project (or so
called Workshop) funded by the European Commission's DG Enterprise through
funding available for standardization activities in the framework of eEurope 2005 and
is overseen by CEN, one of three European ICT standards organizations (the others
being CENELEC and ETSI) from May to February 2006.

The aim of the Workshop ADNOM is to deliver a Workshop agreement, to
establish and maintain a network between European government translation units,
terminology organizations, etc. with the purpose of developing and disseminating
European *Administrative Nomenclature*, built as far as possible on the basis of
existing networks and resources.

L. Maicher and J. Park (Eds.): TMRA 2005, LNAI 3873, pp. 177–182, 2006.

The prototype ADNOM (Administrative Nomenclature) network, a pan-European semantic resource to increase interoperability in applications and in terminological activities in governmental institutions is planned to be in place by the begin of 2006: this will provide relevant information to citizens on European and national administrations, in many European languages. ADNOM is a small size project and the goal is to make it a long-term network. ADNOM uses Topic Maps and Published Subjects to enable governmental specialists working in eGovernment, terminology and information management to manage the concepts and update the content.

Defining mappings between existing resources, designing cross-lingual resources and guaranteeing reliable distributed knowledge exchange is where a Topic Maps approach will solve several problems. Related work has been done in the SNS project [2] but in this project the advantage of Published Subjects has not been utilized. Published Subjects [3] are a method of establishing semantic identity using URIs in an open, democratic, bottom-up, and distributed process. Standards Norway provides the ADNOM Secretariat. For information on participation contact the Secretary Håvard Hjulstad, who is also chair of ISO TC37 "Terminology and language and content resources" or see [1].

First we will explain the need for ADNOM's suspected outcome in the working field of Terminology and which resources are already available so that the approaches in the project can be introduced. The requirements that we list here will give the reader an idea why this is a classic application for topic maps. Then we will go deeper into how a topic maps based, cross-border approach to administration can help in establishing terminological interoperability. The last subsection will give insight in how large the impact of ADNOM might be on all Topic Maps activities in Europe.

2 ADNOM Approaches

Persons working at Governmental organisations in Europe need an administrative nomenclature serving relevant terminology, listing terms with detailed information and explanation. Ideally they should be supported by an interactive system (component c, see later), enabling them to identify terms, make a list of designations, excerpts terms, reduce differences between concepts, harmonise them and process them. ADNOM reuses existing resources and takes a faceted approach with topics like: Governmental function (e.g. Defence, Police, Finance, etc), Jurisdictions (Countries), Organization types (e.g. Parliament, Ministry, Agency). For these, widely used UN [4] and EU reference classifications like Classification of Outlays by Functions of Government, European Nomenclatures (COFOG) [5], Nomenclature of Units for Territorial Statistics (NUTS) [6] are used and it will also build on EUROVOC, AGROVOC and GEMET Topic Maps from the European Parliament Thesaurus available at [7].

ADNOM will provide and integrate the following components with topic maps:

a) a concise guide to typical government activities in terminology across Europe, part of the standard-type document (a CEN Workshop Agreement)

b) content on specific government activities in specific countries in this field. (which organisation types, names do we find in a country, which standards, which terminologies do they use, which functions, which languages)

c) an interactive system for handling topics, terms, codes and content

d) a meta-terminology for European Administrative Nomenclature
e) an active registry and repository functionality for the meta-terminology
f) a long-term network of translators, terminologists, and systems providers

Within ADNOM a lot of principal facets based on existing codes are reused (see [8] and [9]) and it has been recognised which impact facets can have on the power and usability of knowledge resources. The faceted classification as described in Garshol [10] has been followed within ADNOM to cross boundaries between systems and connect terms in a subject-based fashion. The paradigm for the power of facets is described as "Busch's golden law of facets." This states that (in an idealized world) "four facets of 10 nodes each have the same discriminatory power as one taxonomy of 10,000 nodes." (a) faceted navigation helps content owners, as faceted organization enables content owners to streamline their information management processes, and (b) faceted navigation helps users more easily find what they're looking for. The human-computer-interaction (HCI) community correctly suggests that facetted classification doesn't necessarily solve all the problems but with Topic Maps the user can navigate subject based over multiple existing faceted classifications. These advantages will be at the heart of human knowledge organization in ADNOM, and will be reflected in the way that the project develops the semantic infrastructure, knowledge resources, and meets the needs of users.

Topic Maps will allow ADNOM participants to integrate different ontologies, classifications, thesauri, and store terminologies in a language-independent way. A phased expansion of ADNOM to provide information in national languages of all EU countries (including candidate countries) and EFTA countries is planned. Using Published Subjects in combination with a distributed database will allow both humans and computerized systems to make use of the knowledge condensed and integrated in Topic Maps from the multitude of terminology efforts across Europe. For Published Subjects Identifiers (PSIs), ADNOM is using and extending OASIS PSI sets (http://psi.oasis-open.org), which currently consist of country codes (ISO 3166) and language codes (ISO 639-1 and ISO 639-2).

The following two components are at the core of ADNOM: (c) an interactive system for handling topics, terms, codes and content and (d) a meta-terminology for European Administrative Nomenclature. This core has been defined as the ADNOM Seamless Knowledge Core (SKC) Model. For the construction of this model a methodology to disambiguate terms and concepts will be followed and this model can be mapped to the Topic Maps Data model quite easily. For the analysis of the methodology the ADNOM project team has followed the steps used in ISO/CD 860.2 (ISO/TC 37 SC 1 N 276): Terminology work - harmonization of concepts and designations. This means to start at the concept level and continue at the designation level, to identify in a feasibility study differences and similarities between concept systems (including contexts), to analyze the context and characteristics of the concept systems, in our case the proposed ADNOM (meta-) nomenclature), containing the material from the then harmonized sources. The comparative analysis of the different concept systems that one has to take into account is really close in how one develops the Topic Maps ontology; one has to identify the relationships between concepts (associations or occurrences); distinguish between the symbol and the thing that refers to it (topics or subjects); think about the depth of structuring; the types of characteris tics used to develop the concept system; and the criteria of subdivision used to develop the concepts.

3 Terminological Interoperability in ADNOM with Topic Maps

When comparing terms with terminological dictionaries one is functionally speaking working knowledge oriented. He uses description of subject fields where one needs to work with terminological entries. These terminological entries are identified by a concept and normally codes or numbers are used for this. For these entries ADNOM defined Published Subjects. It has been recognized that COFOG acts as a high-level structure where the other concept systems (EUROVOC, NACE, NUTS) can be inserted in their appropriate place in the harmonized concept system, forming an overall ADNOM nomenclature. Topic Maps and Published Subjects act as flexible binding points between all these systems. We use a Published Subject Identifier for one term in one system and when one needs to use it on another system we can use the Topic Maps Remote Access Protocol (TMRAP) [13] or merge Topic Maps.

Only adopting a system like NUTS is not sufficient enough within ADNOM since it will break in what we call the Seamless Knowledge principle. This principle is that one can make a statement and use an indicator without being forced to stick to one hierarchy or one subject within too many boundaries, the user must be able to choose or publish flexible and bottom up. For example a user working with NUTS will quickly face the problem with different systems of internal boundaries where, e.g., say Croatia has no regional division. This example applies cross-domains in much of eGovernment. ADNOM will ensure that it is flexible enough to accommodate these differences in the concept systems within the administrative domain, and one important step towards achieving this goal – namely to allow for cultural differences rather than making a country fit a model – goes via the use of topic maps. With the ADNOM approach using topic maps will fit the concepts and terms, rather than concepts and terms being forced to fit the model, the past problem within administration.

An Administration Module that is running on the Ontopia Knowledge Suite (OKS) will maintain the ADNOM core topic maps. ADNOM terminologists will firm up in additional concepts in these existing European codes, and deal with the maintenance of these, both during the project, and in its long-term phase after the initial phase.

Figure 1 shows an example how a user within ADNOM can connect several terms with fragments of facets for functions, jurisdictions, organs and the role of Published Subjects and Topic Maps. The example will be motivated next, just note the hierarchies for the faceted classifications in the upper part. For most hierarchical relations ADNOM will use the PSI's available at [11]. Multiple hierarchies used in different systems and maintained between several organisations can be navigated seamlessly. For the organisations it becomes possible to integrate their Web-portals since their content is partly and becomes completely subject based. The concept "Parliament" appears here in two hierarchies: in the Administrative functions hierarchy and in the Government hierarchy (in the lower part of the figure) defined by ISO 860 CD2 Terminology work - Harmonization of concepts and terms. ADNOM will also implement some parts of the meta-model from the Terminology Markup Framework of ISO 16642:2003 to express structural organisation of meta-model, to specify data categories and how they relate to meta-model and to indicate which vocabularies are used.

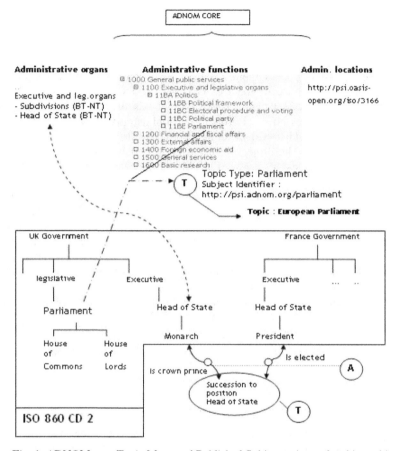

Fig. 1. ADNOM core Topic Maps and Published Subject to interrelate hierarchies

The hierarchies for UK and France are connected to the ADNOM levels with Published Subjects. The lower part illustrates how one can make assertions between hierarchies. In this example we wish to designate or represent a term "Succeed" to assert the succession of the position "Head of State" and how to become one. The ADNOM functionalities will enable organisations to publish their terminology work on-demand; they can make statements around subjects with their point of view, terms that organisations need to share can be published with functionalities that have similarities with RSS news feeds like TMRAP [13]. In the ADNOM nomenclature we have for instance the identifiers http://psi.adnom.org/code/a11BA for the term "Politics" and we convert this same identifier when doing upconversion of the EUROVOC thesaurus where "Politics" appears as well to connect the systems.

Different assertions about concepts and terms can be made by several terminologists and can be selected from the PSI sets in the distributed repository. Reaching group consensus on the published concepts is then for next stages in which increasingly more and more stable and trustworthy PSI sets will be developed for European Administrative Nomenclature.

4 Conclusion and Further Work

Using Topic Maps and a faceted approach for existing classifications, thesauri, and vocabularies enables the users in the ADNOM project to identify their own terms and to harmonise, list and process them for their own activities. By reusing reliable existing resources like those of the COFOG and NUTS nomenclatures, ADNOM already can list terms in 23 languages (see part of this list at [8]. For registry and repository functionalities for European Administrative Nomenclature, the effectiveness of Topic Maps will be combined with other approaches such as the ebXML registry service. The project results with ebXML will be compared with the Topic Maps Remote Access Protocol (TMRAP). Organizations willing to exchange knowledge and that are using Published Subjects will be able to get information from remote repositories of those other organizations automatically. First efforts in the ADNOM workshop need to show how TMRAP/ebXML services will fuse in the architecture. These technologies will probably prove to be orthogonal approaches.

In ADNOM Terminologists will be able to make concept-oriented equivalences like presented in [12]. Nowadays there are over 50 nationally recognised languages in the EU with historical, cultural and legal differences among the various states and regions. CEN emphasises the importance of a long-term project undertaking to link government nomenclatures and terminologies throughout the EU. Input into ISO, W3C and OASIS standards are also planned. ADNOM's influence may also be felt in eGovernment circles during the EU presidencies of the UK (2005) and Austria (2006), and long-term development of ADNOM after that is also planned.

References

1. CEN/ISSS ADNOM Workshop http://www.cenorm.be/isss/ADNOM/
2. Bandholtz, T. : Final Report Implementation of a Semantic Network Service (SNS) in the context of the German Environmental Information Network; 2003, http://www.semantic-network.de/sns-summary-2003-06-06.pdf
3. OASIS Published Subjects Technical Committee Recommendation http://www.oasis-open.org/committees/download.php/3050/pubsubj-pt1-1.02-cs.pdf
4. United Nations Nomenclatures http://unstats.un.org/unsd/cr/registry/regcst.asp?Cl=4
5. European Nomenclatures, http://europa.eu.int/comm/eurostat/ramon/
6. NUTS, http://europa.eu.int/comm/eurostat/ramon/nuts/home_regions_en.html
7. European Parliament's "Interoperability Forum" multi-lingual thesauri, http://www1.europarl.eu.int/forum/interop/dispatch.cgi/sw_km_lib
8. ADNOM COFOG coded nomenclature, codes edited by John Clews and information about Terminology and Nomenclature conference available at http://mssm.nl/materials/adnom/
9. ADNOM Seamless Knowledge Core Model, http://www.adnom.org/adnom-skc/
10. Garshol, L.M. : Metadata? Thesauri? Taxonomies? TopicMaps! Making Sense of it all; 2004, Paper available at: http://www.ontopia.net/topicmaps/materials/tm-vs-thesauri.html
11. Ahmed, K. : Topic Map Design Patterns For Information Architecture, XML 2003; 2003, Paper available at http://www.techquila.com/tmsinia3.html
12. Wright, S.E. : The basic principles of Terminology Management, Open Forum 2005 on Metadata registries; 2005, Paper available at http://www.berlinopenforum.de/
13. Garshol, L. M. : TMRAP - Topic Maps Remote Access Protocol; 2006, In Proceedings of TMRA'05, LNCS, Springer

tolog – A Topic Maps Query Language

Lars Marius Garshol

Ontopia AS, Oslo, Norway
larsga@ontopia.net
http://www.ontopia.net

Abstract. This paper describes a query algebra for tolog, a query language for Topic Maps inspired by Prolog and very similar to Datalog. The language is based on binding variables by matching predicates against the topic map being queried, and contains predicates for querying any aspect of the Topic Maps Data Model (TMDM) [ISO13250-2], as well as support for user-defined predicates. SQL-like features like aggregate functions, projection, ordering, and result set paging are also supported. The paper uses a formal model for Topic Maps called Q to formally define the semantics of tolog. The standard tolog predicates are defined, together with a query algebra. This gives the query language a firm basis, enables interoperable implementations, and serves as the starting point for further work on the language.

1   Introduction

tolog is a query language for Topic Maps originally inspired by Prolog. It is much more similar to Datalog, however, in that no particular evaluation algorithm is required, there is no backtracking, the order of clauses is irrelevant, and complex terms cannot be arguments to predicates. The language supports standard Horn clauses, but also supports NOT, OR, and SQL features like projection, counting, sorting, and paging of result sets.

Predicates are of three kinds: user-defined (through predicate declarations), built-in (this includes comparison predicates as well as predicates based on TMDM), and dynamic predicates (created from occurrence and association types in the topic map).

The language has seen three independent implementations, and has been the foundation for several commercial Topic Maps applications. The language forms the core of the OKS, a commercial suite of Topic Maps tools from Ontopia, and is also implemented in TM4J, an open source Topic Maps engine. The third implementation is part of Concept Glossary Manager from Rodans [Strychowski05]. An effort has also begun to create a fourth Java implementation based on TMAPI by porting the TM4J implementation. It was also selected as the basis for the standard TMQL language to be defined by ISO.

1.1   Brief Tutorial

In order to make this paper more self-contained we give a brief tolog tutorial here. For a fuller introduction to the language, see [Garshol05b].

L. Maicher and J. Park (Eds.): TMRA 2005, LNAI 3873, pp. 183–196, 2006.

Among the simplest possible tolog queries is:

```
instance-of($C, composer)?
```

This uses the built-in predicate `instance-of`, which relates types to their instances. In this case the second argument is the topic reference `composer` and the first is the variable `$C`. The query result is all values for `$C` that make the query true, that is, all instances of the topic type composer, or, informally, all composers.

Predicates can be chained with the AND operator, syntactically represented by comma, just as in Prolog and Datalog, so the following query would also give the birthdate for each composer:

```
instance-of($C, composer), birthdate($C, $D)?
```

As the comma translates to AND it follows that any composers which have no birthdate occurrence will not be included in the query results. Likewise, people other than composers which have a birthdate are not included.

Note that the `birthdate` predicate used above is actually a *dynamic* predicate, in the sense that it's an occurrence type in the topic map that becomes a predicate in tolog. The same happens with association types, as can be seen in the query below:

```
instance-of($C, composer), born-in($C : person, $P : place)?
```

This uses the `born-in` association type to give us the birthplace of the composer. `person` and `place` are association role types.

Another useful operator is the OR operator, which can be used as follows:

```
instance-of($C, composer), born-in($C : person, $P : place),
{ located-in($P : containee, norway : container) |
  located-in($P : containee, sweden : container) }?
```

This query finds all composers born in Norway or Sweden, and the place they were born. In some cases not all variables bound by the query are wanted, and in these cases the SELECT clause can be used to project down to only the wanted variables, as in this example:

```
select $C from
  instance-of($C, composer), born-in($C : person, $P : place),
  { located-in($P : containee, norway : container) |
    located-in($P : containee, sweden : container) }?
```

In this example only the composers will be returned by the query.

Another useful operator is the NOT operator, which makes it possible to find all matches which do not satisfy a particular condition, as shown in this example, which finds all composers not born in Italy:

```
select $C from
  instance-of($C, composer), born-in($C : person, $P : place),
  not(located-in($P : containee, italy : container))?
```

In the case where birth dates are not given for all composers we may still want to display it for those which have birth date, without losing the composers who do not have any. This can be done with the OPTIONAL construct, as follows:

```
instance-of($C, composer), { birthdate($C, $D) }?
```

It's also possible to define new predicates, which can then be used in queries and also in the definition of still more predicates. This is how recursion is implemented in the language, and also how more complex queries can be written.

An example might be a predicate stating whether or not a person is Italian, which could be defined as follows:

```
italian($C) :-
  instance-of($C, person),
  born-in($C : person, $P : place),
  located-in($P : containee, italy : container).
```

This predicate can now be used to find Italian composers, all Italians, every person who is not an Italian, etc etc.

In addition, tolog supports ordering the query result, as in the query below.

```
instance-of($P, person) order by $P?
```

This would list all persons in alphabetical order. Each value type has its own ordering rules, which are used in the sorting. The **asc** and **desc** keywords can be used as in SQL. The same applies to **limit** and **offset**. So the following query:

```
instance-of($P, person) order by $P limit 5?
```

would produce only the 5 first persons (ordered alphabetically).

So far, topics have only been referenced using IDs, which map to item identifiers in TMDM. However, it is considered best practice to refer to topics using subject identifiers, which are much more stable and reliable. Using this approach we could rewrite the first example as:

```
instance-of($C, i"http://psi.ontopia.net/music/#composer")?
```

However, using topic references in this way can be difficult to read, especially when referencing occurrence and association types as predicate names. To simplify this prefix declarations can be used:

```
using music for i"http://psi.ontopia.net/music/#"
instance-of($C, music:composer)?
```

1.2 Related Work

There is quite a variety of work that is related to tolog, falling in three main categories outlined below.

Work on Prolog has been going on since the early 1970s, and is still progressing. Datalog has likewise seen extensive work since 1978, especially in the late

80s and early 90s [Liu99]. tolog is only loosely connected with these languages, in that Prolog served as the initial inspiration, and the design was later found to be very similar to that of Datalog. The query algebra given here is not related to the formal semantics of Datalog in any way.

Several other query languages have been developed for Topic Maps [N0492], such as AsTMa?, Toma, TMPath, and TMRQL [Ahmed05]. These languages are quite varied, ranging from path-based languages, through SQL-inspired languages, functional languages, and even a SQL function library. An attempt was also made to show that Topic Maps queries could be implemented with XQuery [Robie01].

Query languages have also been developed for the W3C's RDF data model, and the present version of the query language that is currently being standardized by the W3C, called SPARQL [Seaborne05], is in many ways quite similar to tolog. It does variable matching in the same way, and supports projection, AND, OPTIONAL, and OR, but does not have NOT, predicate definitions, or ordering.

The key contribution of this paper is the formal definition of tolog, rather than the query language itself. Of the query languages discussed here only SPARQL can claim to have the same, although Robie's work as well as TMRQL were of course developed using formally defined languages.

1.3   The Q Model

A formal definition of the semantics of a Topic Maps query language is impossible without a formal model of Topic Maps on which the query language can operate. This paper uses the Q model [Garshol05] as its foundation, since this is the only formal model for which there exists a defined mapping from TMDM. Given that tolog queries TMDM this was an absolute requirement.

Q represents Topic Maps as a set of five-tuples. The tuples can be thought of informally as a kind of extended RDF, with the following structure:

$$(subject, property, identity, context, object)$$

Here, *subject*, *property*, and *object* are as in RDF, *identity* is the identity of the statement, and *context* is the context in which the statement is considered true. In fact, the context is the identifier representing the set of topics making up the scope in a topic map. One difference with RDF, however, is that the values in the first four elements of a tuple can only be identifiers, which are propertyless objects used only as identifiers. Values, such as strings and URLs, are restricted to the last field.

More formally, a Q instance is a subset of $\mathcal{I} \times \mathcal{I} \times \mathcal{I} \times \mathcal{I} \times \mathcal{A}$ where $\mathcal{I}$ is the set of all identifiers (like blank nodes in RDF), $\mathcal{L}$ is the set of all values (strings etc), and $\mathcal{A} = \mathcal{L} \cup \mathcal{I}$.

In [Garshol05] a procedure for converting any TMDM instance into a Q instance is given, together with the reverse procedure, and also the same transformations for RDF models.

2   Query Algebra

This section defines a query algebra that will be used in the next section to define the tolog language semantics. To do this, it is necessary to introduce some new concepts.

A variable is a token used in a query to identify a particular unknown value in a match to the query. Variables are written as upper-case identifiers preceded by a dollar sign: $A. The set of all variables is $\mathcal{V}$.

A *match* to a query is a set of tuples, where the first element of each tuple is a variable and the second is the value the variable is bound to in that match. More formally, the set of all matches is known as $\mathcal{M}$, and defined as follows:

$$\mathcal{M} = \{m \in \mathcal{V} \times \mathcal{A} \mid \nexists k, v_1, v_2 : (k, v_1) \in m \wedge (k, v_2) \in m \wedge v_1 \neq v_2\}$$

The function $vars : \mathcal{M} \to \mathcal{V}$ is defined as:

$$vars(m) = \{k \mid \exists v : (k, v) \in m\}$$

The function $val : \mathcal{V} \to \mathcal{A}$ is defined as:

$$val(k) = \begin{cases} v & \exists v \mid (k, v) \in m \\ null & \text{otherwise} \end{cases} \tag{1}$$

In the query algebra query results are represented by *match sets*, which are sets of matches. The set of all match sets is $\mathcal{S} = 2^{\mathcal{M}}$.

2.1   Predicates

Predicates are represented in the query algebra by functions which take the Q instance representing the topic map as the first argument and an argument tuple as the second argument.

2.2   The ⊕ Operator

The ⊕ operator combines match sets and is consistent with the semantics of the AND operation. To define it we first define the concept of two matches being *compatible*. Two matches are compatible if they do not contradict each other; that is, they do not contain different values for the same variable.

Formally there is a relation $\sim$ over $\mathcal{M}$, such that:

$$m_1 \sim m_2 \Leftrightarrow \nexists k, v_1, v_2 \mid (k, v_1) \in m_1 \wedge (k, v_2) \in m_2 \wedge v_1 \neq v_2$$

The negation, $m_1 \nsim m_2$, means that the two matches are not compatible; that is, they contradict each other.

Using this concept we can define the ⊕ operator:

$$M_1 \oplus M_2 = \{m_1 \cup m_2 \mid \exists m_1 \in M_1, m_2 \in M_2 \wedge m_1 \sim m_2\}$$

2.3 The $\odot$ Operator

The $\odot$ operator combines match sets in a way that matches the semantics of the OPTIONAL operation. The formal definition is:

$$M_1 \odot M_2 = \{m_1|m_1 \in M_1 \wedge \not\exists m_2 \in M_2 : m_1 \subset m_2\} \cup$$
$$\{m_2|m_2 \in M_2 \wedge \not\exists m_1 \in M_1 : m_1 \subseteq m_2 \wedge \not\exists m_1' \in M_1 : m_1' \not\subset m_2\}$$

2.4 Projection

The $\pi : \mathcal{M} \times 2^{\mathcal{V}} \to \mathcal{M}$ function does projection for an individual match and is defined as follows:

$$\pi(m, s) = \{(k, v) \in m|k \in s\}$$

The $\Pi : \mathcal{S} \times 2^{\mathcal{V}} \to \mathcal{S}$ function does projection for match sets and is defined as follows:

$$\Pi(M, s) = \{m|\exists m' \in M : m = \pi(m', s)\}$$

2.5 The κ Function

The $\kappa : \mathcal{M} \times \mathcal{V} \to \mathcal{M}$ function essentially does counting. However, to define it, some new concepts are necessary.

First, we need the concept of a partition of a match set by a variable, which is effectively a set of subsets (blocks) of the match set where each block has all matches in the match set whose only difference is their value for that variable. The function $P : \mathcal{M} \times \mathcal{V} \to \mathcal{S}$ produces the partition of a match set by a given variable, and is defined as follows:

$$P(M, k) = \{ M' \subset M|\forall m_1, m_2 \in M' : \exists k \in vars(m_1) = vars(m_2) :$$
$$\pi(m_1, vars(m_1) - k) = \pi(m_2, vars(m_2) - k)\}$$

For any block in a partition there is a match that represents the common subset which all matches in the block share. The function $c : \mathcal{S} \times \mathcal{V} \to \mathcal{M}$ produces the common subset for any block in a partition, and is defined as follows:

$$c(M', k) = \{(k', v)|k \neq k' \wedge \forall m \in M' : (k', v) \in m\}$$

Given these concepts we can define the counting function as follows:

$$\kappa(M, k) = \{m|\exists M' \in P(M, k) : m = c(M', k) \cup \{(k, |M' - c(M', k)|)\}\}$$

The cardinality computation to set the value of k in the count may look strange; the rationale is to exclude the match where k has no value, ie: the match that is the common subset. This ensures that OPTIONAL operator can be used to produce the variable being counted, and that when there is no value for k the count becomes 0 instead of 1.

3   Language Semantics

In this section we will define the semantics of tolog queries from the bottom up, starting with literals and eventually progressing to full queries. In each case, a mapping from the tolog query expressions to the query algebra will be given.

3.1   Variables, Literals, and References

Variables are written in tolog as `$NAME`.

Two types of literals are supported: strings, written `"abc"`, and numbers, written in the usual fashion.

In addition, references to topic map objects are allowed. These can use several syntaxes, where the most common is simple ID reference, like `foo`. In each case the effect is the same: the reference evaluates to the topic map object referred to.

In the query algebra literals and topic map object references map to constants representing their values.

3.2   Predicate Application

Predicate applications are uses of a predicate, where the predicate is supplied with an argument tuple. An example of this might be:

`instance-of($A, person)`

In the query algebra, each predicate is a function which given a Q instance and an argument tuple produces a match set binding the variables in the argument tuple. The query above would therefore translate to the following in the query algebra if applied to the topic map Q:

$$instance - of(Q, (\$A, person))$$

The result would be a set of matches where $\$A$ is bound to all person topics in Q.

In the syntax predicates can be referenced in the same ways as topics. The details of the different syntaxes and the scope rules are a little involved, and so we will only focus on the semantics here.

When parsing a predicate application, the predicate function for this application is produced as follows:

1. If there is a user-defined predicate with this name, that predicate is used.
2. If there is a built-in predicate with this name, that predicate is used.
3. Interpret the predicate reference as a topic reference, and find the referenced topic t.
4. If t is an association type, produce a dynamic association predicate as defined in 3.8 on page 194.
5. If t is an occurrence type, produce a dynamic occurrence predicate as defined in 3.8 on page 194.
6. If t is a name type, produce a dynamic name predicate as defined in 3.8 on page 194.
7. If all else fails, use this predicate: $empty(Q, p) = \emptyset$

3.3 Predicate Expressions

A predicate expression is formed by combining predicate expressions using the AND, OR, NOT, and OPTIONAL operators. The mappings of these to the query algebra is relatively straightforward.

AND. The AND operator maps to the $\oplus$ query algebra operator, such that any predicate expression of the form given below

```
e1, e2, ..., en
```

maps to the following query algebra expression: $e_1 \oplus e_2 \oplus ... \oplus e_n$

OR. The mapping of OR is very straightforward: it maps to the $\cup$ operator. Given a predicate expression as follows:

```
{ e1 | e2 | ... | en }
```

the corresponding query algebra expression is:

$e_1 \cup e_2 \cup ... \cup e_n$

NOT. The mapping of NOT is a little more involved than might be expected. To be able to map NOT we need two sets of variables: V being the set of all variables used in the query outside the NOT, and V' being the set of variables used in the NOT. Given this the predicate expression

```
not(e)
```

would translate into the query algebra as follows:

$$\Pi(\beta(\mathcal{A}^{|V'|}, V) - e, V \cap V')$$

This makes NOT produce all match sets for which e is not true, then project these down to the variables used outside the NOT. In this translation NOT can produce infinite match sets, but only formulated in terms of variables also used elsewhere in the query.

OPTIONAL. The mapping of OPTIONAL is relatively straightforward; given a predicate expression as follows:

```
e1, { e2 }
```

the corresponding query algebra expression is:

$e_1 \odot e_2$

3.4 Predicate Definitions

Predicate definitions effectively use a parameter list and a predicate expression to define a predicate. In the query algebra each predicate definition becomes a function whose body is defined using the query algebra.

A predicate definition takes the form

```
name(parameters) :- predicate-expression .
```

In the query algebra, let the name be n, the parameter tuple p, and the predicate expression e. The difficulty here is that e produces match sets using the variables internal to the defined predicate, which are usually different from those used in the predicate application. This means that we need to translate the match set from the internal variables to the external ones (and also filter the match set using the literals provided in the argument tuple). The function that does this is τ, defined as follows, where M is a match set and a the argument tuple:

$$\tau(M, p, a) = \{ \ m | \exists m' \in M : \forall i \in [1, 2, 3, ..., |p|] :$$
$$((p[i] \in \mathcal{V} \wedge (a[i], val(m', a[i])) \in m' \wedge (p[i], val(m, p[i])) \in m) \vee$$
$$(p[i] \in \mathcal{A} \wedge (a[i], p[i]) \in m')\}$$

Given this function we can define the function resulting from a predicate definition as:

$$n(Q, p) = \tau(\Pi(e, p), a)$$

3.5   Queries

The overall structure of a query is:

```
SELECT select-clause FROM
   predicate-expression
ORDER BY order-clause
LIMIT limit-clause
OFFSET offset-clause?
```

A query algebra expression e_1 for the **predicate-expression** is created as described above.

The next expression e_2 is produced as follows:

- If there is no **select-clause** then $e_2 = e_1$.
- If there is a **select-clause** containing the set of variables s but no counted variables then $e_2 = \Pi(e_1, s)$.
- If there is a **select-clause** containing the set of variables s and the counted variable is k then $e_2 = \kappa(\Pi(e_1, s), k)$. (Only one counted variable is allowed.)

The **order-clause**, **limit-clause**, and **offset-clause** are not mapped to the query algebra, as these are relatively straightforward to understand, and have only a very limited impact on optimization.

3.6   Built-in Comparison Predicates

tolog has a number of comparison predicates which mirror those in other query and programming languages. These predicates are all reflections of infinite subsets of $\mathcal{A} \times \mathcal{A}$, and so are what the Datalog literature calls *unsafe*. This means that they cannot be used alone, as they do not sufficiently constrain the result set to guarantee that query results are not infinite in size.

The value sets are sets of tuples and so to define the predicate functions we need somehow to filter such sets based on the literals given in the predicate arguments, and then to produce a match set with variable bindings. This is done by the β function. This function takes the predicate result set and a specification tuple, filters it with any literals given in the specification tuple, and produces a set of matches with each position in the n-tuples bound to any variables given in the specification tuple.

The β function is defined as follows:

$$\beta(R, s) = \{m | \exists t \in R : m = b(t, s) \land (\nexists i : s[i] \notin \mathcal{V} \land s[i] \neq t[i])\}$$

The b function is here a helper function which produces a match from a result tuple from a predicate, defined as:

$$b(t, s) = \{(k, v) | \exists i : s[i] = k \neq * \land s[i] \in \mathcal{V} \land t[i] = v\}$$

With this in hand we can define the predicate functions as follows:

$$= (Q, s) = \beta(\{(v_1, v_2) | \exists v_1, v_2 \in \mathcal{A} \land v_1 = v_2\}$$
$$/ = (Q, s) = \beta(\{(v_1, v_2) | \exists v_1, v_2 \in \mathcal{A} \land v_1 \neq v_2\}$$
$$< (Q, s) = \beta(\{(v_1, v_2) | \exists v_1, v_2 \in \mathcal{A} \land v_1 < v_2\}$$
$$> (Q, s) = \beta(\{(v_1, v_2) | \exists v_1, v_2 \in \mathcal{A} \land v_1 > v_2\}$$
$$<= (Q, s) = \beta(\{(v_1, v_2) | \exists v_1, v_2 \in \mathcal{A} \land v_1 <= v_2\}$$
$$>= (Q, s) = \beta(\{(v_1, v_2) | \exists v_1, v_2 \in \mathcal{A} \land v_1 >= v_2\}$$

Note that in the syntax these predicates are infix predicates.

3.7   Built-in Topic Map Predicates

tolog has a number of built-in predicates that are used to access the detailed structure of the topic map. They are only defined formally here, with no further explanation. More information on these predicates can be found in [Garshol05c].

Supporting Predicates. In order to define the built-in predicates some supporting predicates which are not visible in the language are needed. These are defined here.

The main supporting predicate is _q, which is formally defined as:

$$q(Q, p) = \beta(Q, p)$$

The _self-or-supertype predicate is easily defined:

```
_self-or-supertype($SUPER, $SUB) :- {
  xtm:superclass-subclas($SUPER :xtm:superclass, $SUB : xtm:subclass) |
  xtm:superclass-subclas($SUPER :xtm:superclass, $MID : xtm:subclass),
  _self-or-supertype($MID, $SUB) |
  $SUPER = $SUB
}.
```

The _is_uri($LOC) predicate is true for URIs. To define it we need the set of all URIs: $\mathcal{U} \subset \mathcal{A}$. Given that, the predicate function is easily defined:

$$is - uri(Q, a) = \beta(\{(u) | u \in \mathcal{U}\}, p)$$

The _is-like predicate is true for a pair of strings if they are similar. Precisely what this means is not defined, as this predicate is used for full-text search, and different full-text search systems have different definitions of similarity.

Built-in Predicates. Now that the supporting predicates are defined we can define the actual predicates. Note that the definition of these rules assume that in the mapping of TMDM to Q binary associations are not defined using templates (as in [Garshol05]), but instead in the same way as n-ary associations. This is necessary in order to provide association roles with their own identities.

```
using xtm for "http://www.topicmaps.org/xtm/1.0/core.xtm#"

association($ASSOC) :- _q($TM, ASSOCIATION, $I, Q, $ASSOC).
association-role($ASSOC, $ROLE) :-
  _q($TM, ASSOCIATION, $I, Q, $ASSOC),
  _q($ASSOC, $TYPE, $ROLE, $SCOPE, $PLAYER),
  _q($TYPE, META_TYPE, $I2, Q, ASSOCIATION_ROLE).

direct-instance-of($INSTANCE, $TYPE) :-
  xtm:class-instance($INSTANCE : xtm:instance, $TYPE : xtm:class).

instance-of($INSTANCE, $TYPE) :-
  xtm:class-instance($INSTANCE : xtm:instance, $DTYPE : xtm:class),
  _self-or-supertype($DTYPE, $TYPE).

occurrence($TOPIC, $OCC) :-
  _q($OTYPE, META_TYPE, $I, Q, OCCURRENCE),
  _q($TOPIC, $OTYPE, $OCC, $S, $V).

reifies($REIFIER, $REIFIED) :- _q($REIFIER, REIFIES, $I, Q, $REIFIED).

resource($OBJ, $URI) :- {
  _q($OTYPE, META_TYPE, $I, Q, OCCURRENCE),
  _q($TOPIC, $OTYPE, $OBJ, $S, $URI) |
  _q($TN, VARIANT, $OBJ, $S, $URI)
}, _is-uri($V).

role-player($ROLE, $TOPIC) :-
  _q($ASSOC, $TYPE, $ROLE, $SCOPE, $PLAYER),
  _q($TYPE, META_TYPE, $I, Q, ASSOCIATION_ROLE).

scope($OBJ, $TOPIC) :-
  _q($SUBJ, $PROP, $OBJ, $SN, $VAL),
  _q($SN, SCOPE_MEMBER, $I, Q, $TOPIC).

source-locator($OBJ, $URI) :- _q($OBJ, ITEM_IDENTIFIER, $I, Q, $URI).

subject-identifier($TOPIC, $URI) :-
  _q($TOPIC, NODE_URI, $I, Q, $URI),
  not(_q($TOPIC, TYPE_INSTANCE, $I, Q, INFORMATION_RESOURCE)).
```

```
subject-locator($TOPIC, $URI) :-
  _q($TOPIC, NODE_URI, $I, Q, $URI),
  _q($TOPIC, TYPE_INSTANCE, $I, Q, INFORMATION_RESOURCE).

topic($TOPIC) :- _q($TM, TOPIC, $I, Q, $TOPIC).

topic-name($TOPIC, $NAME) :-
   _q($NTYPE, META_TYPE, $I, Q, TOPIC_NAME),
   _q($TOPIC, $NTYPE, $NAME, $S, $V).

topicmap($TM) :- _q($TM, TOPIC, $I, Q, $TOPIC).

type($OBJ, $TYPE) :- {
  /* topic name, occurrence, or association role */
  _q($PARENT, $TYPE, $OBJ, $S, $VAL),
  _q($TYPE, META_TYPE, $I2, Q, $METATYPE) |
  /* association */
  ($OBJ, TYPE, $I, $S2, $TYPE)
}.

value($OBJ, $VAL) :- {
   _q($TYPE, META_TYPE, $I, Q, $METATYPE),
   { $METATYPE = TOPIC-NAME | $METATYPE = OCCURRENCE },
   _q($TOPIC, $TYPE, $OBJ, $S, $V) |
   _q($TN, VARIANT, $OBJ, $S, $V)
}, not(_is-uri($V)).

value-like($OBJ, $VAL) :- value($OBJ, $REALVAL), _is-like
                          ($REALVAL, $VAL).
variant($TN, $VAR) :- _q($TN, VARIANT, $VAR, $S, $VAL).
```

There is a base-locator predicate in tolog which corresponds to the [base locator] property of TMDM. This property no longer exists in TMDM, and so it is not defined here.

The object-id($OBJ, $ID) predicate produces a unique ID for every topic map object. There are no constraints on the ID beyond that it must be unique within the current topic map, and that it must be a string.

3.8 Dynamic Predicates

Producing a dynamic association predicate from a topic t requires a supporting predicate that not visible in the language, called _pair($PAIR, $T1, $T2). The arguments to dynamic association predicates are pairs (written topic1 : topic2 in the syntax), and the predicate is used to get the components of the pair.

For a dynamic association predicate with one parameter, use the following predicate definition:

```
t($P) :-
  _pair($P, $TOPIC, $ROLETYPE),
```

```
role-player($ROLE, $TOPIC),
type($ROLE, $ROLETYPE),
association-role($ASSOC, $ROLE),
type($ASSOC, t).
```

For dynamic association predicates with two parameters, use the following predicate definition:

```
t($P1, $P2) :-
  _pair($P1, $TOPIC1, $ROLETYPE1),
  _pair($P2, $TOPIC2, $ROLETYPE2),
  role-player($ROLE1, $TOPIC1),
  type($ROLE1, $ROLETYPE1),
  association-role($ASSOC, $ROLE1),
  type($ASSOC, t).
  association-role($ASSOC, $ROLE2),
  $ROLE1 /= $ROLE2,
  type($ROLE2, $ROLETYPE2),
  role-player($ROLE2, $TOPIC2),
```

How to extend this to any number of parameters should be obvious.

To produce a dynamic occurrence predicate from the topic t, use the following predicate definition:

```
t($T, $V) :- occurrence($T, $O), type($O, t),
             { value($O, $V) | resource($O, $V) }.
```

To produce a dynamic name predicate from the topic t, use the following predicate definition:

```
t($T, $V) :- topic-name($T, $N), type($N, t), value($N, $V).
```

4   Conclusion and Further Work

This paper has presented a query algebra for tolog based on the Q model. This gives the query language a formal definition, which gives implementors a much better foundation for producing interoperable implementations. It can also serve as the foundation for work on optimization of tolog queries and type inferencing in tolog queries. Some implementations already support both optimization and type inferencing, but a formal basis is needed to improve both aspects. For this, however, further study of the properties of the query algebra is needed.

Some algebraic properties are immediately obvious. For example, the $\sim$ relation is obviously both reflexive and symmetric, but clearly neither transitive nor total. This implies that the $\oplus$ operator is commutative. It's also clear that $M \oplus M = M$ for all $M \in \mathcal{M}$. $\oplus$ should also be associative, but proving this requires more work. The properties of $\cup$, representing OR, are already known, but more work is required to establish whether $\cup$ is distributive over $\oplus$. The current definition of OPTIONAL is also sub-optimal, in that it presents significant obstacles for optimizations. More work is necessary to determine whether this can be overcome.

More work is also required in order to precisely specify the circumstances under which a tolog query is safe, in the sense that it does not produce infinite results.

Finally, more work is needed in order to establish what the possible sets of values for each variable in a tolog query is, based on the possible sets of values for the parameters to the predicates used in the query. This would make it possible to do type inferencing on a query to tell what types of values a variable may have, which is useful both for optimization and to help programmers find logical errors in their queries.

References

[Ahmed05]   Ahmed, Kal: *Topic Map Relational Query Language – TMRQL*. NetworkedPlanet white paper, 2005. http://www.networkedplanet.com/download/TMRQL.pdf

[Garshol05]   Garshol, Lars Marius: *Q: A model for Topic Maps*. Proceedings of Extreme Markup 2005, IDEAlliance, August 1-5, Montréal, Canada. http://www.ontopia.net/topicmaps/materials/quads.html

[Garshol05b] Garshol, Lars Marius: *tolog – Language tutorial*. Ontopia Knowledge Suite documentation, published on Ontopia web site. http://www.ontopia.net/omnigator/docs/query/tutorial.html

[Garshol05c] Garshol, Lars Marius: *The Built-in tolog Predicates – Reference Documentation*. Ontopia Knowledge Suite documentation, published on Ontopia web site. http://www.ontopia.net/topicmaps/materials/tolog-predicate-reference.html

[ISO13250-2] ISO 13250-3: Topic Maps – Data Model; International Organization for Standardization; Geneva. http://www.isotopicmaps.org/sam/sam-model/

[Liu99]   Liu, Mengchi. *Deductive database languages: problems and solutions*. ACM Computing Survey 31, 1 (Mar. 1999), 27-62. DOI=http://doi.acm.org/10.1145/311531.311533

[N0492]   *TMQL Use Case Solutions*. ISO JTC1/SC34, document N0492, 2004-03-16. http://www.jtc1sc34.org/repository/0492.htm

[Robie01]   Robie, Jonathan; Garshol, Lars Marius; Newcomb, Steve; Biezunski, Michel; Fuchs, Matthew; Miller, Libby; Brickley, Dan; Christophides, Vassillis; Karvounarakis, Gregorius. *The syntactic web*. Markup Languages 3, 4 (Sep. 2001), 411-440. DOI=http://dx.doi.org/10.1162/109966202760152176.   Available from http://www.w3.org/XML/2002/08/robie.syntacticweb.html

[Seaborne05] Seaborne, Andy; Prud'hommeaux, Eric. *SPARQL Query Language for RDF*. W3C Working Draft 21 July 2005. http://www.w3.org/TR/2005/WD-rdf-sparql-query-20050721/

[Strychowski05] Strychowski, Jakub. *Concept Glossary Manager – Topic Maps Engine and Navigator*. forthcoming, to be published in proceedings of TMRA'05.

A TMDM Disclosure Using T+

Robert Barta[1] and Lars Heuer[2]

[1] Bond University,
Faculty of Information Technology
rho@bond.edu.au
[2] Semagia
heuer@semagia.com

Abstract. Both the more pragmatic Topic Map data model (TMDM) and the more fundamental Topic Map Reference Model (TMRM), have reached now a certain degree of maturity. Unfortunately, the development of these models did not occur in lockstep as they address very different needs and communities. This work tries to be the missing link by faithfully mapping TMDM instances into TMRM. For this purpose we formally introduce a refinement of the existing T model by adapting it to the latest TMRM version and by extending it to cover TMRM disclosures.

1 Introduction

On a historical timeline, the Topic Map Data Model (TMDM [7]) is only a rather recent development. Its rather pragmatic approach is to define a set of object classes (using Infoset [5] terminology), such as *topic items* or *association items* by listing their properties. Additional value constraints and so called *computed values* (which are value constraints in disguise) constrain an abstract data structure which is supposed to authoritatively define *Topic Maps*. Based on TMDM, syntaxes like XTM [8] and their deserialization rules can then be properly formulated.

In a parallel effort, another model, TMRM (TM Reference Model [10]), was developed. It abstracts away from particular properties such as 'name' or 'URI occurrences' and only mandates the existence of properties as key/value pairs which are then organized into so-called proxies. Interestingly, these proxies are equally well equipped to capture topics, topic characteristics as well as associations.

The T model [3] serves as an attempt to formalize TMRM, but it does not include a mathematical coverage of the concept of *disclosure* which has been detailed in later versions of TMRM. This is done in section 3. That itself is based on the T+ model which we define before in section 2. Section 4 then tackles the TMDM disclosure by providing a mapping from TMDM instances to maps according to T+. This is followed by critical discussion and summarized suggestions for improvements to make the disclosure less painful.

L. Maicher and J. Park (Eds.): TMRA 2005, LNAI 3873, pp. 197–209, 2006.

On a notational side, we use greyed out text for explanatory text whereas the normal text is authoritative. We also use references like TMRM:*n*:*term* to reference a concept in the original TMRM specification.

2   T$^+$ Model

The T$^+$ model is an extension of the original T model and follows the change of terminology in the latest versions of TMRM. Instead of *assertions*, maps now consists of *proxies* which we formally define in this section. T$^+$ carries over the whole mechanics of T path expressions which facilitate to navigate through maps and which can serve as constraints. That, and the inclusion of explicit value sets for properties is necessary to cover formally disclosures.

Informally, maps consists of proxies and these, in turn, consist of properties. In our formalism a property has two components: a key and a value. The key helps to identify the property inside a proxy (such as "a particular individual has a shoesize"); attached to it is the actual value (such as "the shoesize is the integer 42"). As such keys must be proxies themselves, which implies that there is a recursive relationship between proxies and properties.

In the following we will recursively define $\mathcal{X}$, the set of all *proxies* (TMRM:2: Subject Proxy) and $\mathcal{P}$, the set of properties as both depend on each other. For convenience only, we will associate with all proxies an identifier which serves as a shorthand for a proxy. Accordingly, we postulate a set $\mathcal{I}$ of those identifiers and functions $id : \mathcal{X} \mapsto \mathcal{I}$ and its inverse $id^{-1} : \mathcal{I} \mapsto \mathcal{X}$ to map between the two sets with the obvious constraint that $id(x) = id(x')$ only iff $x = x'$. In the following we treat proxies and their identifiers interchangeably.

2.1   Properties and Proxies

The *trivial proxy* belongs to $\mathcal{X}$. It has the id $\bot$ and is equal to the empty set, $id(\emptyset) = \bot$. Given a set of values V and a set of proxies $\mathcal{X}$, we define a *property* to be a pair $\langle k, v \rangle \in (\mathcal{X} \times V)$. We call the first component in such tuples the *key* and the second the *value* of the property. We denote all such properties with $\mathcal{P}$.

Properties in TMRM are labelled values. For the values we have no particular requirements, except that they themselves are opaque to the formalism and there must be later a way to combine two (or more) of them when properties have to be combined during merging maps (TMRM:3.3). *Opaque* means that objects have no other characteristics than being distinguishable from each other. Internally they may be composite, such as, say, spatial coordinates, but the formalism does not expect any structure to be present. Note that values can also be proxies themselves.

A *subject proxy* (or short *proxy*, TMRM:2:Subject Proxy) is a finite set of properties, $\{p_1, \ldots, p_n\}$, with $p_i \in \mathcal{P}$. Obviously, proxies are only equal if they have identical properties. For the set of all proxies $\mathcal{X}$ consequently $\mathcal{X} = 2^{\mathcal{P}}$ holds.

Properties are not ordered inside a proxy and a particular property may only appear once. A particular proxy is characterized by the totality of its properties. This is quite natural when we consider subject proxies which represent subjects; here we are familiar to attaching properties to objects and expect that the properties characterize the object sufficiently.

It should be noted, that with proxies subjects such as *books, cars, love* and *hate* can be represented structurally identical to statements connecting subjects.

Generic equality between proxies is trivially that of sets. This is not the same as *equivalence*. *Equality* here only makes sure that there is no redundant information in the map. As we detail later, equivalence of proxies triggers a merging process in a map.

To access the keys in the properties of a proxy $x = \{p_1, \ldots, p_n\}$ we define the function $keys(x) = \{k_1, \ldots, k_n\}$ where each k_i is the key of property p_i. Note that the result is a bag, not a set as keys may occur more than once in a proxy. In a similar way we define a function to access all property values inside a proxy: $values(x) = \{v_1, \ldots, v_n\}$ with v_i being the values of properties in x. This, again, is a bag and not a set.

The base model does not impose any restrictions on property values. While not necessary for the formalism itself, we might later want to put additional constraints on the form of proxies to only *meaningful* combinations. Examples of such meaningful constraints are "there may be only one value for a particular property key" or "in one and the same proxy a particular thing cannot be used as value *and* as key": $\forall x \in \mathcal{X}, keys(x) \cap values(x) = \emptyset$. Another useful constraint could avoid that the identifier for a proxy appears in that proxy itself: $\forall x \in \mathcal{X}, id(x) \notin (keys(x) \cup values(x))$.

2.2 Maps

We now consider proxies to be atoms from which *topic maps* (or short *maps*, TMRM:2:Topic Map) can be constructed. A *map* is a finite (possibly empty) set of of proxies. The set of all maps is denoted by $\mathcal{M}$. To build bigger maps, we define the *elementary composition*, denoted by $\oplus$, of two maps $m, m' \in \mathcal{M}$. It is defined as set union $m \oplus m' = m \cup m'$. We also say that m is a *submap* of m' if $m \subseteq m'$.

The merging defined here is naive and generic; only exactly identical proxies in the operand maps will be identified (in the sense "regarded to be about the same thing") and hence automatically merged into the result. To define a more specific merging, two things have to occur: First, proxies have to be identified based on some criterion. That may depend on certain properties, combinations of properties or even on information involving other parts of the map. Secondly, the proxies have to be combined according to a prescription.

Exactly this interpretation of merging is mandated by TMRM:3. In this process it is actually not relevant whether two or more maps are to be *merged*. Rather, this operation is applicable to a single map once all necessary merging information is available.

A *merger* is a commutative, partial function $\bowtie \colon \mathcal{X} \times \mathcal{X} \mapsto \mathcal{X}$ which fullfils two purposes: first it identifies pairs of proxies and then it defines how two such proxies should be replaced by a new one. Any map m can now be subjected to *induced merging*, $m|_{\bowtie}$, as defined by

$$m|_{\bowtie} = \{x \in m \mid \neg \exists y \in m, x \bowtie y \;\; isdefined\} \cup \{x \bowtie y \mid x, y \in m\} \qquad (1)$$

We do not constrain how proxies are effectively combined. In many applications this will involve to actually merge properties by computing new values.

2.3   Map Navigation and Path Expressions

The original T model also defines navigation mechanisms for maps via a path expression language. The language is aware of a small set of predefined constants (proxies), *instance, class, subclass,* and *superclass,* which can be used to model subclassing and class-instance relationships in maps. Honoring so subclassing (a transitive and reflexive closure thereof, to be precise), the language $\mathcal{P}_{\mathcal{M}}$ can be used to extract information from maps.

When a path expression p is applied to a map m, this is written as $m \otimes p$. Obviously, there will only be a result, if the path expression is *asking* for something which is in the map. That can also be seen as a way to *constrain* maps. We regard a given path expression as *constraint* and define a *satisfaction relation* $\models \, \subseteq \mathcal{P}_{\mathcal{M}} \times \mathcal{M}$ between a path expression c and a map m, such that

$$c \models m \qquad \Longleftrightarrow \qquad m \otimes c \neq \emptyset \qquad (2)$$

A *constraint set* is then simply a set of path expressions.

3   T$^+$ Disclosures

TMRM is rather generic. It only tries to capture the *essence of Topic Maps*, namely that every map forms a network of proxies, each of them being a distinct set of properties. The reference model does not assume any particular data type(s) from which the values of properties are taken; and it also does not have assumptions on the kind of properties themselves. To disclose TMDM later, we need to make these ontological commitments.

3.1 Base Vocabulary

The first step in this process is to define a vocabulary with which to build individual properties. For TMDM these will be things like *occurrence*, *association* and a few more (section 4.2). This implies that every map instance will implicitly hold these concepts as proxies and that, in turn, gives us a means to formally mandate their existence with a path expression constraint.

So, for example, to constrain that the concept *scope* must be part of the map m we would use the following constraint:

$$\text{scope} \models m \tag{3}$$

This will be repeated for every primitive concept we introduce.

3.2 Types

TMRM introduces *types* as those sets from which property values are taken. Practically, types are simply algebras a disclosure has to characterize. If, for example, values can be strings over a particular character set, then we have to postulate such a set, possibly together with a comparison operator to allow for sorting strings. One potential type is implicitly defined by the T$^+$ model: the set of proxies itself.

In the following we assume that all such selected sets are disjunct, so that for every value its type can be implicitly inferred (TMRM:2). This has the notational advantage that we do not have to carry on in the following with a whole collection $\{T_1, \ldots, T_m\}$ of types, but only one which contains all values.

A map $m = \{x_1, \ldots, x_n\}$ *conforms* to a given type T, $m \approx T$, if all property values in m are from T, i.e. $\forall x \in m, values(x) \subseteq T$.

3.3 Disclosures

Both ontological commitments, the base vocabulary and (the set of) type(s), is bundled into a disclosure. Given a type T and a constraint set C, the tuple $\langle T, C \rangle$ is a *disclosure of ontological commitment* (or short *disclosure*, TMRM:3). The set of all such disclosures will be denoted as $\mathcal{D}$.

We say that a *disclosure governs a map*, $d \models m$, for $d = \langle T, C \rangle$ if m conforms with T and m also satisfies all constraints in C. The *governance* of a disclosure d, $gov(d)$, is the set of all maps which are governed by d.

4   Disclosing TMDM

To provide a mapping of all information items within TMDM to the formalism provided by T$^+$ we have to undergo the following process. First, preparatory steps are to be taken to canonicalize TMDM map instances in terms of scope and default value handling.

We also have to detail the terms (taxonomy) TMDM is using for itself and to define the algebras to characterize the types TMDM is postulating. Only then we can detail the structural mappings where we actually connect TMDM information items with T^+ proxies.

4.1 Canonicalization

TMDM has the concept of scope which consists of a set of scoping topics. The latest version prescribes 'AND' semantics, i.e. that applications should interpret such sets in such a way that a particular scoped information item only is valid if all scoping topics are *active*.

Conceptually clean is to model this compound scope with a dedicated topic representing the set. To reduce this structural redundancy and to streamline the mapping below, we will treat the scope property in association items and topic characteristics always as one separate and newly generated topic which stands for the whole set of scoping topics. That is to say, that the new topic is playing the role `whole` in an association of type `consists-of` and all the scoping topics are playing a role `part`. If an item has no scope (unlimited validity) the topic `ucs` (unconstrained scope) will be used.

TMDM uses *item identifiers* to address items. As maps may result from various merging processes, an item may potentially acquire any number of these locators, while others may be empty. For the purpose of canonicalization we assume that this set will never be empty and that there is a mechanism which computes a unique identifier from these item identifiers.

4.2 Vocabulary

TMDM uses a specific set of concepts, some of them at the instance level (such as *type-instance* and *supertype-subtype*, TMDM:7.2 and 7.3), some of them inherent in the model (such as *scope sets* or *unconstrained scope*).

We have to formalize the existence of all these concepts using path expressions consisting only of the concept names. While sufficient for the mapping to follow, we choose a slightly extended approach and organize all the relevant concepts into a separate topic map, the *TMDM ontology* (we use AsTMa= [2] as notation):

```
#-- TMDM ontology (version 0.1)

#-- the root of all good, this can be connected
#-- to any top-level ontology
subject

association         is-a       subject

topic               is-a       subject

role                subclasses topic
```

```
instance              is-a       role

type                  is-a       role

subclass              is-a       role

superclass            is-a       role

scope                 is-a       role

# the unconstrained scope
ucs                   is-a       scope

characteristic        subclasses association

occurrence            subclasses characteristic

name                  subclasses characteristic

variant               subclasses name

#-- subject indication and identification
reifies               subclasses subject

indirectly-reifies    subclasses reifies

locator               is-a       role

#-- strings
string                is-a       subject

uri                   subclasses string

xml                   subclasses string

#-- values
value                 is-a       role

#-- set containment
consists-of           is-a       association

whole                 is-a       role

part                  is-a       role
```

Hereby we postulate only the relationship `is-a` (which is equivalent with TMDM *type-instance*, TMDM:7.2) and `subclasses` (*supertype-subtype*, TMDM:7.3).

4.3   Types

TMDM introduces several intrinsic data types (TMDM 4.4), strings, URIs and XML document fragments but allows applications to use any other type in variant and occurrences items as long as there is a locator for it. It is important to understand that TMDM instances store *only* text representations of values.

One possible option to translate TMDM data into T^+ property values is to use the data string representation and to find a way to encode the data type separately. A much more truthful translation, though, is to convert the strings into the *value* itself using a deserialization procedure. Such procedures are assumed to be defined for every type, although TMDM itself does to mandate this.

4.4   Structures

In this section we will cover individual TMDM information items and show how they can be mapped structurally into T^+ proxies. In this process one or more TMDM items might be mapped to one or more proxies.

To streamline the presentation we use the following notation and terminology. We will call here properties of TMDM items *components*, only to avoid confusion with T^+ properties. Given a particular item m we can select a particular component c with the syntax m.c. If a component c contains a set of items, then we use a list syntax m.c[i].

We automatically convert (deserialize) all (string) values in TMDM components into their deserialized form according to the specified data type. How this is accomplished is local policy of the involved data type.

As shorthand notation we use items as property values inside the proxies we generate. In such cases, these items have to be replaced with the id of the proxy which stands for the item.

Scoping. Technically, there are two options to model scope components within information items (associations, characteristics, ...). The simpler method is to dedicate a property $\langle scope, s \rangle$ for any scope property with value s and add such a property to any proxy which correspond to the information item.

The other possibilty is to model *scoping* with a separate proxy. In that we build a dedicated proxy to capture the fact that an information item i is to be valid only in a particular scope s:

$$\{\langle scope, s \rangle, \langle subject, i \rangle\} \tag{4}$$

We model scoping with the simpler method (scope property embedded into proxy) to avoid that the proxies for occurrences and topic names get collapsed into one.

Association Items. The `roles` component of an association item *assoc* contains a set of role items, each of those consisting of topic items for the type (`assoc.roles[i].type`) and the player (`assoc.roles[i].player`). For each association item we build a proxy

$$a = \{r_1, \ldots, r_n, \langle \text{scope}, \text{assoc.scope} \rangle\} \qquad (5)$$

whereby the individual properties $r_i = \langle \text{assoc.roles[i].type}, \text{assoc.roles[i].player} \rangle$ are built from the ith role item. As every association item has a type component, this relationship is modelled by another proxy,

$$\{\langle \text{instance}, a \rangle, \langle \text{type}, \text{assoc.type} \rangle\} \qquad (6)$$

Occurrence Items. Every occurrence item, *occur*, we model with a dedicated proxy,

$$o = \{\langle \text{value}, \text{occur.value} \rangle, \langle \text{topic}, \text{occur.parent} \rangle, \langle \text{scope}, \text{occur.scope} \rangle\} \qquad (7)$$

Hereby we use the **parent** as one value and the actual (deserialized) occurrence value as the other.

As every occurrence item has a type, we model this relationship with a second proxy:

$$\{\langle \text{instance}, o \rangle, \langle \text{type}, \text{occur.type} \rangle\} \qquad (8)$$

Name Items. Name items are special occurrences, in the sense that the value is organized into the actual value component and a set of variant name items. As variants are modelled separately, we only need to consider name values v as strings here:

$$n = \{\langle \text{value}, v \rangle, \langle \text{topic}, \text{name.parent} \rangle, \langle \text{scope}, \text{name.scope} \rangle\} \qquad (9)$$

As every name item has also a **type**, we model this relationship with a second proxy:

$$\{\langle \text{instance}, n \rangle, \langle \text{type}, \text{name.type} \rangle\} \qquad (10)$$

Variant Items. Variant items are specialized names which are attached to a name item. Unlike names, though, they can carry any data which is indicated via a data type component. We model a variant v as a special characteristic which is attached to the name it belongs to:

$$v1 = \{\langle \text{value}, v \rangle, \langle \text{topicname}, \text{v.parent} \rangle, \langle \text{scope}, \text{v.scope} \rangle\} \qquad (11)$$

The value v is built as usual by deserializing the **v.value** component in the variant according to the data type provided by **v.datatype**. To model the type we use

$$\{\langle \text{instance}, v1 \rangle, \langle \text{type}, \text{variant} \rangle\} \qquad (12)$$

Topic Identification. TMDM uses the component `subject locators` to address a specific resource if the subject *is* that resource. We use the conventional *reification* mechanism (not to be confused with the 'reification' of items within TMDM) to model this. For every subject locator `l` in a topic *t* we create a proxy:

$$r = \{\langle \text{topic}, t \rangle, \langle \text{reifier}, l \rangle\} \tag{13}$$

$$\{\langle \text{instance}, r \rangle, \langle \text{type}, \text{reifies} \rangle\} \tag{14}$$

Topic Indication. TMDM uses this mechanism to *indirectly* address subjects. A `subject identifier` is not the address of the subject, but of something which helps to identify it, such as a picture. To faithfully mirror these intentions we have to model this in a dedicated pair of proxies:

$$r = \{\langle \text{topic}, t \rangle, \langle \text{reifier}, l \rangle\} \tag{15}$$

$$\{\langle \text{instance}, r \rangle, \langle \text{type}, \text{indirectly} - \text{reifies} \rangle\} \tag{16}$$

Topic Items. Topic items can be completely ignored as all information is implicit from the above.

Topic Map Items. Topic Map items are simply containers for topic and association items. All proxies we have created with the above recipes are collected in a set which compounds a T^+ map.

5   Discussion

The approach taken has a couple of issues. On the upside, almost all containment information — that which is usually modelled with a `parent` property — has been absorbed by the equivalent set of proxies. The only exception is the set of scopes and the attachment of variants to their names. The side effect is that all *TMDM computed properties* (which mirror particular dependencies) have disappeared.

Also on the positive side we would see that all assumptions made within TMDM are made explicit. This includes the used vocabulary, the different ways how to identify topics with the subject they stand for, the special position *scope* has within TMDM and the data types TMDM defines implicitly. Finally, more on the implementation side, the mapping seems to scale linear with the number of items.

There are a number of open questions and problems, though. A minor one concerns the modelling of scope. While choose to attach the scope *directly* as property into the statement proxy it might be possible to model the scope as dedicated proxy that connects the scoping proxy with the statement that is supposed to scope. We have choosen the embedded variant to avoid that the occurrence proxies and topic name proxies get merged into one proxy.

More serious is the number of additional assumptions we had to postulate. One set is related to the choices of default values (section 4.1). Here we would argue that this can be interpreted as omissions on the side of TMDM.

A second friction point are data types and their implicit deserialization. It arises out of the discrepancy beween the treatment of arbitrary data between TMDM and TMRM. While TMRM always had a completely transparent attitude towards data types (other than strings), TMDM *only* supports string representation of data.

In the mapping outlined above it would have been possible to somewhat mitigate this discrepancy by using strings on the T$^+$ level only. As a price, though, we would have to model somewhere the data type property which exists in the latest versions of TMDM. One could reasonable argue that any data type used within a TMDM instance *always* includes should include a deserialization method. Whether those should be made explicit within TMDM itself remains questionable, though.

A major point of confusion may revolve around *reification*. Again, in the TMDM sense reification means that (some) information items, such as name items or even variant items can be represented by a separate topic and these can consequently be used within associations.

Due to the nature of the mapping provided, most of the items finally correspond to one particular proxy. Its id can then be used either as key or as value in further proxies. But not all information items within TMDM are modelled as separate proxies. Specifically *role items* are completely absorbed by the association they are in. In T$^+$ instances it is not possible anymore to select the fact that *a particular topic plays a particular role in a particular association*.

We are tempted to argue that this is acceptable, especially since this feature within TMDM is very specific and may even in some sense contradict the spirit of Topic Maps. While, for instance, it is possible to reify one involvement of a topic in an association, it is not possible to reify the fact that two particular topics are involved in one assocation. Or, for that matter, that one is and some other is not. This strongly conflicts with the view taken in TMRM, namely that proxies (and consequently associations) are a unit of discourse.

6 Related Work

Since the standardization work started in 2000, the TM community has seen a number of formalizations. At that time, topic maps were mostly understood as rather complex graphs, so many of these approaches used hypergraphs, such as [1] and [12]. Background for most of this work was a precursor of TMRM, called RM4TM (and then PMTM) [11] which lent itself to a graph-theoretic description.

A set-theoretic coverage of more recent versions for TMRM was provided in [9]. In this work the different kinds of nodes in TMRM (a-node, ...) were modelled with disjunct sets, additional predicates modelled constraints on certain constellations to faithfully mirror the intent of TMRM. Also [3] is using set theory to describe assertions. The original T model does not closely follow TMRM; instead it performs a number of conceptual simplifications first.

A very different approach has been taken by [13]. In this thesis the XML elements in XTM were chosen to build a fundament for a formalism which allowed TM encoded information to be viewed in formal concept analysis.

Other models try to abstract directly from the mainstream model, TMDM [7]. Examples of such attempts are [6] and [4] (among various unpublished adhoc proposals). The latter uses sets of quadruples to capture all content within a topic map. Quadruples there are atomic and are in themselves a slight extensions of the triple model used in RDF. It can be shown that TMDM instances can be mapped into such tuples (using *subject, predicate, identity* and *object* components). It remains unclear, though, whether it is possible to formulate constraints on tuple sets in such a way that they model (and not just represent) maps.

7 Summary

This work is an attempt to characterize formally the relationship between the 'programming' model TMDM and T^+ which orients itself towards TMRM. The practical value of this missing link may be low; it at least connects various pieces in the TM standardization landscape.

While the overall mapping is straightforward, it may be even more streamlined if TMDM would adopt some of the procedures outlined in section 4.1. Specifically, multiple scopes and their implicit AND semantics, many of the default situations and source locators as sets (and not single identifiers) could be fixed there. Such would not only benefit the translation process towards T^+ but also towards any other low-level model. The same applies to the vocabulary which TMDM is using for itself.

A question unanswered by this work is whether the proposed translation sufficiently *models* TMDM. The only thing actually shown is that for every TMDM instance an equivalent T^+ instance can be created. To model TMDM, it would also be necessary to have a mechanism to constrain T^+ instances in such a way, that the mapping also works to other way. While this is obviously subject to further research, one avenue is to use path expressions again as constraint language.

References

1. Pascal Auillans, Patrice Ossona de Mendez, Pierre Rosenstiehl, and Bernard Vatant. A formal model for Topic Maps. ISWC Conference, 2002.
2. Robert Barta. Astma = language definition. http://astma.it.bond.edu.au/astma=-spec-xtm.dbk.
3. Robert Barta and Gernot Salzer. The Tau model, formalizing Topic Maps, 2005. http://crpit.com/confpapers/CRPITV43Barta.pdf.
4. Dmitry Bogachev. TMAssert Basic Assertion Model, 2004. http://homepage.mac.com/dmitryv/TopicMaps/TMRM/TMAssert.pdf.

5. John Cowan and Richard Tobin. XML information set (second edition), W3C recommendation, 2004. http://www.w3.org/TR/xml-infoset/.
6. Lars Marius Garshol. A proposed foundational model for Topic Maps, 2004-07-22. http://www.jtc1sc34.org/repository/0529.htm.
7. Lars Marius Garshol and Graham Moore. ISO 13250-2: Topic Maps - data model, 2003-11-02. http://www.isotopicmaps.org/sam/.
8. Lars Marius Garshol and Graham Moore. ISO/IEC JTC1/SC34, Topic Maps - XML syntax, 2004-01-25. http://www.isotopicmaps.org/sam/sam-xtm/.
9. Neill A. Kipp. A mathematical formalism for the Topic Maps reference model. 2003. http://www.isotopicmaps.org/tmrm/0441.htm.
10. Steven R. Newcomb, Sam Hunting, Jan Algermissen, and Patrick Durusau. ISO/IEC JTC1/SC34, Topic Maps - reference model, editor's draft, revision 3.10, 2003. http://www.isotopicmaps.org/tmrm/.
11. Steven R. Newcomb, Sam Hunting, Jan Algermissen, and Patrick Du- rusau. Reference model for iso 13250 topic maps (rm4tm), 2003. http://www.isotopicmaps.org/tmmm/TMMM-1.28/TMMM-1.28.html/.
12. Bernard Vatant. HG4TM - a mathematical model for topic maps, based on hypergraphs and reference model RM4TM. XML Europe, 2002. http://www.idealliance.org/papers/xmle02/dx xmle02/papers/02-01-04/02- 01-04.html.
13. Bastian Wormuth. A conceptual information system for Topic Maps. 2004. http://www.kvocentral.org/kvopapers/wormuth04conceptual.pdf.

TM/XML – Topic Maps Fragments in XML

Lars Marius Garshol[1] and Dmitry Bogachev[2]

[1] Ontopia AS, Oslo, Norway
larsga@ontopia.net
http://www.ontopia.net
[2] Omega Consulting
dmitryv@cogeco.ca

Abstract. This paper describes TM/XML, an XML syntax for Topic Maps that is very close to the natural, or colloquial, XML representation of the information in the topic map. It can be used to process Topic Maps data with XML tools, and integrate non-Topic Maps systems with Topic Maps systems.

Further, TM-Views, a mechanism for describing what to include when extracting a fragment from a topic map, is described. TM-Views improves the usability of TM/XML in the described use cases, but can also be used independently of TM/XML.

1 Introduction

Topic Maps is often described as ideal for information integration, because of the clear conceptual model and built-in support for merging. However, one of the key challenges for those who wish to build Topic Maps-based applications is making the Topic Maps application communicate with other applications, which are nearly invariably not Topic Maps-based. Solutions can of course be developed, but generally require labour- and knowledge-intensive custom programming against the Topic Maps engine API [TMAPI].

XML is today the lingua franca for information interchange, and so this paper attempts to simplify such integrations by making it easier to move data between XML and Topic Maps representations. The rationale is that any pre-existing applications will most likely be able to export and import some form of XML, or at least find XML data easier to work with.

Admittedly, an XML representation of Topic Maps already exists. The XTM syntax for Topic Maps is defined in the Topic Maps ISO standard [ISO13250-3] and is the de facto standard for interchange of Topic Maps today. This syntax is, however, difficult to process with existing XML tools [Robie01] and requires an in-depth understanding of Topic Maps to both produce and interpret.

This paper therefore proposes a more natural XML representation of Topic Maps, called TM/XML, which aims to make it easier to integrate Topic Maps into XML-capable environments. The TM/XML syntax is a private proposal, to be implemented by anyone who is interested, and not an official standard.

L. Maicher and J. Park (Eds.): TMRA 2005, LNAI 3873, pp. 210–230, 2006.

Most scenarios where TM/XML is useful (described in the following use cases section) involve integration with remote systems, which also requires a web service interface for accessing the Topic Maps system. This is provided by TMRAP [Garshol05], and TM/XML is designed to be used together with TMRAP. In TMRAP operations clients can request to receive the retrieved fragment in a specific Topic Maps syntax, and TM/XML is one of the possible syntaxes.

The web service interface operates on fragments of topic maps, which is what TM/XML is used to represent, and this requires an ability to describe the boundaries of the fragments. This paper also describes a syntax, called TM-Views (see section 4 on page 221), for defining views of topic maps that also determine the fragment boundaries.

1.1   Applications of the Syntax

The uses of the TM/XML syntax are theoretically the same as those for XTM, but in practice TM/XML is intended and optimized for a particular set of uses, which are described below. Simply stated, TM/XML is meant for use when Topic Maps are processed with normal XML tools rather than with Topic Maps-aware tools.

Implementing presentation using XML tools. In most cases, a Topic Maps application contains a presentation layer developed using a Topic Maps-aware tool. However, in some cases, this may not be practical, for example because:

- The Topic Maps application is part of a larger application or infrastructure where all presentation is implemented using XML tools, for example XSLT. The choice to use XML tools for all processing effectively precludes the use of Topic Maps-aware tools.
- The presentation layer is deployed in some application server or framework for which no Topic Maps support is available, either because it does not exist, or because the Topic Maps software used by the organization runs on a different platform.
- The presentation layer is developed by a team which has no skill in Topic Maps, and where it is not considered cost-effective to train them on Topic Maps and related technology necessary to implement presentation of Topic Maps content. The presentation team is most likely already familiar with XML technologies, however.

In all of these cases, extracting fragments from the topic map and passing them to the presentation layer in XML form and processing them with standard XML tools is the preferred solution. TM/XML greatly simplifies this, as shown below.

Building knowledge hubs. One very interesting use case is creating "knowledge hubs" where information from many sources is brought together and integrated. In this scenario, information providers invoke operations on a Topic Maps server to add information coming from outside sources, and the server then integrates this information into the existing topic map. Information consumers invoke other operations to retrieve fragments of information which are extracted from the topic map.

A very important variation on this scenario is using the knowledge hub to create a common view of some information domain across many different portals. (This has often been referred to as "portal integration".) In this scenario the knowledge hub (often itself part of a portal) contains the topic map of the information domain, whereas the client portals use information from this central topic map as part of their own presentation. This enables common subjects to be presented in a larger context than that possessed by an individual portal.

A key question in this scenario is how the client portals should present the Topic Maps fragments they retrieve from the hub. In many cases, purchasing separate Topic Maps software licenses and training the developer teams for each portal is out of the question for economic reasons. However, since the Topic Maps fragments are in any case being transmitted in XML syntax, a natural alternative is to let the client portals use ordinary XML tools to present the fragments.

Again, TM/XML supports this use case by enabling information to be inserted (going XML-to-TM) and retrieved (going TM-to-XML) using a natural XML representation that is easily processable with existing XML tools and also easily understood by developers who have little understanding of Topic Maps. This greatly simplifies creation of the knowledge hubs.

When to use XTM. It is not the intention of the authors that TM/XML should replace XTM as the standard XML syntax for Topic Maps. Instead, the intention is that TM/XML should be used in use cases like those described in this section, whereas XTM should continue to be used for interchange of topic maps between Topic Maps-aware tools. In the latter case, the difficulties of extracting domain-specific information from XTM (learning curve, complexity of processing, etc) are irrelevant, as the processing is done by Topic Maps-aware software. That software will provide Topic Maps-specific means of processing the content, such as TMQL and TMAPI, which are much simpler than working directly with XTM.

1.2   Design Principles

The goals for TM/XML were to produce an XML syntax for Topic Maps that

- is easy to learn, and does not require in-depth knowledge of Topic Maps,
- represents information close to the way it would naturally be represented in XML by someone not having Topic Maps in mind, and
- is compact and easy to process with common XML tools, like XSLT.

Essentially, the TM/XML syntax is a mapping between two data models: that of Topic Maps, and that of XML. The two main ways to approach this, in the terminology of [RDFTM], are object mappings and semantic mappings. XTM effectively represents an object mapping, in that the constructs of the Topic Maps data model are represented directly using XML constructs[1].

For TM/XML we have chosen a semantic mapping, as such mappings generally generally score higher on naturalness and compactness[RDFTM], which again leads to ease of learning and processing.

Choosing a semantic mapping effectively means that instead of getting a generic domain-independent representation of the topic map in XML (like XTM), in which all topic maps use the same XML vocabulary, we get a domain-specific representation. In other words, XTM is generic, while TM/XML adapts itself to the domain vocabulary of the domain.

2   Introduction to the Syntax

The TM/XML syntax for Topic Maps is inspired by the RDF/XML syntax for RDF [RDF/XML]. RDF/XML is the standardized XML syntax for interchange of RDF content, like XTM for Topic Maps, but unlike XTM it represents a semantic mapping from RDF to XML. The general principles of RDF/XML are thus rather similar to those of TM/XML, but due to the nature of Topic Maps, the details are rather different.

The status of the syntax at the moment is that it exists as a fully-developed and specified private proposal. A prototype implementation in Jython based on the Ontopia Topic Maps Engine exists, as does an XSLT stylesheet converting TM/XML into XTM. Productized implementations are likely to follow shortly.

Note that TM/XML is not defined as a serialization of an entire topic map, but as a serialization of a set of topics. This is because the use cases described above all involve the use of TM/XML with fragments. Serializing an entire topic map is no harder than making the set of topics to be serialized the set of all topics in the topic map.

2.1   How It Works

The general principle for the syntax is that each topic is represented by an XML element whose type is derived from the topic's type. The characteristics of the topic are represented as child elements of the topic element, again with element types derived from the type of the characteristic. This gives a simple, compact, and natural XML representation for Topic Maps data. Untyped constructs (like variant names) have built-in elements defined as part of TM/XML.

Another principle is that where possible element type names are formed from the subject identifiers of typing topics using namespaces. Where no subject identifiers are available, simple IDs are used.

Below is a simple topic map in LTM syntax:

---

[1] Of course, in reality the mapping went from XTM to TMDM, rather than vice versa, as XTM predates TMDM.

```
#TOPICMAP ~tm
#PREFIX dc @"http://purl.org/dc/elements/1.1/"

[tm : topicmap = "TM/XML example topic map"]
{tm, dc:description,[[This topic map is a simple example of
the use of TM/XML.]]}

[lmg : person = "Lars Marius Garshol"; "garshol, lars marius"]
{lmg, homepage, "http://www.garshol.priv.no"}

created-by(tm : work, lmg : creator)
presentation(lmg : presenter, tmxml : presented, tmra05 : event)
```

In TM/XML, this topic map would be represented as follows:

```
<topicmap xmlns:iso="http://psi.topicmaps.org/iso13250/model/"
          xmlns:tm="http://psi.ontopia.net/xml/tm-xml/"
          xmlns:core="http://www.topicmaps.org/xtm/1.0/core.xtm#"
          xmlns:dc="http://purl.org/dc/elements/1.1/"
          reifier="tmtopic">

  <topicmap id="tmtopic">
    <iso:topic-name>
      <tm:value>TM/XML example topic map</tm:value>
    </iso:topic-name>
   <dc:description>This topic map is a simple example
   of the use of TM/XML.</dc:description>
  </topicmap>

  <person id="lmg">
    <iso:topic-name>
      <tm:value>Lars Marius Garshol</tm:value>
      <tm:variant scope="core:sort">garshol,
          lars marius</tm:variant>
    </iso:topic-name>
    <homepage datatype="http://www.w3.org/2001/XMLSchema#anyURI"
      >http://www.garshol.priv.no</homepage>

    <created-by role="creator" topicref="tmtopic"
        otherrole="work"/>

    <presentation role="presenter">
      <presented topicref="tmxml"/>
      <event topicref="tmra05"/>
    </presentation>
  </person>
</topicmap>
```

The `reifier` attribute on the `topicmap` element refers to the ID of the topic reifying the topic map. This is the opposite of the XTM representation, where the reifying topic would refer to the topic map. (See the XTM version in 2.2.)

The second `topicmap` element represents a topic of type `topicmap` (the one that reifies the topic map). The `iso:topic-name` element name appears because this is the PSI of the default topic name type in TMDM [ISO13250-2], given to topic names which have no type (like those in the LTM fragment). The `tm:value` element is introduced as a wrapper element for the topic name value in order to ensure that topic names and occurrences can be distinguished, and that variant names can be accomodated together with the topic name value without difficulty.

The `tm:variant` element is used to represent variants, and the `scope` attribute contains the scope of the variant. The same attribute can be used throughout TM/XML to represent scope.

The `dc:description` and `homepage` elements represent occurrences. The element type name `dc:description` is a QName, so this refers to the occurrence type by PSI, where the PSI is the concatenation of the namespace URI and the local name.

The `created-by` and `presentation` elements both represent associations. The `presentation` element has one sub-element for each role in the association not played by the parent topic.

2.2   Comparison with XTM

That TM/XML provides a simpler, and more easily understandable, representation of the topic map information than the equivalent XTM representation should be self-evident. However, for those wanting evidence, the following shows the same topic map in XTM. (We describe this as being "the same" topic map, as the XTM and TM/XML representations would produce identical TMDM instances.)

```
<topicMap xmlns="http://www.topicmaps.org/xtm/1.0/"
          xmlns:xlink="http://www.w3.org/1999/xlink"
          id="id2588719">
  <topic id="tmtopic">
    <instanceOf>
      <topicRef xlink:href="#topicmap"/>
    </instanceOf>
    <subjectIdentity>
      <subjectIndicatorRef xlink:href="#id2588719"/>
    </subjectIdentity>
    <baseName>
      <baseNameString>TM/XML example topic map</baseNameString>
    </baseName>
    <occurrence>
      <instanceOf>
        <subjectIndicatorRef
        xlink:href="http://purl.org/dc/elements/1.1/description"/>
```

```
    </instanceOf>
    <resourceData>This topic map is a simple example of the
    use of TM/XML.</resourceData>
  </occurrence>
</topic>
<topic id="lmg">
  <instanceOf>
    <topicRef xlink:href="#person"/>
  </instanceOf>
  <baseName>
    <baseNameString>Lars Marius Garshol</baseNameString>
    <variant>
      <parameters>
        <subjectIndicatorRef
          xlink:href="http://www.topicmaps.org/xtm/1.0/core.
              xtm#sort"/>
      </parameters>
      <variantName>
        <resourceData>garshol, lars marius</resourceData>
      </variantName>
    </variant>
  </baseName>
  <occurrence>
    <instanceOf>
      <topicRef xlink:href="#homepage"/>
    </instanceOf>
    <resourceRef xlink:href="http://www.garshol.priv.no"/>
  </occurrence>
</topic>
<association>
  <instanceOf>
    <topicRef xlink:href="#created-by"/>
  </instanceOf>
  <member>
    <roleSpec>
      <topicRef xlink:href="#creator"/>
    </roleSpec>
    <topicRef xlink:href="#lmg"/>
  </member>
  <member>
    <roleSpec>
      <topicRef xlink:href="#work"/>
    </roleSpec>
    <topicRef xlink:href="#tmtopic"/>
  </member>
```

```
    </association>
    <association>
      <instanceOf>
        <topicRef xlink:href="#presentation"/>
      </instanceOf>
      <member>
        <roleSpec>
          <topicRef xlink:href="#presenter"/>
        </roleSpec>
        <topicRef xlink:href="#lmg"/>
      </member>
      <member>
        <roleSpec>
          <topicRef xlink:href="#presented"/>
        </roleSpec>
        <topicRef xlink:href="#tmxml"/>
      </member>
      <member>
        <roleSpec>
          <topicRef xlink:href="#event"/>
        </roleSpec>
        <topicRef xlink:href="#tmra05"/>
      </member>
    </association>
  </topicMap>
```

The complexity of the syntax affects the ease of processing with standard XML tools quite dramatically, and more than may be immediately obvious. For example, the XPath to find all creators of a work is shown below. (The $work variable contains the ID of the work.)

```
//xtm:association
  [xtm:member[xtm:roleSpec / xtm:topicRef / @xlink:href = '#work']
             [xtm:topicRef / @xlink:href = concat('#', $work)]]
  [xtm:instanceOf / xtm:topicRef / @xlink:href = '#created-by']
  / xtm:member[xtm:roleSpec / xtm:topicRef / @xlink:href
                                             = '#creator]
  / xtm:topicRef / @xlink:href
```

This query actually only finds the IDs of the creators, rather than the creators themselves. It also makes the simplifying assumption that no subject IndicatorRef and resourceRef elements are used to refer to topics. In reality, this assumption is often wrong.

For comparison, a query that returns the elements representing the creators (as opposed to just the IDs as above) in the same situation on TM/XML would look as follows:

```
//person [created-by/@topicref = $work]
```

XPath is only one way among many to process XML, but we here assume that implementing the same operation using other XML tools would be equally complex.

3   Formal Definition

This section defines the syntax and its processing more precisely. All TM/XML documents will be valid according to the RELAX-NG [ISO19757-2] schema shown below[2].

```
default namespace = "http://psi.ontopia.net/xml/tm-xml/"
datatypes xsd = "http://www.w3.org/2001/XMLSchema-datatypes"

start = topicmap

topicmap = element * { reifier?, topic+ } reifier = attribute
reifier { text }

# some form of identifier is required
topic = element * { ((id, identifier*, locator*) |
                     (id?, ((identifier+, locator*) |
                            (identifier*, locator+)))),
                   topicname*, occurrence*, association* }
id = attribute id { xsd:ID }
identifier = element identifier { xsd:anyURI }
locator = element locator { xsd:anyURI }

topicname = element * { reifier?, scope?, value, variant* }
scope = attribute scope { text }
value = element value { text }
variant = element variant { scope, reifier?, datatype?, text }
occurrence = element * { reifier?, scope?, datatype?, text }
datatype = attribute datatype { xsd:anyURI }

association = unary | binary | nary
unary = element * { reifier?, scope?, role }
role = attribute role { text }
binary = element * { reifier?, scope?, role, otherrole, topicref }
otherrole = attribute otherrole { text }
nary = element * { reifier?, scope?, role, assocrole, assocrole+ }
assocrole = element * { topicref }
topicref = attribute topicref { text }
```

---

[2] RELAX-NG was used because DTDs can not describe a vocabulary where element types are defined by their signature instead of by their names, nor can W3C XML Schema.

3.1   The Serialization Process

The input to the serialization process is an element type name, and a set of topics. The element type name is used for the root element, since there is nothing in the set of topics that could tell us what root element type name would be suitable, and since the element type name is in any case not meaningful.

To produce the output, perform the steps below in order for each topic in the input set, and wrap the entire output in an element of the type given as input to the process. If the topic map is reified, add a `reifier` attribute containing a topic reference to the reifying topic (procedure below).

All specific elements mentioned in the steps below belong to the `http://psi.ontopia.net/xml/tm-xml/` namespace. The conventional namespace prefix for this namespace is `tm`, although any prefix may be used.

1. Produce the element type name from the type of the topic (following the procedure described below). If it has no type, use `topic`. If it has more than one type, pick one arbitrarily. (The remaining types will be captured as associations.)
2. If the topic has no subject identifier or subject locator, produce a unique ID for the topic.
3. Output the start tag for the element with the element type name produced in step 1, and, if an ID was produced in step 2, an `id` attribute with that ID as the value.
4. For each subject identifier of the topic, output the identifier in an `identifier` element.
5. For each subject locator of the topic, output the locator in a `locator` element.
6. For each topic name of the topic, produce an element name (procedure below) from the type of the topic name. If the name's scope is non-empty, add a `scope` attribute, containing whitespace-separated topic references (as defined below). Add `reifier` as for the topic map. Then do the following:
   - Output a child element `value` containing the string value of the name.
   - For every variant of the topic name, output a `variant` element, with the `reifier` and `scope` attributes produced the same way as for the topic name. The string value of the variant is output as the content of the element, and if the datatype is not string, the datatype URI is output in the `datatype` attribute.
7. For each occurrence of the topic, produce an element type name (procedure below) from the occurrence type topic. Add scope, reifier, and datatype as above. The string value of the occurrence becomes the element content.
8. For each association role of the topic, except that in the type-instance association used to produce the element type name for the current topic, produce a new element as described below.

   Produce the element type name of the new element from the association type. Add an attribute named `role` containing a topic reference to the type of the role played by the current topic. The `scope` and `reifier` attributes are added as above (with the scope and reifier of the association the role is part of).

(a) If the association has only one role, output an empty element with the attributes and name described above.

(b) If the association has two roles, add a `topicref` attribute with a reference to the topic playing the other role, and a `otherrole` attribute with a reference to the type of the other role. Then output the element with the name and attributes as given above, and no content.

(c) If the association has more than two roles, output the element with the name and attributes as given above. Then, for each other role in the association output an empty child element with an element type name produced from the role type. Give each element a `topicref` attribute with a reference to the topic playing the role.

9. Output the end tag for the topic element.

No particular requirements are placed on whitespace, except that whitespace must not be added to the contents of elements with text content. All text content must of course be properly escaped to ensure that the resulting XML is well-formed.

3.2   Producing Element Type Names

To make an element type name from a topic follow the procedure below:

– If the topic has a subject identifier, use that. If it has more than one, pick one at random. Divide the URI in two at the first '#' or '/' character from the end. The first part becomes the namespace URI, the second part the local name. The choice of namespace prefix is undefined.

– Failing that, use the last part of the topic's item identifier (if there is one; if there is more than one again pick randomly) after the first '/' or '#' from the end. If the result is not unique, add a numeric suffix (starting with 1) to ensure uniqueness.

– Failing that, auto-generate an element type name from the topic's name (again taking care not to create duplicates).

– It is an error if no element type name can be assigned.

3.3   Producing Topic References

Given a topic, a reference to it is produced according to the procedure below:

1. If the topic has a subject identifier, use it. If it has more than one, select one at random. Create a qualified name as for element type names.

2. Failing this, produce a unique ID. How this is done is left to the implementation to determine.

3.4   Deserialization

Producing a topic map from a TM/XML instance is simply the reverse of the serialization process described above. The document element can be ignored (except its **reifier** attribute, if present). Its child elements all create topics. The child elements of topics can be tracked in order, and the various kinds of elements are all structurally different, in such a way that each can be correctly mapped to the corresponding Topic Maps construct.

4   Filtering Fragments with Views

Topic Maps servers can be integrated with external systems by providing basic operations such as "get-topic", "get-topic-list", "update-topic", "add-topic" and "delete-topic" [Garshol05]. In simple cases these operations can use a predefined set of rules to determine what kind of information about a topic can be retrieved from or submitted to a topic map server.

For example, a typical rule for the "get-topic" operation could be:

1. Retrieve all information about main topic including identifiers, names, occurrences, and associations.
2. For all referenced topics retrieve identifiers and names only.

External systems can use a sequence of "get-topic" operations if additional information about referenced topics is required. If the topic map server is restricted by these basic rules then support of interesting use cases would require implementing quite "chatty" sessions between external systems and a topic map server. Client applications would also receive a lot of information about topics which this client is not interested in. Another problem occurs with updates: different external systems can be responsible for updates of different slices of information about topics. A requirement to submit complete information about topic can complicate the communication protocol between external systems and a topic map server.

This section introduces TM-Views – a mechanism for defining flexible filtering rules which can be used in combination with TM/XML for serialization/deserialization of topic map fragments.

4.1   TM-Views – What Is It?

The main goal of TM-Views is to provide the ability to specify which pieces of information about a topic of interest and related topics to include in fragments during communication between external systems and a topic map server.

TM-Views includes an XML vocabulary for defining views and a procedural component which implements filtering rules and integration with TM/XML serialization/de-serialization.

Views enable users to specify which specific topic map constructs should be selected from a topic map for a topic in question. Views also help manage traversal of required associations.

Views consist of a set of patterns. Each pattern selects some constructs from a topic (identifiers, names, occurrences, or associations). Using TM/XML these constructs are mapped to a natural XML syntax.

Views allow patterns to be specified not only for the starting topic but also for topics referenced by associations, thus allowing "path-based" filtering rules. For example, we can specify that if the main topic is a person then a topic for a company-employer and topic for location of this company should be included in the fragment.

Generally speaking, some topics can be referenced several times by different paths during association traversing. Information from different paths is combined for each referenced topic in one topic element.

The example below demonstrates how a view can be defined.

4.2   Example of View Definition

```
<view xmlns="http://psi.ontopia.net/xml/tm-views/"
      id="person_view" name="Person view">

  <topic type="person">
    <identifier type="subjectIdentifier" />

    <basename type="*">
      <except>
        <basename type="nickname" />
      </except>
    </basename>

    <occurrence type="homepage" />

    <association type="employed-by" role="employee"
                 otherrole="employer">
      <topic type="company">
        <identifier type="*"/>
        <basename type="*"/>
        <occurrence type="homepage"/>
        <association type="located-at" role="object"
                     otherrole="location"
                     playertype="city town location"/>
      </topic>
    </association>

    <association type="knows-person" role="person"
                 otherrole="person" playertype="person"/>
  </topic>
</view>
```

This view defines fragments for a main topic of type "person". The **type** attribute on **topic** and the **playertype** attribute on **association** provide "hints" for choosing the type during TM/XML serialization.

If a topic is an instance of the specified type then this type is used as the basis for a mapping to an XML element. If there are several type hints, then they are validated in some order. If there is no valid type hint, then the general TM/XML rule is used.

View definitions allow patterns to be specified based on the types of names, occurrences, identifiers, and associations. Wild card "*" and exceptions are supported to simplify definition of filtering rules.

4.3   View Definition Language

In this section we define the syntax for the view definition language using RELAX-NG schema.

```
default namespace = "http://psi.ontopia.net/xml/tm-views/"
datatypes xsd = "http://www.w3.org/2001/XMLSchema-datatypes"

start = view

view = element view {
    attribute id { xsd:ID },
    attribute name {text}?,
    topic*
}

topic = element topic {
        attribute type {text},
        identifier-pattern*,
        topicname-pattern*,
        occurrence-pattern*,
        association-pattern*
}

identifier-pattern =  element identifier{
        attribute type{text}
}

topicname-pattern =  element basename{
        attribute type{text},
        element except{
            element basename{attribute type{text}}+
        }?
}

occurrence-pattern =  element occurrence{
```

```
        attribute type{text},
        element except{
            element occurrence{attribute type{text}}+
        }?
}

association-pattern =  unary-pattern | binary-pattern |
                       nary-pattern

unary-pattern= element association{
        attribute type{text},
        attribute role{text},
        element except{
            element association{
                    attribute type{text},
                    attribute role{text}
            }+
        }?
}

binary-pattern = element association{
        attribute type{text},
        attribute role{text},
        attribute otherrole{text},
        attribute playertype{text}?,
        topic*,
        element except{
            element association{
                    attribute type{text},
                    attribute role{text},
                    attribute otherrole{text}
            }+
        }?
}

nary-pattern= element association{
        attribute type{text},
        attribute role{text},
        other-role-pattern,
        other-role-pattern+,
        element except{
            element association{
                    attribute type{text},
                    attribute role{text},
                    attribute otherroles{text}
```

```
        }+
      }?
}

other-role-pattern=element otherrole{
    attribute type{text},
    attribute playertype{text}?,
    topic*
}
```

4.4 Applying a View to a Topic Map

The example below demonstrates the result of applying the previously defined
view to an example topic map. (Some details in the example have been replaced
with ... for readability.)

```
<topicmap view="person_view" ...>
   <person id="lmg" top_topic="true">
     <iso:topic-name>
       <tm:value>Lars Marius Garshol</tm:value>
     </iso:topic-name>
     <homepage datatype="...">http://www.garshol.priv.no</
      homepage>
     <employed-by topicref="ontopia" role="employee" otherrole=
      "employer"/>
     <knows-person topicref="dmitrybv" role="person" otherrole=
      "person"/>
   </person>

   <person id="dmitrybv">
     <iso:topic-name><tm:value>Dmitry Bogachev</tm:value></iso:
      topic-name>
   </person>

   <company id="ontopia">
     <iso:topic-name><tm:value>Ontopia</tm:value></iso:topic-name>
     <homepage datatype="...">http://www.ontopia.net</homepage>
     <located-at topicref="city_Oslo" role="object" otherrole=
      "location"/>
   </company>

   <city id="city_Oslo">
      <iso:topic-name><tm:value>Oslo</tm:value></iso:topic-name>
   </city>
</topicmap>
```

The XML elements at the top level of this fragment represent topics. Sub-elements are used to encode identifiers, names, occurrences and associations. The only pieces of information requested by the view definition provided above are presented in this fragment (combined with the default filtering rules).

4.5   The Fragmentation Process

In this section we define the fragmentation process. The input to the fragmentation process is a set of "top topics" and a view definition.

To produce the output:

1. "normalize" the view definition by replacing each "playertype" attribute with a "topic" sub-element which has a "type" attribute equal to the value of the "playertype" attribute; add "any identifier" and "any name" patterns to created "topic" sub-element;
2. let Topic Description List denote an empty list of topic descriptions;
3. let Topic View List denote a list of topic view definitions ("topic" sub-elements inside of a "view" element);
4. for each topic in the "top topics" set apply Create a Topic Description procedure described below with the "view-list" argument binded to the Topic View List and the "top-topic" argument bound to the "true" value;
5. for each topic description in the Topic Description List produce a "topic wrapper" element with an "id" attribute based on the TM/XML serialization rules;
6. for each construct inside of the topic description produce its XML representation based on TM/XML serialization rules;
7. create a "fragment wrapper" element based on TM/XML serialization rules and insert the results of the serialization of the topic descriptions inside of the "fragment wrapper" element;

"Create a Topic Description" procedure:

1. if there is no topic description for a given topic in the Topic Description List then create an empty topic description;
2. if the "top-topic" argument is "true" then mark the topic description as "top_topic";
3. for a given topic and a given list of topic view definitions find a first topic view definition which matches the topic based on the "type" attribute and types of the topic;
4. if a matching topic view definition is found then add matching topic type to the topic description;
5. if a matching topic view definition is found then use it to add identifier, name, occurrence and association descriptions based on the procedures described below;
6. if there is no matching topic view definition or the topic view list is empty then add all identifiers and names from the given topic to the topic description;

"Create an Identifier Description" procedure:

1. for each identifier related to a given topic find a first identifier pattern which matches the identifier based on the "type" attribute;
2. if there is a matching pattern then include a description of the identifier into a topic description;

"Create a Topic Name Description" procedure:

1. for each topic name related to a given topic find a first name pattern which matches the topic name based on the "type" attribute;
2. if there is a matching pattern then include a description of the topic name into a topic description;
3. if the topic name has a scope, for each topic in the scope apply "Create a Topic Description" procedure with an empty topic view list;
4. if the topic name is reified by a topic, apply "Create a Topic Description" procedure for this topic with an empty topic view list;

"Create an Occurrence Description" procedure:

1. for each occurrence related to a given topic find a first occurrence pattern which matches the occurrence based on the "type" attribute;
2. if there is a matching pattern then include a description of the occurrence into a topic description;
3. if the occurrence has a scope, for each topic in the scope apply "Create a Topic Description" procedure with an empty topic view list;
4. if occurrence is reified by a topic, apply "Create a Topic Description" procedure for this topic with an empty topic view list;

"Create an Association Description" procedure:

1. for each association related to a given topic find a first association pattern which matches the association based on "type", "role", and "otherrole" attributes;
2. if there is a matching pattern then include a description of the association into a topic description;
3. for each other role player of the association create a list of topic view definitions based on "topic" sub-elements of the "association" element (can be empty);
4. apply recursively "Create a Topic Description" procedure for the role player and the topic view definition list;
5. if association has a scope, for each topic in the scope apply "Create a Topic Description" procedure with an empty topic view list;
6. if association is reified by a topic, apply "Create a Topic Description" procedure with an empty topic view list; x.

4.6   TM-Views and Updates

TM-Views support remote editing use cases when some information can be extracted from a topic map as a fragment, transformed into an XML resource using domain-specific vocabulary, modified by users or other systems as an XML resource, and pushed back to a topic map as a modified topic map fragment. Views effectively describe boundaries of the information that can be transferred from and into a topic map. When modified fragment is pushed back, only topic map constructs defined by these boundaries need to be changed.

5   Related Work

The Topic Maps syntax in the original Topic Maps standard was similar to XTM 1.0, but unlike XTM 1.0 it was defined as an SGML architecture. This meant that the architectural forms facility in HyTime could be used to map domain syntaxes to the SGML architecture declaratively. The actual mapping would be performed by the SGML/XML parser, or an associated architectural forms processor. The workings of this were actually similar to those of TM/XML, with element type names of element types mapped to topics becoming the topic type, etc. However, architectural forms is more or less dead today, and also requires either modifying the DTD or the instance document, and so is less attractive.

Another obviously related syntax is RDF/XML, which is the standard interchange syntax for RDF[RDF/XML]. It is very similar to TM/XML, but is for RDF only, and is not directly applicable to Topic Maps.

Meaning Definition Language (MDL)[Worden01] provided a means to annotate an XML vocabulary to describe its mapping into an object model, which can then be connected to either UML or RDF Schema. The language relies heavily on XPath for describing the cases in which individual mappings apply. The language has clear similarities with TM/XML, but is not an XML data syntax and more of a method for mapping near-arbitrary XML into an object model.

Other syntaxes have been defined for both RDF and Topic Maps, but all of them have been object mappings (like XTM) instead of semantic mappings like RDF/XML and TM/XML. Some work has also been done on mapping XML to RDF [Miller2004], but this relied on manually writing XSLT stylesheets for each mapping. An earlier work by one of the authors showed how to use XPath to create complex mappings from near-arbitrary XML to RDF using XPath, which could then be converted from RDF to Topic Maps[Pepper02].

The fragmentation process described in this paper is close to other approaches for defining Topic Maps fragments, for example TMShare [Ahmed01] and XTM Fragment Interchange [Garshol02]. The main difference with the solution proposed in this paper is the ability to filter topics being included in fragments and the ability to selectively traverse associations.

6   Conclusion

This paper presents a syntax for Topic Maps, called TM/XML, that can represent all of Topic Maps without loss of information[3], formulated in terms of the

---

[3] Or nearly so. Reification of association roles is deliberately not supported.

information domain. TM/XML is far easier to read for human beings, and also to process with XML tools such as XSLT, than is XTM.

The TM/XML syntax is already integrated with the TMRAP protocol, and can thus meet our use cases. However, for improved usability, more work on updating fragments with new information that only partially replaces existing information is necessary. Further, in order to make it easier for those receiving TM/XML fragments to process these (whether for presentation or other purposes), conversion from the Topic Maps schema to an XML schema for the received fragments would be desirable.

It is not the intention of the authors that TM/XML become a standardized Topic Maps syntax. If it should be widely adopted, and standardization proposed by others, the authors would not oppose this, but for the time being standardization seems premature.

References

[Ahmed01]   K. Ahmed; TMShare - Topic Map Fragment Exchange In a Peer-To-Peer Application; XML Europe 2003, London, England. http://www.idealliance.org/ papers/dx_xmle03/papers/02-03-03/02-03-03.html

[Garshol05]   L. M. Garshol; TMRAP – Topic Maps Remote Access Protocol; forthcoming, to be published in proceedings of TMRA'05.

[Garshol02]   L. M. Garshol; XTM Fragment Interchange 0.1 Ontopia Technical Report 2002-09-23; http://www.ontopia.net/topicmaps/materials/xtm-fragments.html

[ISO13250-2]   ISO 13250-3: Topic Maps – Data Model; International Organization for Standardization; Geneva. http://www.isotopicmaps.org/sam/sam-model/

[ISO13250-3]   ISO 13250-3: Topic Maps – XML Syntax; International Organization for Standardization; Geneva. http://www.isotopicmaps.org/sam/sam-xtm/

[ISO19757-2]   ISO 19757-2: Document Schema Definition Languages (DSDL) – Part 2: Regular-grammar- based validation – RELAX NG; International Organization for Standardization; Geneva. http://www.y12.doe.gov/sgml/sc34/document/0362_files/relaxng-is.pdf

[Miller2004]   E. Miller, C. M. Sperberg-McQueen; On mapping from colloquial XML to RDF using XSLT; Extreme Markup 2004. http://www.mulberrytech.com/Extreme/Proceedings/html / 2004 / Sperberg-McQueen01/EML2004Sperberg-McQueen01.html

[Pepper02]   S. Pepper, L. M. Garshol; The XML Papers: Lessons on Applying Topic Maps; XML USA 2002, Baltimore, USA. http://www.ontopia.net/topicmaps/materials/xmlconf.html

[RDFTM]   S. Pepper, F. Vitali, L. M. Garshol, V. Presutti; A Survey of RDF/Topic Maps Interoperability Proposals; W3C Note; World Wide Web Consortium, 2005-03-29; http://www.w3.org/TR/rdftm-survey/

[RDF/XML]   D. Beckett; RDF/XML Syntax Specification (Revised); W3C Recommendation, World Wide Web Consortium, 10 February 2004; http://www.w3.org/TR/rdf-syntax-grammar/

[Robie01]   J. Robie, et al; The Syntactic Web; Markup Languages: Theory & Practice 3.4 (2002): 411-440. http://www.w3.org/XML/2002/08/robie.syntacticweb.html

[TMAPI]   TMAPI. http://www.tmapi.org

[Worden01]   R. Worden; Meaning Definition Language; in *Professional XML Meta Data*; Wrox Press, 2001.

Navigating Through Archives, Libraries and Museums: Topic Maps as a Harmonizing Instrument

Salvatore Vassallo

University of Pavia, Corso Strada Nuova 65,
27100 Pavia, Italy
salvatore_vassallo@tin.it

Abstract. The paper deals with the possibility of creating a topic map based system where different sectors of cultural heritage would interact with users, by monitoring the navigation histories of users and the statistics on the searches, in order to authorize variant form of names. The problem of managing different sectors and harmonizing them both from a structural and a semantic view point, by using topic maps, is also discussed. With regards to this, we are introducing two projects, which are largely based on the above mention use of topic maps.

1 Introduction

The paper considers use of topic maps in the area of cultural heritage from three view points:

- To manage the variant forms of a name, caused by the users' search itself. According to this, we carried out an analysis through questionnaires in order to test a hypothetical system built on this logics;
- To allow the management and the navigation through an archive: we will present a model finalized to the production of a guide for the exploitation of the archival fonds as well as the reorganization of the library, both owned by the "Archivio di Stato di Pavia";
- To navigate through archives, libraries and museums: using topic maps as a harmonizing instrument in conformity with the specific descriptive standards, but at the same time creating a logical framework enabling the interactions of various objects. This idea is at the basis of the CeDECA[1] project: a census about cultural heritage in the Oltrepò pavese.

---

[1] Centro di Documentazione Etnografica e di Cultura Appenninica, developed on behalf of Pavia University by Maria Antonietta Arrigoni, Federica Biava, Ester Bucchi de Giuli, Marina Chiogna, Paola Ciandrini, Elettra de Lorenzo, Elena Giavari, Flavia Giudice, Marco Savini and Salvatore Vassallo with the coordination of professors Pierangelo Lombardi and Paul Gabriele Weston.

L. Maicher and J. Park (Eds.): TMRA 2005, LNAI 3873, pp. 231–240, 2006.

2   Topic Maps and Variant Forms of Names: A Permanent Renovation

In this case our study started from the analysis of the solutions adopted by products such as Aquabrowser[2]: the peculiar graphic layout of the latter showing the variant name options, led us to foresee the possibility of incorporating some of those functions into a topic map.

One of the aims of Aquabrowser (which, according to the scopes of our analysis is just an example) is to use the words related with the search to discover new information and to help users to formulate a new query. The discover function works like the associations in a topic map. The problem is that the software uses also the spelling variations (probably based on Levensthein distance ≤ 2) to determine the associations. Such an approach will necessarily cause a great deal of noise: for example, a search based on the string "Kenedi" (meaning Aaron Kenedi) will produce as an alternative form, the name "Kennedy". Another example is the case of "queen": here Aquabrowser uses as alternative form the term "queer" to generate other associations, which is quite obviously a problem.

Our idea is to overcome this limit, through a statistical analysis of the users' behaviors, in order to certificate the variant forms, no matter how they have been generated. For instance, if, among the average sample, a significant percentage of users research "Kenedy" and accept the option which is suggested, (i.e., the form "Kennedy") by selecting it and not leaving the page within the first 30 seconds[3], then "Kenedy" will be considered a variant forms of the name certified by the users, and will be included into the "Kennedy" topic (as variant or as basename) and used to generate the net of associations (as in Aquabrowser).

We have prepared a questionnaire with the aim of simulating users' approach to the research: five known personalities were indicated and the user was asked to write down how he would search each name into a hypothetical informative system. The test was carried out on famous people, but could have dealt with any other term (indeed, the idea of an automatic certification of variant forms of a name refers to any research term, even though it is undeniable that people's names seem to be among the most researched terms).

We tried to find an empirical formula to define the minimum rate to become a certified variant form: the main idea is to find an equation that decreases slowly when the number of questionnaires increases. In this meaning we analyzed in increasing groups the questionnaires, determining and testing, step by step, the minimum rate. The formula upon which the minimum rate varies according to the number of searches was calculated by interpolating such results.

---

[2] Aquabrowser, <http://www.medialab.nl/>, is developed by Medialab as a non conventional library OPAC interface. It appears like a system that allows the contextualization of terms, using a graphic environment comparable to graphic topic maps. Besides it offers the chance of navigating through variant name forms, trying to cater for accidental mistyping. It's indeed on this function that we based our first analysis.

[3] It is the time estimated so to exclude non profitable searches, evidenced by the quick leave of the page.

$$P = \frac{1}{k^{\log x}} \tag{1}$$

where P is the minimum rate, x is the number of questionnaires (in our case or the number of searches in the case of an information system) and k is a constant value (empirical range calculated between 2.0 and 3.0). This range is a consequence of the impact of the constant value on the inclination of the curve: in the presence of a highly homogeneous group of users one should decrease k to increase P and to refine the sample (for i.e. to exclude dialect form, typical of a homogeneous groups).

This solution and the equation now exposed were tested through a questionnaire filled in by nearly 600 persons, of different age and social extraction. So, with an average k = 2.5, according to the formula the minimum rate is 8%.

Significant results that were obtained in relation to the above mention function were the following:

Table 1. Shakespeare – name form certified by users searches ($\geq$8%)

Name form certified	Per cent of questionnaires
Shakespeare	82%
Shakespear	13%

Table 2. Krusciov – name form certified by users searches ($\geq$8%)

Name form certified	Per cent of questionnaires
Krushov	50%
Kruscev	13%
Krusciov	13%
Crusciov	8%

Table 3. Beethoven – name form certified by users searches ($\geq$8%)

Name form certified	Per cent of questionnaires
Beethoven	76%
Beethowen	11%

Table 4. Ceausescu – name form certified by users searches ($\geq$8%)

Name form certified	Per cent of questionnaires
Ceausescu	32%
Ciausescu	29%
Chausescu	17%
Causescu	9%

Table 5. Tchaikovsky – name form certified by users searches (≥5%)[4]

Name form certified	Per cent of questionnaires
Tchaikovsky	6,5%
Chaicoski	5%
Tchaikowsky	5%

This idea could be integrated into a real system through the automatic analysis of statistic researches, thus certificating the variant forms of the name, according to users' "mistakes".

Undoubtedly a choice of this kind is laid open to criticism from the language purists' side, who could accuse our approach of laxity and of encouraging the language natural degeneration. Anyway our first aim is users' satisfaction and, in this case, the research success. If you better consider it, topic maps can turn into a didactic instrument, since – navigating through the variant forms of names (or, to better say it, through usual errors) – you can recognize and consequently avoid the most common spelling mistakes.

A system such as Aquabrowser, for example, can evolve, by showing through graphs only the options and the associations included in the topic maps (we could say certified by the users).

3 Navigating Through an Archive

In this paragraph our intent is to illustrate the possibility of creating an informative system that highlights different aspects and services offered by an archive.

This idea was later realized into a project which was submitted to the Archivio di Stato di Pavia but what concerns us here is to explain difficulties and propose a pattern that beyond this specific case.

Starting point is how to link the descriptions of the fonds (for example described in a finding aid, as well as in a pre-existent more complex information system) with the library's catalogue of the archive itself or with an OPAC.

In fact, I have always considered frustrating being unable to navigate through the bibliography which is supplied for each fonds, accessing directly to bibliographic records or to the lending service. Anyway – as you'll see from the model – the targets we appointed concern different aspects, not only literary works or fonds.

In this case we can identify three groups of entities: agents, objects (fonds, works, documents and exhibitions) and access points (places, events and keywords).

It's to be noticed that we provided a single entity for the agents group: this is extremely important with regard to the debate among archivists; the point – as we have often repeated - is to identify one single ontology with different descriptions and relations. This may seem a trivial conclusion, but I think that managing as a single ontology "Comune di Pavia" as creator and as custody represents a result that would

---

[4] The case of Tchaikovsky suffers obvious problem of transliteration, so we need to refine less the sample increasing K and consequently decrease minimum rate (P).

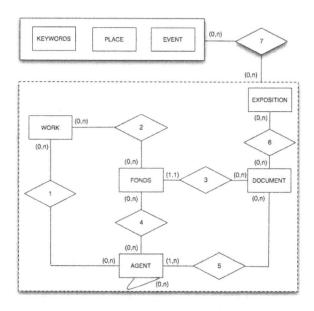

Fig. 1. Entity/Relation model. The relations are: 1- writes/is written by; 2 – is bibliography of/has as bibliography; 3 – is part of/has as part; 4 – created by/has as creator; 5 – writes/is written by; 6 - is part of/has as part; 7 - is related to/has as subject.

make lots of archivists seethe. This could be expressed in a topic map through a single topic with different descriptions (and with the two different scopes: creator and custody).

For what concerns the "objects", the most important connection is between work and fonds (represented by the relationship "is bibliography of/has as bibliography"), whose purpose is to solve the problem of separating the fonds bibliography from the catalogue we emphasized previously. Work is a concept included in the first group of entities (work, expression, manifestation, item) of FRBR model[5][1]. We can easily map FRBR in a topic map and Alexander Siegel provided a lot of example in this sense[6]. We will create a set of PSIs to map the FRBR model, based on his researches, but we need to define PSI for all the relations between the entities of the first group and the others.

It's worth mentioning the idea of online exhibitions[7], whose advantage is to navigate from shown documents to the fonds (or to the series, according to the description level) they belong to.

Finally, in this case there are three contextualization entities, a sort of simplification of those of the FRBR third group: concept, object, event, place. In this

---

[5] Functional Requirements for Bibliographic Records.

[6] See <http://kpeer.wim.uni-koeln.de/~sigel/Projects/FRBR_and_XTM.html> in particular
<http://kpeer.wim.uni-koeln.de/~sigel/Projects/FRBR/FRBR_with_SIPs.ltm> and
<http://kpeer.wim.uni-koeln.de/~sigel/Projects/FRBR/FRBR_examples.ltm>.

[7] About online exhibition see <http://www.archivescanada.ca/english/virtual/search.asp>
<http://www.aabc.bc.ca/aabc/exhibit.html>.

case the most important entity is keywords, with the aim of defining and create some research pathway to guide the inexpert user in navigating the archive.

About the implementation and the management of the topic map, several factors are to be considered:

- Topics on works will be extracted from MARC[8] records. There still exist a few projects on the subject, however the cataloguing software used in this case is based on a MySql database, so the creation of a topic map can be realized with no big difficulty, either converting first MySql database into XML database and then working with a stylesheet XSL-T, or through a script querying the database to extract a topic map (the latter solution is the one we opt for at the moment);
- Agents will be extracted from EAC[9] or EAG[10] documents (using a XSL-T stylesheet) and from MARC records itself;
- Fonds will be extracted from descriptions realized in EAD[11] or EAG (using again XSL-T);
- Some associations can be automatically created from MARC records (for what concerns the relationship author-work) or from EAD and EAG file (analysing the tags addressed to relationships between fonds and creators);
- Documents are codified in TEI[12] and DALF[13] so again we can use a stylesheet to extract topics;
- Exhibitions and contextualization entities will be included manually.

Quite obviously each entity will be linked to its description realized in its own standard format; in this way it will be possible to navigate directly from a fond description to its bibliography, to the single record MARC, all the way to the lending service or to the document delivery, if provided.

4   Managing Related Terms in a Cultural System with a Topic Map

The CeDECA project, mentioned in the introduction, is a census of the cultural patrimony located in the mountain community of the province of Pavia.

In this project the principal issues deal with processing objects of a heterogeneous nature requiring different descriptive representations and different standards.

In order to develop a system that will manage the relationships between different areas of cultural heritage (for example archives, libraries and museums), it is necessary to solve various problems [2]: first of all, it is necessary to manage entities of various nature (for example, classes of objects as fonds, works, their creators,

---

[8] MAchine-Readable Cataloging see <http://www.loc.gov/marc/>.
[9] Encoded Archival Context, see also <http://www.iath.virginia.edu/eac>.
[10] Encoded Archival Guide see also
      <http://aer.mcu.es/sgae/jsp/censo_guia/Documentos/EAG.DTD.txt> and
      <http://aer.mcu.es/sgae/jsp/censo_guia/Documentos/Repertorio_de_etiquetas_EAG_Alfa_0.
      2.doc >.
[11] Encoded Archival Description see also <http://www.loc.gov/ead/>.
[12] Text Encoding Initiative see <http://www.tei-c.org/>.
[13] Digital Archive of Letters in Flanders see <http://www.kantl.be/ctb/project/dalf/>.

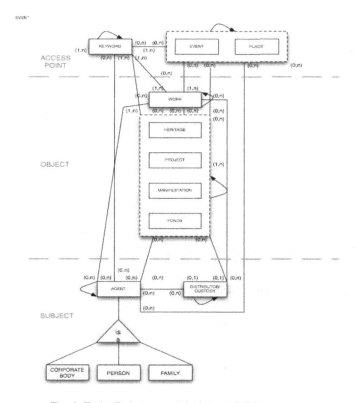

Fig. 2. Entity/Relation model of the CeDECA project

publishers, rights owners, etc.). In the case of cultural heritage repositories the challenge consists in favouring and allowing searches between analogous, though not completely overlapping, areas [3].

Another key factor towards experimenting topic maps is that the CeDECA project doesn't apply only to archival, library and museum collections, but includes a variety of cultural resources, dynamic as well as static, such as those defined in the Minerva Project[14] [4].

The pattern this project is based on, provides three groups of entities: agent, object, access points (**fig. 2**). Regarding the agents, we chose to distinguish between custody and creator, following the well-established archivist tradition: however, in a second stage, it is possible to create on the topic map level one single ontology with different relations (associations) and different descriptions (occurrences), properly characterised through the use of scopes.

The third group of entities – access point – means contextualization entities, after the style of those of FRBR third group, we mentioned previously.

Each entity serves as the focal point for a cluster of data. The model is largely based on the principles expressed in FRBR and <indecs>[15] [5]., as well as on

---

[14] <http://www.minervaeurope.org/>.
[15] INteroperability of Data in E-Commerce Systems <http://www.indecs.org/>.

standards such as ISAD(G) for the multilevel description and ISAAR(CPF)[16] [6] for the treatment of creators, publishers, custodians, etc.

The analysis of attributes and relations has given evidence of many dynamic aspects related to the life cycle of an entity, to the flow of an event or even to the chronological validity of a relation. The simple use of relations and attributes defined a priori was considered inadequate because static. The need for a dynamic approach has led to consider the ABC Harmony[17] model and once again the use of topic maps. It was decided to treat the descriptions of the individual entities through a database and to manage the relations through topic maps, where topics will be automatically extracted from the database. Therefore topic maps play a twofold role, being not just subject maps, but also structure maps, through which the hierarchical complexity should be rendered.

Great affords and time were spent in developing standards aiming at enabling interoperability between archives, libraries and museums. As a matter of fact, these attempts turned out to be grids that did not entirely satisfy the requirements of either of these institutions.

We believe that topic maps, or at least the concept of a net of relationships, independent from the level of the occurrences, allow the description of a single object to be carried out in conformity with the specific descriptive standard, but at the same time they create a net that enables the cohabitation of various objects. For i.e. we could have a topic "Liliana Grassi" (types: agent, creator) separated from the description level, the latter could be managed as an occurrence pointing to an EAC document, compliant ISAAR(CPF) standard.

The harmonization between different cultural heritage areas can be expressed at three levels:

- The entity level: it is necessary to produce an authority file [7] acting as the pivot between different "scopes", within different disciplinary areas, of the entity (for example a corporate body playing the role of creator, publisher, custodian, distributor, etc.). From the point of view of the description, this can be obtained in two ways: either designing a single descriptive record encompassing different[18] fields and interests, or safeguarding the specificities of every party involved and taking advantage, in a later phase, of the possibilities offered by topic maps used as a harmonization device. From the point of view of the topic map this situation will consist, either in different "scopes" or in different "topics" connected according to the degree of diversity involved in the changing role. With respect to harmonizing between variant forms of names arising from different cataloguing tradition and rules, the ADE project (Archivio Delle Entità) [8] under development in Italy, is based on the recognition of different forms, differently described, though under one single ontology. In a topic map we could have for instance the basename "Homer" scoped as AACR2 compliant together with the basename "Homerus" scoped as RICA compliant.

---

[16] International Standard Archival Authority Record for Corporate Bodies, Persons and Families.

[17] <http://metadata.net/harmony/ABCV2.htm>.

[18] Also through a map between standards of description afferent to different words. For this purpose Paul Getty's works can be helpful for the first analysis <http://www.getty.edu/research/conducting_research/standards/intrometadata/3_crosswalks/index.html>.

- The structure level [9]: one could apply descriptive models of the structure in different sectors. Particularly interesting is the application of the ISAD(G)[19][10] model, in its general rather than its specific features, to sectors different from the archives. An effort in this direction is offered, for example, by the UKOLN - RSLP[20] model. Topic maps offer the instrument to represent hierarchical relations of this type, allowing cross searches on various fields (such would be the case of a search showing on the one hand the hierarchical structure of a fonds and on the other hand the ramification of the creator connected to the latter). Moreover it is possible to deal with the single object as a monad[21] described through the appropriate specific language, but at the same time to insert it in a network providing the context. Again the works of Paul Getty can be used as the initial scheme, notwithstanding the difficulties, also of a linguistic nature, one has to cope with in order to interrelate different ontologies (it is the case of the relationship "creator – archival fonds" as opposed to the one "author - work").

- The semantic level: it is by far the level at which topic maps are used with greater profit. The difficulty, in this case, is limited to the definition of the subject terms and to their organization within a taxonomy[11], mapping whenever possible the library subject headings to the corresponding access points in archival or museum systems. In short, the aim is to supply the contextualization elements that in the librarianship field are represented by the third group entities of FRBR concept, object, event, place. We think that the realization of a semantic network, in which the objects of the speech are to be put, can't avoid confronting with these four entities.

References

1. FRBR Functional Requirements for Bibliographic Record. 1998. <http://www.ifla.org/VII/s13/frbr/frbr.pdf>.
2. Ahmed, K.: Topic map design patterns for information architecture. XML Conference & Exposition 2003. <http://www.idealliance.org/papers/dx_xml03/papers/05-03-05/05-03-05.pdf>.
3. Simovaara, J., Vakaari, M.: Interoperability potential in data repositories of archives, libraries and museums. In: Archivi & computer. San Miniato: Archilab, 2 (2004)
4. Minerva Working Group 5: Handbook for quality in cultural web sites: improving quality for citizens. 2003. <http://www.minervaeurope.org/publications/qualitycriteria1_2draft/qualitypdf1103.pdf>.
5. Brickley, C., Hunter, J., Lagoze, C.: An Event-Aware Model for Metadata Interoperability. In: Research and Advanced Technology for Digital Libraries, 4th European Conference, ECDL 2000, Lisbon, Portugal, September 18-20, 2000, Proceedings. Lecture Notes in Computer Science 1923 (2000) 103-116.
6. ISAAR (CPF) International Standard Archival Authority Record for Corporate Bodies, Persons and Families. 2004. <http://www.icacds.org.uk/eng/isaar2ndedn-e_3_1.pdf>.
7. FRAR Functional Requirements for Authority Records. 2005. <http://www.ifla.org/VII/d4/FRANAR-Conceptual-M-Draft-e.pdf>.

---

[19] International Standard for Archival Description (General).
[20] Research Support Libraries Programme, see also <http://www.ukoln.ac.uk/metadata/rslp>.
[21] Meaning a single entity.

8. Galeffi, A., Weston, P.G.: Il controllo d'autorità come raccordo fra sistemi descrittivi. In: Archivi & computer. San Miniato: Archilab, 2 (2004).

9. Ahmed K.: Topic maps for repository. XML Europe 2000. <http://www.gca.org/papers/xmleurope2000/pdf/s29-04.pdf>.

10. ISAD (G) General International Standard Archival Description. 2000. <http://www.icacds.org.uk/eng/ISAD(G).pdf>.

11. Garshol, L.M.: Metadata? Thesauri? Taxonomies? Topic maps! Making sense of it all. Oslo: Ontopia, 2004, <http://www.ontopia.net/topicmaps/materials/tm-vs-thesauri.html>.

MARCXTM: Topic Maps Modeling of MARC Bibliographic Information

Hyun-Sil Lee[1], Yang-Seung Jeon[2], and Sung-Kook Han[2]

[1] University Library, Wonkwang University, 344-2 Sinyong Dong,
Iksan, Chonbuk, Korea
hyunsil@wonkwang.ac.kr
[2] Semantic Web Services Lab., Department of Computer Engineering,
Wonkwang University, 344-2 Sinyong Dong
{globaljeon, skhan}@wonkwang.ac.kr

Abstract. MARC has played an important role as the standard for the description of bibliographic information for a long time. This paper describes a Topic Maps-based bibliographic framework which is compatible with MARC21 formats and the same expressive power as metadata. The MARC record formats are modeled with aggregation relationships. This paper describes the implementation of this model into MARCXTM. MARCXTM consists of two modules: the implementation of MARC21 specification and the representation of real MARC record data. MARCXTM shows how to realize a compatible framework with MARC21 at the level of metadata within the current information technology environment.

1 Introduction

Machine-processible semantics based on metadata or ontology is expected to realize the dream of Semantic Web and intelligent agents. The semantic or conceptual representation and organization of information resources plays a vital role in bibliographic information systems to store, to exchange, and to share various types of bibliographic data.

The Machine-Readable Cataloging (MARC) standards have been widely used for the representation and interchange of bibliography, authority, classification, community information, and holding data in machine-readable form. MARC was originally designed in the late 1960's to aid in the transfer of bibliographic data onto magnetic tape, and also to replace the printed catalog cards with electronic forms[2]. Through continuous updates to MARC21, MARC accommodates extensive data elements describing all forms of materials susceptible to bibliographic description, as well as related information. Despite these strengths for capturing bibliographic properties, MARC reveals limitations for cataloging bibliographic collections: lack of expandability due to rigorous record formats, difficulties in representing bibliographic relationships, ambiguities in describing MARC records, incompatibilities between other MARC formats, weaknesses in describing bibliographic attributes of digitized

L. Maicher and J. Park (Eds.): TMRA 2005, LNAI 3873, pp. 241–252, 2006.
© Springer-Verlag Berlin Heidelberg 2006

resources, and so on[1, 8, 9]. The lack of semantic representation capability especially is an obstacle to realizing knowledge-based bibliographic information systems and achieving interoperability among library systems. Nowadays, the library catalog is no longer a tool for library's own collection; it has become a node serving as an information resource via the Internet[1, 9, 11].

With the advent of XML technologies that can represent the semantic structures of information resources, the Library of Congress' Network Development and MARC Standards Office[1] has developed a framework for working with MARC data in an XML environment. This MARCXML framework is intended to be flexible and extendable to allow users to work with MARC data in ways specific to their needs[5]. However, as MARCXML simply represents MARC records in XML style, it seems that is does not chive its original goals. The Library of Congress (LOC) has also developed a more advanced descriptive metadata standard for bibliographic element set that may be used for a variety of purpose. Metadata Object Description Schema (MODS) that has a richer bibliographic element set than Dublin Core is intended for metadata representation of the existing MARC21 records[6]. In addition to these approaches, the Functional Requirements for Bibliographic Records (FRBR) framework[2] is proposed to provide a clearly defined, structured framework for relating the data that are recorded in bibliographic records to the needs of the users of those records, and to recommend a basic level of functionality for records created by bibliographic agencies. The FRBR framework uses an entity-relationship model of metadata for bibliographic information entities, instead of the single flat record concept used in MARC formats and includes 4 levels of representation: work, expression, manifestation and item[3].

These approaches to represent semantic information in MARC records are not sufficient to achieve their goals. MARCXML is only the XML-style representation of traditional MARC records and does not consider semantic properties of bibliographic elements. Although MODS takes into account the rapid growth of metadata models, it offers only a subset of MARC bibliographic elements. On the other hand, FRBR is a conceptual framework applicable to any metadata about a product of intellectual and/or artistic endeavor.

MARC contains abundant bibliographic elements and is widely used as the fundamental record structure of library systems. Considering the usability of MARC in library systems, a representation schema is required which is highly compatible with MARC21 and can represent semantic information in an XML environment. The Topic Maps paradigm is suitable for conceptual modeling of MARC bibliographic elements. Multi-dimensional representation of relationships among topics is effective in capturing diverse bibliographic relations, and its incremental merging capability is useful to construct large bibliographic information resources[7].

This paper proposes MARCXTM, XTM model of MARC21 bibliographic elements. The major research efforts to enhance the representation of MARC record formats is reviewed to derive the functional requirements necessary for modeling MARC formats. Based on these requirements, the topic map model of MARC bibliographic elements is presented. This paper also describes the implementation of MARCXTM and demonstrates the usability of MARCXTM. MARCXTM can retain

---

[1] http://www.loc.gov/marc

[2] http://www.iflz.org/VII/s13/frbr/frbr.htm

all bibliographic elements in MARC21, and represent their concepts and relationships. MARCXTM also gives insight into metadata and ontology for bibliographic resources. This paper is organized as follows. Section 2 provides introductory information on MARC and its new frameworks. In Section 3, Topic Maps modeling of MARC is discussed. Section 4 presents the implementation of MARCXTM and finally the conclusion and discussion in Section 5.

2   Description of Bibliographic Information Based on MARC

Although MARC standards constitute a solid foundation for the description of bibliographic information, they are forced to accommodate state-of-the-art technology such as metadata and ontology. This section reviews the core MARC format and a framework for working with MARC in XML environment so as to apprehend more effective descriptions of bibliographic information.

2.1   MARC Formats: Standards for the Representation of Bibliographic Information

Although the MARC format was originally developed to facilitate the printed catalog cards and to assist in the exchange of bibliographic data, various related MARC formats were successively developed for authority, classification, community information and holding data. According to the dissemination of MARC formats, a number of dialects such as USMARC, CAN/MARC((, and UKMARC((emerged to meet their own local requirements. After discussions and minor changes to USMARC and CAN/MARC, MARC21 was evolved to harmonize both formats and to cover diverse types of resources including digital materials and Internet resources. MARC21 defines the record structure that describes information containers, i.e., books manuscripts, maps, serials, movies, music scores, audio/video recordings, 2D/3D images and microforms. MARC21 as an implementation of ANSI/NISO Z39.2 and its international counterpart, ISO 2709, strongly ensures its position in the standards of cataloging bibliographic information.

Though MARC21 standards are composed of 5 record formats and 6 code lists, a MARC record consists of three main components: the Leader, the Directory, and the Variable Fields[2].

- **Leader:** The leader is the first 24 characters of the record defining parameters for processing the record. The leader consists of data elements that contain coded values and are identified by relative character position.
- **Directory:** The directory consists of directory entries that contain the tag used in variable fields, starting location, and length of each field within the record. The directory is constructed by computer from the bibliographic record, and can be reconstructed in the same way if any of the cataloging information is altered. The length of a directory entry is 12 characters.

---

[3] http://www.collectionscanada.ca/marc/index-e.html
[4] http://www.bl.uk/services/bibliographic/exchange.htm#ukmarc

- **Variable Fields:** The variable fields contain the actual substance of the catalog record. Each variable field is identified by a three-character numeric tag that is stored in the Directory entry for the field, and ends with a field terminator character (ASCII 1D hex). There are two types of variable fields: *variable control fields* and *variable data fields*. Variable control fields, which are the tagged 00X fields, may contain either a single data element or a series of fixed-length data elements identified by relative character position. Variable data fields describe bibliographic data components.

Within variable data fields, the following two kinds of content designation are used:

- **Indicators:** The first two character positions contain values which interpret or supplement the data found in the field. Indicator values are interpreted independently, that is, meaning is not ascribed to the two indicators taken together.
- **Subfield codes:** Two characters that precede each data element within a field that requires separate manipulation. A subfield code consists of a delimiter '$', followed by a data element identifier. Data element identifiers are lowercase alphabetic or numeric characters. Subfield codes are defined independently for each field; however, parallel meanings are preserved where possible.

As the MARC record format focuses on the description of the contents rather than the structure of bibliographic information, no formal definitions for MARC structures and data types are available. It is impossible to derive general rules for repeatability of record elements since their specification is distinctively defined in MARC. However, the overall structure of MARC formats can be defined as in Fig. 2.1.

<Marc21Record>::=<Leader><Directory><VariableField>
  <Directory>::=<DirectoryElement>*
  <DirectoryElement>::=<Tag><Length><Position>
  <VariableField>::=<ControlField><DataField>*
<ControlField>::=<ControlNumber><ControlFieldElement>
  <DataField>::=<Tag><Indicator><SubField>*
  <Indicator>::=<FirstIndicator><SecondIndicator>
  <SubField>::=<SubFieldCode><SubFieldValue>

Fig. 2.1. Structure of MARC record formats

The definition of MARC record formats can be applied to modeling MARC structure. In Fig. 2.2, a typical example of MARC record annotated with the signpost is shown[2]. The MARC record is composed by attaching various field codes to bibliographic data elements. The MARC record represents only the descriptive information, neither semantic representation of bibliographic data nor relationships among them.

Despite many arguments about MARC formats, MARC has been the standard for the representation and communication of bibliographic and related information, and, as yet, nothing standardized has been developed or agreed upon to replace it. MARC

"SIGNPOSTS"				"MARC DATA"
Personal Name	100	1#	$a	Arnosky, Jim.
Title Statement	245	10	$a	Raccoons and ripe corn /
			$c	Jim Arnosky.
Edition Statement	250	##	$a	1st ed.
Publication, Distribution	260	##	$a	New York :
			$b	Lothrop, Lee & Shepard Books,
			$c	c1987.
Physical Description	300	##	$a	25p. :
			$b	col. Ill. ;
			$c	26 cm.
Summary	520	##	$a	Hungry raccoons feast at night in a field or ripe corn.
Subject Added Entry	650	#1	$a	Raccoons.
	900	##	$a	599.74 ARN
	901	##	$a	8009
	903	##	#a	$15.00

Fig. 2.2. The typical example of MARC record

can be regarded as the treasury of bibliographic information since MARC has continuously discovered diverse bibliographic data elements for over 30 years. MARC may play a vital role in the development of metadata or ontology for bibliographic resources.

2.2 MARCXML Framework

According to the advent of the XML paradigm in information technology, the Network Development and MARC Standards Office in LOC developed the MARCXML framework for working with MARC data in an XML environment, which is shown in Fig. 2.3.

The core of the MARCXML framework has a simple XML schema structure which contains MARC data[5]. The schema that supports MARC21 record formats with tags and subfield codes plays the role of the bridge between MARC21 and other formats. The base XML schema output can be used where full MARC records are

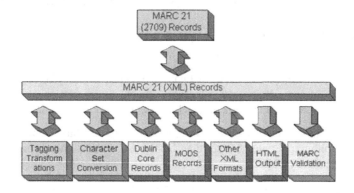

Fig. 2.3. MARC XML architecture

needed or it can act as a "*bus*" to enable MARC data records to go through further transformations such as to Dublin Core and/or processes such as validation. The software tools maintained by LOC will support transformations to and from MARC21 records and other metadata approaches, including Dublin Core and MODS. In Fig. 2.4, the typical schema representation of MARC21 record is shown.

The main objective of MARCXML is to work with MARC bibliographic data in an XML environment. The schema simply represents MARC record structure in XML style as shown in Fig. 2.4.

The schema does not support semantic properties of the MARC tags and subfield codes. It can be regarded as XML implementation of MARC structure of Fig. 2.1.

```
<record xmlns="http://www.loc.gov/MARC21/slim">
  <leader>00967cam 2200277 a 4500</leader>
  <controlfield tag="001">3471394</controlfield>
  <controlfield tag="005">19990429094819.1</controlfield>
  <controlfield tag="008">931129s1994    wauab      001 0 eng </controlfield>
  <datafield tag="020" ind1=" " ind2=" ">
      <subfield code="a">0898863872 (acid-free, recycled paper) :</subfield>
      <subfield code="c">$14.95</subfield>
  </datafield>
  <datafield tag="040" ind1=" " ind2=" ">
      <subfield code="a">DLC</subfield>
      <subfield code="c">DLC</subfield>
      <subfield code="d">DLC</subfield>
  </datafield>
  <datafield tag="100" ind1="1" ind2=" ">
      <subfield code="a">Slavinski, Nadine,</subfield>
      <subfield code="d">1968-</subfield>
  </datafield>
  <datafield tag="245" ind1="1" ind2="0">
      <subfield code="a">Germany by bike :</subfield>
      <subfield code="b">20 tours geared for discovery /</subfield>
      <subfield code="c">Nadine Slavinski.</subfield>
  </datafield>
  ...................
  <datafield tag="650" ind1=" " ind2="0">
      <subfield code="a">Bicycle touring</subfield>
      <subfield code="z">Germany</subfield>
      <subfield code="x">Guidebooks.</subfield>
  </datafield>
</record>
```

Fig. 2.4. MARCXML schema representation of MARC21 record

2.3 MODS: Metadata Objects Description Schema

MODS is the XML-based descriptive metadata standard that includes a subset of data elements derived from MARC21[6]. MODS is intended to carry selected data from existing MARC21 records as well as to enable metadata description of bibliographic information under XML environment. MODS has many notable features:

- MODS is intended to complement other metadata formats. MODS provides a richer bibliographic element set than Dublin Core and is more compatible with library data than ONIX.
- MODS has a high level of compatibility with MARC records because it inherits the semantics of the equivalent data elements in the MARC21 bibliographic

format. But it is also simpler than the full MARC format. It allows for a conversion from MARC21 fields to MODS, while other MARC 21 fields may be dropped or carried in a less specific manner.

- In MODS some elements that appear in various fields in MARC have been repackaged into one. So MODS can define 19 upper metadata elements.
- MODS takes advantage of the XML environment. It uses language-based tags rather than the numeric tags traditional to MARC. It also has flexible linking mechanisms by providing for all the top-level elements with attributes such as xlink and ID.
- MODS accommodates special requirements for digital resources.

The typical MODS record is shown in Fig. 2.5. MODS is viewed as an evolutionary pathway forward for bibliographic metadata and revision of MARC21 formats.

However, MODS has some limitations that it includes only a subset of bibliographic data elements from MARC21 and it does not include business rules for populating the elements.

```
<mods xmlns="http://www.loc.gov/mods/">
  <titleInfo><title>Germany by bike : 20 tours geared for discovery /</title></titleInfo>
  <name type="personal">
      <namePart>Slavinski, Nadine,</namePart>
      <namePart type="date">1968-</namePart>
      <role><roleTerm type="text">creator</roleTerm></role>
  </name>
  <typeOfResource>text</typeOfResource>
  <originInfo>
      <place><placeTerm type="code" authority="marc">wau</placeTerm></place>
      <place> <placeTerm type="text"> Seattle, Wash. :</placeTerm></place>
      <publisher>Mountaineers,</publisher>
      <dateIssued>c1994</dateIssued>
      <issuance>monographic</issuance>
  </originInfo>
  ....................
  <classification authority="lcc">GV1046.G3 G47 1994</classification>
  <classification authority="ddc" edition="20">796.6/4/0943</classification>
  <identifier type="isbn">0898863872 (acid-free, recycled paper) :</identifier>
  <identifier type="lccn">93047676</identifier>
  <recordInfo>
      <recordContentSource>DLC</recordContentSource>
      <recordCreationDate encoding="marc">931129</recordCreationDate>
      <recordChangeDate encoding="iso8601">19990429094819.1
      </recordChangeDate>
      <recordIdentifier>3471394</recordIdentifier>
  </recordInfo>
</mods>
```

Fig. 2.5. Example of MODS record

3   Topic Maps Modeling of MARC21

MARC formats contain abundant bibliographic data elements. This section describes the requirement analysis for MARC modeling with consideration of other approaches such as MARCXML and MODS. This section also presents the conceptual model of MARC to be used in Topic Maps modeling.

3.1   Requirement Analysis for MARC Modeling

In spite of many problems, MARC as standards for the representation of bibliographic information is the foundation of most library catalogs used today. Considering the present circumstances of bibliographic information management and the innovation of information technology, a broker is required that can encapsulate MARC functionality and accommodate the current technology environment. The MARCXML bus is one of such approaches.

MARC reveals idiosyncratic features in tags and subfield codes as discussed in the previous section. However, the record structure of MARC is relatively simple unless the dependency relation between indicators and subfield codes need to be explicitly represented. The followings are the summarization of core concepts underlying other modeling approaches.

- A model should be able to support the full set of data elements in MARC21 to achieve seamless compatibility with MARC formats. This is a practical requirement in order to embrace the current circumstances even though it is awkward.
- It should have the same expressive power as metadata. This implies that the model should be realized with semantic descriptors to be used in an XML environment instead of obsolete alphanumeric codes.
- The use of attributes should be minimized to maintain consistency and increase readability.
- While a model does not intend to develop bibliographic metadata system based on MARC, it should be able to maintain the structure of MARC record format.
- A model can be handled without expertise in MARC to achieve the usability of the model. However, due to the idiosyncratic relationships between indicators and subfields, this causes a model to be incompatible with MARC records.
- A model should be simple and lightweight for system implementation and harmonization with other models.

Since the aim of the model is to refine bibliographic data elements of MARC, not to define metadata such as Dublin Core or MODS, the compatibility with MARC is important. The model may give some insight into bibliographic metadata.

3.2   Conceptual Model of MARC Structure

Considering the primitive features of MARC and its record structure in Fig.2.1, MARC is inherently based on an aggregation relationship among data elements. For example, <DataField> can be represented with the aggregation of <Tag>, <Indicator> and <SubField>. In this case, the data elements of MARC can be easily classified into two types: one for aggregation classes and the other for their properties. The UML diagram of MARC structure model is viewed as in Fig. 3.1.

Two properties, Repeatability and Description, are included to capture MARC specification. Repeatability of data elements is individually defined in MARC specification, it cannot be uniformly modeled. It is appropriate to regard Repeatability as a property necessary for the validation of MARC records. In Fig. 2.6, the model uses the common indicator item for two indicators because they have the same structure for supplying additional information about the subfield and there are no dependency relations between them. However, for seamless compatibility with MARC record, the model defines two indicators distinct.

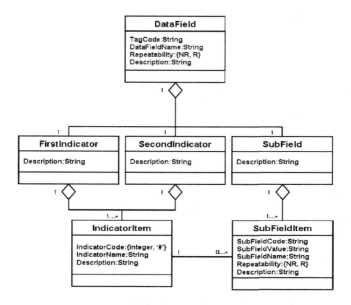

Fig. 3.1. UML diagram of MARC structure model

4   Implementation of MARCXTM

The MARCXTM as the implementation of the MARC structure model with XTM 1.0., consists of two modules. One is the implementation of MARC specification itself and the other is the representation of real MARC record data.

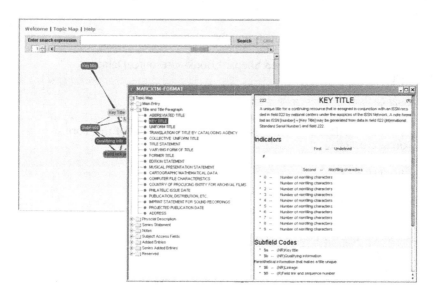

Fig. 4.1. MARCXTM implementation of MARC Specification

```
<topic id="M357">
 <instanceOf> <topicRef xlink:href="#bibData" /> </instanceOf>
 <occurrence>
  <scope>
   <topicRef xlink:href="#personalName" />
   <topicRef xlink:href="#Surname" />
  </scope>
  <resourceData>Arnosky, Jim</resourceData>
 </occurrence>
 <occurrence>
  <scope>
   <topicRef xlink:href="#Title" />
   <topicRef xlink:href="#addedEntry" />
  </scope>
  <resourceData>Raccoons and ripe corn</resourceData>
 </occurrence>
 <occurrence>
  <scope>
   <topicRef xlink:href="#statementOfResponsiblitiy" />
   <topicRef xlink:href="#addedEntry" />
  </scope>
  <resourceData>Jim Arnosky</resourceData>
 </occurrence>
 <occurrence>
  <scope> <topicRef xlink:href="#editionStatement" /> </scope>
  <resourceData>1st ed</resourceData>
 </occurrence>
 <occurrence>
  <scope> <topicRef xlink:href="#placeOfPublication" /> </scope>
  <resourceData>New York</resourceData>
 </occurrence>
 <occurrence>
  <scope>
   <topicRef xlink:href="#nameOfPublisher" />
  </scope>
  <resourceData>Lothrop, Lee&Shepard Books</resourceData>
 </occurrence>
    ....................
 <occurrence>
  <scope> <topicRef xlink:href="#Summary" /> </scope>
  <resourceData>Hungry raccoons feast at night in a field of ripe corn.
    </resourceData>
 </occurrence>
 <occurrence>
  <scope>
   <topicRef xlink:href="#topicalTerm" />
   <topicRef xlink:href="#LCsubjectHeading" />
  </scope>
  <resourceData>Raccoons</resourceData>
 </occurrence>
</topic>
```

Fig. 4.2. MARCXTM representation of MARC record

The MARCXTM implementation of MARC21 specification defines bibliographic data elements and is used as the knowledge base of MARC information. In this module based on Fig. 2.6, the aggregation class is implemented with topic and their properties with occurrence, while aggregation relation is implemented with n-ary association of Topic Maps. For example, the Field 222(Key Title) will be implemented as in Fig. 4.1. MARCXTM provides navigation within bibliographic data elements of MARC as shown in Fig. 4.1.

The representation of real MARC record data bears some problems due to the role of indicators. The indicator is usually regarded as a modifier to restrict the interpretation of subfield codes. However, its function is implicitly defined against subfield codes in MARC specification. The role of indicators makes topic representation complex and requires expertise in MARC.

Considering the compatibility with MARC, in MARCXTM the indicators and sub-field codes are regarded as the scope, and the real bibliographic data are represented as the occurrence within these scope. The MARC record example shown in Fig. 2.2 will be represented as in Fig. 4.2 and 4.3.

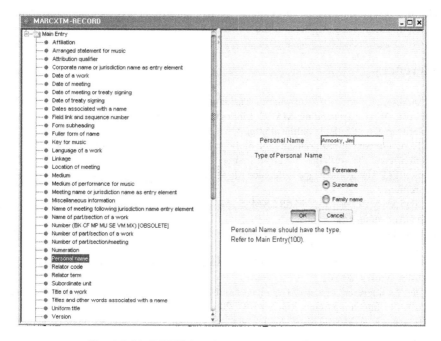

Fig. 4.3. MARCXTM implementation of MARC record

5   Conclusion

This paper presents Topic Maps-based implementation of MARC21, MRACXTM, for the description of bibliographic information. MARCXTM intends to develop a biblio-graphic framework compatible with MARC21 formats in Topic Maps paradigm, which has the same expressive power as metadata instead of obsolete alphanumeric codes of MARC record formats. MARCXTM consists of two modules: the implementation of MARC21 specification and the representation of real MARC record data.

Since the MARC21 specification can be modeled with aggregation relationships, MARCXTM accommodates all the features of MARC formats and provides the functionality as knowledge base of bibliographic data elements. Although MARCXTM can handle the real MARC record data, the Topic Maps representation of real data is complex due to the idiosyncratic dependency between indicators and subfield codes. MARCXTM shows how to realize the compatible framework with MARC21 at the level of metadata, but the application of MARCXTM requires expertise in abundant bibliographic data elements of MARC.

The future of the MARC formats is recently a matter of some debate in the world-wide library science community. The metadata framework compatible with MARC such as MODS and especially, the conceptual framework for bibliographic resources such as FRBR attract remarkable attention beyond MARC formalism. In any case, Topic Maps paradigm will lead the representation and communication of bibliographic information.

Acknowledgements. The authors thank the Korean Ministry of Science and Technology for financial support through the Center for Healthcare Technology Development.

References

1. Andresen, L.: After MARC-what then?, Library Hi Tech, 22(1):40-51, 2004.
2. Furrie, B.: Understanding MARC Bibliographic: Machine-Readable Cataloging, Follett Software Co., available online at http://www.loc.gov/marc/umb/.
3. IFLA, Functional requirements for bibliographic records: final report, available online at http://www.ifla.org/VII/s13/wgfrbr/finalreport.htm
4. ISO/IEC, The Topic Maps Reference Model, available online at http://www.isotopicmaps.org/tmrm/.
5. Library of Congress, MARCXML: MARC21 XML Schema, http://www.loc.gov/standards/marcxml/.
6. McCallum, S.: An introduction to the Metadata Object Description Schema, Library Hi Tech, 22(1):82-88, 2004.
7. Park, J., Hunting, S., XML Topic Maps: Creating and Using Topic Maps for the Web, Addison-Wesley. 2003.
8. Qin, J.: Representation and Organization of Information in the Web Space: From MARC to XML, Informing Science, 3(2):83-87, 2000.
9. Tennant, Roy: MARC Must Die. Library Journal, October 15, 2002.
10. TopicMaps.Org, XML Topic Maps (XTM) 1.0, available online at http://www.topicmaps.org/xtm/1.0/.
11. Weinstein, P: Ontology-Based Metadata: Transforming the MARC Legacy. Proceedings of the Third ACM Digital Library conference, Pittsburgh, PA, USA, June 1998.

Improving Information Retrieval Using XML and Topic Maps

Ralf Schweiger and Joachim Dudeck

Institute of Medical Informatics,
Justus-Liebig-University Giessen, Germany

Abstract. The bulk of clinical data is available in an electronic form. About 80% of the electronic data, however, is narrative text and therefore limited with respect to machine interpretation. As a result, the discussion has shifted from "electronic versus paper based data" towards "structured versus unstructured electronic data". The XML technology of today paves a way towards more structured clinical data and several XML based standards such as the Clinical Document Architecture (CDA) emerge. The implementation of XML based applications is yet a challenge. This paper will focus on XML retrieval issues and describe the difficulties and prospects of such an approach. The result of our work is a search technique called "topic matching" that exploits structured data using Topic Maps in order to provide a search quality that is superior to established text matching methods. With this solution we are able to utilize large numbers of heterogeneously structured documents with only a minimum of effort.

1 Introduction

More and more healthcare data become available in an electronic form. The data range from weakly structured text to highly structured messages and databases. The eXtensible Markup Language (XML) seems to become the standard format for electronic data interchange. The Clinical Document Architecture (CDA), for example, provides an exchange model for clinical documents such as discharge summaries and pathology reports [1]. CDA documents are XML documents. The document-oriented view of XML corresponds well with the organization of healthcare data. In addition, XML is easy to process due to the growing number of free XML tools. The exploitation of electronic data, on the other hand, is still limited. Despite existing communication standards and commercial application systems clinical data are often not accessible and searchable at the clinical workstation. Most healthcare data is narrative text and requires structural preparation. Moreover, the relationships between the resources are often implicit and vary from site to site. We therefore developed a pragmatic and flexible approach, which is based on standards such as XML and Topic Maps. The approach aims to combine the simplicity of a web search with the accuracy of customized applications.

L. Maicher and J. Park (Eds.): TMRA 2005, LNAI 3873, pp. 253–262, 2006.
© Springer-Verlag Berlin Heidelberg 2006

2 Methods and Materials

2.1 Representing Relationships Between Data Using XML

In our use case model a healthcare professional simply enters search terms into a web browser and a search engine selects the "appropriate" information resources. A resource in this context is anything that has a Uniform Resource Identifier (URI), e.g. a document, an image or even a service. Existing text matching methods relate search terms to resources and have limitations to identify relationships between the terms. Search results are often inaccurate. Figure 1 illustrates the limitation of simple text matching. The pathology report contains two findings "Basaliom" and "Keratose" that refer to different sample excisions with the locations "Stirn" (forehead) and "Nase" (nose) respectively. Numbers 1, 2 are used to express the relationships between findings and locations. Existing search engines simply relate terms to document addresses, e.g. [basaliom]=>[report.txt], [keratose]=>[report.txt], [stirn]=>[report.txt] and [nase]=>[report.txt] where "report.txt" is the relative URI of the pathology report. If the clinical user now enters the query "Keratose Stirn" she or he probably wants to find those reports in which the given terms are related with each other.

The document in Figure 1 is therefore less relevant to the query because the fnding "Keratose" relates to the wrong location "Nase". The search engine, on the other hand, relates the given terms to "report.txt" and returns the document as a relevant search result. Search engines have still severe limitations to automatically detect relationships between the terms within plain text documents. More sophisticated search engines consider the distance of the words in the text (proximity) as a relationship indicator. The proximity measure works well in many cases. In the pathology example, however, it fails.

Gießen, den 14. April 1999

Prof. Dr. med. A. Schulz
Institut für Pathologie
am Klinikum der Justus-Liebig-Universität

Institut für Pathologie
Langhansstraße 10
35385 Gießen

Prof. Dr. Glanz

Sekretariat: +49-641-9941101
Befundauskunft: +49-641-9941103
Fax: +49-641-9941109

HNO-Klinik
Zentrum HNO und Augenheilkunde
Feulgenstr. 10

Dr. Dreyer

Patient: Thomas Müller, 10.04.1970

Einsendung vom 12. April 1999
Kennung 9907946
1 PE Stirn li.
2 PE Nasenflügel re.

Es handelt sich um ein multizentrisch wachsendes oberflächl. Basaliom (1) sowie eine aktinische Keratose mit bis zu leichten Epitheldysplasien (2).

Fig. 1. Is this pathology report relevant to the query „Keratose Stirn"?

The eXtensible Markup Language (XML) offers many possibilities to represent relationships between the data in a way that a machine can understand [2]. The markup `<location   id="2">Nase</location>` and `<finding ref="2">Keratose</finding>`, for example, relates the finding "Keratose" to the right location "Nase". A search engine would now be able to detect the relationships between the findings and locations and return more accurate search results. Other XML standards such as the Resource Description Framework (RDF) allow to express even more sophisticated relationships between the data. XML structured documents consequently enable new search techniques that are superior to existing text matching methods [3].

The organizational cost of inserting XML markup into plain text documents has been described in [4]. Producing structure always requires some initial effort. The document oriented view of XML, however, suggests structuring the data in a stepwise, i.e. more flexible manner. The resulting structures are maintainable with web browsers (XML forms) and reusable in different applications. In this paper we will focus on retrieval issues. The subsequent section outlines a search method called "topic matching" that exploits XML structures to compute higher search quality and calls attention to the difficulties with such an approach.

2.2 Exploiting XML Represented Relationships Using Topic Maps

Many XML standards have established since 1998 and search engines increasingly have to deal with structured data. At this point another limitation of existing search engines reveals. Search engines parse the given text into single words and directly relate the words to the address of the document in which they occur (indexing). More advanced search engines can also manage a list of synonymous terms. More complex relationships, however, can not be represented. The relationship between the finding "Keratose" and the location "Nase", for example, is not of type "synonym". Another example is the more precise location "Stirn links" (forehead left) which should be represented as one concept and related as a whole to the finding "Basaliom". We consequently need a data model for the representation of arbitrary relationships between terms and other resources. The International Organization for Standardization (ISO) provides a standardized notation, called Topic Maps (ISO13250:1999), for interchangeably defining topics, and the relationships between topics [5, 6]. Figure 2 shows the fundamental elements of the Topic Maps model. Topics are perceived as abstract, meaningful and reusable concepts (subjects) described by a number of "meaningless" words (reification). Topics may be related to one another (associations) and to documents or other information resources such as databases (occurrences). Advanced Topic Maps elements such as "classifications" and "scopes" allow to express even more specific relationships between the data items. The Topic Maps standard provides a simple, yet flexible data model to represent semantic networks that meaningfully link the data with each other.

The representation of data relationships is only part of the solution. We also need methods that exploit the given knowledge in an efficient way. Due to our experience semantic networks grow very fast and may comprise millions of single relationships. The challenge with such an approach is therefore the efficient searching and refreshing of very large semantic networks. Efficiency is a result of many details that will not be presented here. Figure 3, however, illustrates the basic idea of our search method that is referred to as "topic matching".

The search method has been subdivided into two steps. The "association step" finds a set of topics that relate the search terms meaningfully with each other. The subsequent "occurrence step" relates the identified topics to resources such as documents and images. As a result, our search method finds meaningful topics rather than meaningless words and captures more meaning than existing text matching methods. In addition, topic matching excludes irrelevant relationships very quickly and is therefore also performant.

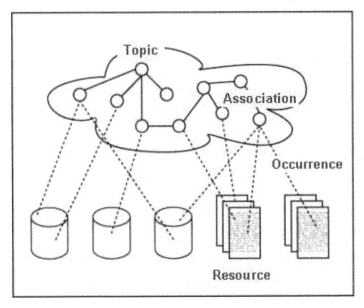

Fig. 2. Topic Maps may relate documents/data with each other

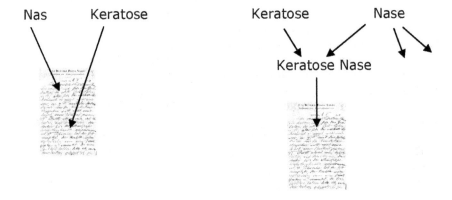

Fig. 3. Text matching compared to "topic matching"

Topic matching exploits documented respectively marked associations between terms to improve the search engine's line of reasoning and to manage large semantic networks. Another key feature of our approach is the automatic categorization of the documents as part of our search engine's indexing method. Internet formats such as RSS 2.0 [7] allow the specification of the categories that a given headline belongs to. Even HTML authors are able to classify their documents using Dublin Core and other meta standards. Due to our experience, however, the majority of the documents remains unclassified. In those cases we use Bayesian Filtering to automatically relate terms and documents to definable category systems. Popular applications of Bayesian Filtering are spam filters, which automatically classify emails into "ham" and "spam" categories. In a similar way, our search engine computes the categories of a given document and represents them using Topic Maps scopes. Such scopes may then be used to further improve information retrieval.

3 Results

3.1 Search Engine for Topic Maps

The key challenge with Topic Maps is the management of very large semantic networks. Our search engine LUMRIX (XML + URI) is able to manage millions of documents and relationships using a single desktop computer [3, 4]. The average search time is always below a second. Furthermore, the search load may be distributed on many computers as the number of documents grows. The freshness and integrity of the semantic network is another challenge, especially if the topics are highly interwoven. Our work consequently meets the Semantic Web Initiative, which addresses the efficient management of very large semantic networks. Using LUMRIX several special search engines (agents) have been established in different domains. Some of these engines are accessible on the web as standalone applications frequently visited by many users. The Topic Maps engines may be subdivided into two kinds. Some engines operate on a Topic Maps database that changes less frequently and is therefore rather static. Examples for static Topic Maps are searches in medical terminologies such as the ICD10, the SNOMED CT or pharmacy databases. Another static engine is dealing with the German Law Code, the "Bürgerliche Gesetzbuch" (BGB). Other engines work with dynamic Topic Maps that change very frequently such as the university library, our news syndication and personalization service (LUFEE derived from LUMRIX Feed) and our Wikipedia search.

Figure 4 shows a web browser interface of our Topic Maps search engine applied to drug information sources at our university hospital. The development of new search services is as simple as listing the addresses (URIs) of the documents that LUMRIX is to search. LUMRIX automatically identifies the topics within the documents and links them meaningfully with each other. Hyperlinks between the documents are considered as well. In addition, LUMRIX controls modifications of the document space and informs the users if new documents emerge or existing documents have changed. The documents may be differently structured. The university hospital's pharmacy, for example, creates XML, HTML and PDF documents. Heterogeneous data are characteristic for clinical environments. Clinical users simply enter search words into the text field and submit the query to the search engine using the "Suchen" button or pressing the return key. LUMRIX tries to match the words with topics ("topic matching") and returns links to appropriate information sources which will be rendered on demand. With such an approach we are able to quickly search, link and utilize arbitrary document collections. The average access rate to the drug documents, for example, has grown in our university hospital from 50 accesses per month up to 200 accesses per day because the information of interest is only a search term or click away from the given user context. It turned out that XML structures improve information retrieval. The hospital's pharmacy maintains XML documents using web browsers and XML forms. The markup allows us, for example, to extract drug substances from the hospital's drug formulary and to search a given substance in the German drug formulary, which contains complementary information such as drug indications and drug interactions. Another use case illustrates the benefit of XML: If a physician enters a clinical diagnosis she or he usually searches for drug indications rather than drug contraindications. If the indications and contraindications of the drugs have been marked in the text LUMRIX will be able to search the given diagnosis in the right context.

Figure 4 shows an interesting approach to the vision of the "Semantic Web" [8]. The user interface is simple and the given query is automatically passed to a number of search agents, i.e. specialty search engines. The query "virus", for example, is passed to our drug agent, to our news agent and to our Wikipedia agent which simultaneously search their specialities. The respective search results are merged into a common user interface. A MEDLINE agent may be added later on and could search for appropriate literature. Such an approach proves simple, fast and useful at the same time. The clinical user is not only informed about the drugs listed in the hospital's drug formulary ("Virustatika"). In addition, she or he will get the latest news and explanations related to the given context. Topic Maps further allow to establish non-trivial associations, e.g. between "Vogelgrippe" and "H5N1", which could make the retrieval even more intelligent.

Fig. 4. Application of our search engine LUMRIX to drug information sources

3.2 News Categorization and Syndication

Our news agent is able to mange millions of headlines in an efficient way. Those headlines may be extracted from web pages or more structured RSS (Really Simple Syndication) feeds. LUMRIX automatically learns the refresh periods of the various information sources to guarantee a maximum of information freshness at a minimum of network traffic. Our news service proves that it is possible to refresh complex Topic Maps in a seamless way. Another experience with our news service is the automatic categorization of the headlines using Bayesian Filtering. The computed categories are surprisingly reliable and allow for specific selection of news. We are able, for example, to establish a "medicine" category and show related news within the drug application. A special category is the user. LUMRIX may automatically learn the click thru of a user and specifically select the news of individual interest. The quality of news personalization depends, among other things, on the granularity of the category system. We aim to maximize the surprise effect including a great number of different news feeds (recall) and to avoid irrelevant news at the same time (precision). The main difficulty in the development of search engines is always the simultaneous optimization of different search criteria such as fuzzy search, search recall, search precision, and search performance that tend to run in opposite directions. A very precise search, for example, often requires many recalls in order to find the information of interest. It turned out that structure in general and Topic Maps in particular may improve the situation.

3.3 Wikipedia Search

Our Wikipedia search[1] is another show case of LUMRIX and has been integrated with the drug application in order to provide the clinical users with comprehensive information and knowledge. Wikipedia offers images, background information, and hyperlinks to related topics and is continuously maintained by a huge number of experts. Our Wikipedia search supports 17 different languages from English over Russian to Chinese. The search technique works independent of the language and is able to automatically correct English and Chinese misspellings in the same way (fuzzy search). Another aspect of complexity is the number of queries against the Topic Maps per time. Our service wiki.lumrix.net currently copes with more than 1.000.000 queries per month with no loss of performance. The scalability problem of semantic networks is consequently manageable with a distributed approach to indexing and searching.

3.4 SNOMED CT

SNOMED CT (Systemized Nomenclature of Medicine – Clinical Terms) is a standardized healthcare terminology including comprehensive coverage of diseases, clinical findings, therapies, procedures and outcomes [9] which will probably replace the currently used medical classification systems like ICD10 and ICPM in the near future. SNOMED CT is represented as a semantic network of medical concepts including and relating findings, diagnoses, diagnostic and therapeutic procedures,

---

[1] http://wiki.lumrix.net

drugs, care management, social behaviour and many other concepts. Concepts have unique numeric (ConceptID) and textual (Fully specified name resp. preferred name) identifiers. They can also be described by an unlimited number of synonyms. The concepts are currently organized into 18 different hierarchies (axes). Relationships between the concepts have semantic meanings like "is-a", "is-part-of", "is-causative-agent" and "has-laterality". The defined relationships between concepts within the same hierarchy and between interrelated concepts in different hierarchies establish the semantic net of concepts in SNOMED CT.

Fig. 5. SNOMED CT user interface

After entering the synonym description "heart attack" the search engine displays the related preferred term "Myocardial Infarction" and the conceptID 22298006. By post-coordination the disease description is refined by the severity specification "Severe" and its related conceptID 24484000. By clicking on the different flag icons the user can switch to different language representations of SNOMED CT at the engine level (upper icon) or at the concept level (lower icons).

Concepts are mapped as topics with the described identifiers, relationships as classes of associations between concepts. The LUMRIX SNOMED CT engine tries to identify those concepts which best fit the entered character string. If there is only one choice, the preferred term, the conceptID and the synonyms are displayed (Figure 1). If necessary the user can start to navigate within the network by clicking on "Specialize", "Generalize" or "Links". He can also refine the concept by adding specifying concepts ("Specify") such as "Severity". This process is called "Post-coordination". The final goal of the SNOMED CT approach is to describe the disease, finding, procedure, therapy etc. as precise and comprehensive as possible by one or more SNOMED CT concepts.

4   Discussion

4.1   Topic Maps Versus XML Database

There are other approaches to information retrieval that use XML. XML databases, for example, may store and retrieve XML documents without the need to map hierarchical XML schemas onto relational database schemas. XML query languages are used to select information from a set of XML resources [10]. XML databases and XML query languages provide a retrieval infrastructure for semi-structured XML data. Nonetheless, there are major differences to our approach. XML databases provide no inference method that directly relates search terms to resources. In addition, developers and users need to learn XML schemas. A key feature of our approach is the ease of development and use. Our inference engine relies on the Topic Maps standard, which allows representing arbitrary relationships between resources. The relationships between the data are no longer fixed in the application logic. As a result, we can start with little requirements and establish new relationships between the data as they become available. New data relationships enable new ways of reasoning; i.e. the intelligence of the search engine grows continuously. Such relationships are often referred to as semantics. Another difference between XML databases and our approach is the level of decentralization. Databases tend to centralize data. Search engines, on the other hand, separate the index from the data; i.e. the data are usually located somewhere else and authored by different individuals. Distributed methods seem to be the key to the management of huge semantic networks and little organized systems.

4.2 Standard Ontologies

Due to our experience, the automatic categorization of documents, news and other resources works fine and may reliably separate relevant from irrelevant resources. In the absence of standardized categorization taxonomies, however, the machine-to-machine communication remains difficult. The RSS 2.0 [7] standard, for example, allows news providers to classify a given headline into one ore more categories and to specify the domain of the taxonomy in use. On the other hand, RSS readers and aggregators will encounter problems joining the information if different news providers employ different category systems. The Open Directory may already suggest useful categories. Crucial, however, is the adoption of a common taxanomy. This is the point where standards bodies come in. We may use XML Topic Maps to describe and exchange standard ontologies. Public Subject Indicators (PSIs) allow to define, relate and encode categories in a language independent way. A standard category system should be simple and could be refined in a stepwise manner starting with a maximum of 10 top level categories. One level of refinement with less than 100 standard categories would probably be sufficient for many use cases.

4.3 Approaching the Semantic Web

Our Topic Maps search engine LUMRIX [3, 4] has been applied to a diversity of knowledge domains such as drug knowledge, medical terminologies, laws and court decisions, libraries, banking establishments, Wikipedia, blogs and news. Developing a knowledge service is as simple as listing the start addresses (URIs) and designing a Web interface. The Topic Maps database allows LUMRIX to better represent and exploit the given data structures. HTML headings, for example, may be regarded as meaningful topics rather than incoherent lists of words. Depending on the requirements, we are able to establish meaningful links and additional search pathways to the resources. Pragmatism and the flexibility of Topic Maps allow for the quick satisfaction of user needs. The creation of a great diversity of knowledge services respectively specialty search engines that are addressable by simple standards such as HTTP and RSS could be a good approach to the Semantic Web [8]. Specialty search agents may automatically operate in the background and collect together the information of interest. Figure 4 shows a first implementation of this idea. The clinical user enters a query which is automatically passed to the drug agent, the news agent and the Wikipedia agent. Each agent simultaneously searches its own knowledge space and feeds the requesting client with the matching resources (URIs) using RSS. The client finally renders the various results in a user friendly way. Such an approach is fast and easy to scale. We are currently about to develop a self-organizing system of distributed agents that allows us to add and remove agents with a minimum of effort (plug-and-play). The ambiguous meaning of single words is another problem. Public Subject Indicators (PSIs) are desirable in the long run. In the absence of standard ontologies, however, our method of automatic resource categorization turned out very useful. The drug application in Figure 4, for example, searches not only for "virus" but more precisely for "category=medicine & query=virus". Even more specific would be the query "category=medicine & query=virus & source=medline". Another application could search for "category=computer & query=virus" and retrieve completely different results. With a common category taxanomy we are obviously able to specify the context of a query and to improve the precision of the search results.

References

[1] Clinical Document Architecture Framework Release 1.0, ANSI/HL7 CDA R1.0-2000, Health Level Seven, Inc. http://www.hl7.org, Accessed 6 Dec 2005.

[2] Dudeck J, Schweiger R. Representation of Relationships between Data in Healthcare Documents. Stud Health Technol Inform. 2003;96:272-279.

[3] Schweiger R, Hölzer S, Rudolf D, Rieger J, Dudeck J. Linking clinical data using XML topic maps. Artif Intell Med 2003;28(1):105-115.

[4] Schweiger R, Brumhard M, Hölzer S, Dudeck J. Implementing health care systems using XML standards. Int J Med Inform 2005;74:267-277.

[5] Park, J [Ed.], Hunting, S. [Techn. Ed.] XML Topic Maps: Creating and using Topic Maps for the Web. Pearson Education Inc. Boston (2003)

[6] Pepper S, Moore G: XML Topic Maps (XTM) 1.0. http://www.topicmaps.org/xtm/1.0/, Accessed 6 Dec 2005.

[7] RSS 2.0 Specification. http://blogs.law.harvard.edu/tech/rss, Accessed 6 Dec 2005.

[8] Berners-Lee T, Hendler J, Lassila O: The Semantic Web. Scientific American, May 2001.

[9] SNOMED Clinical Terms, User Guide, College of American Pathologists, 2004.

[10] Boag S, Chamberlin D, Fernandez MF, Florescu D, Robie J, Siméon J: XQuery 1.0: An XML Query Language, W3C Candidate Recommendation 3 November 2005.

Visualizing Search Results
from Metadata-Enabled Repositories
in Cultural Domains

Lynne C. Howarth and Thea Miller

Faculty of Information Studies, University of Toronto, Toronto
{lynne.howarth, thea.miller}@utoronto.ca

Abstract. With the rapid increase in the number of metadata-enabled cultural repositories, the need for systems that can display larger, content-rich sets of results has grown correspondingly. At the same time, the ability to access objects from repositories in multiple cultural domains suggests an opportunity for innovative approaches to the visualization of search results drawing on heterogeneous conceptual frameworks, metadata structures, naming devices and end-user requirements. We describe the development and testing of a two-tier semantic mediating device to support searches of multiple cross-cultural metadata-enabled repositories. Seventeen common categories provide a semantic bridge linking different content metadata schemes, while a topic map-enabled search interface facilitates the access of digital objects in diverse repositories.

1 Introduction and Background to the Research

As Buckland, et al. (1999, 1) have noted, "There is a massive investment worldwide in making repositories accessible over networks and . . . in providing indexing, categorizing, and other metadata. So the number and proportion of network accessible repositories with unfamiliar metadata vocabularies are rapidly growing. The amount of searching can be expected to rise, but diminishing search effectiveness is the predictable result." While the extent of investment and work has remained in evidence as the number of digital libraries, enterprise portals, and metadata-enabled knowledge repositories has grown, the challenge of "unfamiliar metadata vocabularies" has also assumed a predictable dimension. Within cultural domains, such as libraries, archives, museums, and art galleries, work has focused primarily on developing content metadata for describing and accessing digital objects. The design of systems that search and display content metadata and their corresponding items has merited less attention. Where systems have been developed, they have tended to be repository-specific, exploiting metadata structure and content, as well as search terminologies unique to a silo of digital objects.

Activities undermining the provenance and validity of data, such as index spamming and pagejacking, have discouraged more generalized access to metadata-enabled resources, calling into question the desirability of using schemas, such as Dublin Core, to mark-up items for consumption beyond the

L. Maicher and J. Park (Eds.): TMRA 2005, LNAI 3873, pp. 263–270, 2006.

local level. For example, while general search engines, such as Google (TM), or enterprise search engines, such as Northern Light (TM) are fully capable of accessing Dublin Core-enabled digital objects, their use is normally restricted to internal repositories where the source and reliability of Dublin Core records describing those objects is well known. Thus, to date, while much metadata exist for representing electronic resources, issues of trust on the Web have detracted from their use and usefulness beyond the known boundaries of a particular institutional context – that is, the repository developed and maintained by an individual library, archive, museum, or art gallery.

Yet, as the number of metadata project implementations have increased with the adoption of standards, such as Dublin Core, TEI (Text Encoding Initiative), and EAD (Encoded Archival Description), the need for systems that can display larger, content-rich results sets has grown in tandem. Likewise, the capability for accessing objects concurrently from repositories in more than one cultural domain has suggested an opportunity for introducing innovative approaches to visualizing search results that draw from very different conceptual frameworks, metadata structures, naming devices, and end-user requirements. For end-users unfamiliar with domain-specific metadata, being able to enter a natural language (free text) query and having search results returned in a language-independent format, such as that offered by current visualization technologies, would offer an alternative to the potential ambiguities of textual labelling.

Having described the motivational context for the research, the remainder of the paper will outline the objectives guiding subsequent work on the development and testing of a two-tier semantic mediating device to support searches of multiple cross-cultural metadata-enabled repositories. Further sections will explore the derivation and validation of the seventeen common categories that provide a semantic bridge for linking different content metadata schemes, and will also detail the design of a topic map-enabled search interface to facilitate access to digital objects in diverse repositories. The paper concludes with a description of future directions and next steps for the research.

2   Objectives of the Research

Recognizing both the wealth of metadata-enabled cultural repositories and the constraints in accessing them by any means other than individually, research was undertaken to create and test mediating models and/or tools for supporting multiple cross-repository searches. A two-tier approach was envisioned wherein a semantic bridge would be developed to link different content metadata schemas, and a search interface would be designed to facilitate access to and retrieval of digital objects in diverse repositories for which metadata records had been created.

2.1   Developing and Testing a Semantic Bridge

In conceptualizing a possible semantic bridge to assist with sorting through or "making sense" of multiple metadata conventions, the research team was mindful of De Mey's (1982, 4) observation that, "The central point of the cognitive view is that *any* such *information processing*, whether perceptual (such as perceiving an object) or symbolic (such as understanding a sentence) *is mediated* by a *system of categories or concepts* which for the information processor constitutes a *representation* or a *model* of his *world*." [emphasis in original]

Consequently the team iteratively crafted a kind of *lingua franca* – a set of seventeen common category labels derived from nine metadata schemes[1] used for organizing digital collections of cultural resources (Howarth, Cronin, and Hannaford, 2002). The seventeen categories represented semantic commonalities between or among the 755 tags of the metadata schemes comprising the cross-walk – that is, the summary "buckets" in which individual elements would logically fit. The researchers chose to name the categories with labels that searchers would be able to understand without a specialized knowledge of either MARC (the target schema) or any of the eight source metadata schemes, *per se*.[2] The "common categories" model that derived from this first stage of the research was intended to relieve the searcher of the responsibility of having to understand the metadata structures and terminology underlying each repository, and also to offer a mediating space that would not be unfamiliar to a searcher's own cognitive world view.

To assess the degree to which the common categories model might align with end-users, and as a next step in the research, focus groups were recruited to review and validate the categories and definitions (see Table 1) for their clarity and relative usefulness (Howarth and Hannaford, 2003, Howarth, 2003; Howarth, 2004). In addition to linking element labels with their corresponding definitions, study participants were asked to assess how well the metatags and concepts captured within each category corresponded with their own mental models of information content. Findings suggested that, while certain categories, such as "Language", "Physical Format", and "Date & Time Period" were readily interpreted and understood, others, including "Methodology", "Genre/Type", and "Roles", proved ambiguous, confusing, or even misleading, particularly where

---

[1] Using crosswalk methodology, eight "source" metadata schemes, including the Encoded Archival Description (EAD), the Dublin Core (DC), the Government Information Locator Services (GILS) metadata scheme [now Global Information Locator Service], the Text Encoding Initiative (TEI) Header, the Visual Resources Association (VRA) Visual Document Description Categories, the Consortium for the Interchange of Museum Information (CIMI) metadata set, the Content Standard for Digital Geospatial Metadata (CSDGM), and the Online Information Exchange (ONIX) publishing standard, were mapped to one "target" standard for encoding and exchanging bibliographic records, namely, the Machine-Readable Cataloging (MARC21) format. Previously validated crosswalks linking one or more of the full nine standards were employed as "benchmarks" in the process to minimize inconsistencies in interpretation and mapping. For a more detailed description see Howarth, Cronin, and Hannaford (2002).

[2] To view both the derived master crosswalk and the detailed description of each of the categories (labels, definitions, background information), see URL: http://www.fis.utoronto.ca/special/metadata/mmo/index.html (Accessed 12/17/05).

Table 1. Element Labels and Definitions: The 17 Common Categories Model

Element Label	Definition
Contact Information	Information on how to communicate with someone about a work, i.e., names, phone numbers, etc.
Rights/Restrictions on Use	Legal limitations/rules that affect how you can use a work after you have been given access to it
Edition	Information on a work's version
Summary & Description	Details about a work that illustrate its main points
Identifiers	Unique names or numbers assigned to a work so that it can be distinguished from others, for example, its ISBN
Sources, References & Related Works	Other works that are related to the work you are seeking or were used to develop the work you are looking for
Language	The language or dialect of a work
Physical Format	The physical appearance of a work
Subject	The topic of a work; its intellectual content
Date & Time Period	Dates associated with a work, as well as time period information regarding a work's content
Terms of Access & Availability	The legal limitations/rules that affect your ability to access a work. This relates to privacy or intellectual property concerns
Methodology	The procedures/techniques used to make or change a work
Genre/Type	The nature or style of a work's intellectual content
Names	Names of individuals or organizations associated with a work, such as creators, publishers, sponsors, etc.
Title	The name or phrase assigned to a work for identification purposes
Place	Locations associated with a work, for example, where a work was created, published, is housed, etc.

some broader context for terminological usage was lacking (Howarth, 2004).
Time and again context was emphasized as the key to clarifying the meaning of
labelled categories.

2.2   Designing the Prototype

Having devised and tested a semantic bridge, the project team proceeded to
design, initially, a proof-of-concept "gateway" or transparent, language neutral
query interface, for searching metadata-enabled repositories of digital objects
collected in cultural domains, and to present search results in visual category

clusters (e.g., topic maps) for an end-user who may know little about the metadata *per se*. The seventeen common categories would provide a first sort of search results, offering semantic mediation between the repositories (and their digital collections) and the diverse array of metadata used to mark-up digital content.

In designing and implementing the search interface a prototype web application was created, which we refer to as the "DUCK" (Device for the Uniform Categorization of Knowledge). Basically, the DUCK presents the user with a simple search interface, consistent with common web practice: after entering the search phrase, a button is clicked which launches a script, this in turn presents the appropriate results. With the DUCK, however, the results are displayed in a graphical form, based on a topic map.

For testing purposes, a repository was created using the 107 documents of the British Women Romantic Poets project of the Library of the University of California Davis, which are marked up according to the TEI SGML document type definition (DTD). Using the Swish-e search engine (UCLA, 2005), this collection was then indexed, specifying the 17 common categories as metadata aliases.

The design of the underlying application was based on a simple model which can be applied to many forms of XML, including XTM (topic maps), and RDF (Resource Description Framework). As a first step, Swish-e is configured in such a way that all individual metadata tags (from any relevant metadata schema) are mapped to appropriate aliases (i.e., in this case, the categories), as outlined in the previous section. In the case of topic maps, the string resulting from the query is split up according to the category aliases, and these are then "packaged" in an XTM document, using a simple Perl program. At the same time (with the same program), HTML documents are created for each of the category tags; these are then available for later use if the user wishes to see all the results for a specific category. Once the XTM document has been created, the script procedes to transform it via XSLT to a SVG (scalable vector graphics) document, which then presents the topic map in a graphical format, consisting of nodes and edges (see Figure 1). After examining the display, the user can click on any node of interest to view the relevant documents (via the HTML pages previously created by the program).

In creating the topic map, two super topic types were identified, namely "category" and "resource". The topic type "category" then consists of the 17 categories as child topic types. Individual documents are instances of the "resource" type; metadata content within the documents is connected to the categories through association topics. In the script, a counter is used to generate a number for each metadata element instance (by category), this is then conjoined with the category identifier to provide a unique identifier for the element content. This same counter is then later used to indicate the total number of occurrences for each category, which allows the subsequent manipulation of the category node representation in the topic map display (for example by size, shape, colour or location), thus providing non-linguistic cues regarding the significance of that node relative to the other nodes.

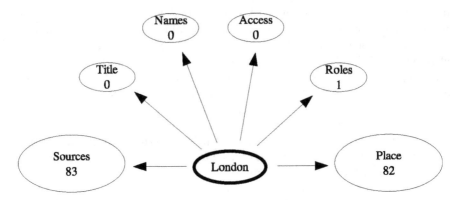

Fig. 1. Presentation of search results from topic map document

For example, if the user enters the search term "London", the results will come back as a graphical display showing nodes and edges (see Figure 1). The centre node contains the actual search term used (in this case, "London"). The surrounding nodes show all of the relevant categories, along with the number of documents associated with each category.[3] In this case, 83 documents were returned where the term "London" occurs in metadata relating to "Source" (as defined by the category), while no documents were returned where the term occurs in metadata relating to "Title" (again, as defined by the category). If the user wishes to examine any of the 83 documents relating to "Source", she can then click on the node, which will open the HTML page with all of the appropriate documents. From this view, she is then able to examine the actual document at any particular repository by clicking on the available link.

3   Next Steps: Evaluating the Common Categories and Topic Map Displays

As work on the proof-of-concept prototype has progressed, it has become clear to the research team that further refinements to the seventeen-element categorization model will be required prior to attempting to have the model serve as a foundation for displaying results in visual topic maps from a search query. In other words, if there is any ambiguity still remaining with any of the core categories, these semantic incongruities would be compounded presumably as we attempted to migrate the model into a language-neutral – i.e., visual – search environment. It has been determined that, only through having end-users evaluate the appropriateness of search results relative to each of the common categories, will it be possible to assess the degree of cognitive consonance associated with

---

[3] At this proof-of-concept level, only six categories were identified for the metadata used in the test repository. In an implementation phase, all seventeen categories would be available.

each element. Consequently, the research will proceed with a subsequent focus on two objectives, namely:

- To assess the relevance of a set of search categories to a series of individual images of information objects; and
- To obtain participant feedback on a series of different visual displays showing results from the same query term.

This next phase of study will provide information concerning the appropriateness of the seventeen-element categorization model for uniquely identifying and retrieving digital cultural objects (i.e., objects in electronic format from libraries, archives, museums, art galleries), and will help to inform the design of visual displays that are more appropriately used in language-neutral search environments. The contextual and semantic validation that derives from focus group data will be key to refining a cross-domain search tool and user interface that exists currently as a proof-of-concept.

4   Conclusions

The ultimate intent of the research is to support the following matrix of search scenarios, with results being grouped within commonly understood core categories, and displayed in scalable topic maps:

- English language query retrieves monolingual English results
- English language query retrieves multilingual results
- Other language query retrieves monolingual results by language of query
- Other language query retrieves multilingual results
- Multiple languages query retrieves results in languages defined by query
- Multiple languages query retrieves multilingual results

Exploiting the wealth of descriptive metadata that are being used in cultural repositories will be important to integrating resource discovery across domains. Additionally, extending the potential of topic maps to represent clusters of search results in context will help in addressing the challenges of accessing digital content in a translingual milieu. Exploring visualization technologies will also offer innovative cross-disciplinary applications to the bibliographic, archival, and museums communities whose own terminological conventions and ways of representing objects unique to their domains will themselves require transparent, semantic bridging.

Acknowledgements

The principal investigator (Howarth) gratefully acknowledges the financial assistance provided by the Social Sciences and Humanities Research Council of Canada in funding this research project (SSHRC SRG 410-03-1413).

References

Buckland, M.K., et al.: "Mapping Entry Vocabulary to Unfamiliar Metadata Vocabularies." *D-Lib Magazine*, 5/1 (January 1999) URL: http://www.dlib.org/dlib/january99/buckland/01buckland.html   Accessed 25/08/2005.

De Mey, M.: *The Cognitive Paradigm*. Dordrecht: D. Reidel, 1982

Howarth, L.C.: "Designing a Common Namespace for Searching Metadata-Enabled Knowledge Repositories: An International Perspective." *Cataloging & Classification Quarterly* 37/1-2 (2003) 19-38

Howarth, L.C.: "Modelling a Natural Language Gateway to Metadata-enabled Resources." In *Knowledge Organisation and the Global Information Society: Proceedings of the Eighth International Conference of the International Society of Knowledge Organization*, University College London, London, England, UK, 13-16 July, 2004. Edited by I. McIlwaine and K. Lottman. Wuerzburg: Ergon Verlag, 2004, 61-66

Howarth, L.C., Cronin, C., and Hannaford, J.: "Designing a Metadata-Enabled Namespace for Accessing Resources Across Domains." In *Advancing Knowledge: Expanding Horizons for Information Science: Proceedings of the 30th Annual Conference of the Canadian Association for Information Science/Association canadienne des sciences de l'information* - held with the Congress for the Social Sciences and Humanities of Canada, University of Toronto, Toronto, Canada, 30 May-1 June, 2002. Edited by L.C. Howarth, A. Slawek, and C. Arsenault. Toronto: CAIS, 2002, 223-232

Howarth, L.C., and Hannaford, J.: "Deriving a Multilingual Gateway to Cultural Repositories." In *Bridging the Digital Divide: Equalizing Access to Information and Communication Technologies: Proceedings of the 31st Conference of the Canadian Association for Information Science/Association canadienne des sciences de l'information* - held with the Congress for the Social Sciences and Humanities of Canada, Dalhousie University, Halifax, Nova Scotia, 30 May-1 June, 2003. Edited by L.Spiteri and W. Peekhaus. Toronto: CAIS, 2003, 196-209

MARC21 Concise Format for Bibliographic Data. Available at URL: http://www.loc.gov/marc/bibliographic/ Accessed 12/17/05

Swish-e: Simple Web Indexing Software for Humans - Enhanced. Available at URL: http://swish-e.org/ Accessed 12/17/2005.

Report on the Open Space Sessions[*]

Alexander Sigel

University of Cologne,
Department of Information Systems and Information Management,
50969 Köln, Germany
sigel@wim.uni-koeln.de

Abstract. This report summarizes the eleven contributions by eight presenters from the two open space sessions that took place during the TMRA'05 workshop on 6th and 7th of October 2005. The contributions were informal and non-refereed, since workshop attendants had been given the opportunity to sign up to short talks on a flipchart, and the suggested format for each presentation was: only one slide, five minutes presentation, and five minutes discussion. The 90 minutes, smoothly chaired by Lars Marius Garshol, were filled with an inspiring exchange of ideas and arguments, since in this "playground for visionaries" new proposals were made and current work in progress was reported and lively discussed. For the purpose of this report, the presentations have been regrouped into the five sections: 1. Resources for the topic maps research community, 2. Authoring topic maps, 3. Querying topic maps, 4. A PSI infrastructure for topic maps, and finally, 5. Topic maps applications.

1 Resources for the Topic Maps Research Community

BibMap: The Bibliography of the Topic Maps Technology Literature
Since one of main objectives of the TMRA'05 workshop was "to chart the landscape of topic maps research", *Lutz Maicher*, University of Leipzig, created bibMap[1], an attempt to capture all known research references to the topic maps technology literature, represented in one topic map. This bibliographic topic map contains 95 persons and 194 sources (version 1.0 revision 1.3.3 of 2005-08-22). It is published in LTM[2] (and also available in XTM[3]) format and can be freely used. To deploy it (e.g. for literature research), it may be loaded into a freely available topic maps browser

---

[*] The corresponding slides for all presentations can be retrieved from http://www.informatik. uni-leipzig.de/~tmra05/prog.html#OSS1 and http://www.informatik. uni-leipzig.de/~tmra05/ prog.html#OSS2. In the preparation of this report, the following two blog entries about this session, published by the session chair, have been used: http://www.garshol.priv.no/blog/8.html and http://www.garshol.priv.no/blog/9.html. In addition, comments by the presenters about an earlier draft of this report have been taken into account.

[1] http://www.informatik.uni-leipzig.de/~maicher/bibliography.html

[2] http://www.informatik.uni-leipzig.de/~maicher/bib/bibmap_latest.ltm

[3] http://www.informatik.uni-leipzig.de/~maicher/bib/bibmap_latest.xtm and http://www.topic-maps.org/lib/exe/fetch.php?cache=cache&media=topic_maps%3Abibmap.xtm.

L. Maicher and J. Park (Eds.): TMRA 2005, LNAI 3873, pp. 271–280, 2006.
© Springer-Verlag Berlin Heidelberg 2006

such as the TM4J/TMNav or the Omnigator, or be viewed online[4] with Tmwiki, developed by Hendrik Thomas (see below). You are also free to write your own application using bibMap. To maintain consistency, modification of the original bibMap is not allowed. In order to extend it with your own documented (subjective) view of the topic maps research literature, you may create your own topic map (with categories, annotations, and comments) and merge it with bibMap. Exchanging such extensions with others in the topic maps community and merging further extensions in is highly encouraged. Please contact Lutz Maicher if you want to collaborate with him on improving bibMap.

2   Authoring Topic Maps

TMEP Disclosure: Disclosing the Process of the Topic Maps Engineering

In order to ease the maintenance of huge topic maps (like his bibMap), Lutz Maicher advocates to also disclose the observation principle applied during the topic map generation, i.e. to document the principles by which a topic map is created. A schema is not sufficient for this purpose, as the editorial guidelines need also to be documented. If a schema, for example, defines that a topic of type "person" exists, a maintainer of the topic map would want to know when such a topic has to be created and how a person should be described accurately.

A TMEP disclosure is a topic map which describes the editing process[5] (the observation of the environment) motivating the topic map modifications. It consists of a set of action items which direct an interactive editing interface. The action items are: action directive, action sequence and action container. A TMEP disclosure defines an operator, an operand and a slot for the result, as well as conditions and the previous action item if the condition holds. Lutz Maicher demonstrated his current TMEP disclosure implementation, using the console, and the corresponding large LTM topic map[6].

A TMEP disclosure is useful to drive generic topic map editing interfaces (customizing the editing interface with TMEP), to disclose how automatic indexing functions (like e.g. in the Semantic Talk [1] system which creates indices of real-time speech streams) were used to improve later integration of indices, and to describe arbitrary workflows.

Tmwiki – a Topic Map Wiki Application

Tmwiki[7], developed and presented by *Hendrik Thomas*, is:

1. A topic map-enhanced wiki system: wiki-like collaborative editing of XTM topic maps and browsing and viewing of topic maps with a generic graphical topic map browser (TMV[8], the "Topic Map Visualiser") as a display and navigation interface;
2. Content in this wiki about topic maps (information which someone needs to understand what topic maps are for and how they can be used).

---

[4] http://www.topic-maps.org/cgi-bin/tmv_graph.pl?id=b1&path=bibmap.xtm
[5] The acronym TMEP stands for: Topic Maps Editing Process.
[6] See http://www.informatik.uni-leipzig.de/~tmra05/PRES/LMc.ppt, slide 3
[7] http://www.topic-maps.org/projects:tmwiki
[8] http://www.topic-maps.org/projects:tmv

Tmwiki extends the PHP wiki DokuWiki[9] (which stores all data in plain text files) by storing topic maps flattened into the file system, and by displaying them.

As seen above, editing and viewing the bibMap topic map is one example. Another example is viewing the entry for this presentation[10] in the TMRA'05 topic map[11], originally created by Robert Cerny.

A clear advantage of Tmwiki is the capability for very easy and fast collaborative development of topic maps, supported by a versioning system and an RSS feed about changes. Current problems are consistency (the topic map may become confusing because additions by many users may lead to an unstructured topic map editing process), and that Tmwiki understands only XTM syntax, since XPath and no topic maps engine is used internally.

AsTMa= 2.0: Authoring Topic Maps

Lars Heuer held a 6-slide tutorial on latest developments towards AsTMa= (version 2.0), created by him and Robert Barta.[12] The AsTMa*[13] language family [3] is designed to support authoring, updating, constraining and querying topic maps. AsTMa= is the authoring language[14], and "=" stands for facts which authors state. Version 2.0 is almost ready, but some work remains to be done. AsTMa= supports definition of a topic by identifier, by subject locator and by subject identifier. An association can be defined as follows:

General:
```
(assoc-type)
role-type: role-player
```
Example:
```
(membership)
member: john
group: beatles
```
Association templates are one of the most powerful features of AsTMa=, since the template URIs (here: ...#left and ...#right) will be replaced by the respective topics:
```
[(born-in)
bio-entity:
http://astma.it.bond.edu.au/authoring/psi/1.0#left
place: http://astma.it.bond.edu.au/authoring/psi/1.0#right
]
```
Named association templates look like this:
```
born-in = [(i'http://psi.example.org/born-in )
... ]
```
To apply an association template:
```
JohnLennon is-a person born-in Liverpool
tn: John Lennon
var @sort: lennon, john
ex (website): http://johnlennon.com
in @en (descr): John Lennon was ...
```

---

[9] http://wiki.splitbrain.org/wiki:dokuwiki

[10] http://www.topic-maps.org/cgi-bin/tmv_graph.pl?id=t713&path=tmra05.xtm

[11] http://www.topic-maps.org/cgi-bin/tmv_graph.pl?path=tmra05.xtm

[12] [2] is a tutorial of the *previous* version of AsTMa=

[13] http://astma.it.bond.edu.au/

[14] A comparable authoring language is LTM [4]. AsTMa= v2.0 will have directives like LTM for prefixes, include etc.

Lars Heuer has also written an AsTMa= parser in Java for TMAPI[15], which will be open source. The alpha version is available upon direct request from the author.

3 Querying Topic Maps

AIOBCT - Q/A Over Topic Maps

Rani Pinchuk reported on how topic map queries are used in the AIOBCT project to support question answering (Q/A). AIOBCT is an ESA project to create a Q/A system to assist astronauts on board the International Space Station (ISS) by answering questions that arise while performing their tasks. Topic maps are populated with knowledge of two subsystems of the Columbus (Europe's laboratory on the ISS) Operations Manual, namely EPDS – Electrical Power Distribution System and MSM – Mechanical Structure and Mechanisms).[16]

The topics and the associations between them provide an excellent structure for extracting answers to questions. The system knows about associations such as:

- Host-location (the location of the device)
- Function-of (which is the function of the PDU)
- Mode-of (the mode of the device)
- Part-of (the parts of the device)
- Controls (the controller of the PDU)
- Provides (the device which provides 28W).

The Q/A system supports a wide range of English natural language queries, since queries are parsed with Context Free Grammar into an internal representation of the question which is later used to generate queries in Toma (Topic Map Query Language) [5]. For example, the natural language query "What is the device which is located in d2?" is transformed to what_is ([device] host-location ([d2])).

Toma is considered as useful input to the development of TMQL, a standard topic map query language[17], since most of the language as described in the specification is already implemented in a prototype topic maps engine running Toma queries.

The system can answer questions like:

- What is ...? (What are the parts of the device which is located in D2?) the value ...? /its mass? / the location of the PDU? / the electrical interface of the device which is located in D2? / What are the commands available on the PDU?
- Where is ...? / Yes/No question – where
- How many?
- View / Show ...? / Can I see please a diagram of the device which controls the PDU?
- Which telemetry is available? (for the device in D2)?
- How to execute (How do I activate the PDU?) / How are the parts of the PDU related to the MLU?

---

[15] TMAPI, Common Topic Map Application Programming Interface. http://www.tmapi.org/

[16] Question Answering System for Astronauts on board the International Space Station. Poster http://www.sas.be/projects-so/37AIOBCT.pdf

[17] http://www.isotopicmaps.org/tmql/

4   A PSI Infrastructure for Topic Maps

Towards a P2P (?) PSI Registry

Alexander Sigel motivated the urgent need for a PSI(D) registry, provided some use cases where such a registry would be advantageous and tried to convince people to start working together on this neglected subject to offer the services of a PSI registry, calling for contributions of work items towards a project. After vigorous discussion on the subject, there was general agreement that this was needed, but no concrete action plan was devised.

A published subject has a machine-readable published subject identifier (PSID, must be a URI) which must resolve to a human-interpretable published subject indicator (PSI) [6]. Consider the following statement from the Published Subjects Technical Committee on the adoption of PSIs: *"Any user that needs a PSI for a particular purpose should first consider adopting one that already exists, and then, if nothing suitable is found, create his or her own."* [6]. How could a user know for sure about an existing PSI without a PSI registry, and how could the "arbitrary proliferation of PSI entries"[18] be avoided without a PSI registry?

He named as main motivations for such a registry:

- PSIs establish identity and lead to better semantic interoperability [8]. A PSI infrastructure supports merging and works towards the aim of SLUO (Subject Location Uniqueness Objective, the collocation objective)[19].
- PSIs support reuse and best practice, e.g. in Distributed Knowledge Management (DKM), Federated Seamless Knowledge, or Content Intelligence.
- PSIs are the infrastructure for emerging collaborative distributed lightweight ontology engineering.

Unfortunately, no long-term public registry ("PSIpedia") and no working group on this exists[20], therefore, not much progress has been seen since the inception of XTM five years ago.

Architectural and technical issues include:

- Should such a registry evolve to a P2P-like system in which topic map fragments are exchanged with TRMAP [11] between peers?
- Which topic map engine should be used as backend for the moment? How should a PSI search engine be implemented, and which topic map query language should be used?

There should be cooperation with content owners, and incentives for publishers and content producers should be discussed. Practical questions include: creating roles

---

[18] *Cf. "The aim with such registries (and services) is to early on forestall the arbitrary proliferation of unrelated but maybe similar topics." [7, 398].*

[19] [9] defines: *"2.26 Subject Location Uniqueness Objective (SLUO): The objective of the topic map paradigm, which is to enable everything that is known about a subject to be accessible from one place",* in other words: *"having one proxy for each unique subject".* However, in the current version of this document [10], this concept can no longer be found.

[20] Meanwhile, Michael Chapman informed this author about his "WWW Virtual Library of Published Subject Indicators", automatically generated from a topic map. http://psi.mchapman.com/vl/

and responsibilities, deciding for an implementation language, setting up a sourceforge project, registering a domain like psi-regisry.net, and hosting the application. Advanced research questions include the realization of P2P trust networks such that subjective mappings between two PSIs can be shared between parties trusting each other.

In some later individual discussions[21], *Lars Marius Garshol* suggested preparing a much simpler problem statement to gain traction on this. *Gabriel Hopmans* pointed out that one might draw some ideas from the openPSI project proposal[22] and current extensions of this idea[23]. He also proposed trying to get EC funding within ADNOM[24] for such a registry. *Lutz Maicher* asked if one should better start with individual published topic maps as a kind of decentralized registry. *Jack Park* wondered how PSI registries registering a rigid semantics can cope with meaning "in a constant flux" and how PSIs for key-value pair types in TMRM for the specification of subject properties might help. One answer to the latter is that notions are stable to the interpreter at the time of describing the PSI, and that upper categories used to describe the characteristics of concepts are more stable than concepts themselves. Hence, more research should be carried out on using "essential characteristics" from knowledge organization (a concept is the sum of all essential statements one can make about a subject) to refine PSIs, e.g. by modelling such statements as topic map expressions within the PSI. Instead of simply writing text into the PSI documentation, we could attach a topic map, e.g. characterizing a person by its birthday, occupation, works produced, or influence it had on the works of other thinkers.[25, 26]

Use of PSI Sets in ADNOM

Gabriel Hopmans asked the audience for best practice on how to define and use PSI sets in the ADNOM project (see also [12]). Questions included:

1. Why should three-digit numbers be used as ISO country identifiers instead of two-letter abbreviations? (Because a given two-letter ISO country abbreviation is not guaranteed to be stable whereas the number is. In addition, upconversion of legacy data is easier, in which three-digit numbers are often used.)

---

[21] See also the blog entry: http://asigel.blogspot.com/2005/10/towards-p2p-psi-registry.html

[22] Open Published Subjects Infrastructure (openPSI). Proposal for the openNet call for seed projects: http://www.agentcities.org/openNetOld/first.php

[23] http://mssm.nl/portfolio/openpsi/

[24] The acronym stands for: **A**dministrative **Nom**enclature, see also below

[25] Bernard Vatant had proposed using properties for establishing identity, instead of restricting to a URI. "*... so far both Topic Maps and RDF (hence OWL) use a very restrictive way of establishing subject identity: use of a single identifier (URI string), although subject identity could be established on more general basis by identical values for a specific subset of properties.*" Cf. "Subject Identity Discrimination Properties - in Topic Maps and in OWL". Posting by Bernard Vatant on 2003-11-05 to the mailinglist public-webont-comments@w3.org, archived at http://lists.w3.org/Archives/Public/public-webont-comments/2003Nov/0001.html See also his univers immedia blog on subject identity at http://universimmedia.blogspot.com/

[26] See also the blog entry: http://asigel.blogspot.com/2005/10/topic-properties-psis-and-more-email.html

2. Why should, in faceted classification, the classification code (e.g. http://psi. adnom.org/code/11ba) rather than the textual explanation (e.g. http://psi.adnom. org/politics/) be used as URI of the PSID? (Again, reasons include stability and ease of administration.)

Systematic documentation of such best practice is needed.

Using PSI in Inferencing

Peter-Paul Kruijsen asked about the relationship between inference rules and PSIs in a topic map:

- Is it possible to link a PSI to a predicate in the head of an inference rule? (E.g., in a first topic map, brother is statically defined with a PSI, and in a second topic map, brother is dynamically defined via an inference rule, using parent-hood associations with father, mother and child role players. To link the two, the PSI in the first topic map should be attached to the inference rule in the second topic map.)
- And in general: Can inference rules be placed within a topic map?

It is natural that one wants to make explicit what one knows about identities, independently of the fact whether a topic characteristic is static or inferred, but so far tolog [13] does not support this well. Further work will extend tolog and/or fulfill this requirement in TMQL.

Peter-Paul Kruijsen illustrated with several examples (comparing various topic maps/ontologies, dynamic topic typing, and the notion of an interface) how his ideas could lead to ontology mapping, i.e. mapping information between sources that use similar (not equal) ontologies. He is collecting requirements and wants to tackle some hard problems there. The requirements include:

- PSIs in inference rules
- Tolog statements and inference rule heads with constants (PSI or strings)
- Use of existing association-types in inference rule heads
- Caching of inferred facts.

5 Topic Maps Applications

Merlino: A Prototype for Semi-automated Generation of Occurrences in Topic Maps Using Internet Search Engines

Hendrik Thomas demonstrated Merlino[27], a system which takes as input a topic map and uses multiple web search engines to automatically identify relevant information resources as occurrences for a given topic. The prototype system, implemented in Perl, combines the ability to express semantic relationships in topic maps with search engine retrieval power. The aim is to accelerate and facilitate the generation process for occurrences.

---

[27] The acronym stands for: **M**ethod for **e**valuation and **r**etrieval of **lin**ks for **o**ccurrences.

The system realizes a five-step workflow: After uploading a topic map via a web form, the system (1) analyzes it for certain knowledge, (2) generates appropriate queries for search engines, and (3) queries the engines correspondingly. Occurrence candidates are pre-ranked (4) and (5) presented for intellectual relevance evaluation, and finally added to the topic map. In the analysis step (1), the information stored in the topic map is extracted via XPath queries from base and variant names of the topic, from already existing occurrences, and from associations in which the topic is involved. During query generation (2), processing rules are applied which describe how to transform the information gained from step (1) into the query syntax of the search engines. To rank the occurrence candidates in step (3) according to estimated relevance, Merlino can either use scoring information extracted from the collected search result sets for internal ranking, or use the external web impact factor, calculated by querying Altavista.

An online demo of Merlino is available[28]. Hendrik Thomas had developed an earlier version of Merlino in his diploma thesis [14], which was further extended together with Patrick Möhn, and demonstrated at the 2nd European Semantic Web Conference [15].

A Software for Personal Knowledge Logging

Robert Cerny has created a personal knowledge logging system.[29] Conceptually, it is a tool for people wanting to record what they know and where they know it from. Technically, it is a web application for creating topics, associations and encounters (his occurrences differ slightly from the standard ones), including a journal to trace the development over time. It is based on REST and topic map ideas, is implemented with PHP, JavaScript, mySQL and Ajax. Robert Cerny sees the following areas into which his system might potentially develop:

- CMS for homepages and weblogs
- Knowledge syndication via HTTP
- Methods for topics in JavaScript or PHP
- E-Learning system, and
- Topic map export to XTM.

Semblogging with Topic Maps

Alexander Sigel presented his ongoing research project kPeer on topic map-based semblogging (semantic blogging).[30] Semblogging is a special case of semantic annotation in line with DKM (Distributed Knowledge Management). To achieve smarter content aggregation, blog entries need more semantics than just tag clouds.[31] Therefore, the blog entries are semantically described by associating topics and associations, held in topic maps, with them.

---

[28] http://staudinger.wirtschaft.tu-ilmenau.de:8080/merlinotest-cgi-bin/m_start.pl

[29] In http://www.cerny-online.com/resume/en/, he describes it as a "Web application for Personal Knowledge Management", a leisure time project started in January 2005.

[30] See also [16] for early ideas on P2P aspects, and [17] for aspects of content intelligence.

[31] For aspects of tagging, see also [18].

Both the seminal semblogging concept and prototype by Steve Cayzer [19] and a first proposal to mine desktop data for semantic blogging [20] uses RDF. However, with topic maps one can do even better[32], therefore the kPeer system builds on topic maps.

In a first diploma thesis, use cases have been described, and a plug-in for the Java blogging framework blojsom has been developed which uses TMAPI and TM4J. A demonstration will be available soon[33]. A further diploma thesis will look into issues of P2P distribution and semantic web services. The aim is to release an open source prototype via sourceforge in the near future and to test and further develop the system with semblogging user communities. Such communities might including the bibMap or the TMRA'05 community semblogging (or even sem-wiki-blogging?[34]) on topic maps, the students in a teaching course in information and knowledge management, or a group of people interested in semblogging in cultural heritage[35].

References

(Online references were last accessed 2005-11-22)
1. Ziegler, J., El Jerroudi, J., Böhm, K.: Generating Semantic Contexts from Spoken Conversation in Meetings, in: Procs. 10th Int. Conference on Intelligent User Interfaces (IUI'05), San Diego, California, USA, January 9–12, 2005. New York: ACM, 290–292. Online: http://doi.acm.org/10.1145/1040830.1040902
2. Barta, R.: AsTMa= Authoring Tutorial, v1.0, 2002-07-10, Revision 1.0. Online: http://astma.it.bond.edu.au/astma=-tutorial.dbk
3. Barta, R.: AsTMa* Language Family (v 1.4 2003/09/14). Online: http://astma.it.bond. edu.au/astma-family.dbk
4. Garshol, L.M.: The Linear Topic Map Notation. Definition and introduction, version 1.3 (2005-09-18) Online: http://www.ontopia.net/download/ltm.html
5. Pinchuk, R.: Toma - Topic Map Query Language, 2004 (Version 0.4.6m 2004-10-04). Online: http://www.spaceapplications.com/toma/Toma.html
6. Published Subjects TC: OASIS Published Subjects Technical Committee: Published Subjects: Introduction and Basic Requirements. OASIS Published Subjects Technical Committee Recommendation, 2003-06-24. Online: http://www.oasis-open.org/committees/ download.php/3050/pubsubj-pt1-1.02-cs.pdf
7. Sigel, A.: Topic Maps in Knowledge Organization, in: Park, J. and Hunting, S. (eds.): XML Topic Maps: Creating and Using Topic Maps for the Web. Boston: Addison Wesley, 2002, 383-476. Draft of an earlier version: http://kpeer.wim.uni-koeln.de/~sigel/veroeff/ XTM-Book/
8. Pepper, S., Schwab, S.: Curing the Web's Identity Crisis: Subject Indicators for RDF, in: Procs. XML Conference and Exposition 2003, Philadelphia; PA, USA, December 7–12. Online: http://www.idealliance.org/papers/dx_xml03/html/abstract/05-01-05.html, http:// www. ontopia.net/topicmaps/materials/identitycrisis.html

---

[32] This is visible e.g. from [21] (semblogging as an example for Augmented Storytelling), Dmitry Bogachev informally discussing semblogging with topic maps, and Lars Marius Garshol realizing a simple semblogging application using OKS (personal communication).
[33] http://semblog.wim.uni-koeln.de/blojsom/blog/
[34] See blog entry: http://asigel.blogspot.com/2005/10/semantic-wikis-semwikis-topic-map.html
[35] See blog entry: http://asigel.blogspot.com/2005/10/semblogging-use-case-40000-digital.html

9. Newcomb, S.R., Hunting, S., Algermissen, J., and Durusau, P.: Topic Maps Model (TMM) (Version 2.30, 2003/03/28, for review and comment). ISO/IEC JTC 1/SC34. Online: http://www.jtc1sc34.org/repository/0393.pdf or http://y12web2.y12.doe.gov/sgml/SC34/document/0393.pdf

10. Durusau, P. and Newcomb S.R.: Topic Maps—Reference Model, 13250-5, version 6.0 (July 13, 2005) Online: http://www.isotopicmaps.org/TMMM/TMMM-latest.html

11. Garshol, L.M.: TMRAP—Topic Maps Remote Access Protocol, in: Procs. TMRA'05, 2006, in this volume. Slides, with title "TMRAP: A Web Service Protocol for Topic Maps": http://www.informatik.uni-leipzig.de/~tmra05/PRES/LMGa.pdf

12. Hopmans, G., Kruisen P.-P., Oud, L., Verhoeff, J, Küster, M.W., and Clews, J.: Topic Maps for European Administrative Nomenclature, in: Procs. TMRA'05, 2006, in this volume. Slides, with title "ADNOM: Topic Maps for European Administrative Nomenclature": http://www.informatik.uni-leipzig.de/~tmra05/PRES/HKOVC.ppt

13. Garshol, L.M.: tolog – a topic maps query language, in: Procs. TMRA'05, 2006, in this volume. Slides, with title "A Query Algebra for tolog. Formalizing tolog": http://www.informatik.uni-leipzig.de/~tmra05/PRES/LMGb.pdf

14. Thomas, H.: Konzeption und Entwicklung eines Prototypen zur Generierung von Occurrences in Topic Maps unter Verwendung von Suchmaschinentechnologien. TU Ilmenau. Institut für Wirtschaftsinformatik. Fachgebiet Informations- und Wisensmanagement. Diploma Thesis. 4.4.2005

15. Markscheffel, B., Thomas, H., Stelzer, D.: Merlino – A Prototype for semi automated Generation of Occurrences in Topic Maps using Internet Search Engines, in: Procs. 2nd European Semantic Web Conference (ESWC 2005), Heraklion, Greece, 29. May – 1. June 2005, Posters and Demos. (LNCS 3532) Springer, 25–27. Online: http://www.wirtschaft.tu-ilmenau.de/deutsch/institute/wi/wi3/forschung/documents/Merlino.pdf

16. Sigel, A.: kPeer (Knowledge Peers): Informationssuche beim verteilten SemBloggen. Presentation at the workshop "P2P Information Retrieval in Deutschland", Leipzig 2005-11-21. Slides: http://www.sempir.informatik.uni-leipzig.de/folien/sigel.pdf.

17. Sigel, A.: Content Intelligence durch Verknüpfung semantischer Wissensdienste am Beispiel von Semblogging. Presentation at "2. Kongress Semantic Web und Wissenstechnologien. Semantic Web Services", Darmstadt 2005-11-30. Slides: http://www.wim.uni-koeln.de/uploads/media/Content_Intelligence_ZGDV05_v16.pdf

18. Park, J.: Just For Me: Topic Maps and Ontologies, keynote, in: Procs. TMRA'05, 2006, in this volume.

19. Cayzer, S.: Semantic Blogging and Decentralized Knowledge Management, in: Communications of the ACM 47(12) (December 2004) Special issue: The Blogosphere. New York: ACM, 47–52. http://doi.acm.org/10.1145/1035134.1035164

20. Möller, K., Decker, S.: Mining Desktop Data for Semantic Blogging, in: Procs. 1st Workshop on the Semantic Desktop – Next Generation Personal Information Management and Collaboration Infrastructure (SemDesk 2005) at ISWC 2005, Galway; Ireland, November 2005. http://www.semanticdesktop.org/index_htm

21. Park, J.: Augmented Storytelling on the Web. Presentation at the National Storytelling Conference, Bellingham, WA, USA, July 2004. Slides: http://www.nexist.org/nsc2004/index.html

Author Index

Lecture Notes in Artificial Intelligence (LNAI)

Vol. 3630: M.S. Capcarrère, A.A. Freitas, P.J. Bentley, C.G. Johnson, J. Timmis (Eds.), Advances in Artificial Life. XIX, 949 pages. 2005.

Vol. 3626: B. Ganter, G. Stumme, R. Wille (Eds.), Formal Concept Analysis. X, 349 pages. 2005.

Vol. 3625: S. Kramer, B. Pfahringer (Eds.), Inductive Logic Programming. XIII, 427 pages. 2005.

Vol. 3620: H. Muñoz-Ávila, F. Ricci (Eds.), Case-Based Reasoning Research and Development. XV, 654 pages. 2005.

Vol. 3614: L. Wang, Y. Jin (Eds.), Fuzzy Systems and Knowledge Discovery, Part II. XLI, 1314 pages. 2005.

Vol. 3613: L. Wang, Y. Jin (Eds.), Fuzzy Systems and Knowledge Discovery, Part I. XLI, 1334 pages. 2005.

Vol. 3607: J.-D. Zucker, L. Saitta (Eds.), Abstraction, Reformulation and Approximation. XII, 376 pages. 2005.

Vol. 3601: G. Moro, S. Bergamaschi, K. Aberer (Eds.), Agents and Peer-to-Peer Computing. XII, 245 pages. 2005.

Vol. 3600: F. Wiedijk (Ed.), The Seventeen Provers of the World. XVI, 159 pages. 2006.

Vol. 3596: F. Dau, M.-L. Mugnier, G. Stumme (Eds.), Conceptual Structures: Common Semantics for Sharing Knowledge. XI, 467 pages. 2005.

Vol. 3593: V. Mařík, R. W. Brennan, M. Pĕchouček (Eds.), Holonic and Multi-Agent Systems for Manufacturing. XI, 269 pages. 2005.

Vol. 3587: P. Perner, A. Imiya (Eds.), Machine Learning and Data Mining in Pattern Recognition. XVII, 695 pages. 2005.

Vol. 3584: X. Li, S. Wang, Z.Y. Dong (Eds.), Advanced Data Mining and Applications. XIX, 835 pages. 2005.

Vol. 3581: S. Miksch, J. Hunter, E.T. Keravnou (Eds.), Artificial Intelligence in Medicine. XVII, 547 pages. 2005.

Vol. 3577: R. Falcone, S. Barber, J. Sabater-Mir, M.P. Singh (Eds.), Trusting Agents for Trusting Electronic Societies. VIII, 235 pages. 2005.

Vol. 3575: S. Wermter, G. Palm, M. Elshaw (Eds.), Biomimetic Neural Learning for Intelligent Robots. IX, 383 pages. 2005.

Vol. 3571: L. Godo (Ed.), Symbolic and Quantitative Approaches to Reasoning with Uncertainty. XVI, 1028 pages. 2005.

Vol. 3559: P. Auer, R. Meir (Eds.), Learning Theory. XI, 692 pages. 2005.

Vol. 3558: V. Torra, Y. Narukawa, S. Miyamoto (Eds.), Modeling Decisions for Artificial Intelligence. XII, 470 pages. 2005.

Vol. 3554: A.K. Dey, B. Kokinov, D.B. Leake, R. Turner (Eds.), Modeling and Using Context. XIV, 572 pages. 2005.

Vol. 3550: T. Eymann, F. Klügl, W. Lamersdorf, M. Klusch, M.N. Huhns (Eds.), Multiagent System Technologies. XI, 246 pages. 2005.

Vol. 3539: K. Morik, J.-F. Boulicaut, A. Siebes (Eds.), Local Pattern Detection. XI, 233 pages. 2005.

Vol. 3538: L. Ardissono, P. Brna, A. Mitrović (Eds.), User Modeling 2005. XVI, 533 pages. 2005.

Vol. 3533: M. Ali, F. Esposito (Eds.), Innovations in Applied Artificial Intelligence. XX, 858 pages. 2005.

Vol. 3528: P.S. Szczepaniak, J. Kacprzyk, A. Niewiadomski (Eds.), Advances in Web Intelligence. XVII, 513 pages. 2005.

Vol. 3518: T.-B. Ho, D. Cheung, H. Liu (Eds.), Advances in Knowledge Discovery and Data Mining. XXI, 864 pages. 2005.

Vol. 3508: P. Bresciani, P. Giorgini, B. Henderson-Sellers, G. Low, M. Winikoff (Eds.), Agent-Oriented Information Systems II. X, 227 pages. 2005.

Vol. 3505: V. Gorodetsky, J. Liu, V.A. Skormin (Eds.), Autonomous Intelligent Systems: Agents and Data Mining. XIII, 303 pages. 2005.

Vol. 3501: B. Kégl, G. Lapalme (Eds.), Advances in Artificial Intelligence. XV, 458 pages. 2005.

Vol. 3492: P. Blache, E.P. Stabler, J.V. Busquets, R. Moot (Eds.), Logical Aspects of Computational Linguistics. X, 363 pages. 2005.

Vol. 3490: L. Bolc, Z. Michalewicz, T. Nishida (Eds.), Intelligent Media Technology for Communicative Intelligence. X, 259 pages. 2005.

Vol. 3488: M.-S. Hacid, N.V. Murray, Z.W. Raś, S. Tsumoto (Eds.), Foundations of Intelligent Systems. XIII, 700 pages. 2005.

Vol. 3487: J.A. Leite, P. Torroni (Eds.), Computational Logic in Multi-Agent Systems. XII, 281 pages. 2005.

Vol. 3476: J.A. Leite, A. Omicini, P. Torroni, P. Yolum (Eds.), Declarative Agent Languages and Technologies II. XII, 289 pages. 2005.

Vol. 3464: S.A. Brueckner, G.D.M. Serugendo, A. Karageorgos, R. Nagpal (Eds.), Engineering Self-Organising Systems. XIII, 299 pages. 2005.

Vol. 3452: F. Baader, A. Voronkov (Eds.), Logic for Programming, Artificial Intelligence, and Reasoning. XI, 562 pages. 2005.

Vol. 3451: M.-P. Gleizes, A. Omicini, F. Zambonelli (Eds.), Engineering Societies in the Agents World V. XIII, 349 pages. 2005.

Vol. 3446: T. Ishida, L. Gasser, H. Nakashima (Eds.), Massively Multi-Agent Systems I. XI, 349 pages. 2005.

Vol. 3445: G. Chollet, A. Esposito, M. Faúndez-Zanuy, M. Marinaro (Eds.), Nonlinear Speech Modeling and Applications. XIII, 433 pages. 2005.

Vol. 3438: H. Christiansen, P.R. Skadhauge, J. Villadsen (Eds.), Constraint Solving and Language Processing. VIII, 205 pages. 2005.

Vol. 3435: P. Faratin, J.A. Rodríguez-Aguilar (Eds.), Agent-Mediated Electronic Commerce VI. XII, 215 pages. 2006.

Vol. 3430: S. Tsumoto, T. Yamaguchi, M. Numao, H. Motoda (Eds.), Active Mining. XII, 349 pages. 2005.

Vol. 3419: B.V. Faltings, A. Petcu, F. Fages, F. Rossi (Eds.), Recent Advances in Constraints. X, 217 pages. 2005.

Vol. 3416: M.H. Böhlen, J. Gamper, W. Polasek, M.A. Wimmer (Eds.), E-Government: Towards Electronic Democracy. XIII, 311 pages. 2005.